国家出版基金项目
"十二五"国家重点图书出版规划项目

孙中山全集

第十四卷
外文著述

尚明轩 主编

人民出版社

总 目 录

第一卷　专论
　　前言
　　凡例
　　目录
　　正文

第二卷　文集
　　凡例
　　目录
　　　论著
　　　传记与回忆
　　　序跋
　　　祭悼
　　　祝词
　　　其他
　　　译著
　　　遗嘱
　　正文

第三卷　文告　规章
　　凡例
　　目录
　　　文告
　　　通电
　　　启事(含声明、讣告等)
　　　其他
　　　规章
　　正文

第四卷　函札(上)
　　凡例
　　目录
　　正文

第五卷　函札(下)
　　凡例
　　目录
　　正文

第六卷　文电
　　凡例
　　目录
　　正文

第七卷　演说

  凡例
  目录
  正文

第八卷 谈话
  凡例
  目录
  正文

第九卷 公牍（上）
  凡例
  目录
  正文

第十卷 公牍（中）
  凡例
  目录
  正文

第十一卷 公牍（下）
  凡例
  目录
  正文

第十二卷 人事任免（上）
  凡例

目录

正文

第十三卷　人事任免（下）
凡例
目录
正文

第十四卷　外文著述
凡例
目录
正文

第十五卷　题词遗墨
凡例
目录
正文

第十六卷　索引　传略
凡例
目录
　索引
　传略
后记

凡　　例

一、本全集共收录孙中山现有著述11500余篇,按文体性质分类(含有多种性质的,据其主要倾向归类),依时间顺序编次,据类别和篇幅列卷。

二、日期与编次。底本有写作日期的,按原日期。无写作日期的,按最后发表日期,或通过考证予以判明;写作日期无从考证的,列于该类之末。著述日期统一采用公历,标于标题下方圆括号内。各卷原则上按时间顺序编次;卷内存在分类的,按各类时间顺序编次。

三、分类与列卷。根据类别和篇幅,分22类,列15卷:第一卷,专论(收录集中反映孙中山政治思想的5种著述);第二卷,文集(含论著、传记与回忆、序跋、祭悼、祝词、译著、遗嘱等);第三卷,文告规章(含文告、通电、启事、规章等);第四、五卷,函札;第六卷,文电;第七卷,演说;第八卷,谈话;第九、十、十一卷,公牍;第十二、十三卷,人事任免;第十四卷,外文著述;第十五卷,题词遗墨。索引和传略单独列卷,为第十六卷。

四、底本的选择。优先采用原始文件、影印件和初刊本;充分吸收现有各种图书报刊的文献成果,如中国社会科学院近代史研究所中华民国史研究室、广东省社会科学院历史研究室(所)、中山大学历史系孙中山研究室合编《孙中山全集》(中华书局1981—1986年出版),秦孝仪主编《国父全集》(台北近代中国出版社1989年版)。发表在不同图书报刊的同内容文献，有歧义之处的，经考证后取其一说，其余在注释中简要介绍；诸说并存的，选择最佳版本；文字内容虽有出入但各具特色的，原则上选择底本来源较权威者为主文，其余作为"同题异文"附录于后。

五、标题。原有标题的，一般保留，个别编者酌改；原无标题的，编者酌拟。标题文字以国家现行文字规范为准。标题中的人名一律统一为现行惯称，文中不另做说明。

六、注释。每篇著述，文末均注明所据底本。文内酌加的注释，均为页下注。人物有多个字、号、别名的，地名有多种译法的，原则上在该卷首次出现时加注，其后不注。【　】内的文字，系编者为避免上下文表意脱节或缺省所加的说明。

七、校勘与标点。文内明显的错漏，编者均予以校勘：订正讹字，置于〔　〕内；增补脱字，置于〈　〉内；衍文加［　］；有疑误、难以确定的，用〔？〕表示；字句残缺或难以辨认的，用□表示。校勘、考释和外文翻译等，部分吸收前人成果，本全集一般不做具体说明。标点符号原则上执行国家现行规范。底本无标点或有标点但与国家现行规范不符的，均重新标点。

八、本全集中文为简体字横排，底本的繁体、古体和异体字，原则上统一为简体字，特殊含义者例外。第十四卷"外文著述"，参考秦孝仪主编《国父全集》（台北近代中国出版社1989年版）编排。全集中插图及题词遗墨，一般据底本影印；质量较差的，适当修版或据原图重新绘制。

九、受时代局限，有的著述中使用的词语及字词用法和个别观点在今天看来欠妥，但因是原文固有，均不做改动。

CONTENTS

Writings

Kidnapped in London, Jan. 1897 ················ 3
China's Present and Future, Mar. 1897 ················ 73
The True Solution of The Chinese Question, Autumn, 1904 ················ 101
China's Next Step, Apr. 1, 1912 ················ 113
Plain Speaking from China, 1919 ················ 119
The International Development of China, July 20, 1920 ················ 125

Letters, Messages And Telegrams

To James Cantlie, Oct. 1896 ················ 373
To James Cantlie, Oct. 1896 ················ 374
To Felix Volkhovzky, Mar. 15, 1897 ················ 375
To Chew, July 12, 1897 ················ 376
To Walter N. Fung, July 12, 1897 ················ 377
To. J. H. Stewart Lockhart, Sept. 1897 ················ 378
To Kamagusu Minakata, Dec. 11, 1900 ················ 379
To Kamagusu Minakata, July 1, 1901 ················ 380
To. Mrs. Aoe McGregor, Dec. 9, 1903 ················ 381

To C. E. MacWilliams, July 22, 1904	383
To C. E. MacWilliams, Aug. 31, 1904	384
To C. E. MacWilliams, Sept. 6, 1904	385
To. C. E. MacWilliams, Sept. 15, 1904	386
To C. E. MacWilliams, Sept. 26, 1904	387
To Sugawara, May 9, 1906	388
To Sewh, Sept. 26, 1906	389
To Sewh, Mar. 17, 1908	391
To Sim Boon Kwang, Jan. 9, 1909	392
To Ahchong, Feb. 11, 1910	393
To General Homer Lea, Feb. 24, 1910	394
To Charles B. Boothe, Mar. 21, 1910	395
To Dr. & Mrs. James Cantlie, Mar. 22, 1910	396
To General Homer Lea, Mar. 24, 1910	397
To Charles B. Boothe, Apr. 5, 1910	399
To Ahchong, Apr. 5, 1910	400
To General Homer Lea, Apr. 10, 1910	401
To Ahchong, Apr. 25, 1910	403
To Ahchong's Wife, Apr. 25, 1910	405
To General Homer Lea, May 9, 1910	406
To General Homer Lea, May 24, 1910	408
To Charles B. Boothe, May 24, 1910	410
To Charles B. Boothe, June 22, 1910	411
To Charles B. Boothe, July 15, 1910	413
To Ahchong, July 21, 1910	415
To General Homer Lea, Aug. 11, 1910	417
To Charles B. Boothe, Sept. 4, 1910	419
To General Homer Lea, Sept. 5, 1910	422

CONTENTS

To General Homer Lea, Sept. 29, 1910 ········· 425
To General Homer Lea, Nov. 7, 1910 ········· 427
To Charles B. Boothe, Nov. 8, 1910 ········· 430
To Mrs. Cantlie, Nov. 20, 1910 ········· 432
To Mrs. Cantlie, Nov. 24, 1910 ········· 433
To Charles B. Boothe, Dec. 16, 1910 ········· 434
To Charles B. Boothe, Mar. 6, 1911 ········· 435
To General Homer Lea, Aug. 10, 1911 ········· 437
To General Homer Lea, Sept. 25, 1911 ········· 439
To Taro R. Otsuka, Oct. 22, 1911 ········· 441
To General Homer Lea, Oct. 31, 1911 ········· 442
To General Homer Lea, Nov. 1, 1911 ········· 443
To Miyazaki, Nov. 28, 1911 ········· 444
To Mrs. Lea, June 27, 1912 ········· 445
To General Homer Lea, Oct. 13, 1912 ········· 447
To Mrs. Lea, Nov. 14, 1912 ········· 449
To James Cantlie, May 2, 1913 ········· 450
To Postmaster, Nov. 12, 1913 ········· 452
To Mrs. Cantlie, Nov. 14, 1913 ········· 453
To Mrs. Lea, Dec. 23, 1913 ········· 454
To Mrs. Lea, June 17, 1914 ········· 456
To James Deitrick, Aug. 14, 1914 ········· 458
To Mrs. Lea, Sept. 13, 1914 ········· 463
To Lee Yuan Swee, Oct. 9, 1914 ········· 465
To James Deitrick, Oct. 12, 1914 ········· 467
To James Deitrick, Oct. 19, 1914 ········· 469
To James Deitrick, Nov. 20, 1914 ········· 472
To President Wilson, Nov. 30, 1914 ········· 474

To James Deitrick, Dec. 19, 1914 ··· 475

To James Deitrick, Dec. 25, 1914 ··· 476

To Mrs. Lea, Dec. 31, 1914 ··· 477

To Mrs. Cantlie, Mar. 19, 1915 ··· 478

To President of Republic Portugal, Apr. 3, 1915 ··································· 480

To Governor of Macao, Apr. 3, 1915 ·· 481

To President of the International Socialist Bureau, Nov. 10, 1915 ·········· 482

To James Deitrick, Nov. 18, 1915 ·· 487

To Mrs. Lea, Nov. 20, 1915 ·· 488

To Yokashi, Dec. 29, 1915 ··· 490

To Chowkok, Dec. 30, 1915 ·· 491

To Mrs. Lea, Jan. 11, 1916 ··· 492

To Mrs. Cantlie, Jan. 18, 1916 ·· 494

To James Deitrick, May 27, 1916 ··· 497

To James Deitrick, July 5, 1916 ·· 500

To Mrs. Lea, Oct. 19, 1916 ·· 502

To Comrades in Singapore, Oct. 31, 1916 ·· 504

To Comrades in Australia, Oct. 31, 1916 ··· 505

To James Deitrick, Nov. 24, 1916 ·· 506

To President Wilson, June 8, 1917 ·· 507

To President Wilson, June 9, 1917 ·· 508

To Baron Kato, June 18, 1917 ·· 509

To Mrs. Cantlie, Oct. 17, 1918 ··· 510

To President Wilson, Nov. 18, 1918 ··· 513

To Paul S. Reinsch, Jan. 10, 1919 ··· 517

To Lady James Cantlie, Mar. 20, 1919 ··· 518

To C. E. MacWilliams, Aug. 26, 1919 ··· 520

To N. E. B. Ezra, Apr. 24, 1920 ·· 521

To Dr. & Mrs. James Cantlie, Aug. 10, 1920 ··············· 522

To James Cantlie, Apr. 2, 1921 ··············· 523

To Mrs. Lea, Aug. 5, 1921 ··············· 525

To James Cantlie, Aug. 12, 1921 ··············· 526

To Lady James Cantlie, Aug. 12, 1921 ··············· 528

To Tchitcheren, Aug. 28, 1921 ··············· 530

To Mrs. Lea, Feb. 11, 1922 ··············· 534

To Paul S. Reinsch, Aug. 26, 1922 ··············· 536

To Maring, Feb. 11, 1923 ··············· 537

To Duff. and Joffe, May 23, 1923 ··············· 538

To Lim Nee Soon, Sept. 18, 1923 ··············· 539

To Mr. Borodin, Oct. 28, 1923 ··············· 540

To Rabindranath Tagore, Apr. 7, 1924 ··············· 541

To Mr. Borodin, May 14, 1924 ··············· 542

To Henry Ford, June 12, 1924 ··············· 543

To Mr. Borodin, Sept. 9, 1924 ··············· 545

To Monsieur Motta, Sept. 24, 1924 ··············· 546

To Mr. Borodin, Sept. 26, 1924 ··············· 548

To Mr. Borodin, Sept. 26, 1924 ··············· 549

To Mr. Borodin, Oct. 12, 1924 ··············· 550

To Mr. Borodin, Oct. 12, 1924 ··············· 551

To Mr. Borodin, Oct. 13, 1924 ··············· 552

To the Central Executive Committee of the Union of Soviet Socialist
   Republics, Mar. 11, 1925 ··············· 553

Others

The Commercial Union of China Bond, Jan. 22, 1895 ··············· 557

Autobiography, Apr. 14, 1904 ·· 558

The Chinese Revolutionary Government Bonds, Jan. 1, 1906 ··············· 559

Certificate for Koki H. Ike, Dec. 12, 1907 ·· 560

Certificate for Charles B. Boothe, Mar. 14, 1910 ································· 561

The Chinese Republic, July 1912 ·· 562

Eulogy on the Death of Homer Lea, Nov. 6, 1912 ······························· 567

Interrogatories in the Court of First Instance for the Judicial
District of Manila, May 6, 1915 ··· 568

Joint Statement with A. A. Joffe, Jan. 26, 1923 ································· 573

Resume of Dr. Sun's Remarks at Canton Christian College,
Dec. 22, 1923, Confidential ··· 576

Русские документы

Письмо Русселю, 8 Ноября, 1906 г. ·· 581

Письмо Русселю, 26 Ноября, 1906 г. ·· 582

Социальное значение китайской революции, 31 Марта, 1912 г. ······ 585

Письмо Ленину, 6 Декабря, 1922 г. ·· 590

Телеграмма Мотте, 24 Сентября, 1924 г. ······································· 592

WRITINGS

KIDNAPPED IN LONDON

Being the Story of My
Capture by,
Detention at,
and
Release from
the Chinese Legation, London

Jan. 1897

CONTENTS

PREFACE ·· 5

CHAPTER Ⅰ
THE IMBROGLIO ·· 6

CHAPTER Ⅱ
MY CAPTURE ·· 15

CHAPTER Ⅲ
MY IMPRISONMENT ·· 21

CHAPTER Ⅳ
PLEADING WITH MY GAOLERS FOR LIFE ························· 26

CHAPTER Ⅴ
THE PART MY FRIENDS PLAYED ··· 33

CHAPTER Ⅵ
THE SEARCH FOR A DETECTIVE ·· 40

CHAPTER Ⅶ
THE GOVERNMENT INTERVENE ··· 45

CHAPTER Ⅷ
RELEASED ·· 51

APPENDIX ··· 57

PREFACE

My recent detention in the Chinese Legation, 49 Portland Place, London, has excited so much interest, has brought me so many friends and has raised so many legal, technical and international points of law, that I feel I should be failing in my duty did I not place on public record, all the circumstances connected with the historical event.

I must beg the indulgence of all readers for my shortcomings in English composition, and confess that had it not been for the help rendered by a good friend, who transcribed my thoughts, I could never have ventured to appear as the Author of an English book.

SUN YAT SEN
London, 1897

KIDNAPPED IN LONDON

Jan. 1897

CHAPTER I

THE IMBROGLIO

When in 1892 I settled in Macao, a small island near the mouth of the Canton river, to practise medicine, I little dreamt that in four years time I should find myself a prisoner in the Chinese Legation in London, and the unwitting cause of a political sensation which culminated in the active interference of the British Government to procure my release. It was in that year however, and at Macao, that my first acquaintance was made with political life; and there began the part of my career which has been the means of bringing my name so prominently before the British people.

I had been studying medicine, during the year 1886, in Canton at the Anglo-American Mission, under the direction of the venerable Dr. Kerr, when in 1887 I heard of the opening of a College of Medicine at Hong Kong, and determined immediately to avail myself of the advantages it offered.

After five years' study (1887-1892) I obtained the diploma entitling me to style myself "Licentiate in Medicine and Surgery, Hong Kong."

Macao has belonged to Portugal for 360 years; but although the Government is Europeanised, the inhabitants are mostly Chinese, and the section of the population which styles itself Portuguese, consists really of Eurasians of several inbred generations.

In my newly selected home, I found the Chinese authorities of the native hospital willing to help me forward in the matter of affording me opportunities to practise European medicine and surgery. They placed a ward at my disposal, supplied me with drugs and appliances from London, and granted me every privilege whereby to secure my introduction amongst them on a fair footing.

This event deserves special notice as marking a new and significant departure in China; for never before had the Board of Directors of any Chinese hospital throughout the length and breadth of the great empire given any direct official encouragement to Western medicine. Many patients, more especially surgical cases, came to my wards, and I had the opportunity of performing several of the major operations before the Directors. On the other hand, I had difficulty from the first with the Portuguese authorities. It was not the obstructive ignorance of the East, but the jealousy of the West, which stepped in to thwart my progress. The law of Portugal forbids the practice of medicine, within Portuguese territory, by any one who is not possessed of a Portuguese diploma, obtainable only in Europe. Under this rule the Portuguese doctors took refuge and fought my claims to practise. They first forbade me to practise amongst, or prescribe for, Portuguese; the dispensers in the pharmacies were not allowed to dispense prescriptions from the pen of a doctor of any alien nationality; consequently my progress was hampered from the first. After futile attempts to establish myself in Macao, and at considerable pecuniary loss, for I had settled down little dreaming of opposition, I was induced to go to Canton.

It was in Macao that I first learned of the existence of a political movement which I might best describe as the formation of a "Young China" party. Its objects were so wise, so modest, and so hopeful, that my sympathies were at once enlisted in its behalf, and I believed I was doing my best to further the interests of my country by joining it. The idea was to bring about a peaceful reformation, and we hoped, by forwarding modest schemes of reform to the Throne, to initiate a form of government more consistent with modern requirements. The prime essence of the movement was the establishment of a form of constitutional government to supplement the old-fashioned, corrupt, and worn-out system under which China is groaning.

It is unnecessary to enter into details as to what form of rule obtains in China at present. It may be summed up, however, in a few words. The people have no say whatever in the management of Imperial, National, or even Municipal affairs. The mandarins, or local magistrates, have full power of adjudication, from which there is no appeal. Their word is law, and they have full scope to practise their machinations with complete irresponsibility, and every officer may fatten himself with impunity. Extortion by officials is an institution; it is the condition on which they take office; and it is only when the bleeder is a bungler that the government steps in with pretended benevolence to ameliorate but more often to complete the depletion.

English readers are probably unaware of the smallness of the established salaries of provincial magnates. They will scarcely credit that the Viceroy of, say, Canton, ruling a country with a population larger than that of Great Britain, is allowed as his legal salary the paltry sum of £ 60 a year; so that, in order to live and maintain himself in office, accumulating fabulous riches the while, he resorts to extortion and the selling of justice. So-called education and the results of examinations are [the] one means of obtaining official notice. Granted that a young scholar gains distinction, he proceeds to seek public employment, and, by bribing the Peking authorities, an official post is hoped for. Once obtained, as he cannot live on his salary, perhaps he even pays so much annually for his post, licence to squeeze is the result, and the man must be stupid indeed who cannot, when backed up by government, make himself rich enough to buy a still higher post in a few years. With advancement comes increased licence and additional facility for self-enrichment, so that the cleverest "squeezer" ultimately can obtain money enough to purchase the highest positions.

This official thief, with his mind warped by his mode of life, is the ultimate authority in all matters of social, political, and criminal life. It is a feudal system, an *imperium in imperio*, an unjust autocracy, which thrives by its own rottenness. But this system of fattening on the public vitals—the selling of power—is the chief means by which the Manchu Dynasty continues to exist. With this legalised corruption stamped as the highest ideal of government, who can wonder at the existence of a strong undercurrent of dissatisfaction among the people?

The masses of China, although kept officially in ignorance of what is going on in the world around them, are anything but a stupid people. All European authorities on this matter state that the latent intellectual ability of the Chinese is considerable; and many place it even above that of the masses in any other country, European or Asiatic. Books on politics are not allowed; daily newspapers are prohibited in China; the world around, its people and politics, are shut out; while no one below the grade of a mandarin of the seventh rank is allowed to read Chinese geography, far less foreign. The laws of the present dynasty are *not* for public reading; they are known only to the highest officials. The reading of books on military subjects is, in common with that of other prohibited matter, not only forbidden, but [is] even punishable by death. No one is allowed, on pain of death, to invent anything new, or to make known any new discovery. In this way are the people kept in darkness, while the government doles out to them what scraps of information it finds will suit its own ends.

The so-called "Literati" of China are allowed to study only the Chinese classics and the commentaries thereon. These consist of the writings of ancient philosophers, the works of Confucius and others. But of even these, all parts relating to the criticism of their superiors are carefully expunged, and only those parts are published for public reading which teach obedience to authorities as the essence of all instruction. In this way is China ruled—or rather misruled—namely, by the enforcement of blind obedience to all existing laws and formalities.

To keep the masses in ignorance is the constant endeavour of Chinese rule. In this way it happened, that during the last Japanese incursion, absolutely nothing was known of the war by the masses of China, in parts other than those where the campaign was actually waged. Not only did the people a short way inland never hear of the war, but the masses had never even heard of a people called Japanese; and even where the whisper had been echoed, it was discussed as being a "rebellion" of the "foreign man."

With this incubus hanging over her, China has no chance of reform except it come from the Throne; and it was to induce the Throne to modify this pernicious state of things that the "Young China" party was formed. Hoping that the Peking authorities, by their more extended contact during recent years with foreign diplomatists, might have learned something of constitutional rule, and might be willing to aid the people in throwing off their deplorable ignorance, I ventured, with others, to approach them, beseeching them, in all humility, to move in this direction for the welfare of China. These petitions only resulted in the infliction of many rigorous punishments. We had seized the moment when the Japanese were threatening Peking, and the Emperor, fearing that harsh dealings with the reformers might alienate many of his people, took no notice of them until peace was assured. Then an edict was issued denouncing the petitioners and commanding the immediate cessation of all suggestions of reform.

Finding the door closed to mild means, we grew more concrete in our notions and demands, and gradually came to see that some degree of coercion would be necessary. In all quarters we found supporters. The better classes were dissatisfied with the behaviour of our armies and fleets, and knew that corruption in its worst forms[form] was the cause of their failure. This feeling was not confined to one locality, but was wide-spread and deep-rooted, and promised to take shape and find expression in decided action.

The headquarters of the "Young China" party was really in Shanghai, but the scene of action was to be laid in Canton. The party was aided in its course by one or two circumstances. First among these was the existence of discontented soldiery. Three-fourths of the Cantonese contingent were disbanded when the war in the North had ceased in 1895. This set loose a number of idle, lawless men; and the small section of their comrades who were retained in service were no better pleased than those dismissed. Either disband all or retain all, was their cry; but the authorities were deaf to the remonstrance. The reform party at once enlisted the sympathies of these men in their cause, and so gained numerical strength to their military resources.

Another [chance] coincidence hastened events. For some reason or other a body of police, discarding their uniform, set to work to loot and plunder a section of the city. After an hour or two, the inhabitants rose, and obtaining mastery of the quondam police, shut some half-dozen of the ringleaders up in their Guildhall. The superintendent of the official police then sent out a force to release the marauders, and proceeded forthwith to plunder the Guildhall itself. A meeting of the inhabitants was immediately held, and a deputation of 1000 men ⟨was⟩ sent to the Governor's residence to appeal against the action of the police. The authorities, however, told the deputation that such a proceeding was tantamount to a rebellion, and that they had no right to threaten their superiors. They thereupon arrested the ringleaders of the deputation, and sent the others about their business. The discontents soon became disaffected, and, the "Young China" party making advance[advances], they readily joined the reformers.

Yet a third and a fourth incident helped to swell their ranks. The Viceroy, Li Han Chang (brother of the famous Viceroy Li), put a fixed tariff on all official posts throughout his two provinces, Kwang-Tung and Kwang-Si. This was an innovation which meant a further "squeeze" of the people, as the officials, of course, made the people pay to indemnify them for their extra payments. The fourth, and the most characteristically Chinese, method of extortion was afforded in [on] the occasion of the Viceroy's birthday. The officials in his provinces combined to give their master a present, and collected money to the amount of a million taels (about £ 200,000). Of course the officials took the money from the richer merchants in the usual way, by threats, by promises, and by blackmailing. A follower of Li Han Chang, Che Fa Nung by name, further angered all the "Literati" by selling, to all who could afford to pay, diplomas of graduation for 3000 taels (about £ 500) each. The richer men and the "Literati" became thereby disaffected and threw in their lot with "Young China".

In this way the reform movement acquired great strength and coherence and wide-spread influence, and brought matters all too soon to a climax. The plan was to capture the city of Canton and depose the authorities, taking them by surprise and securing them in as quiet a way as possible, or, at any rate, without blood-shed. To ensure a complete *coup*, it was considered necessary to bring an overwhelming force to bear; consequently, two bodies of men were employed, one in Swatow and the other from the banks of the West river. These places were fixed upon as the Swatow men, for instance, were totally ignorant of the Cantonese language. Although only 180 miles north of Canton, the language of Swatow differs as much from that of Canton as English does from Italian. It was deemed wise to bring strangers in, as they were more likely to be staunch to the cause, since they could not communicate with, and therefore could not be tampered with by, Cantonese men. Nor would it be safe for them to disband or desert, as they would be known as strangers, and suspicion would at once fall on them were they found in Canton after the disturbance.

It was arranged that on a certain day in October, 1895, these men should march across country, one body from the south-west, the other from the north-east, towards Canton. All proceeded satisfactorily, and they commenced their advance. Frequent meetings of the Committee of Reformers were held, and arms, ammunition and dynamite were accumulated at the headquarters. The soldiers advancing across the country were to be still further strengthened by a contingent of four hundred men from Hong Kong. The day for the assemblage came and the southern men were halted within four hours march of the city. A guard of one hundred men, fully armed, was stationed around the Committee in their Guild; runners, some thirty in number, were despatched to the disaffected over the city to be ready for the following morning. Whilst the conspirators sat within their hall a telegram was received to the effect that the advancing soldiers had been stayed in their progress, and the reform movement forthwith became disconcerted. It was impossible to recall the messengers, and others could not be found who knew where the disaffected were resident. Further news came to hand rendering it impossible to proceed, and the cry arose "*Sauve qui peut.*" A general stampede followed, papers were burnt, arms hidden, and telegrams despatched to Hong Kong to stop the contingent from that place. The telegram to the Hong Kong agent, however, only reached him after all his men had been got on board a steamer, which also carried many barrels of revolvers. Instead of dismissing the men as he should have done, he allowed them to proceed, and they landed on the wharf of Canton only to find themselves placed under arrest. The leaders in Canton fled, some one way, some another; I myself, after several hairbreadth escapes, getting [got] on board a steam launch in which I sailed to Macao. Remaining there for twenty-four hours only, I proceeded to Hong Kong, where, after calling on some friends, I sought my old teacher and friend, Mr. James Cantlie. Having informed him that I was in trouble through having offended the Cantonese authorities, and fearing that I should be arrested and sent to Canton for execution, he advised me to consult a lawyer, which I immediately proceeded to do.

CHAPTER II

MY CAPTURE

I did not see Mr. Cantlie again, as Mr. Dennis, who directed my steps, constrained me to get away at once.

In two days time l went by Japanese steamer to Kobe, whence, after a few days' stay, I proceeded to Yokohama. There I changed my Chinese attire for a European costume *à la* Japanese. I removed my queue, allowed my hair to grow naturally and cultivated my moustache. In a few days I sailed from Yokohama for the Hawaiian Islands and there took up my quarters in the town of Honolulu, where I had many relations, friends and well-wishers. Wherever I went, whether in Japan, Honolulu, or America, I found all intelligent Chinese imbued with the spirit of reform and eager to obtain a form of representative government for their native land.

Whilst walking in the streets of Honolulu I met Mr. and Mrs. Cantlie and family, who were then on their way to England. They did not at first recognise me in my European dress, and their Japanese nurse at once addressed me in the Japanese language, taking me for a countryman. This happened frequently, Japanese everywhere at first taking me for one of themselves and only finding their mistake when they spoke to me.

I left Honolulu in June, 1896, for San Francisco, where I remained for a month before proceeding eastward. There I met many of my countrymen and was well received by them. I spent three months in America, and came to Liverpool by the *S. S. Majestic.* In New York I was advised to beware the Chinese Minister to the United States, as he is a Manchurian, and has but little sympathy with Chinese generally and a reformer in particular.

On October 1st, 1896, I arrived in London and put up at Haxell's Hotel in the Strand. I went next day to Mr. Cantlie's, at 46 Devonshire Street, Portland Place, W., where I received a hearty welcome from my old friend and his wife. Lodgings were found for me at 8 Gray's Inn Place, Gray's Inn, Holborn. Henceforward I proceeded to settle down to enjoy my stay in London and to become acquainted with [the] many sights, the museums and the historical relics in [this] the very centre of the universe. What impressed me, a Chinaman, most was the enormous vehicular traffic, the endless and unceasing stream of omnibusses [omnibuses], cabs, carriages, wagons, and wheeled conveyances of humbler character which held the streets; the wonderful way in which the police controlled and directed the traffic, and the good humour of the people. The foot passengers are, of course, many, but they are not in such crowds as we find in Chinese streets. For one thing, our streets are much narrower, being, in fact, mere alleys; and, in the second place, all our goods are conveyed by human carriage, everything being slung from a bamboo pole carried across the shoulders. Yet even in the wide streets of Hong Kong our foot passenger traffic is in swarms.

I was just beginning to know Holborn from the Strand, and Oxford Circus from Piccadilly Circus, when I was deprived of my liberty in the fashion so fully described by the public press of the country.

I had been frequently at Mr. Cantlie's, almost daily in fact, and spent most of my time in his study. One day at luncheon he alluded to the Chinese Legation being in the neighbourhood, and jokingly suggested that I might go round and call there; whereat his wife remarked, "You had better not. Don't you go near it; they'll catch you and ship you off the [to] China." We all enjoyed a good laugh over the remark, little knowing how true the womanly instinct was, and how soon we were to experience the reality. While dining one evening at Dr. Manson's, whom I had also known in Hong Kong, as my teacher in medicine, I was jokingly advised by him also to keep away from the Chinese Legation. I was well warned, therefore; but as I did not know where the Legation was, the warning was of little use. I knew that to get to Devonshire Street I had to get off the omnibus at Oxford Circus, and from thence go straight north up a wide street till I found the name Devonshire on the corner house. That was the extent of my knowledge of the locality at this time.

On Sunday morning, October 11th, at almost half-past ten, I was walking towards Devonshire Street, hoping to be in time to go to church with the doctor and his family, when a Chinaman approached in a surreptitious manner from behind and asked, in English, whether I was Japanese or Chinese. I replied, "I am Chinese." He then inquired from what province I came, and when I told him I was from Canton, he said, "We are countrymen, and speak the same language; I am from Canton." It should be observed that English or "Pidgin", that is "business" English, is the common language between Chinamen from different localities. A Swatow and a Cantonese merchant, although their towns are but [writes] 180 miles apart (less than the distance between London and Liverpool), may be entirely ignorant of each other's spoken language. The written language is the same all over China, but the written and spoken languages are totally different, and the spoken languages are many. A Swatow merchant, therefore, doing business in Hong Kong with a Cantonese man, speaks English, but writes in the common language of China. While upon this subject it may be well to state that the Japanese written language is the same in its characters as that used by the Chinese; so that a Chinaman and a Japanese when they meet, although having no spoken words in common, can figure to each other on the ground or on paper, and frequently make imaginary figures on one hand with the forefinger of the other to their mutual understanding.

My would-be Chinese friend, therefore, addressed me in English until he found my dialect. We then conversed in the Cantonese dialect. Whilst he was talking we were slowly advancing along the street, and presently a second Chinaman joined us, so that I had now one on each side. They pressed me to go in to their "lodgings" and enjoy a smoke and chat with them. I gently demurred, and we stopped on the pavement. A third Chinaman now appeared and my first acquaintance left us. The two who remained further pressed me to accompany them, and I was gradually, and in a seemingly friendly manner, led to the upper edge of the pavement, when the door of an adjacent house suddenly opened and I was half-jokingly and half-persistently compelled to enter by my companions, one on either side, who reinforced their entreaties by a quasi-friendly push. Suspecting nothing, for I knew not what house I was entering, I only hesitated because of my desire to get to Mr. Cantlie's in time for church, and I felt I should be too late did I delay. However, in good faith I entered, and was not a little surprised when the front door was somewhat hurriedly closed and barred behind me. All at once it flashed upon me that the house must be the Chinese Legation, thereby accounting for the number of Chinamen in mandarin attire, and for the large size of the house; while I also recollected that the Minister resided somewhere in the neighbourhood of Devonshire Street, near to which I must then be.

I was taken to a room on the ground floor whilst one or two men talked to me and to each other. I was then sent upstairs, two men, one on either side, conducting and partly forcing me to ascend. I was next shown into a room on the second floor and told I was to remain there. This room, however, did not seem to satisfy my captors, as I was shortly afterwards taken to another on the third floor with a barred window looking out to the back of the house. Here an old gentleman with white hair and beard came into the room in rather a bumptious fashion and said:

"Here is China for you; you are now in China."

Sitting down, he proceeded to interrogate me.

Asked what my name was, I replied "Sun."

"Your name," he replied, "is Sun Wen; and we have a telegram from the Chinese Minister in America informing us that you were a passenger to this country by the *S. S. Majestic*; and the Minister asks me to arrest you."

"What does that mean?" I enquired.

To which he replied:

"You have previously sent in a petition for reform to the Tsung-Li-Yamen in Peking asking that it be presented to the Emperor. That may be considered a very good petition; but now the Tsung-Li-Yamen want you, and therefore you are detained here until we learn what the Emperor wishes us to do with you."

"Can I let my friend know I am here?" I asked.

"No," he replied; "but you can write to your lodging for your luggage to be sent ⟨to⟩ you."

On my expressing a wish to write to Dr. Manson, he provided me with pen, ink and paper. I wrote to Dr. Manson informing him that I was confined in the Chinese Legation, and asking him to tell Mr. Cantlie to get my baggage sent to me. The old gentleman, however, —whom I afterwards learned to be Sir Halliday Macartney, —objected to my using the word "confined", and asked me to substitute another. Accordingly I wrote: "I am in the Chinese Legation; please tell Mr. Cantlie to send my luggage here."

He then said he did not want me to write to my friend, and asked me to write to my hotel. I informed him that I was not at a hotel, and that only Mr. Cantlie knew where I was living. It was very evident my interrogator was playing a crafty game to get hold of my effects, and more especially my papers, in the hope of finding correspondence whereby to ascertain who my Chinese accomplices or correspondents were. I handed him the letter to Dr. Manson, which he read and returned, saying, "That is all right." I put it in an envelope and gave it to Sir Halliday Macartney in all good faith that it would be delivered.

CHAPTER III

MY IMPRISONMENT

Sir Halliday then left the room, shut the door and locked it, and I was a prisoner under lock and key. Shortly afterwards I was disturbed by the sound of carpentry at the door of my room, and found that an additional lock was being fixed thereto. Outside the door was stationed a guard of never less than two people, one of whom was a European; sometimes a third guard was added. During the first twenty-four hours the Chinese guards at the door frequently came in and spoke to me in their own dialect, which I understood fairly well. They did not give me any information as to my imprisonmentnor did I ask them any questions further than that the old gentleman who had locked me up was Sir Halliday Macartney, the Ma-Ta-Jen, as they called him: *Ma* standing for "Macartney," *Ta-Jen* being the equivalent for "His Excellency". This is in the same category with the name under which the Chinese Minister passes here, Kung-Ta-Jen. *Kung* is his family name or surname; *Ta-Jen* indicates his title, meaning "His Excellency". He never gives his real name in public matters, thereby compelling every foreigner to unconsciously style him "His Excellency". I often wonder if he deals with the British government under this cognomen solely; if he does, it is a disparagement and slight that is meant. Court and diplomatic etiquette in China is so nice, that the mere inflection of a syllable is quite enough to change the meaning of any communication to the foreigner from a compliment to a slight. This is constantly striven after in all dealings with foreigners, and it requires a very good knowledge of Chinese literature and culture indeed, to know that any message delivered to a foreigner does not leave the Chinese diplomatist hugging himself with delight at having insulted a foreigner of high rank, without his knowing it. To the people around him he thereby shows his own preeminence, and how the "foreign devils"—the Yang Quei Tze—are his inferiors.

Several hours after my imprisonment, one of the guard came into my room and told me that Sir Halliday Macartney had ordered him to search me. He proceeded to take my keys, pencil and knife. He did not find my pocket in which I had a few bank notes; but he took the few unimportant papers I had. They asked me what food I wanted, and at my request brought me some milk which I drank.

During the day two English servants came to light the fire, bring coals and sweep the room. I asked the first who came to take a letter out for me, and being promised that this would be done, I wrote a note addressed to Mr. Cantlie, 46 Devonshire Street, W. When the second servant came I did the same thing. I did not, of course, know till later what had happened to my letters, but both men said they had sent them. That (Sunday) evening an English woman came in to make up my bed. I did not address her at all. All that night I had no sleep, and lay with my clothes on.

On the following day—Monday, 12th October—the two English servants came again to attend to the room, and brought coals, water and food. One said he had sent the note with which I had entrusted him, while the other, Cole, said he could not get out to do so. I suspected, however, that my notes had never reached their destination.

On Tuesday, the 13th, I again asked the younger manservant—not Cole—if he had delivered my letter and had seen Mr. Cantlie. He said he had; but as I still doubted him, he swore he had seen Mr. Cantlie, who on receiving the note said, "All right!" Having no more paper, I wrote with pencil on the corner of my handkerchief, and asked him to take it to my friend. At the same time I put a half-sovereign in his hand, and hoped for the best. I was dubious about his good faith, and I found that my suspicions were but too well-founded; for I ascertained subsequently he went immediately to his employers and disclosed all.

On the fourth day of my imprisonment Mr. Tang, as he is called, came to see me, and I recongised in him the man who had kidnapped me. He sat down and proceeded to converse with me.

"When I last saw you," he began, "and took you in here, I did so as part of my official duty; I now come to talk with you as a friend. You had better confess that you are Sun Wen; it is no use denying it, everything is settled." In a vein of sarcastic-pseudo flattery he continued: "You are well known in China, the Emperor and the Tsung-Li-Yamen are well acquainted with your history; it is surely worth your while dying with so distinguished a name as you have made for yourself upon you." (This is a species of Oriental flattery scarcely perhaps to be appreciated by Western minds; but it is considered everything in China, how and under what name and reputation you *die*.) "Your being here," he proceeded, "means life or death. Do you know that?"

"How?" I asked. "This is England, not China. What do you propose to do with me? If you wish extradition, you must let my imprisonment be known to the British Government; and I do not think the Government of this country will give me up."

"We are not going to ask legal extradition for you," he replied. "Everything is ready; the steamer is engaged; you are to be bound and gagged and taken from here, so that there will be no disturbance; and you will be placed on board in safe keeping. Outside Hong Kong harbour there will be a Chinese gunboat to meet you, and you will be transferred to that and taken to Canton for trial and execution."

I pointed out that this would be a risky proceeding, as I might have the chance of communicating with the English on board on the way. This, however, Tang declared would be impossible, as, said he, "You will be as carefully guarded as you are here, so that all possibility of escape will be cut off." I then suggested that the officers on board might not be of the same mind as my captors, and that some of them might sympathise with me and help me.

"The Steamboat company," replied Tang, "are friends of Sir Halliday Macartney's and will do what they are told."

In reply to my questions he told me that I should be taken by one of the "Glen" Line of Steamers, but that my departure would not take place that week (this was October 14th), as the Minister was unwilling to go to the expense of exclusively chartering the steamer, and he wished to have the cargo shipped first, so that only the passenger tickets would have to be paid for.

"Some time [Sometime] next week," he added, "the cargo will be embarked and you will go then."

On my remarking that this was a very difficult plan to put into execution, he merely said:

"Were we afraid of that, we could kill you here, because this is China, and no one can interfere with us in the Legation."

For my edification and consolation he then quoted the case of a Korean patriot, who, escaping from Korea to Japan, was induced by a countryman of his to go to Shanghai, where he was put to death in the British concession. His dead body was sent back by the Chinese to Korea for punishment, and on arrival there it was decapitated, while the murderer was rewarded and given a high political post. Tang was evidently fondly cherishing the belief that he would be similarly promoted by his government for arresting me and securing my death.

I asked him why he should be so cruel, to which he replied:

"This is by order of the Emperor, who wants you captured at any price, alive or dead."

I urged that the Korean case was one of the causes of the Japanese war, and that my capture and execution might lead to further trouble and great complications.

"The British Government," I said, "may ask for the punishment of all the members of this Legation; and, as you are a countryman of mine, my people in the province of Kwang Tung may revenge themselves on you and your family for your treatment of me."

He then changed his tone, desisted from his arrogant utterances, and remarked that all he was doing was by the direction of the Legation, and that he was merely warning me in a friendly way of my plight.

CHAPTER IV

PLEADING WITH MY GAOLERS FOR LIFE

At twelve o'clock the same night Tang returned to my room and re-opened the subject. I asked him, if he was really a friend of mine, what he could do to help me.

"That is what I came back for," he replied, "and I want to do all I can, and will let you out by-and-by. Meantime," he continued, "I am getting the locksmith to make two duplicate keys, one for your room and one for the front door."

Tang had to take this step, he said, as the keys were kept by the confidential servant of the Minister, who would not part with them.

To my inquiry as to when he could let me out, he stated that it would be impossible till the following day, and that he could probably manage it at two a. m. Friday morning.

As he left the room he counselled me to be ready to get out on the Friday.

After his departure I wrote down a few words on a paper to give to the servants to take to Mr. Cantlie.

Next morning, Thursday, October 15th, I gave the note to the servant;

but, as Tang told me on the afternoon of that day, it was handed by the servant to the Legation authorities.

Tang declared that by my action I had spoiled all his plans for rescuing me, and that Sir Halliday Macartney had scolded him very much for telling me how they intended to dispose of me.

I thereupon asked him if there was any hope for my life, to which he replied:

"Yes, there is still great hope; but you must do what I tell you."

He advised me to write to the Minister asking for mercy. This I agreed to do, and asked for pen, ink and paper. These Tang told Cole to bring me.

I asked, however, that Chinese ink and paper should be supplied ⟨to⟩ me, as I could not write to the Chinese Minister in English.

To this Tang replied:

"Oh, English is best, for the Minister is but a figure-head; everything is in Macartney's hands, and you had better write to him."

When I asked what I should write, he said:

"You must deny that you had anything to do with the Canton plot, declare that you were wrongly accused by the mandarins, and that you came to the Legation to ask for redress."

I wrote to his dictation a long letter to this effect in Tang's presence.

Having addressed the folded paper to Sir Halliday Macartney (whose name Tang spelt for me, as I did not know how) I handed it to Tang, who went off with it in his possession, and I never saw the intriguer again.

This was no doubt a very stupid thing to have done, as I thereby furnished my enemies with documentary evidence that I had come voluntarily to the Legation. But as a dying man will clutch at anything, as I, in my strait, was easily imposed upon.

Tang had informed me that all my notes had been given up by the servants, so that none of them had reached my friends outside. I then lost all hope, and was persuaded that I was face to face with death.

During the week I had written statements of my plight on any scraps of paper I could get and throw them out of the window. I had at first given them to the servants to throw out, as my window did not look out on the street; but it was evident all of them had been retained. I therefore attempted to throw them out at my own window myself, and by a lucky shot one fell on the leads of the back premises of the next house.

In order to make these missives travel further I weighted them with coppers, and, when these were exhausted, two-shilling pieces, which, in spite of the search, I had managed to retain on my person. When the note fell on the next house I was in hopes that the occupants might get it. One of the other notes, striking a rope, fell down immediately outside my window. I requested a servant—not Cole—to pick it up and give it ⟨to⟩ me; but instead of doing so he told the Chinese guards about it, and they picked it up.

Whilst searching about, the letter on the leads of the next house caught their attention, and, climbing over, they got possession of that also, so that I was bereft of that hope too. These notes they took to their masters.

I was now in a worse plight than ever, for they screwed up my window, and my sole means of communication with the outside world seemed gone.

My despair was complete, and only by prayer to God could I gain any comfort. Still the dreary days and still more dreary nights wore on, and but for the comfort afforded ⟨to⟩ me by prayer I believe I should have gone mad. After my release I related to Mr. Cantlie how prayer was my one hope, and told him how I should never forget the feeling that seemed to take possession of me as I rose from my knees on the morning of Friday, October 16th—a feeling of calmness, hopefulness and confidence, that assured me my prayer was heard, and filled me with hope that all would yet be well. I therefore resolved to redouble my efforts, and made a determined advance to Cole, beseeching him to help me.

When he came in I asked him: "Can you do anything for me?"

His reply was the question: "What are you?"

"A political refugee from China," I told him.

As he did not seem to quite grasp my meaning, I asked him if he had heard much about the Armenians. He said he had, so I followed up this line by telling him that just as the Sultan of Turkey wished to kill all the Christians of Armenia, so the Emperor of China wished to kill me because I was a Christian, and one of a party that was striving to secure good government for China.

"All English people," I said, "sympathise with the Armenians, and I do not doubt they would have the same feeling towards me if they knew my condition."

He remarked that he did not know whether the English Government would help me, but I replied that they would certainly do so, otherwise the Chinese Legation would not confine me so strictly, but would openly ask the British Government for my legal extradition.

"My life," I said to him, "is in your hands. If you let the matter be known outside, I shall be saved; if not, I shall certainly be executed. Is it good to save a life or to take it? Whether is it more important to regard your duty to God or to your master? —to honour the just British, or the corrupt Chinese Government?"

I pleaded with him to think over what I had said, and to give me an answer next time he came, and tell me truly whether he would help me or not.

He went away, and I did not see him till next morning. It may well be imagined how eager I was to learn his decision. While engaged putting coals on the fire he pointed to a paper he had placed in the coal scuttle. On the contents of that paper my life seemed to depend. Would it prove a messenger of hope, or would the door of hope again be shut in my face? Immediately he left the room I picked it up and read:

"I will try to take a letter to your friend. You must not write it at the table, as you can be seen through the keyhole, and the guards outside watch you constantly. You must write it on your bed."

I then lay down on my bed, with my face to the wall, and wrote on a visiting card to Mr. Cantlie. At noon Cole came in again, and I pointed to where my note was. He went and picked it up, and I gave him all the money I had about me—£ 20. Mr. Cantlie's note in reply was placed by Cole behind the coal scuttle, and by a significant glance he indicated there was something there for me. When he had gone, I anxiously picked it up, and was overjoyed to read the words: "Cheer up! The Government is working on your behalf, and you will be free in a few days." Then I knew God had answered my prayer.

During all this time I had never taken off my clothes. Sleep came but seldom, only in snatches, and these very troubled. Not until I received my friend's cheering news did I get a semblance of real rest.

My greatest dread was the evil that would befall the cause for which I had been fighting, and the consequences that would ensue were I taken to China and killed. Once the Chinese got me there, they would publish it abroad that I had been given up by the British Government in due legal fashion, and that there was no refuge in British territory for any of the other offenders. The members of "the Party" will remember the part played by England in the Taiping rebellion, and how by English interference that great national and Christian revolution was put down. Had I been taken to China to be executed, the people would have once more believed that the revolution was again being fought with the aid of Britain, and all hopes of success would be gone.

Had the Chinese Legation got my papers from my lodgings, further complications might have resulted to the detriment of many friends. This danger, it turned out, had been carefully guarded against by a thoughtful lady. Mrs. Cantlie, on her own responsibility, had gone to my lodgings, carefully collected my papers and correspondence, and within a few hours of her becoming acquainted with my imprisonment, there and then destroyed them. If some of my friends in various parts of the world have had no reply to their letters, they must blame this considerate lady for her wise and prompt action, and forgive my not having answered them, as I am minus their addresses, and in many cases do not even know their names. Should the Chinese authorities again entrap me, they will find no papers whereby my associates can be made known to them.

I luckily did not think of poison in my food, but my state of mind was such that food was repulsive to me. I could only get down liquid nourishment, such as milk and tea, and occasionally an egg. Only when my friend's note reached me could I either eat or sleep.

CHAPTER V

THE PART MY FRIENDS PLAYED

Outside the Legation, I of course knew nothing of what was going on. All my appeals, all my winged scraps I had thrown out at the window, all my letters I had handed officially to Sir Halliday Macartney and Tang, I knew were useless, and worse than useless, for they but increased the closeness of my guard and rendered ⟨the⟩ communication with my friends more and more an impossibility.

However, my final appeal on Friday morning, October 16th, had made an impression, for it was after that date that Cole began to interest himself in my behalf. Cole's wife had a good deal to do with the initiative, and it was Mrs. Cole who wrote a letter to Mr. Cantlie on Saturday, October 17th, 1896, and so set the machinery going. The note reached Devonshire Street at 11 p.m. Imagine the Doctor's feelings when he read the following:

"There is a friend of yours imprisoned in the Chinese Legation here since last Sunday. They intend sending him out to China, where it is certain they will hang him. It is very sad for the poor man, and unless something is done at once, he will be taken away and no one will know it. I dare not sign my name; but this is the truth, so believe what I say. Whatever you do must be done at once, or it will be too late. His name is, I believe, Lin Yin Sen."

No time was evidently to be lost. Late as it was, after ascertaining Sir Halliday Macartney's address, Mr. Cantlie set out to find him. He little knew that he was going straight to the head centre of all this disgraceful proceeding. Luckily or unluckily for me, one will never know which, he found the house, 3 Harley Place, shut up. It was 11:15 p. m. On Saturday night, and the policeman on duty in the Marylebone Road eyed him rather suspiciously as he emerged from the compound in which the house stands. The policeman said that the house was shut up for six months, the family having gone to the country. Mr. Cantlie asked how he knew all this, and the policeman retorted that there had been a burglary attempted three nights previously, which led to close enquiries who the tenants were; therefore, the information he had, namely a six months' "anticipated" absence, was evidently definite and precise. Mr. Cantlie next drove to Marylebone Lane Police Office, and laid the matter before the Inspector on duty. He next went to Scotland Yard and asked to see the officer in charge. A Detective Inspector received him in a private room, and consented to take down his evidence. The difficulty was to get anyone to believe so improbable a story. The Police authority politely listened to the extraordinary narrative, but declared that it was impossible for Scotland Yard to take the initiative, and Mr. Cantlie found himself in the street about 1 a. m. , in no better plight than when he set out.

Next morning Mr. Cantlie went to Kensington to consult with a friend as to whether or not there was any good in asking the head of the Chinese Customs in London to approach the Legation privately, and induce them to reconsider their imprudent action and ill-advised step.

Not receiving encouragement in that direction, he went again to 3 Harley Place, in hopes that at least a caretaker would be in possession, and in a position to at least tell where Sir Halliday Macartney could be found or reached by telegram. Beyond the confirmation of the policeman's story that burglary had been attempted, by seeing the evidence of "jemmies" used to break open the door, no clue could be found as to where this astute orientalised diplomatist was to be unearthed.

Mr. Cantlie then proceeded to Dr. Manson's house, and there, at his front door, he saw a man who proved to be Cole, my attendant at the Legation. The poor man had at last summoned up courage to disclose the secret of my imprisonment, and in fear and trembling sought out Mr. Cantlie at his house; but being told he had gone to Dr. Manson's, he went on there and met both the doctors together. Cole then presented two cards I had addressed to Mr. Cantlie, stating:

"I was kidnapped on Sunday last by two Chinamen, and forcibly taken into the Chinese Legation. I am imprisoned, and in a day or two I am to be shipped off to China, on board a specially-chartered vessel. I am certain to be beheaded. Oh! woe is me."

Dr. Manson heartily joined with his friend in his attempt to rescue me, and proceeded to interrogate Cole. Mr. Cantlie remarked:

"Oh, if Sir Halliday Macartney were only in town, it would be all right. It is a pity he is away; where can we find him?"

Cole immediately retorted:

"Sir Halliday is in town, he comes to the Legation every day; it was Sir Halliday who locked Sun in his room, and placed me in charge, with directions to keep a strict guard over the door, that he should have no means of escape."

This information was startling, and placed the difficulty of release on a still more precarious footing. The proceedings would have to be still more carefully undertaken, and the highest authorities would have to be called in, were these crafty and masterful men to be outwitted.

Cole, in answer to further interrogations, said that it was given out in the Legation that I was a lunatic; that I was to be removed to China on the following Tuesday (that was in two days more); that he did not know by what line of ships I was going, but a man of the name of McGregor, in the City, had something to do with it. It also came out that two or three men dressed as Chinese sailors had been to the Legation during the week, and Cole had no doubt their visit had something to do with my removal, as he had never seen men of that description in the house before.

Cole left, taking a card with the names of my two friends upon it to deliver to me, in the hopes that its advent would allay my fears, and serve as a guarantee that Cole was actually working on my behalf at last. The two doctors then set out to Scotland Yard to try the effects of a further appeal in that direction. The inspector on duty remarked: "You were here at 12:30 a.m. this morning. I am afraid it is no use your coming here again so soon." The paramount difficulty was to know where to go to represent the fact that a man's life was in danger; that the laws of the country were being outraged; that a man was to be practically given over, in the Metropolis of the British Empire, to be murdered.

On quitting the premises they took counsel together, and decided to invade the precincts of the Foreign Office. They were told the resident clerk would see them at five p.m. At that hour they were received, and delivered their romantic tale to the willing ears of the courteous official. Being *Sunday*, of course nothing further could be done, but they were told that the statement would be laid before a higher authority on the following day. But time was pressing, and what was to be done? That night might see the tragedy completed and the prisoner removed on board a vessel bound for China. What was most dreaded was that a foreign ship would be selected; and under a foreign flag the British authorities were powerless. The last hope was that, if I were removed before they succeeded in rousing the authorities and the vessel actually got away, that it might be stopped and searched in the Suez Canal; but, were I shipped on board a vessel under a flag other than British, this hope would prove a delusion. With this dread upon them, they decided to take the decisive step of going to the Legation, and telling the Chinese that they were acquainted with the fact that Sun was a prisoner in their hands, and that the British Government and the police knew of their intention to remove him to China for execution. Dr. Manson decided he should go alone, as Mr. Cantlie's name in connection with Sun's was well known at the Legation.

Accordingly Dr. Manson called alone at 49 Portland Place. The powdered footman at the door was asked to call one of the English-speaking Chinamen. Presently the Chinese interpreter, my captor and tormentor, Tang himself, appeared. Dr. Manson said he wanted to see Sun Yat Sen. A puzzled expression fell over Tang's face, as though seeking to recall such a name. "Sun! Sun! there is no such person here." Dr. Manson then proceeded to inform him that he was quite well aware that Sun was here; that he wished to inform the Legation that the Foreign Office had been made cognisant of the fact; and that Scotland Yard was posted in the matter of Sun's detention. But a Chinese diplomatist is nothing if not a capable liar, and Tang's opportunity of lying must have satisfied even his Oriental liking for the *role*. With the semblance of truth in his every word and action, Tang assured his interrogator that the whole thing was nonsense, and that no such person was there. His openness and frankness partly shook Dr. Manson's belief in my condition, and when he got back to Mr. Cantlie's he was so impressed with the apparent truthfulness of Tang's statement, that he even suggested that the tale of my imprisonment might be a trick by myself to some end—he knew not what. Thus can my countrymen lie; Tang even shook the belief of a man like Dr. Manson, who had lived in China twenty-two years; who spoke the Amoy dialect fluently; and was thereby more intimately acquainted with the Chinese and their ways than nine-tenths of the people who visit the Far East. However, he had to dismiss the thought, as no ulterior object could be seen in a trick of the kind. Tang is sure to rise high in the service of his country; a liar like that is sure to get his reward amongst a governing class who exist and thrive upon it.

It was seven o'clock on Sunday evening when the two doctors desisted from their labours, parted company, and considered they had done their duty. But they were still not satisfied that I was safe. The danger was that I might be removed that very night, especially since the Legation knew the British Government were now aware of the fact, and that if immediate embarkation were not possible, a change of residence of their victim might be contemplated. This was a very probable step indeed, and, if it had been possible, there is no doubt it would have been accomplished. Luckily for me, the Marquis Tseng, as he is called, had shortly before left London for China, and given up his residence. Had it not been so, it is quite possible the plan of removal to his house would have recommended itself to my clever countryman; and when it was accomplished, they would have thrown themselves upon the confidence and good friendship of the British, and asked them to search the house. That ruse could not be carried out; but the removal to the docks was quite feasible. It was expected I was to sail on Tuesday, and, as the ship must be now in dock, there was nothing more likely than that the "lunatic" passenger should be taken on board at night, to escape the excitement and noise of the daily traffic in the streets.

CHAPTER VI

THE SEARCH FOR A DETECTIVE

With all this in his mind Mr. Cantlie set forth again, this time to search out some means of having the Legation watched. He called at a friend's house and obtained the address of Slater's firm of private detectives in the City. Hither he went; but Slater's office was closed.

On Sunday it would seem no detectives are required. Can no trouble arise on Sunday in England? It must be remembered that the division of the month is but an artificial and mundane convenience, and crime does not always accommodate itself to such vagaries of the calendar as the portioning ⟨of⟩ the month into weeks. However, there was the hard fact, Slater's office was shut, and neither shouting, bellringing, nor hard knocks could elicit any response from the granite buildings in Basinghall Street.

A consultation in the street with a policeman and the friendly cabman, who was taken into the secret of my detention, ended in a call at the nearest police station. Here the tale had to be unfolded again, and all the doubts as to the doctor's soberness and sanity set at rest before anything further could be attempted.

"Where was the place?"

"Portland Place, West."

"Oh! it is no good coming here, you must go back to the West End; we belong to the City police."

To the doctor's mind neither eastern nor western police were of any avail.

"However," he persisted, "could a detective not be obtained to watch the house?"

"No. It was out of the power of the City police to interfere in the West End work."

"Have you not [got] some old police constable, a reserve man, who would be willing to earn a little money at a job of the kind?" Mr. Cantlie asked.

"Well, there might be—let us see."

And here a number of men fell good-naturedly to discussing whom they could recall to memory. Well, yes; they thought so-and-so would do.

"Where does he live?"

"Oh! he lives in Leytonstone. You could not get him tonight; this is Sunday, you know."

Sunday I should think it was, and my head in the balance. After a long discussion a man's name was suggested, and they got rid of the persistent doctor. The man's address was Gibston Square, Islington.

But before starting thence, Mr. Cantlie thought he would give the newspapers the whole tale, so he drove to the *Times* Office and asked for the sub-editor. A card to fill in was handed 〈to〉 him as to the nature of his business; and he wrote:

"Case of Kidnapping at the Chinese Legation!"

This was 9 p.m., and he was told no one would be in until 10 p.m.

Away then he went to Islington in search of his "man". After a time the darkly-lit square was found, and the number proving correct, the abode was entered. But again disappointment followed; for "he could not go, but he thought he knew a man that would." Well, there was no help for it; but where did this man live? He was a wonderful chap; but the card bearing his address could not be found. High and low was it looked for: drawers and boxes, old packets of letters and unused waist-coats were searched and turned out. At last, however, it was unearthed, and then it was known that the man was not at home, but was watching a public-house in the City.

Well, even this was overcome, for the Doctor suggested that one of the numerous children that crowded the parlour should be sent with a note to the home address of the detective, whilst the father of the flock should accompany the Doctor to the City in search of the watcher. At last the hansom cab drew up at a little distance from a public-house, somewhere in the neighbourhood of the Barbican, and the place was reconnoitred. But no watcher could be seen around, and a futile search was settled in this way: that the public-house should be watched until eleven o'clock, when the house closed, at which time in all probability the "man" would be forthcoming. Mr. Cantlie left his erstwhile friend outside the house and set off again for the *Times* Office. There he was received in "audience" and his statement was taken down, and the publication of the tale was left to the *Times'* discretion. By this time it was 11:30 p. m. on Sunday, and at last the restless Doctor sought his home. He was somewhat chagrined to find that at 12 midnight his expected detective had not yet appeared, but, nothing daunted, he prepared to keep watch himself. He said good-night to his wife, and set out to observe the Legation, ready to interfere actively if need be.

However, as he strode forth with valiant intent, the Doctor encountered his expected "man" in the street, and immediately posted him. His Gibston Square friend had proved himself reliable and sent his deputy. The windows of the Legation, late as it was,—past twelve at night,—were still lit up, indicating a commotion within, the result, no doubt, of Dr. Manson's intimation that their evil ways were no longer unknown. The "man" was placed in a hansom cab in Weymouth Street, under the shadow of a house on the south side of the street, between Portland Place and Portland Road. It was a beautiful moonlight night, and both the Legation entrances could be clearly seen. The hansom cab was a necessary part of the sentinel on duty, as, supposing I had been hurried from the house across the pavement and into a carriage, I should have been carried beyond the reach of a person on foot in a few minutes. Cabs cannot be had at any moment in the early morning hours; hence the necessary precaution of having the watchman in a position by which he could follow in pursuit, if he were required [so] to do ⟨so⟩. The newspapers had it, that the cab was intended to carry me off when the rescue party had freed me, but this is another part of the story which I will relate later on.

At 2 a. m. the Doctor got to bed, and having informed the Government, told the police, given the tale to the newspapers, posted private detectives for the night, his day's work was finished and practically my life was saved, although I did not know it.

CHAPTER VII

THE GOVERNMENT INTERVENE

On Monday, October 19th, Slater's office was again asked for detectives, and, when they came, they were posted with instructions to watch the Legation night and day.

At 12 noon, by appointment at the Foreign Office, Mr. Cantlie submitted his statement in writing. The Foreign Office were evidently anxious that some less official plan of release should be effcted than by their active interference, in the hopes that international complications might be averted.

Moreover, the proofs of my detention were mere hearsay, and it was unwise to raise a question which seemed to be founded on an improbable statement. As a step in the evidence, enquiry was made at the "Glen" Line Office, and when it was found that a passage had been asked for, the Government then knew by direct evidence that the tale was not only true, but that actual steps for its execution had been carefully laid. From this moment the affair passed into Government [Government's] hands, and my friends were relieved of their responsibility.

Six detectives were told off by Government for duty outside the Legation, and the police in the neighbourhood were made cognisant of the facts and apprised to be vigilant.

The police had, moreover, my photograph, which I had had taken in America in my European dress. To 〔In〕 the eye of the foreigner, who has not travelled in China, all Chinese are alike, so that an ordinary photograph was not likely to be of much assistance; but in this photograph I wore a moustache and had my hair "European fashion".

No Chinaman wears a moustache until he has attained the "rank" of grandfather; but even in the country of early marriages, I, who have not yet attained the age of thirty, can scarcely aspire to the "distinction".

On Thursday, October 22nd, a writ of *Habeas Corpus* was made out against either the Legation or Sir Halliday Macartney, I know not which, but the Judge at the Old Bailey would not agree to the action, and it fell through.

On the afternoon of the same day a special correspondent of the *Globe* called at Mr. Cantlie's house and asked him if he knew anything about a Chinaman that had been kidnapped by the Chinese Legation. Well, he thought he did; what did the *Globe* know about it? The Doctor said he had given the information to *The Times* on Sunday, October 18th, five days before, and further supplemented it by additional information on Monday, October 19th, and that he felt bound to let *The Times* make it public first. However, Mr. Cantlie said, "Read over what you have written about the circumstance, and I will tell you if it is correct." The information the *Globe* had received proving correct, the Doctor endorsed it, but requested his name not to be mentioned.

Of course many persons were acquainted with the circumstances long before they appeared in print. Some two or three hundred people knew of my imprisonment by Tuesday morning, and it was a wonder that the ever eager correspondents did not know of it before Thursday afternoon. However, once it got wind there was no hushing the matter up, for from the moment the *Globe* published the startling news, there was no more peace at 46 Devonshire Street, W.

Within two hours after the issue of the fifth edition of the *Globe*, Mr. Cantlie was interviewed by a *Central News* and a *Daily Mail* reporter. He was too reticent to please them, but the main outlines were extracted from him.

The two searchers after truth next called at the Chinese Legation and asked to see Sun. They were met by the everready and omnipresent Tang, who denied all knowledge of such a man. Tang was shown the report in the *Globe*, at which he laughed merrily and said the whole thing was a huge imposition. The *Central News* reporter, however, said it was no good denying it, and that if Sun was not given up, he might expect 10,000 men here tomorrow to pull the place about his ears. Nothing, however, moved Tang, and he lied harder than ever.

Sir Halliday Macartney was next unearthed at the Midland Hotel and interviewed. His statements are [were] best gathered from the Press reports.

Interviews with Sir Halliday Macartney

Sir Halliday Macartney, Counsellor of the Chinese Legation, visited the Foreign office at 3:30 yesterday afternoon. In conversation with a press representative, Sir Halliday said: I am unable to give you any information about the man detained at the Legation, beyond what has already appeared in print. On being informed that the Foreign office had just issued an announcement to the effect that Lord Salisbury had requested the Chinese Minister to release the prisoner, Sir Halliday admitted that this was so, and in answer to a further question as to what would be the result of the request, replied: "The man will be released, but this will be done strictly without prejudice to the rights of the Legation involved."

In course of a later conversation with a representative of the press, Sir Halliday Macartney said: Sun Yat Sen is not the name of the man whom we have in detention upstairs. We have no doubt of his real identity, and have been from time to time fully informed of all his movements since he set foot in England. He came of his own free will to the Legation, and was certainly not kidnapped or forced or inveigled into the premises. It is quite a usual thing for solitary Chinamen in London to call here to make casual inquiries, or to have a chat with a countryman. There appears, moreover, to be some ground for suspecting that this peculiar visitor, believing himself unknown, came with some idea of spying on us and getting some information. Nobody knew him by sight. When he called he got into conversation with one of our staff, and was afterwards introduced to me. We chatted for a while, and some remarks he made led me after he had gone to suspect he might be the person we were having watched. These suspicions being confirmed, he was, on returning the following day, detained, and he is still under detention pending instructions from the Chinese Government.

Speaking on the international side of the matter, Sir Halliday said: The man is not a British, but a Chinese subject. We contend that for certain purposes the Legation is Chinese territory, where the Chinese Minister alone has jurisdiction. If a Chinaman comes here voluntarily, and if there are charges or suspicions against him, we contend that no one outside has any right to interfere with his detention. It would be quite different if he were outside this building, for then he would be on British territory, and we could not arrest him without a warrant.

Answering further questions, Sir Halliday mentioned that the man was not treated like a prisoner, and every consideration had been paid to his comfort. Sir Halliday ridiculed the statement which has appeared that the captive might be subjected to torture or undue pressure. He added a statement that a letter of inquiry had been received from the Foreign office on the subject, which would receive immediate attention.

The *Central News* says: Sir Halliday Macartney, on his return to the Chinese Legation from the Foreign Office, proceeded to the bedside of the Minister Kung Ta Jen, and explained to him that Lord Salisbury had insisted upon the release of Sun Yat Sen.

It is not for me to discuss the behaviour of Sir Halliday Macartney; I leave that to public opinion and to his own conscience. In his own mind, I have no doubt, he has reasons for his action, but they seem scarcely consistent with those of a sane man, let alone the importance of the position he occupies. I expect Tang expressed the position pretty exactly when he told me that "the Minister is but a figure-head here, Macartney is the ruler."

Various reports of an intended rescue crept into the newspapers. The following is an example:

An Intended Rescue

In reference to the arrest of Sun Yat Sen, it has been ascertained that his friends had arranged a bold scheme to bring about his rescue. Had they not been definitely assured by the Foreign Office and Scotland Yard that no harm whatever should come to him, his rescue was to be effected by means of breaking the window of his room, and descending from the roof of No. 51 Portland place, the residence of Viscount Powerscourt. His friends had succeeded in informing him of the plan they intended to pursue, and although information which was subsequently obtained pointed to the fact that Sun Yat Sen was being kept handcuffed, a promise of inside assistance in opening the window satisfied his friends of the feasibility of the plan. Indeed, so far matured was the scheme, that a cab was held in waiting to convey Sun Yat Sen to the home of a friend. By the prisoner's friends it is declared that Long, the interpreter at the Legation, was one of the Chinamen who actually decoyed Sun into the Legation, though he was invariably the most positive subsequently in denying that such a man had ever been inside the Legation walls. His friends declare that Sun was dressed in English clothes, and so far from his being a typical Oriental, when dressed according to Western fashion was invariably taken for an Englishman. He is declared to be a man of unbounded good nature and of the gentlest disposition in Hong Kong, and the various places where he practised medicine he obtained a reputation for skill and benevolence towards the poor. He is believed to have been in a great extent the tool of the Canton conspirators, though he never hesitated to condemn the cruel and oppressive Government of the Viceroy of Canton. He is said to have journeyed throughout

Canton in the interests of his society, and the plot itself is declared to be the most widespread and formidable since the present Emperor commenced to reign.

The real facts are these. Cole sent the following communication to Mr. Cantlie on October 19th, 1896: "I shall have a good opportunity to let Mr. Sun out on to the roof of the next house in Portland Place to-night. If you think it advisable, get permission from the occupants of the house to have someone waiting there to receive him. If I am to do it, find means to let me know." Mr. Cantlie went with this letter to Scotland Yard and requested that a constable be posted with himself on the roof of the house in question; but the Scotland Yard authorities, thinking it was an undignified proceeding, dissuaded him from his purpose, and gave it as their firm conviction that I should walk out by the front door in a day or two.

CHAPTER VIII

RELEASED

On October 22nd Cole directed my attention to the coal scuttle, and when he left the room I picked up a clipping from a newspaper, which proved to be the *Globe*. There I read the account of my detention, under the heading: "*Startling Story*! *Conspirator Kidnapped in London*! *Imprisonment at the Chinese Embassy*!" And then followed a long and detailed account of my position. At last the Press had interfered, and I felt that I was really safe. It came as a reprieve to a condemned man, and my heart was full of thankfulness.

Friday, October 23rd, dawned, and the day wore on, and still I was in durance. At 4.30 p.m., however, on that day, my English and Chinese guards came into the room and said, "Macartney wants to see you downstairs." I was told to put on my boots and hat and overcoat. I according [accordingly] did so, not knowing whither I was going. I descended the stairs, and as it was to the basement I was being conducted, I believed I was to be hidden in a cellar whilst the house was being searched by the command of the British Government. I was not told I was to be released, and I thought I was to enter another place of imprisonment or punishment. It seemed too good to be true that I was actually to be released. However, Mr. Cantlie presently appeared on the scene in company with two other men, who turned out to be Inspector Jarvis from Scotland Yard, and an old man, the messenger from the Foreign Office.

Sir Halliday Macartney then, in the presence of these gentlemen, handed me over the various effects that had been taken from me, and addressed the Government officials to the following effect:

"I hand this man over to you, and I do so on condition that neither the prerogative nor the diplomatic rights of the Legation are interfered with," or words to that effect. I was too excited to commit them to memory, but they seemed to me then, as they do now, senseless and childish.

The meeting related above took place in a passage in the basement of the house, and I was told I was a free man. Sir Halliday then shook hands with us all, a post-Judas salutation, and we were shown out by a side-door leading to the area. From thence we ascended the area steps, and issued into Weymouth Street from the back door of the Legation.

It will perhaps escape observation and pass out of mind as but a minor circumstance that we were sent out by the *back* door of the Legation.

The fact of the rescue was the all important measure in the minds of the little group of Englishmen present; not so, however, with my astute countryman; not so especially with Sir Halliday Macartney, that embodiment of retrograde orientalism.

The fact that the representatives of the British Government were shown out by the back door, as common carrion [carrier], will redound to the credit of the Minister and his *clientelle* in the high courts of their country. It was intended as a slight and insult, and it was carried out as only one versed in the Chinese methods of dealing with foreigners can appreciate. The excuse, no doubt, was that the hall was crowded with reporters; that a considerable throng of people had assembled in the street outside the building; that the Foreign Office was anxious that the affair should be conducted quietly without demonstration. These, no doubt, were the reasons present in the ever-ready minds of these Manchurian rapscallions and their caretaker Macartney.

To English ways of looking at things, the fact of my release was all that was cared for; but to the Chinese the manner of the release wiped out all the triumph of British diplomacy in obtaining it. Both had their triumph, and no doubt it brought them equal gratification.

It was not an imposing party that proceeded to the Chinese Legation that Friday afternoon in October; but one member of it, the venerable old messenger from the Foreign Office, had a small note concealed in the depths of his greatcoat pocket that seemed to bear great weight. It must have been short and to the point, for it took Macartney but two or three seconds to master its contents. Short it may have been, but it bore the sweet message of freedom for me, and an escape from death, and what I dreaded more, the customary exquisite torture to which political prisoners in China are submitted to procure confession of the names of accomplices.

In Weymouth Street a considerable crowd had assembled, and the everpresent newspaper reporter tried to inveigle me there and then into a confession. I was, however, speedily put into a fourwheeled cab, and, in company with Mr. Cantlie, Inspector Jarvis, and the messenger, driven off towards Scotland Yard. On the way thither Inspector Jarvis gravely lectured me on my delinquencies, and scolded me as a bad boy, and advised me to have nothing to do any more with revolutions. Instead of stopping at Scotland Yard, however, the cab drew up at the door of a restaurant in Whitehall, and we got out on the pavement. Immediately the newspaper men surrounded me; where they came from I could not tell. We had left them a mile away in Portland Place, and here they were again the moment my cab stopped. There is no repressing them; one man had actually, unknown to us, climbed up on the seat beside the driver. He it was 〔It was he〕that stayed the cab at the restaurant, knowing well that if once I was within the precincts of Scotland Yard they could not get at me for some time. Unless the others—some dozen in number—were on the roof of my cab, I cannot understand where they sprang from. I was hustled from the pavement into the back premises of the hostelry with much more violence than ever was expended upon me when originally taken within the Chinese Legation, and surrounded by a crowd thirsting for knowledge as eagerly as my countrymen thirsted for my head. Pencils executed wonderful hieroglyphics which I had never seen before, and I did not know until that moment that English could be written in what seemed to me cuneiform characters. I found out afterwards it was in shorthand they were writing.

I spoke until I could speak no more, and it was only when Mr. Cantlie called out "Time, gentlemen!" that I was forcibly rescued from their midst and carried off to Scotland Yard. At the Yard I was evidently regarded as a child of their own delivery, and Jarvis's honest face was a picture to behold. However, the difficult labour was over, and here I was free to make my own confession. I was detained there for an hour, during which time I made a full statement of the circumstances of my capture and detention. This was all taken down and read over to me, and I appended my signature and bade a cordial adieu to my friends in the police force. Mr. Cantlie and myself then hied ourselves homewards, where a hospitable welcome was accorded 〈to〉 me, and over an appetising dinner, a toast to my "head" was drunk with enthusiasm.

During the evening I was frequently interviewed, and it was not until a late hour that I was allowed to rest. Oh! that first night's sleep! Shall I ever forget it? For nine hours did it last, and when I awoke it was to the noise of children romping on the floor above me. It was evident by their loud, penetrating voices some excitement was on hand, and as I listened I could hear the cause of it. "Now, Colin, you be Sun Yat Sen, and Neil will be Sir Halliday Macartney, and I will rescue Sun." Then followed a turmoil; Sir Halliday was knocked endways, and a crash on the floor made me believe that my little friend Neil was no more. Sun was brought out in triumph by Keith, the eldest boy, and a general amnesty was declared by the beating of drums, the piercing notes of a tin whistle, and the singing of "The British Grenadiers." This was home and safety, indeed; for it was evident my youthful friends were prepared to shed the last drop of their blood on my behalf.

During Saturday, October 24th, I was interviewing all day. The one question put was, "How did you let the doctors know?" and the same question was addressed to Mr. Cantlie many scores of times. We felt, however, that our tongues were tied; as, by answering the query, we should be incriminating those who, within the Legation walls, had acted as my friends, and they would lose their positions. However, when Cole resolved to resign his appointment, so that none of the others should be wrongly suspected, there was no object in hiding who had been the informant. It is all very well to say that I bribed him; that is not the case. He did not understand that I gave him the money by way of fee at all; he believed I gave it him [him it] to keep for me; he told Mr. Cantlie he had the £ 20 the day he got it, and offered to give it to him for safe keeping. When I came out Cole handed the money back to me, but it was the least I could do to urge him to keep it. I wish it had been more, but it was all the ready money I had. Cole had many frights during this time, but perhaps the worst scare he got was at the very first start. On the Sunday afternoon, October 18th, when he had made up his mind to help me practically, he took my notes to Mr. Cantlie, in his pocket, at 46 Devonshire Street. The door was opened and he was admitted within the hall. The doctor was not at home, so he asked to see his wife. Whilst the servant was gone to fetch her mistress, Cole became conscious of the presence of a Chinaman watching him from the far end of the hall. He immediately suspected that he had been followed or rather anticipated, for here was a Chinaman, pigtail and all 〔tall〕, earnestly scrutinising him from a recess. When Mrs. Cantlie came down she beheld a man, trembling with fear and pale from terror, who could hardly speak. The cause of this alarm was a model of a Chinaman, of most life-like appearance, which Mr. Cantlie had brought home with him amongst his curios from Hong Kong. It has frightened many other visitors with less tender consciences than Cole's, whose overwrought nerves actually endowed the figure with a halo of terrible reality. Mrs. Cantlie relieved Cole's mind from his fear and sent him in to find her husband at Dr. Manson's. My part of the tale is nearly ended; what further complications in connection with this affair may arise I cannot say. There is not time, as yet, to hear how the papers in other English-speaking countries will deal with the subject, and as Parliament has not yet assembled I cannot say what questions appertaining to the event may be forthcoming. I have, however, found many friends since my release. I have paid several pleasant visits to the country. I have been dined and feasted, and run a good chance of being permanently spoiled by my well-wishers in and around London.

APPENDIX

I append a few of the numerous articles called forth by my arrest. The first is a letter from Professor Holland to *The Times*, and is headed:

The Case of Sun Yat Sen
——To the Editor of *THE TIMES*

Sir, the questions rasied by the imprisonment of Sun Yat Sen are two in number. First, was the act of the Chinese Minister in detaining him an unlawful act? And secondly, if so, what steps could properly have been taken to obtain his release had it been refused?

The reply to the former question is not far to seek. The claim of an Ambassador to exercise any sort of domestic jurisdiction, even over members of his suite, is now little heard of, although, in 1603, Sully, when French Ambassador, went so far as to sentence one of his *attachés* to death, handing him over to the Lord Mayor for execution. I can recall but one instance of an attempt on the part of a Minister to exercise constraint against a person unconnected with his mission. In 1642, Leitao, Portuguese Minister at the Hague, detained in his house a horse-dealer who had cheated him. The result was a riot, in which the hotel was plundered, and Wicquefort remarks upon the transaction that Leitao, who had given public lectures on the Law of Nations, ought to have know *qu'il ne luiestoit pas permis de faire une prison de sa maison*. Sun Yat Sen, while on British soil as a *subditus temporarius*, was under the protection of our Laws, and his confinement in the Chinese Legation was a high offence against the rights of the British Crown.

The second question, though not so simple, presents no serious difficulty. A refusal on the part of the Chinese Minister to release his prisoner would have been a sufficient ground for requesting him to leave the country. If this mode of proceeding would have been too dilatory for the exigencies of the case, it can hardly be doubted that the circumstances would have justified an entry upon the Legation premises by the London police. An Ambassador's hotel is said to be "extra-territorial," but this too compendious phrase means no more than that the hotel is for certain purposes inaccessible to the ordinary jurisdiction of the country in which it stands. The exemptions thus enjoyed are, however, strictly defined by usage, and new exemptions cannot be deduced from a metaphor. The case of Gyllenburg, in 1717, showed that if a Minister is suspected of conspiring against the Government to which he is accredited he may be arrested and his cabinets may be ransacked. The case of the coachman of Mr. Gallatin, in 1827, establishes that, after courteous notice, the police may enter a Legation in order to take into custody one of its servants who has been guilty of an offence elsewhere. There is also a general agreement that, except possibly in Spain and in the South American Republics, the hotel is no longer an asylum fox even political offenders. Still less can it be supposed that an illegal imprisonment in a Minister's residence will not be put an end to by such action of the local police as may be necessary.

It seems needless to inquire into the responsibility which would rest upon the Chinese authorities if Sun Yat Sen was, as he alleges, kidnapped in the open street, or would have rested upon them had they removed him through the streets, with a view to shipping him off to China. Acts of this kind find no defenders. What is admitted to have occurred is sufficiently serious, and was doubtless due to excess of zeal on the part of the subordinates of the Chinese Legation. International law has long been ably taught by Dr. Martin at the Tung-wen College of Peking, and the Imperial Government cannot be supposed to be indifferent to a strict conformity to the precepts of the science on the part of its representatives at foreign Courts.

I am, Sir, your obedient servant,

T. E. HOLLAND

Oxford, October 24th.

Another legal opinion is referred to below:

Legal Opinion

Mr. Cavendish, one of the best authorities on the law of extradition, informed an interviewer at Bow Street yesterday that, speaking from memory, he could cite no case at all parallel with the case of Sun Yat Sen. The case of the Zanzibar Pretender was, of course, in no way parallel, for he took refuge in the German Consulate. He threw himself on the hospitality of the German Government, which, following the procedure sanctioned by International Law, refuses to give him up, and conveyed him to German territory on the mainland. Sun Yat Sen's case was that of an alleged Chinese subject, having come within the walls of the Legation of his own country, was arrested by representative of his own Government for an offence against that Government. Mr. Cavendish assumed that if the facts were as stated, the case could only be dealt vith by diplomatic representation on the part of our Foreign Office, and not by any known legal rule.

The next is a letter from Mr. James G. Wood to the same paper discussing some of the points of law rasied in Professor Holland's letter:

To the Editor of *THE TIMES*

Sir, —The second question proposed by Professor Holland, though fortunately, under the circumstances, not of present importance, is deserving of careful consideration. I venture to think his answer to it unsatisfactory.

It is suggested that on a refusal by the Chinese Minister to release his prisoner, "it can hardly be doubted that the circumstances would have justified an entry on the Legation premises by the London police. " But why there should not be such a doubt is not explained. This is not solving the question but guessing at its solution. The London police have no roving commission to release persons unlawfully detained in London houses; and anyone attempting to enter for such a purpose could be lawfully resisted by force.

The only process known to the law as applicable to a case of unlawful detention is a writ of *habeas corpus*, and this is where the real difficulty lies. Could such a writ be addressed to an Ambassador or any member of the Legation? Or if it were, and it were disregarded, could process of contempt follow? I venture to think not; and I know of no precedent for such proceeding.

I agree that the phrase that an Ambassador's hotel is extra-territorial is so metaphysical as to be misleading. It is, in fact, inaccurate. The more careful writers do not use it. The true proposition is not that the residence is extraterritorial in the sense in which a ship is often said to be so, but the Minister himself is deemed to be so; and as a consequence he and the members of his family and suite are said to enjoy a complete immunity from all civil process. It is not a question of what may or may not be done in the residence, but what may or may not be done to individuals. That being so, the process I have mentioned appears to involve a breach of the comity of nations.

To adduce cases where the police have under a warrant entered an Embassy to arrest persons who have committed an offence elsewhere to found the proposition that "the local police may take action to put an end to an illegal imprisonment," begun and continued within the Embassy, does not land us on safe ground. There is no common feature in the two cases.

I am, Sir, your obedient servant,

JAMES G. WOOD

October 27th.

The Supposed Chinese Revolutionist

(From the *China Mail*, Hong Kong, Dec. 3rd, 1896)

Sun Yat Sen, who has recently been in trouble in London through the Chinese Minister attempting to kidnap him for execution as a rebel, is not unlikely to become a prominent character in history. Of course, it would not be right to state, until a duly constituted court of law has found, that a man is definitely Connected with any illegal movement, or that any movement with which he is connected is definitely anti-dynastic. The only suggestion of Dr. Sun Yat Sen being a rebel in any sense comes from the Chinese Legation in London and the officials of Canton. But without any injury to him it may be safely said that he is a remarkable man, with most enlightened views on the undoubtedly miserable state of China's millions, and that there are many Chinese who feel very strongly on the subject and try now and then to act very strongly. The allegation of the officials is that these people tried to accomplish a revolution in October, 1895, and that Sun Yat Sen was a leader in the conspiracy. Foreigners, even those resident in the Far East, had little knowledge how near the long-expected break-up of China then was. As it happened, the outbreak missed fire, and what little attention it did attract was of the contemptuous sort. The situation was, however, one of as great danger as any since the Tai Pings were suppressed, and the organisation was much more up-to-date and on a more enlightened basis than even that great rebellion. In fact, it was the intelligence of the principal movers that caused the movement to be discountenanced at an early stage as premature, instead of struggling on with a more disastrous failure in view, for the revolution is only postponed, not abandoned for ever. The origin of the movement cannot be specifically traced; it arose from the general dissatisfaction of Chinese with Manchu rule, and it came to a head on the outbreak of war between China and Japan. The malcontents saw that the war afforded an opportunity to put their aspirations into shape, and they promptly set to work. At first, that is to say before China had been so soundly thrashed all along the line, they had in view purely lawful and constitutional measures, and hoped to effect radical changes without resort to violence. Dr. Sun worked hard and loyally to fuse the inchoate elements of disaffection brought into existence by Manchu misgovernment, and to give the whole reform movement a purely constitutional form, in the earnest hope of raising his wretched country out of the Slough of Despond in which it was and is sinking deeper daily. His was the master mind that strove to subdue the wild uncontrollable spirits always prominent in Chinese reactionary schemes, to harmonise conflicting interests, not only as between various parties in his own country but also as between Chinese and foreigners, and as between various foreign Powers. The most difficult problem was to work out the sequel of any upheaval—to anticipate and be ready in advance to deal with all the complications bound to ensue as soon as the change took place. Moreover he had to bear in mind that any great reform movement must necessarily depend very largely on the aid of foreigners, of nations and individuals as well, while there is throughout China an immense mass of anti-foreign prejudice which would have to be overcome somehow. The task was stupendous, hopeless in fact, but he recognised that the salvation of China depended and still depends on something of the sort being some day rendered possible, and that the only way to accomplish it was to try, try, try again. That is to say, last year's attempt was not likely to succeed, but was likely to bring success a stage nearer, and in that sense it was well worth the effort to an ardent patriot. Dr. Sun was the only man who combined a complete grasp of the situation with a reckless bravery of the kind which alone can make a national regeneration. He was born in Honolulu, and had a good English education. He has travelled extensively in Europe and America, and is a young man of remarkable attainments. He was for some time a medical student in Dr. Kerr's School in Tientsin, and afterwards was on the staff of the Alice Memorial Hospital in Hong Kong. He is of average height, thin and wiry, with a keenness of expression and frankness of feature seldom seen in Chinese. An unassuming manner and an earnestness of speech, combined with a quick perception and resolute judgment, go to impress one with the conviction that he is in every way an exceptional type of his race. Beneath his calm exterior is hidden a personality that cannot but be a great influence for good in China sooner or later, if the Fates are fair. In China, any advocate of reform or any foe of corruption and oppression is liable to be regarded as a violent revolutionist, and summarily executed. It has been the same in the history of every country when freedom and enlightenment were in their infancy, or not yet born. The propaganda had therefore to be disseminated with the greatest care, and at imminent peril. First, an able and exhaustive treatise on political matters was published in Hong Kong, and circulated all over China, especially in the south, where it created a sensation, early in 1895. It was most cautiously worded, and the most censorious official could not lay his finger on a word of it and complain; but it depicted in vivid colours the beauties of enlightened and honest government, contrasted with the horrors of corrupt and tyrannical misgovernment. This feeler served to show how much voluntary reform could be expected of Chinese officialdom, for it had as much effect as a volume of sermons thrown among a shoal [school] of sharks. Then it became no longer possible to control the spirits of insurrection. Steps were at once taken to organise a rebellion, with which it is alleged, but not yet proved, that Dr. Sun Yat Sen was associated. Before the war there had been insurrectionary conspiracies—in fact, such things are chronic in China. The navy was disaffected, because of certain gross injustices and extortions practised on the officers and men by the all-powerful mandarins. The commanders of land forces and forts were not much different, and many civilian officials were willing to join in a rising. No doubt much of the support accorded to the scheme was prompted by ulterior motives, for there are more of that sort than of any other in China. The rebellion was almost precipitated in March, when funds were supplied from Honolulu, Singapore, Australia, and elsewhere; but men of the right sort were still wanting, and arms had not been obtained in great quantity, and wiser counsels prevailed. It would have been better perhaps if wiser counsels had prevailed in October, but wisdom cannot come without experience, and for the sake of the experience the leaders of the abortive revolution do hot greatly regret their action. Some indeed drew out as soon as it became certain that violent measures were to be adopted; but the penalty of death would not be obviated by that, and it was at imminent risk of his life that Dr. Sun had been travelling throughout the length and breadth of China, preaching the gospel of good government and gathering recruits for constitutional reform. His allies, never very confident in pacific methods, planned a bold *coup d'etat*, which might have gained a momentary success, but made no provision for what would happen in the next few moments. Men were drafted to Hong Kong to be prepared for an attack on Canton; arms and ammunition were smuggled in cement-casks; money was subscribed lavishly, foreign advisers and commanders were obtained, and attempts were made, without tangible result, to secure the co-operation of the Japanese Government. What would have been the result if the verbal sympathy of Japanese under-officials had been followed by active sympathy in higher quarters, none can tell; the indemnity, the Liaotung Settlement, the commercial treaty, the whole history of the relations between Japan and China and Europe since the war might have been totally different. Every detail of the plot was arranged, but before the time for striking the blow, treachery stepped in. A prominent Chinese merchant of Hong Kong had professed adherence to the reform movement, for he had much to gain by it; then he concluded that he could gain more by playing into the hands of the official vampires, for he was connected with one of the many syndicates formed to compete for railway and mining concessions in China after the war. So he gave information, and the cement was examined, with the result that the whole *coup d'etat* was nothing more than a flash in the pan. Dr. Sun happened to be in Canton at the time, and was accused of active participation in the violent section of the reform movement. In China, to be innocent is not to be safe; an accusation is none the less dangerous for being utterly unfounded. Sun had to fly for his life, without a moment's deliberation as to friends or property or anything else; and for two or three weeks he was a fugitive hiding in the labyrinthine canals and impenetrable pirate-haunts of the great Kwang-Tung Delta. A report has been published that forty or fifty of his supposed accomplices were executed, and a reward was offered for his arrest, but he got away to Honolulu and thence to America. The story goes that this indomitable patriot immediately set to work converting the Chinese at the Washington Embassy to the cause of reform, and that afterwards he tried to do the same in London; that one of the Chinese in the Legation at Washington had professed sympathy with the apostle of enlightenment, and then thought more money could be made on the other side, and so telegraphed to the London Embassy to arrest Sun and kidnap him back to China by hook or by crook. However that may be, he was captured and confined in a most outrageous manner in the London Legation, whatever Plausible piffle may be put forward by Sir Halliday Macartney, or any servile prevaricator; and it is due to Dr.

Cantlie, Sun's friend and teacher in Hong Kong, that one of the best men China has ever produced was rescued by British justice from the toils of treacherous mandarindom. All who know Dr. Cantlie—and he is well known in many parts of the world—agree that a more upright, honourable and devoted benefactor of humanity has never breathed. Dr. Sun is in good hands, and under the protection of such a man as Dr. Cantlie there can be little doubt that he will pursue his chosen career with single-hearted enthusiasm and most scrupulous straight-forwardness of methods, until at last the good work of humanising the miserable condition of the Chinese Empire is brought to a satisfactory state of perfection.

A leading article in *The Times* of Saturday, October 24th, 1896, discusses the question very fully:

While the "Concert of Europe" is supposed to be making steady progress towards the establishment of harmony amongst the constituent Powers, the ordinarily smooth course of diplomatic intercourse has been ruffled by a curious violation of law and custom at the Chinese Legation—a violation which might have led to tragic cousequences, but which has so turned out as to present chiefly a ludicrous side for our consideration. Through a communication made on Thursday to our contemporary the *Globe*, it became known that a Chinese visitor to England, a doctor named Sun Yat Sen, was imprisoned at the house of the Chinese Minister, and that it was supposed to be the intention of his captors to send him under restraint to his own country, there to receive such measure of justice as a Chinese tribunal might he expected to extend to an alleged conspirator. Fortunately for the prisoner, he had studied medicine at Hong Kong, where he had made the acquaintance and had won the friendly regard of Mr. Cantlie, the Dean of the Hong Kong Medical College, and of Dr. Manson, both of whom are now residing in London. Sun Yat Sen was sufficiently supplied with money, and he succeeded in finding means of communication with these English friends, who at once took steps to inform the police authorities and the Foreign Office of what was being done, while, at the same time, they employed detectives to watch the Legation, in order to prevent the possibility of the prisoner being secretly conveyed away. Lord Salisbury, as soon as he was informed of what had occurred made a demand for the immediate release of the prisoner, who was forthwith set at liberty, and was taken away by Mr. Cantlie and Dr. Manson, who attended in order to identify him as the person they had known. He has since furnished representatives of the

Press with an account of the circumstances of his capture and detention, an account which differs in important respects from that of the Chinese authorities. If the Chinese had accomplished their supposed object, and had smuggled Sun Yat Sen on shipboard, to be tried and probably executed in China, our Foreign Office would have had to deal with an offence against the comity of nations for which it would have been necessary to demand and obtain the punishment of all concerned. The failure of the attempt may perhaps be held to bring it too near the confines of comic opera to furnish a subject for anything more than serious remonstrance.

The offence alleged against Sun Yat Sen is that his medical character is a mere cloak for other designs, and that he is really Sun Wen, the prime over [mover] in a conspiracy which was discovered in 1894, and which had for its object the dethronement of the present reigning dynasty. The first step of the conspirators was to be the capture of the Viceroy of Canton, who was to be kidnapped when inspecting the arsenal; but the plot, like most plots, leaked out or was betrayed, and fifteen of the ringleaders were arrested and decapitated. Sun Wen saved himself by timely flight, and made his way through Honolulu and America to this country, being all the time carefully watched by detectives. On reaching England, at the beginning of the present month, he called upon his old friends, Mr. Cantlie and Dr. Manson, and prepared to commence a course of medical study in London. A few days later he disappeared, and on the evening of last Saturday Mr. Cantlie was informed of his position. Sun Wen, or Sun Yat Sen, whichever he may be alleges that he was walking in or near Portland Place on the 11th inst., when he was accosted in the street by a fellow-countryman, who asked whether he was Chinese or Japanese; and, being told in reply that he was Chinese and a native of Canton, hailed him as a fellow provincial, and kept him in conversation until a second and then a third Chinaman joined them. One of the three left, while the other two walked slowly on until they reached the Legation, when the others invited Sun to enter, and supported the invitation by the exercise of a certain amount of force. As soon as he was inside, the door was shut and he was conveyed upstairs to a room where, as he alleges, he was seen by Sir Halliday Macartney, and in which he was afterwards kept close prisoner until released by the intervention of Lord Salisbury. The officials of the Chinese Legation, on the other hand, assert that the man came to the Legation of his own accord on Saturday, the 10th, and entered into conversation, talking about Chinese affairs, and appearing to want only a chat with some of his fellow-countrymen, after having which he went away; and that it was not until after he had gone that suspicion was excited that he might be the notorious Sun Wen, who had fled from justice at home, whose passage through America and departure for England had already been telegraphed to the Legation, and who was actually then being watched by a private detective in the employment of the Chinese Government. Sun came to the Legation a second time, on Sunday, the 11th, and then, evidence of his identity having been obtained, he was made ⟨a⟩ prisoner. It had been supposed that he was about to return to Hong Kong as to a convenient base for further operations; and it was the intention of the Chinese Government to ask for his extradition as soon as he arrived there. In the meanwhile the actual presence of the supposed conspirator in the Legation furnished a temptation which it was found impossible to resist, and he was locked up until instructions with regard to him could arrive from Peking. There can be little doubt that these instructions, if they had been received and could have been acted upon, would have effectually destroyed his power to engage in any further conspiracies; and it may be assumed that the intervention of Lord Salisbury was not too early. Even as it was Sun appears to have suffered considerable anxiety lest the food supplied to him at the Legation should be unwholesome in its character.

The simple process of cutting a knot is often preferable to the labour of untying it, and we are not very much surprised that the Chinese Minister or his representative should have authorized the adoption of the course which has happily failed of success. But we cannot conceal our surprise that Sir Halliday Macartney, himself an Englishman, should have taken any part in a transaction manifestly doomed to failure, and the success of which would have been ruinous to all engaged in it. The Chinese Minister is said to have surrendered his prisoner "without prejudice," as lawyers say, to his assumed rights; but he appears to have claimed a right which is not acknowledged by any civilized country, and which would be intolerable if it were exercised. It would be a somewhat similar proceeding if the Turkish Ambassador were to inveigle some of the leading members of the Armenian colony in London into the Embassy, in order to despatch them, gagged and bound, as an offering to his Imperial Majesty the Sultan, or if Lord Dufferin had in the same way made a private prisoner of Tynan, and had sent him to stand his trial at the Old Bailey. It is well recognised that the house of a foreign mission is regarded as a portion of the country from which the mission is sent, and that not only the Minister himself, but also the recognised members of his state, enjoy an immunity from liability to the laws of the country to which the Ambassador is accredited; but this hardly entitles the Ambassador to exercise powers of imprisonment or of criminal jurisdiction, and the privileges of the Embassy as a place of refuge for persons unconnected with it are strictly limited to the ground on which it stands. Even if the Chinese Minister could not have been prevented from keeping Sun in custody, he would have been liberated by the police as soon as he was brought over the threshold to be conveyed elsewhere. It is fortunate that he did not suffer from any form of illness; for if he had died during his imprisonment, it is very difficult to say what could have been done in consequence. Evidence would have been very hard to procure; and, even if it had been procured, the persons of the Minister and of his servants would have been sacred. Probably the only course would have been to demand that the Minister should be recalled, and that he should be put upon his trial in his own country; a demand which might perhaps have been readily complied with, but which might not improbably have led to what Englishmen would describe as a miscarriage of justice. We think that this country, almost as much as the prisoner, may be congratulated upon the turn of events; and we have no doubt that the Foreign Office will find ways and means of making the rulers of the Celestial Empire understand that they have gone a little too far, and that they must not commit any similar offence in the future.

This Article called forth a remonstrance from Sir Halliday Macartney, in which he stated his views:

To the Editor of *The Times*

Sir, —In your leading article of to-day, commenting on the alleged kidnapping of an individual, a Chinese subject, calling himself, amongst numerous other aliases, by the name of Sun Yat Sen, you make some remarks with regard to me which I cannot but consider as an exception to the fairness which in general characterises the comments of *The Times*.

After stating the case as given by the two opposite parties, in the surprise which you express at my conduct, you take it for granted that the statement of Sun Yat Sen is the correct one and that of the Chinese Legation the wrong one.

I do not know why you make this assumption, for you undoubtedly do so when you say the case is as if the Turkish Ambassador had inveigled some of the members of the Armenian colony of London into the Embassy with a view to making them a present to his Majesty the Sultan.

Now, I repeat what I have said before—that in this case there was no inveiglement. The statement of Sun Yat Sen—or, to call him by his real name, Sun Wen—that he was caught in the street and hustled into the Legation by two sturdy Chinamen is utterly false.

He came to the Legation unexpectedly and of his own accord, the first time on Saturday, the 10th, the second on Sunday, the 11th.

Whatever the pundits of international law may think of his detention, they may take it as being absolutely certain that there was no kidnapping and that he entered the Legation without the employment of force or guile.

I am, Sir, your obedient servant,

Halliday Macartney

Richmond House
49 Portland Place, W.
Oct. 24th

Sir Halliday Macartney's remarks about my going under various aliases, is no doubt intended to cast a slur upon my character; but Sir Halliday knows, no one better, that every Chinaman has four names at least to which he is entitled. 1st, the name one's parents bestow on their child. 2nd, the name given by the school master. 3rd, the name a young man wishes to be known by when he goes out into society. 4th, the name he takes when he is married. The only constant part of the name is the first syllable—the surname, really the family name; the other part of the name varies according [accordingly] as it is ⟨what⟩ the parent, the schoolmaster, etc., chooses. Whilst upon this subject it may not be without interest to know that my accuser has various aliases by which he is known to the Chinese. In addition to the name Ma-Ta-Jen, which means Macartney, His Excellency, he is also known as Ma-Ka-Ni, and as Ma-Tsing-Shan, showing that no name is constant in China except the family name.

From *THE SPEAKER*, October 31st, 1896
The Dungeons of Portland Place

Sir Halliday Macartney is an official in the service of the Chinese Government. That fact seems to have deprived him of any sense of humour he might otherwise have had, which, we imagine, would in no circumstances have been conspicuous. The Secretary of he Chinese Legation has struck an attitude of injured innocence in *The Times*. He is like Woods Pasha, when that undiscerning personage stands up for the Turkish Government in an English newspaper. What in a true Oriental would seem natural and characteristic, in the sham Oriental is merely ridiculous. Sir Halliday Macartney assures the world that the Chinese medical gentleman who was lately released from the Portland Place Bastille was not inveigled into the institution. To the obvious suggestion that Sun Yat Sen would never have walked into the Chinese Embassy of his own accord, had he known the real identity of his entertainers, Sir Halliday vouchsafes no reply. It is unquestionable that he saw the captive, and took no measures to set him at liberty, till a peremptory requisition came from the Foreign Office. If it was not intended to deport Sun Yat Sen to China, why was he kept a prisoner? Sir Halliday Macartney is in the pitiable position of an Englishman who is forced by his official obligations to palliate in London what would be the ordilnary course of justice at Canton. A purely Chinese emissary would have said nothing. Having failed in his manoeuvre, he would have accepted the consequences of defeat with the fatalism of his race and native climate. The spectacle of Sir Halliday Macartney fussing and fuming in *The Times* like an Englishman, when he ought to hold his peace like a Chinaman, can only suggest to the authorities at Peking that their English representative here is a rather incompetent person.

On the other hand, there is something in this Chinese kidnapping which is irresistibly diverting. Englishmen can never take the Chinaman seriously, in spite of Charles Pearson's prediction that the yellow man will one day eat us up. The personality of Ah Sin, especially when he wears a pigtail and his native costume, is purely comic to the average sightseer. If the men who decoyed Sun Yat Sen were pointed out to a London crowd, they would be greeted not with indignation, but with mildly derisive banter, It might go hard with any Europeans who had tried the same game; but Ah Sin, the childlike and bland, is a traditional joke. His strategy excites no more resentment than the nodding of the ornamental mandarin on the mantelpiece. The popular idea of Lord Sahshuly's intervention in this case is probably that the Chinaman's pigtail has been gently but decisively pulled, and that such a lesson is quite sufficient without any public anger. Had a German or a Frenchman been kidnapped in similar circumstances the situation would at once have been recognised as extremely serious. The capture and incarceration in Portland Place simply excite a smile. The newspapers have treated the incident as they treat the announcement that Li Hung Chang, promoted to be Imperial Chancellor of China, had at the same time been punished for an unauthorised visit to the Empress Dowager. How can you be angry with a people whose solemnities frequently strike the Occidental mind as screaming farce? It is impossible to pass No. 40 Portland Place with a romantic shudder. That middle-class dwelling, of substantial and comfortable aspect, is now a Bastille *pour rire*, and excites the mirth of tradesmen's boys, who must feel strongly tempted, by way of celebrating the Fifth of November, to ring the bell and introduce a Celestial guy to the puzzled servitors of the Embassy, with a fluent tirade in pigeon-English.

As for Sun Yat Sen, it cannot escape his notice that there is little curiosity to know the precise reason why he is obnoxious to the Chinese Government. He is said to have taken part in a conspiracy against the Viceroy of Canton, a statement which conveys no vivid impression to the popular mind. Political refugees—Italians, Poles, Hungafians—have commonly inspired a romantic interest in this country. They have figured in our fiction, always a sure criterion of public sympathies. When the storyteller takes the foreign conspirator in hand, you may be sure that the machinations, escapes, and so forth touch a responsive chord in the popular imagination. But no storyteller is likely to turn the adventures of Sun Yat Sen to such account, though they may be really thrilling, and though this worthy Celestial medico may have been quite a formidable person in his native land. Even the realistic descriptions by travellers of Chinese administration, the gentle coercion of witnesses in his courts by smashing their ankles, the slicing of criminals to death, have not given a sinister background to the figure of the Heathen Chinese. The ignominious defeat of the Chinese arms in the late war has strengthened the conception of the yellow man as a rather grotesquely ineffectual object. If Sun Yat Sen were to deliver a lecture on his adventures, and paint the tyranny of the Viceroy of Canton in the deepest colours, or if Sir Halliday Macartney were to show that his late prisoner was a monster of ferocity, compared to whom all the Western dynamiters were angels in isguise [disguise], we doubt whether either story would command the gravity of the public. The Chinese have their virtues; they are a frugal, thrifty, and abstemious people; they practise a greater respect for family ties than Western nations. The custom of worshipping their ancestor [ancestors], though one of the chief stumbling-blocks to the Christian missionaries, probably exercises a greater moral influence than the reverence for genealogy here. But no audience in England or America would accept these virtues as rebukes to the short-comings of the Anglo-Saxon civilisation. So deep is the gulf between Occident and Orient that the pride of neither will learn from the other, and both are indifferent to the warnings of prophets who foretell the triumph of the Caucasian in the Flowery Land or the submergement of Europe by the yellow flood of immigration. All Western notions are regarded in China with a contempt which even the travels of Li are not likely to dispel; and No. 40 Portland Place can never recover that prestige of harmless nonentity it enjoyed before the pranks of the Chinese Embassy made it a centre of the ludicrous.

The following is a copy of the letter I sent to the newspapers thanking the Government and the Press for what they had done for me:

To the Editor of the—

Sir, —Will you kindly express through your columns my keen appreciation of the action of the British Government in effecting my release from the Chinese Legation? I have also to thank the Press generally for their timely help and sympathy. If anything were needed to convince me of the generous public spirit which pervaded Great Britain, and the love of justice which distinguishes its people, the recent acts of the last few days have conclusively done so.

Knowing and feeling more keenly than ever what a constitutional Government and an enlightened people mean, I am prompted still more actively to pursue the cause of advancement, education, and civilisation in my own well-beloved but oppressed country.

Yours faithfully,

Sun Yat Sen

46 Devonshire Street

Portland Place, W.

Oct. 24

CHINA'S PRESENT AND FUTURE
THE REFORM PARTY'S PLEA FOR BRITISH BENEVOLENT NEUTRALITY

Mar. 1897

CHINA'S PRESENT AND FUTURE
THE REFORM PARTY'S PLEA FOR BRITISH BENEVOLENT NEUTRALITY *

Mar. 1897

* This article, which will probably form part of a book we are writting 〔writing〕 together, is the result of a collaboration between Dr. Sun Yat Sen and myself, in which he is responsible for the facts and for the opinions expressed; I, only for their selection from the mass of material, for their arrangement, and for the form in which they now appear. —Edwin Collins.

It is generally admitted that China's present condition and future prospects are far from satisfactory; but, as I venture to think, no European has yet fully realized the extent and far-reaching consequences of the corruption which makes China a reproach and danger among nations, or knows the extent of her latent recuperative forces, and of the possibilities that exist for her salvation from within.

By adducing facts which none but a Chinaman can fully know or adequately interpret, and of which the full significance can only become clear when they are described in detail, I hope to show that even China's physical evils are of moral origin; and that, nevertheless, the apparent inability and unwillingness of the Chinese to develop the country's vast internal resources and to resist external attack, are not inherent in the Chinese, but are entirely due to artificially produced causes and to artificially induced tendencies, which the Reform Party exists to remove or counteract.

It is too generally forgotten that the Chinese and the Chinese Government are not convertible terms; but that the throne and all the highest offices, military and civil, are filled by foreigners. These facts should always be allowed their due weight in passing judgment on the Chinese for conduct and characteristics which the Tartars have made prevalent; and, even more especially, when calculating the chances of internal reform, supposing it possible to effect the radical change of government for which we, of the Reform Party, hope. This only by way of parenthesis; but it is worth remembering, when the character of all Chinese official life, which I am about to delineate is under consideration.

Nothing short of the entire overthrow of the present utterly corrupt regime, and the establishment of good government and a pure administration by native Chinese with at first, European advice, and, for some years, European administrative assistance, can effect any improvement whatever. The mere introduction of railways or any such appliances of the material civilization of Europe, would (even were it as feasible as those who put their faith in Li Hung Chang seem to think) rather make matters worse, by opening up new channels for extortion, fraud, and peculation. That this is no overstatement of the case for the Reform Party's contention will perhaps only become clear when I have cited concrete examples of such failure in the past, and described, from my own personal knowledge and experience, the public and official life of China, and that with a minuteness of detail which might prove wearisome but for the startling—nay, almost incredible—nature of the facts to be revealed.

Since the written law of China is fairly good, and most of the worst abuses are cleverly worked into compatibility with the observance of its strict letter, it is not wonderful that the majority of Englishmen whose stay in China is only temporary, and who mostly have for their informants members of the very class whose interest [it] is to conceal the truth, gain but a very imperfect knowledge of the true state of affairs. There are, indeed, Englishmen who know the truth; but they have become, for the most part, to all intents and purposes, Chinese and members of a corrupt official class, who, like many I could name, out-Mandarin the Mandarins. Of myself it may be sufficient to say that before I adopted the study of medicine, my early years were spent in intimate association with members of the Chinese official class, and that my friends were anxious for me to purchase an entry into public life, as very many of my acquaintance have done within the last ten years. Thus I have had every opportunity and incentive to study the subject on which I am now writing.

The people of China suffer from four great and chronic afflictions: famine, flood, pestilence, and insecurity of life and property. This is a matter of common knowledge. Not so, however, to what an enormous extent all these troubles—even the first three—are preventible and are secondary as to their causation. There is, in truth, one and one only [only one] cause of these—and I may say of all—China's ill: that is the universal and systematic corruption which is directly responsible for famine, flood, and pestilence, no less than for the perennial flourishing of large hordes of armed robbers and banditti.

The connection may not by strikingly obvious between official corruption and such physical evils as pestilence, scarcity of food, and supe abundance of water in the wrong place; yet it is not the less real, and is that of cause and effect. For it cannot be too strongly insisted on that none of these is a necessary consequence of the physical features or climatic characteristics of the country; or even of indolence and ignorance among the masses; but that they are brought about mainly by the official corruption, which is also answerable, in great measure, for such ignorance and indolence as prevail and which may, doubtless, be rightly named among contributing causes.

Take, first, the case of the floods arising from the overflowing of the Hwang Ho (Yellow River). There is an official known as the Ho-tao-tchung-tu (Viceroy of the course of the River), with a large number of subordinate officers, whose special duty [it] is to preserve and keep in order the banks of the river and to guard against accidents, by seeing that the embankments are adequate and sound. These officials are, however, practically without salary *, and have purchased their positions at immense cost. They must, therefore, make money, and this they can do in many ways when an embankment bursts and has to be reconstructed. Thus it is their constant hope that floods may come, and far from taking precautions to prevent these terrible visitations which lay [may] waste whole provinces and cost thousands of lives, they actually take care to produce a flood by artificial means if, for the demands of their ruthless cupidity. Nature seem too dilatory in the matter. When there is not enough rain to make the river overflow its banks, it is quite common for men to be sent out to damage the embankments and so cause "an accident". This is a source of profit in a variety of ways. First, there is the pay received for repairing the breach, then there is the profit obtained by docking the wages of the workmen employed and by employing fewer workmen than are supposed to be paid; and, yet another, on the cost of materials, etc.; then the lack of food consequent upon the destruction of rice-fields causes widespread distress, and relief funds pour in both from Government and from charitable individuals—relief funds which never, in anything like their full amount, reach the people for whom they are intended. Finally, there is always a promotion, by way of "recompense for public services", conferred on the officers under whom an embankment has been repaired.

* Further on it will be seen that nearly all Chinese officials find it pays best not to draw, at all, their small salaries, but to leave them as a set-off against fines.

All this may sound incredible, but so well known is it in China that there is a popular saying which runs—"The best cure for the Hwang Ho, and the best safeguard against floods, would be to behead all the officials and leave the river to itself."

For famine in China, neither overpopulation, nor any scarcity of food due to natural causes, is responsible. It is generally the result of exorbitant local taxation(Liken [Likin]) added to faulty as well as inadequate means of communication—want of railways and roads and imperfectly developed and artificially obstructed water transit. All these tributary causes will presently be seen to rise in the dead sea of corruption whose foul mists form the miasmatic atmosphere of our official life, and whose phosphorescence it is, alone, that serves to gild the obscurity in which the Court of Peking is veiled.

At the present time there is famine in Kwang-si, formerly China's great rice-producing province, whence many others drew their supplies. Now the rich rice fields have gone out of cultivation. For so exorbitant have become the duties levied, that the farmers long since found it did not pay to grow more rice than was actually needed for their own consumption and to meet the immediate local demand. Even "Free Trade", when only partial and imposed from without, has, in this case, defeated its own object; for before the treaty of foreign commerce admitted rice duty free from Siam and Annam, Kwang-tung (Canton) was entirely dependent on Kwang-si for its supply. Now, the foreign rice being admitted free while that from Kwang-si has to pay heavy Liken [Likin], the latter has been so completely driven out of the market as to cause fertile land to fall below the margin of cultivation. Yet native rice could be grown at a prime cost of far less than that of foreign rice. It is the Liken [Likin] only that has ruined the Kwang-si farmer, and is responsible for the famine.

Again, often there is famine in one district and a superabundance of food in another not far distant; but the people who are starving cannot for want of railways, or even of proper roads, get at the food which may be wasting a few miles off. Although I shall elsewhere deal fully with the subject, I may here say that it is not native superstition among the masses, as is generally supposed, but official corruption and Tartar fear of reform, added to the notorious insecurity of all invested capital, that alone prevents the development of a proper railway system. Why, however, the excellent natural facilities for water transit and communication are not further developed and are practically useless, may be surmised from the state of affairs of which the following experience of my own is only a typical example:

I was staying in the city of Siukwan on the North River of Canton, and wished to go, by boat, to the next city, Ying-Tak—a distance of from thirty to forty English miles, the regular fare for the journey being about 5 or 6 tael [taels] (15s. or 18s.). Yet the boatmen, one and all, refused to take me, even when offered 20 tael [taels] (£ 3), because of their well-justified fear of detention by the river police for the purpose of levying blackmail. To understand this it must be explained that all boatmen can legally be called upon to assist the Government by the transport of prisoners with their escort, from town to town, upon the rivers. They are also bound to wait until the prisoner and his guard are ready to start. This practice is made the excuse for a most vexatious system of blackmail. The police do not ask for money—they simply order the boatmen to "wait, as there is a prisoner to take back" to the port whence they came. There may be no prisoner at all, but that does not matter; the boatmen, unless they offer a sufficiently large bribe for permission to return, are kept waiting for perhaps a month or more until there is one. That fear of this system was the only reason of my being refused by the boatmen is proved by the fact that, as soon as I could convince them I was a *persona grata* with the magistrate of Ying-Tak, and could guarantee immunity from the river police, a boat took me thither for the small sum of 4 tael [taels] (12s.)!

There are cargo boats, chartered by merchants who have already bribed the Customs (under whom are the river police), which are exempt from this kind of blackmail; but they have to pay very heavy duties as well as bribes, the combined burden of which is so great as to totally paralyse all trade—foreign as well as native.

Nominally, the duties are not very high, but when it is remembered that the same article has to pay duty many times over, and that each *douane* is a centre of complex bribery, it can be easily imagined how the cost is enhanced long before the consumer is reached. Between places as near to each other as Fatshan and Canton (about twelve English miles), there are one regular *douane* for the collection of duty, and at least four or five "searching stations" where, unless satisfactory bribes are paid, goods are wilfully destroyed in the process of "examination" and delays, detentions and vexatious charges make the life of the merchant a misery, and profitable trade an impossibility. Suppose, for instance, a bottle containing oil be found on which duty has been paid; if the certificate only mentions the oil, the merchant to whom it belongs will be charged with attempting to smuggle "lassware [glassware]", and may be imprisoned for attempting to defraud the customs, until he pays a bribe.

Not only is famine in China caused by this interference with internal communication and traffic on the rivers, but also the loss inflicted upon European trade is very great indeed. China has, at present, much commerce at her treaty ports on the sea coast and on the Yangtze River; but this only affects a narrow strip of land adjacent to these ports, and foreign goods rarely reach the interior. Imagine the effect on trade in England if goods sent from London to Brighton not only had to pay duty several times over, but involved their dealers in a risk of imprisonment and exposure to all kinds of extortion at four or five intermediate stations. The effect on English trade in China, produced by the working of the internal customs system, may be judged by noting what happens to goods of English manufacture sent, say, from Canton to Siukwan, a distance of about 200 miles. Before entering Canton they have paid 5 per cent maritime duty. They have then to pay Liken [Likin] to the Canton authorities before being sent *out* of the city. At Fatshan (12 miles out) they have to pay duty, and again at Sinam, about 30 miles further on, and again on entering the North River at Lupau, after only another 30 or 40 miles they have to pay duty, and yet again destination duty on reaching Siukwan. In addition to these five regular stations for the collection of dues, there are numerous "inspection stations" where bribes are also exacted, as above described. Naturally, by the time the goods reach the interior, their price has been increased by considerably over 100 per cent, and no less naturally, except in the case of articles absolutely necessary to life, they are practically unsaleable.

Since, even in these circumstances, China is regarded as a good market for

English goods, how would not the trade of England benefit if these exorbitant duties and the system of bribery were altogether abolished?

If floods and famine result from artificial, rather than from natural causes, this can certainly be shown to be no less true of pestilence, which need not be more common at present in China than elsewhere. The climate is not unhealthy—at any rate for natives—and in the country districts the health of the people is generally excellent. It is in the towns and cities only that pestilence arises, owing to the total lack, in them, of anything like sanitation or official organization of preventive means. In almost every part of the Chinese Empire the country districts are entirely free from pestilence until disease is imported from the towns which are overcrowded, filthy in the extreme, and supplied with unspeakably polluted water.

That official corruption is solely responsible for the insanitary condition of the towns may readily be seen from the case of the water supply. In the European sense of the term there is no water supply in the whole of the Chinese Empire. In Canton and Shang-hai, for instance, where things are somewhat better than elsewhere, the sewage flows direct into the river, and from the very place of the outflow the people take their drinking water! In Canton, about ten years ago, a Chinese company was formed for the purpose of establishing waterworks to supply the city with uncontaminated water. For such a scheme, quiescent toleration, at least, might have been expected from the authorities; but official greed is not to be daunted even by the fear of pestilence. A well-known official demanded such an enormous bribe before he would allow any work to be begun, that the company, unable to pay it, had to give up the undertaking. Another company was formed a few years ago in Canton, also by native merchants. It was called the "Fertiliser Company," and had as its object the contracting for sweeping and cleansing all the streets of the city and the conversion of the refuse, so obtained, into manure. So enamoured of the scheme were the masses of the people that they called meetings of their guilds, and through their representatives, expressed their willingness to pay for the proposed work of scavenging; and, as the company would have also made a profit on the sale of its fertilisers, it would doubtless have proved a flourishing concern. Here, again, however, the Mandarins interfered and demanded bribes to such an impossible figure that this undertaking had also to be dropped.

When even financial and industrial enterprises, undertaken more in the interests of public health than in those of the shareholders, are made abortive by the corrupt greed of the civil authorities, it is hardly to be wondered at that purely commercial enterprise should meet with a similar fate, and that would be capitalists should fear to risk their money in a country where the rights of property are as little regarded as are those of life and public health, by the authorities who should safeguard both.

But the effects of corruption in making property and life insecure throughout the country, are more directly felt through the creation of robber-bands already alluded to. Most of these robbers are disbanded soldiers, left armed and starving, often thousands of miles away from their homes. The Government, it is true, allows each soldier a certain sum to pay his expenses home; but this money is generally kept by the officers who simply turn the soldiers loose when done with to shift for themselves, and shifting for themselves means preying on the public. But there are other banditti as well who are regularly protected by each district magistrate so long as they confine their depredations to districts outside that over which he rules. Did the space allotted to me permit I could give some curious details illustrative of this statement. I must, however, pass on to the consideration of other matters, merely noting here that some of the worst robbers are soldiers, still in the Imperial service, who go on their marauding expeditions with their coats turned inside out, and then, when pursued, again turn their coats so that, being in uniform, no one dare molest them. Both in the cities and in the rural districts, rich people keep their own guards, while the large manufacturers, and the owners of plantations, passenger boats, etc., not only have to pay the Government taxes, but also a regular annual tribute to the robber chiefs in return for immunity and protection from attack. The police, or rather those city soldiers who are supposed to do the work of the police, are often the organizers of daring and extensive robberies. An incident of this kind occurred quite recently in Canton, when the police superintendent and his men robbed the local silk weaving factory of all they could lay hands on, and the Governor when appealed to for redress, punished the leaders, not of the robbers, but of his petitioners.

So universal and deeply rooted is the corruption from which all these evils spring, that partial and gradual reform is impossible and no change for the better can be hoped for except from a radical alteration in the administrative system. For under the present *regime* any official who wishes to be honest is, nevertheless, compelled to follow in the footsteps of the dishonest ones, or retire from public life altogether. He must accept bribes in order to pay the bribes exacted of him by his superiors; and he must connive at all kinds of corruption both in his subordinates and in those who hold higher rank or office than his own.

How inevitable is all this will be obvious when some account has been given of the paths by which official life can be entered upon, and of the different methods of promotion.

There are four ways of entering public life in China, and of secaring [secuning] promotion:

Through examination.
Through military service.
Through obtaining recognition of "distinguished merit".
By purchase pure and simple.

The first of these avenues to public life is the oldest, and, in every way, the purest and the best. In former years, even since the Manchu Dynasty began their rule in China, the literary examinations were, generally speaking, honestly conducted and the official did not begin his career of corruption until after the end of his course of study and examination. But, even here, corruption has, of recent years, crept in; so that now it is not at all uncommon for the "students" to be personated at the examinations by learned but dishonest professors who make a living by being examined, under different names, over and over again. The examiners are also not infrequently bribed.

When the student has in his own district, passed the examinations entitling him to take the first degree, he must present himself, at intervals of three years, to be examined for the second and third degrees, at the provincial centre and at the capital, respectively. When the third degree has been conferred the candidate is a Mandarin, and is eligible for an official position. At this point, however, begins the bribery, without which the most brilliant examinee might just as well have remained an ignoramus or stayed at home, for all the chances he has of holding any office, however humble, in the State. There is, however, one more examination to pass at Peking, after the third degree has been conferred. This is the Imperial Examination, as a result of which the Emperor divides the candidates into three classes: (1) Fellows of the Imperial College, to remain in Peking; (2) the Magistrate class; (3) those whom the Emperor rejects altogether. The third class must either retire into private life or enter official life by one of the more corrupt avenues indicated above. It is from the second class that the district magistrates and all the local officials outside Peking—so far as they have entered by way of examination—are drawn. Each of these is at once sent off to the capital of one of the provinces, dignified by the rank of "district magistrate," and eligible for any appointment which the provincial authority may see fit to confer on him.

Immediately on arrival he has to bribe the Viceroy and his subordinates, and since many candidates may be sent to the same district at the same time, the few vacant appointments are, of course, conferred upon those who pay the highest bribes. But even were there no competition for posts, the candidate would have to bribe the Governor; for if he refused to do so, the latter could indefinitely postpone giving him a berth. Even the Emperor's special warrant, assigning him a special district, would not save him. A candidate with great family influence might succeed in prevailing upon the Official Board at Peking to protest; but even then the governor need only reply that so-and-so "is too young," or "too inexperienced," and "that a deputy has been temporarily (i. e., for an indefinite period) appointed to allow the magistrate time to make a further study of official and administrative business." If he be at once successful in obtaining a position, promotion follows, automatically, at the end of three years. There is also, however, a triennial "general calculation of merit" in each district; so that promotion for recorded merit may fall to the lot of a magistrate who has only been appointed one or two years. This triennial calculation of merit is a very profitable affair for the Governor. The officials under him are "meritorious" in proportion to the amount they pay him, and anyone who refused altogether to bribe the Governor would certainly be declared "unfit to continue in office," and dismissed; and from the decision of the Governor there is no appeal. In such circumstances an honest man disgusted with the corruption of official life, would retire; a bad one would simply make a fresh start, re-entering public life by purchase.

Prior to each promotion the official has to be received in audience by the Emperor. But this is a very costly affair. For no one's presence in the Capital City is recognised until he has bribed the gatekeeper to register his name as having passed into the city and duly report his advent. That Li Hung Chang had to pay an enormous sum in tips and bribes—over one million sterling—at his last visit to Peking is a matter of common knowledge; but the narration of two instances that have come directly under my notice, may perhaps serve to make the English reader realise, even more vividly, how inexorable and how shamelessly open, is the systematic corruption.

The governor of Kiang-su Province, who was an intimate friend of Prince Kung, thought to take advantage of his great influence by coming into the city without bribing the gatekeeper. When he called upon his royal friend, Prince Kung exclaimed: "When did you come? I cannot possibly recognise your presence, for I have not seen your name in the Chung-Wen Men Report," and he had to return and pay double the usual bribe to the gate keeper before Prince Kung would receive him. Even more remarkable is the case of Tso Tchung Tong, one of the greatest of our generals, who having suppressed the Mahommedan rebellion in Turkestan, had acquired for the Celestial Empire territory about half as large as China itself. The Emperor, who held him in high esteem, wished to see him, and sent a special sommons [summons] calling him to an audience at Peking. When on his coming to the city, the Chung-Wen Men, or gatekeeper, demanded 80,000 tael [tales], he refused to pay anything. But even he was not officially reported, and after he had remained several months in Peking, waiting for an audience, the Emperor issued another edict, asking why he had never come. Tso Tchung Tong responded by telling the whole story, adding that having spent all his own and his family's money on the support of soldiers during the war, he had no means with which to pay such a bribe. He appealed to the Emperor graciously to relieve him of the imposition. In reply the Emperor said: "This(the feeing of the gate keeper) is a general and ancient usage, and the viceroy and generalissimo must submit to it like another"; and as Tso Tchung Tong really had not the money, his friends raised a subscription, the Dowager Empress herself contributing half the required sum.

This lengthy digression may, perhaps, be excused for the sake of the light it throws on the imperial attitude towards corrupt practices.

Of course no newly-promoted magistrate even attempts to evade payment of the bribes that alone can open the way into the presence of the Emperor, and after feeing and bribing a whole army of court officials, he has his audience and takes his new title of say, Taotai or Prefect Magistrate. A process, similar to that indicated above, only each time more costly than before, has to be gone through with every promotion, and all this to obtain appointments that are practically unsalaried. It is true that, nominally, there is a salary attached to each appointment. Not only, however, are these salaries small out of all proportion to the mere expenses incidental to holding office, but they are hardly ever claimed at all, for reasons, the force of which it will not be difficult to appreciate. The salary of any official, before it can be drawn at the Provincial Treasury, has had to pass through so many hands and pay so many commissions that the payee would only receive about 30 or 40 percent, of the original amount. Now it is quite common for an official to be fined a whole year's salary. This he would have to pay in full, unless he could show that his past year's salary still lay unclaimed at the office of the Provincial Treasury. Thus an official with £100 a year, on being fined a year's salary, would lose about £60 or £70 by having drawn his pay.

Thus, although there are salaries and even a fund for expense—called "a support of purity" —attached to all the offices of State, civil and military, it is no exaggeration to say that the officials, one and all, are somewhat similarly placed to the waiters at some English restaurants, who pay liberally and work without wages, only for the privilege of being in a position to receive tips.

It will be readily seen that as soon as the new Taotai is back in his district he must begin "squeezing" all those below him; not only to recoup himself for the expenses incurred, and to live himself and support his numerous relatives, clansmen, and dependants, but also to meet the expenses of his next promotion at the end of another three years.

If all this is true of the section of the official class that has entered public life through the comparatively clean and narrow way of hard work, genuine, if useless study, and literary examination, with how much more force must it apply to the men who have come in by the other more devious paths?

Promotions for military service are perhaps the most rapid.

It was in this way that Li Hung Chang entered public life. Immediately on passing his third examination, instead of becoming "an outside officer" (District Magistrate) or an "inside officer" (Member of the Imperial College at Peking) he returned home, entered the army through the influence of Marquis Tseng's father, and was, in a few months, promoted to be Taotai of Fukien, to reach which position by the regular method of promotion would have taken six years. He never even visited Fukien at all, and yet in another month or so he was again promoted; this time to be Futai(Governor) of Kiang-su. It was while he was military adviser, or Secretary to Marquis Tseng(General-in-Chief) that, the former Governor of Kiang-Su having been killed, Li Hung Chang had the opportunity of recommending himself for the vacant appointment. The General, who liked and admired him, forwarded a memorial to the Emperor craving the appointment for him, but, on reflection, saw that this was perhaps stretching favoritism too far, since it meant the transformation of a Taotai straightway into a Fu-tai, a process that should take at least nine years. A second messenger was, therefore, dispatched to recall the memorial. Too late, however; for Li, anticipating that this might happen, had taken care to induce the first messenger to travel post haste.

With the aid of General Gordon and other foreigners Li succeeded in freeing his new province from the Tai Ping, and was soon promoted to the position of Viceroy. How immense a fortune Li has been able to amass is too widely known to need farther mention here. One source of official wealth I had ample opportunity of observing when I was in Tientsin just before the beginning of the Japanese war. Officers of all ranks, both military and civil, came flocking in from all parts of the Empire to seek commands, but before their petitions could even reach Li, they had to pay immense bribes to his attendants.

When a military appointment has been made, and the warrant is ready for issue in the hands of the Clerk of the Yamun, the officer has to pay for its delivery a sum proportionate to the value of the appointment. Then, as soon as he has his warrant, the officer commences business by selling the commands under him. Only those who have some kind of military *rank* can, however, buy commands in the army; but, as will presently appear, military rank can be acquired in many curious ways. It is, for example, not at all uncommon for men who have never seen a battle in their lives to be promoted to the rank of Colonel. By citing one out of many instances that have come directly under my own observation, I can, perhaps, best illustrate the possibility of such promotions.

A young man from my native town entered the army, and, by dint of hard fighting and real merit rose to the rank of Brigadier-General; but with him, at every promotion, rose his brother, whom I will call X, who had not met him for years, and who was peacefully occupied as cook in a distant opium den. This is how it was done. The soldier, after each engagement in which he distinguished himself, reported imaginary deeds of valour performed by this brother, and his word was taken. One day the cook in the opium den, who had never even seen a battle, read his name in the *Gazette*, and found, to his surprise, that he had attained the ank [rank] of Colonel in the Imperial forces.

Military service is, in many ways, very remunerative to the officers. They enrol any men they like, and they always draw the pay for many more men than are actually in the army. About 70 percent, of the full number of men nominally serving and for whom pay is drawn is the average strength of the forces, even under Li Hung Chang's comparatively honest officers, while elsewhere, 100 men on paper usually menas [means] but 40 or 50 in the flesh. On review days the officers engage a sufficient number of soldiers *by the day* to make the army *look* all right. But there are other sources of profit besides dealing in dummy soldiers. The live ones have to wear uniforms, and to eat, and both food and clothes are supplied at extortionate prices by the officers; so that of the five tael [taels] per month paid by Government for each soldier, about one-fifth or less reaches the pockets of the men. All this refers to the "braves [bravers]" who are only engaged during war time and are disbanded the moment the fighting is over wherever they may happen to be, and nearly always without the means of returning to their homes, thus keeping up the supply of armed robbers all over the Empire. As to the soldiers of the standing army in times of peace, they are, with the exception of the Manchu garrison, so wretchedly paid, that its strength exists only on paper. The men enlist and regularly draw their pay—about 3s. a month—and have scarcely any further connection with the military service. The few that go on duty, in the city gates live entirely on bribes. The Manchu force under the Tartar General, on the other hand, is well paid; but these soldiers do no fighting; they are only engaged in guarding the city against Chinese rebles [rebels]. They live in a separate quarter to that occupied by the Chinese, on whom they often make unprovoked attacks. Thus fights between the Chinese and the Tartar soldiery are of common occurrence, and as these Tartar soldiers are not under the jurisdiction of the Givil Law, their outrages invariably go unpunished. Naturally there is no love lost between the city guards and the native Chinese.

That promotion for military service means, in China, little more than a decent pretext for the purchase of entry into official life, and of posts of profit, is, perhaps, by this time sufficiently obvious, yet another fact will help to make it even more clear. The Generals in the Chinese army are in the habit of mentioning for promotion a large number of soldiers who exist only in their imagination. They thus obtain possession of a large number of promotion papers made out for non-existent soldiers bearing the most common Chinese names. The paper-Corporal Smith or Private Jones continues to be regularly promoted, so that in time the General has a whole collection of commissions for various ranks of the service, ready for sale to the first applicant whose family or clan name is, say, Smith or Jones, and who is willing to pay the market price. Private soldiers also who prefer money to promotion are in the habit of changing their names and selling their papers to civilians desirous of acquiring military rank by combined purchase and personation. Thus there is little to favourably distinguish "promotion for military service" from the fourth avenue to official life, or mere purchase. It has, however, a semblance of decency and is sometimes combined with a certain amount of public service.

The third method of rising in the world, "promotion for special merit," is even less honest, and need hardly be considered by itself; for the "special merit" has to be recorded by officials who are, without exception, corrupt and dependent for their livelihood on bribes; so that, unless they recommend members of their own family or clan, they will certainly only see "special merit" in those who open their eyes with gold.

The fourth method of entering public life, i. e. , by purchase pure and simple, is quite recognised by law, and is becoming more common every year. Even such a highly-placed official as Chang, the late minister to the United States, had passed no examinations, but had simply bought his first official post.

Whenever the Government is in financial difficulties, and requires money for a specific purpose, it "opens a subscription," and those who give a certain sum obtain a rank. Moreover, it is not uncommon for companies to be formed for the purpose of paying the bribes and other expenses attendant upon the purchase of a civil appointment. One of the members of this Magistrate Manufacturing Limited Liability Company(or, as it is called in Chinese, backflogging company, because of the prospective magistrate's methods of extracting money from the people), gets the appointment, and the other shareholders divide with him the spoils of office. Other would-be officials borrow the necessary money and pay it back with interest before many years have elapsed.

It costs rather more to buy one's way into the Chinese civil service than to enter by examination; otherwise the chances of obtaining promotion for the two classes of candidates are practically equal. When once the rank of District Magistrate and an appointment have been bought, further promotions follow regularly, as already described.

I have tried to made it clear that corruption and bribery, nepotism, and the unblushing sale and purchase of influence and position, are, in China, no mere accident, or result of occasional or individual cupidity, circumstance, or temptation, but are universal, and the only possible condition of accepting or retaining of public service—whether civil or military—under the present *regime*—that to be a public man in China, however high or low, means to be incurably corrupt, and that to renounce corrupt practices is to renounce public life altogether.

Thus no change for the better can be hoped for from the infusion of new blood into the official class, since the very conditions of official existence exclude the possibility of honesty. Nor can improvement be hoped for from the spread of education; for not only is it the recognised interest of the official class to keep the masses ignorant, but also the officials themselves are absolutely ignorant, some of them even unable to read and write, and even those that have passed the examinations being only trained in a useless "literature and literary style of composition," but totally without knowledge of the world's affairs or even of the needs and possibilities of their own country, and of the laws administered in their names by poorly-paid clerks.

What has been said of the condition of the army and of the way in which military commands are given and used, has perhaps made it unnecessary to explain that it is not want of physical courage or of patriotism in the native Chinese, but the prevalence of an incurably corrupt system, kept up by their Tartar rulers, that makes China a ready prey for any other nation, and explains our easy defeat at the hands of the Japanese. I may in this place allude to the attempted regeneration of the navy under the English Admiral Lang, who only failed because the presence of an incorruptible officer was felt to be intolerable, and led therefore to an intrigue and series of insults that practically compelled his resignation. Some idea of how official corruption affects China's preparedness for resisting external attack, may be gathered from the recital of an incident that took place shortly before the outbreak of the Japanese war. A young naval officer, one of my personal friends, who shortly afterwards quitted the service in disgust, told me that he had just had to sign a receipt for several tons of coal-dust, described and paid for as gunpowder! I may add that the officers of the Government gunboats have practically a monopoly in smuggling, in which they do a large and lucrative business; and the southern squadron of the navy is entirely and exclusively employed in carrying the mandarins and their families whither they wish to go, and in smuggling.

Here in England it seems to be supposed that China's regeneration will begin, and the development of her vast natural resources will become possible, when Li Hung Chang and others who may be convinced of the utility of railways and telegraphs, European military and naval organization, etc., [etc.,] enlighten their compatriots and attempt the introduction of all this machinery of civilisation. As well might one expect the conversion of cannibals to vegetarianism by the introduction of silver forks and Sheffield cutlery.

A concrete example or two may perhaps better serve to carry conviction than many arguments.

European innovations have been introduced within the past thirty years. We have arsenals and docks opened in Tientsin, Foochow, and Shanghai; there are military and naval colleges in Tientsin and Nanking, and there are now telegraphs all over the Empire; there is a railway between Tientsin and Shan-Hai-Kwan; and there are steamers on the coast and on the rivers, belonging to the Government and to merchants; but there is no improvement resulting, or to be hoped for, from any or all of these modern improvements. In the arsenals no real work has been done; only a large number of appointments and "jobs" have been created. The permanent expert heads of departments, engineers, and so forth, are badly paid, and have absolutely no freedom or voice in the man agement of work they understand, but are altogether governed by "superior" officials, who are not only entirely ignorant, but have no time to learn before they are promoted and their place is taken by others. These temporary officials issue contradictory orders which have to be obeyed by the skilled foremen, so that, so far as any manufacture is attempted, waste of materials is the sole result. That however, is not very often, since it pays the *officials* better to import arms and ammunition on which they can make both profit and commission.

The telegraphs were first established by merchants under Government sanction, but afterwards came into the hands of the Government. Since that time all the local superintendents have been appointed through the nomination of relatives or through "influence", and no annual balance-heet〔balance-sheet〕has been issued. The execution of repairs is here, as in the case of the river, a very profitable part of the business. When, however, a new station is established, little or no profit can be made as the material is supplied by the central authority. This accounts for a curious phenomenon that strikes the foreigner: In the country districts the telegraph posts are much lower than in the towns, though all were of the same length when supplied. A case explaining the shrinkage came under my personal observation. The superintendents cut a few feet off each telegraph post before its erection and sell the wood to local carpenters. It is thought that native superstition and conservatism form the chief obstacle in the way of telegraph and railway enterprise, but this is not the case. When the telegraph was first set up in Hunan the posts and wires were immediately pulled down by the people, and it was publicly reported that the masses were too anti-foreign in their sentiments to allow such an innovation. The private and true reason was very different. The superintendent had not paid his workmen in full, and it was these workpeople who started the riots and destroyed the product of their unpaid labour. It is the officials and not the masses who are anti-foreign, the Tartars and not the native Chinese; and it is these officials whom England defended from the Taipings, who instigate the anti-Christian risings and massacres, afterwards throwing all the blame upon the people. Chow Han, the famous anti-foreign agitator, is a Taotai, and is looked upon by the official class as one of the greatest heroes in China. The Tientsin Railway is appreciated by the people, and has a large traffic, but it is bankrupt because it is in the hands of the unscrupulous official administration, whose members manage to appropriate all the profits, with the result that, of course, the railway is bankrupt; and Chinese capitalists, who understand the reason why, will not be likely to invest in any similar undertaking. As the railways now under construction are to be financed entirely by Russian and Chinese capital, it is not very difficult to foresee what will be the nationality of those who will pay for and control the line.

The Steam Navigation Company was originally established by the famous merchant, Tong-King-Sing; and, at first, no official interference was allowed. The concern, however, seemed likely to be a success. Then the Government got hold of it, as it does of every private undertaking that shows signs of becoming profitable; and, of course, the steamboat company is now as corrupt as any other

Government Department, and each commander must buy his appointment. It is thus evident that China cannot be reformed by the introduction of material civilisation, but only by the extirpation of official corruption, ⟨since⟩ this official corruption becomes worse every year. Things that would have been regarded as shocking even ten years ago, are now quite common. Never, until quite recently, was there a fixed tariff of bribes in connection with the granting of official positions. Now, so shameless have the authorities grown, that the late viceroy, Li Han Chang—brother of Li Hung Chang—has actually fixed a regular price for every office in the provinces of the two Kwangs(Kwang-Si and Kwang-Tung).

The whole people is ready for a change; there are plenty of honest men ready and willing to enter public life; the army is so corrupt, that even were it not to a great extent leavened with sympathisers with the Reform Party, it could not be depended on by the Government. It is only from the Manchu soldiers or from shortsighted selfish interference of foreigners that the Reform Party has anything whatever to fear. Indeed, one object I have in writing this article is to prove to the English people that it is in the interests of Europe generally, and of England in particular, to allow us to succeed, and that the policy often recommended(as, for instance, by "L." in the August number of this Review), that of protecting the present Government, is entirely mistaken. That writer says that England ought to protect the present *regime* from every attack, native or foreign. One thing he fails to recognise is that it is the Manchu or Tartar element alone, and the officials whose bread depends on the maintenance of the present system, who are inimical to other races, and that if the pure Chinese were left to themselves, and left to consolidate their own country, they would be at peace, and be ready to cultivate friendly relations with all the world.

To adequately describe the aims and ideals of the Reform Party would alone, require a separate article. Here it may be enough to say that the benevolent neutrality of Great Britain, and the other Powers, is all the aid needed to enable us to make the present system give place to one that is not corrupt, and that even if trade were temporarily disorganized it would soon be vastly improved. While the development of the natural wealth of China would enrich the whole world, the reform of her government and administration, and of her army would make her impregnable to any foreign attack—even from Russia—and prevent the disruption which, like the partition of Turkey, could hardly fail of producing serious European complications.

Sun Yat Sen

THE TRUE SOLUTION

OF

THE CHINESE QUESTION

Autumn, 1904

THE TRUE SOLUTION
OF
THE CHINESE QUESTION

Autumn, 1904

The attention of the whole world is at present directed towards the Far East, not only because of the war which is now going on between Russia and Japan, but also because of the fact that China will ultimately be the main field of struggle between those countries striving for the mastery in Asia. European possessions in Africa which had hitherto been the bone of contention between the European powers having now been pretty well defined, a new field for territorial aggrandizement and colonial expansion must therefore be sought. China, long known as the "Sick Man of the Far East", affords naturally such a field for the satisfaction of European ambitions. America, notwithstanding her traditional seclusive policy in international politics, is, however, by no means disinterested in it, although in a way somewhat different from that of the other countries. In the first place, the passing of the Philippine Islands under American control makes the United States one of the nearest neighbors of China, and it is therefore impossible for her to shut her eyes to the state of things in that country. In the second place, China is a great market for American goods, and if America intends to extend her commercial and industrial activity to other parts of the world, China is the first country that she must look to. Hence the so-called "Far Eastern question" is of peculiar importance to this country.

The problem is as important as it is difficult of solution, owing to the many conflicting interests involved therein. The ultimate outcome of the present war between Russia and Japan has been considered by many as the probable solution of the question. But, from a Chinese standpoint, the war raises more difficulties than it solves; if it decides anything at all, it would decide, at the most, the question of supremacy between those two countries only. What about the interests of Great Britain? of France? of Germany? of the United States? As to these questions, the war is far from being a solution.

In order to arrive at a satisfactory solution of the whole question, we must find out the root of all these difficulties. The most superficial knowledge of Asiatics affairs will convince any one that this lies in the weakness and corruptness of the Manchu government which threatens, by the very fact of its weakness, to disturb the existing political equilibrium of the world. Paradoxical it is, it is not without foundation, as a proof of this, we would only mention the present Russo-Japanese war. Had it not been for the utter inability of the Manchu government over Manchuria, the war might have been avoided. And it is but the beginning of the long series of conflicts which are likely to arise between the different powers interested in the Chinese question.

We say the Manchu government, and not the Chinese government, with intention. The Chinese have at present no government of their own, and the term "Chinese Government", if applied to the present government of China, is a misnomer. This seems to be startling to one who is not well acquainted with Chinese affairs, but it is a fact—a historical fact. In order to convince you of this, let us give you a short account of the establishment of the Manchu Dynasty.

Before they came in contact with the Chinese, the Manchus were a savage, nomadic tribe roaming in the wilds of the Amoor region. They often raided and plundered the peaceful Chinese inhabitants along the frontier. Towards the close of the Ming Dynasty there was a great civil war in China, and taking advantage of this golden opportunity they suddenly came down and captured Peking in much the same way as the barbarians overran the Roman Empire. This was in the year 1644. The Chinese were unwilling to submit to this foreign yoke and offered to the invaders the most stubborn resistance. In order to force them to yield, the barbarous Manchus ruthlessly massacred millions of people, combatants and non-combatants, young and old, women and children; set fire to their dwellings; ransacked their houses and forced them to adopt their costume. It has been estimated that for disobeying the order of keeping the queue, tens of thousands of persons were slaughtered. It was not until after must bloodshed and barbarity that the Chinese finally submitted to the Manchu rule.

The next measure the Manchus adopted was to keep the conquered people in ignorance as much as possible by burning and destroying all the Chinese books and literature concerning their dealings with and their invasion of China. They also prohibited the people to form associations or to hold meetings for the discussion of public affairs. Their object was to stamp out the patriotic spirit of the Chinese, so that in course of time they might forget that they were subject to a foreign rule. The Manchus number ⟨is⟩ at present not more than five millions, while the Chinese have a population of not less than four hundred millions. It is therefore their constant fear that the Chinese might rise up some day and regain their country. To safeguard against this, many precautious measures have been and are still being adopted. Such has been the policy of the Manchus towards the Chinese.

There is a general misapprehension among western peoples that the Chinese are by nature a seclusive people, unwilling to have any intercourse with outsiders, and that it was only at the point of the bayonet that a few ports along the coast were opened to foreign trade. This misapprehension is due more to the ignorance of Chinese history than to anything else. History furnishes us abundant proof that from the very earliest times up to the establishment of the present dynasty the Chinese entertained close relations with the neighboring countries and did not appear to have the least ill disposition towards foreign traders and missionaries. The Nestorian Tablet at Si-an Fu give [gives] us an excellent record of the evangelistic works of foreign missionaries among the people there as early as the seventh century after christ[Christ]. Again, the Buddist religion was introduced into China by the Emperor in the Han Dynasty, and the people welcomed the new religion with great enthusiasm. It has since continued to flourish until now it is one of the three leading religions in China. Not only missionaries but traders also were allowed to travel freely throughout the length and breadth of the Empire. Even as late as the Ming Dynasty there was no sign of antiforeign spirit among the Chinese. The Prime Minister, Hsu Kwang Che, himself embraced the Catholic faith, and his intimate friend, Mathew Ricci, a Jesuit missionary in Peking, was held in great esteem by the people.

With the establishment of the Manchu Dynasty came a gradual change of policy. The whole country was closed to foreign trade; missionaries were driven out; native Christians were massacred; and no Chinese was allowed to emigrate outside the Chinese border under pain of death. Why was this? Simply because the Manchus wanted to exclude foreigners from their jurisdiction and instigate the people to hate them, lest the Chinese might be enlightened and realize their own nationality through coming in contact with them. The anti-foreign spirit fostered by the Manchus finally culminated in the Boxer trouble of 1900. It is only well known that the leaders of the movement were nobody else than the members of the reigning family. Hence it may be seen that the seclusive policy of China is the outcome of selfishness on the part of the Manchus and does not represent the will of the majority of the Chinese people. Foreigners traveling in China have often noticed the fact that those people who are farther away from official influence are always more friendly to them than those nearer.

Since the Boxer war many have been led to believe that the Tartar government is beginning to see the sign of time and to reform itself for the betterment of the country, just from the occasional imperial edicts for reform, not knowing that they are mere dead letters made for the express purpose of pacifying popular agitations. It is absolutely impossible for the Manchus to reform the country, because reformation means detriment to them. By reformation they would be absorbed by the Chinese people and would lose the special rights and privileges which they are enjoying. The still darker side of the government can be seen when the ignorance and corruption of the official class is brought to light. These fossilized, rotten, good-for-nothing officials know only how to flatter and bribe the Manchus, whereby their position may be strengthened to carry on the trade of squeezing. A very striking evidence can be seen from the proclamation issued recently by the Chinese Minister at Washington prohibiting the Chinese in this country from having anything to do with the Patriotic Society under the severe penalty that their families and distant relatives will be arrested and beheaded in China. Such a barbarous act coming from such an educated man as Sir Liang Ching, the Chinese Minister, cannot be accounted for except upon the probable assumption that he wishes to flatter the government so that his position as a minister may be secured. Where is the hope for reform by the government and its officials? During the two hundred and sixty years of Tartar rule we have suffered innumerable wrongs, chief of which are following.

(1) The Tartars run the government for their own benefit and not for the benefit of the governed.
(2) They check our intellectual and material development.
(3) They treat us as a subjected race and deny us equal rights and privileges.
(4) They violate our inalienable rights of life, liberty and property.
(5) They practise or connive at official corruption and bribery.
(6) They suppress the liberty of speech.
(7) They impose heavy and irregular taxes on us without our consent.
(8) They practise the most barbarous tortures in the trial of an alleged offender for the purpose of compelling him to give evidence to incriminate himself.
(9) They deprive us of our rights without due process of law.
(10) They fail in their duty to protect the lives and property of all persons residing within their jurisdiction.

Notwithstanding all these grievances, we have tried every possible means to become reconciled with them, but to no purpose. In view of this fact, we, the Chinese people, in order to redress our wrongs, and to establish peace in the Far East and in the world generally, have therefore determined to adopt adequate measures for the attainment of those objects, "peaceably if we may, forcibly if we must".

The whole nation is ripe for revolution. Look at the Weichow uprising of 1900, the attempted *Coup de Main* at Canton in 1902, and the Kwang-si movement which is now still going on with ever increasing force and encouragement.

The newspapers and the recent publications in China are also full of democratic ideas. Furthermore, there is the Chee Kung Tong (Chinese Patriotic Society), commonly known in this country as the Chinese Freemason, which has for its object "the overthrow of the Ching (Manchu) and the restoration of the Ming (Chinese) Dynasty". This political organization has lasted for over two hundred years and it has now a membership of tens of millions of people, spreading all over Southern China. About 80 percent of the Chinese in this country belong to this league. Those Chinese who favor revolutionary ideas may be roughly divided into three classes. The first class, the most numerous of the three, comprises those persons who cannot even obtain a bare livelihood because of the extortions and exactions of the officials. To the second belong all those who are provoked by racial prejudice against the Manchus, while to the third class belong those who are inspired by noble thoughts and high ideas. These three factors, co-operating together in different directions, with increasing force and velocity, will ultimately produce the desired result. It is evident, therefore, that the downfall of the Manchu government is but a question of time.

The theory has sometimes been advanced with some show of plausibility that China, with her immense population and her vast resources, would be a menace to the whole world, if she would wake up and adopt western methods and ideas; that if the foreign countries should do anything towards the uplifting and enlightening of the Chinese people, they would thereby creat a sort of Frankenstein; and that the wisest policy for other countries to pursue is to keep the Chinese down as much as possible. This is, in short, the substance of what is known as the "Yellow peril". The theory sounds very well; but it will be found upon examination to be untenable from whatever standpoint you may view it. Apart from the moral side of the question as to whether it is right for one country to hope for the downfall of another, is the political side to it. The Chinese are by nature an industrious, peaceful, law-abiding people. They are by no means an aggressive race. If ever they go to war at all, it is only for self-defence. The Chinese would be a menace to the peace of the world only if they were properly drilled by some foreign country and made use of as an instrument for the gratification of its own ambition. It left to themselves they would prove to be the most peaceful people in the world. Again from an economic standpoint, the awakening of China and the establishment of an enlightened government is beneficial not only to the Chinese but also to the world at large. The whole country would be open to foreign trade; railroads would be built; natural resources would be developed; the people would be richer and their standard of living would be higher; the demand for foreign goods would be greater, and international commerce would be increased a hundred fold above its present rate. Is this a peril? Nations are to each other as individuals. Is it economically better for a man to have a poor, ignorant neighbor than it is for him to have a wealthy intelligent one? Viewed from this light, theory falls at once to the ground and we may safely assert that the yellow peril may after all be changed into the yellow blessing.

There are two conflicting policies pursued by the foreign powers in regard to China. The one favors the partitioning and colonizing; the other advocates the integrity and colonizing; the other advocates the integrity and independence of China. To those maintaining the former policy it is needless to remind them that it is fomented [fermented] with danger and disaster, as the ease of colonizing Manchuria by Russia exhibits; while to those maintaining the latter policy we venture to predict that it is impossible for them to realize their object so long as the present government exists. The Manchu Dynasty may be likened to a collapsing house; the whole structure is thoroughly rotten to its very foundation. Is it possible for any one to prevent the house from falling just by supporting the walls collaterally outside with a few beams? We fear this very act of supporting it might hasten its tumbling. The dynastic life in China, as shown from history, is much the same as all individual; it has its birth, growth, maturity, declining and dying. The present Tartar rule has begun to decline since the beginning of the last century and is dying fast now. Therefore we say that even this benevolent and chivalric act of maintaining the integrity and independence of China, if such is meant, as we understand, to support the present tottering Tartar house, is doomed to failure.

Now it is evident, in order to solve this burning question, and to remove the source of disturbance to the peace of the world, that a new, enlightened and progressive government must be substituted in place of the old one. In such a case China would not only be able to support herself, but would also relieve the other countries of the trouble of maintaining her independence and integrity. There are many highly educated and able men among the people who would be competent to take up the task of forming a new government, and carefully thought-out plans have long been drawn up for the transformation of this out-of-date Tartar Monarchy into a "Republic of China". The general masses of the people are also ready to accept the new order of things and are longing for a change for better, to uplift them from their present deplorable condition of life. China is now on the eve of a great national movement, for just a spark of light would set the whole political forest on fire to drive out the Tartar from our land. Our task is indeed great, but it will not be an impossible one. It needed fewer than twenty thousand troops of the allied army in the Boxer war in 1900 to break down the Tartar resistance, to march into Peking and capture that city. There is no doubt we could do the same with double or triple that number of men; furthermore, we could easily raise a hundred or a thousand times more men from our patriots. And it is evident from recent experiences that the Tartar soldiers are not our match in every field. The present uprising of patriots in the province of Kwang Si is a striking proof. They are far away from the coast and cannot get supplies of arms and ammunition from any source. The only means of getting such materials depends exclusively upon capturing those of the enemy. Even thus they have continued the fight for the last three years and repeatedly defeated expedition after expedition of imperial troops sent against them⟨from⟩ various parts of the Empire. By possessing such a wonderful fighting capacity, who could say that they could not vanquish the Tartar power from China if sufficient supplies could be forthcoming? When our great object of revolutionizing China shall have been accomplished not only a new era would down[dwell] on our beautiful country, but a brighter prospect also would be shared by the whole human race. Universal peace will surely follow the step of the regeneration of China, and a grand field hitherto never dreamed of will be opened to the social and economic activities of the civilized world.

To work out the salvation of China is exclusively a duty of our own, but as the problem has recently involved a world wide interest, we, in order to make sure of our success, to facilitate our movement, to avoid unnecessary sacrifice and to prevent misunderstanding and intervention of foreign powers, must appeal to the people of the civilized world in general and the people of the United States in particular for your sympathy and support, either moral or material, because you are the pioneers of western civilization in Japan; because you are a Christian nation; because we intend to model our new government after yours; and above all because you are the champion of liberty and democracy. We hope we may find many Lafayettes among you.

Sun Yat Sen

CHINA'S NEXT STEP

Apr. 1, 1912

CHINA'S NEXT STEP *

Apr. 1, 1912

＊ In the following article the founder and temporary President of the new Republic of China indicates that in laying down that office he does not consider his task done, but plans for a new social and industrial revolution for China which shall put that ancient nation in the very van of the nations of the world and achieve results which could not be achieved without bloodshed in countries with a fixt〔fixed〕 social system. This remarkable utterance appeared first in the form of an address at the farewell banquent〔banquet〕 given in his honor at Shanghai by the Revolutionary Association, April 18, 1912. —Editor of *The People*

The republic is established in China, and though I am laying down the office of Provisional President, this does not mean that I am going to cease to work for the cause. After laying down my office, still greater affairs demand my attention. China has been under the domination of the Manchus for 270 years. During that time many attempts have been made to regain independence. Fifty years ago the Taiping Rebellion was such an attempt, but this was merely a revolution of the race (Chinese against Manchus). Had the revolution been successful, the country would still have been under an autocratic government. This would not count success.

Some years ago a few of us met in Japan and founded the Revolutionary Society. We decided on three great principles: (1) The (Chinese) people to be supreme as a race (i. e., not to be under the domination of an alien race). (2) The people supreme in government. (3) The people supreme in wealth production. Now the Manchus have abdicated, we have succeeded in establishing the first two of these principles, and it now remains for us to accomplish the revolution of society. This subject is being much discussed in the world today, but many people in China are ignorant of what is involved in such a question. They suppose that the aim of the regeneration of China is only that this may become a great and powerful country, on an equality with the great Powers of the West; but such is not the end of our effort. Today there are no wealthier countries than Britain and America; there is no more enlightened than France. Britain is a constitutional monarchy; France and America are perfect republics; but the gap betwixt [between] the poor and the wealthy in these countries is too great. And so it comes to pass that thoughts of revolution still rankle in the minds of many. For, if this revolution of society be not effected, the many cannot enjoy complete joy and happiness. Such felicity is not for the few capitalists. The mass of laborers continues to suffer bitterness and cannot be at rest. Now, the revolution of the race and the revolution of government are easy, but the revolution of society is difficult. This is because it is only a people of high attainments that can work out a revolution of society. Some will say, "We have succeeded so far in our revolution, why not be content and wait? Why seek to accomplish what Britain and America, with all their wealth and knowledge, have not yet undertaken?" This would be a mistaken policy. For in Britain and America civilization is advanced and industry flourishes, it is therefore difficult to accomplish a revolution of society. In China we have not yet reached this stage, so such a revolution is easy for us. In Britain and America capitalists with their vested interests are intrenched and it is therefore difficult to dislodge them. In China, capitalists and vested interests have not yet appeared; hence the revolution of society is easy. I may be asked, "To accomplish such a revolution as you foreshadow, will military force be necessary?" I reply, "In Britain and America it will be necessary to use military force, but not in China." The coal strike in Britain is a proof of what I say. Yet the coal strike cannot be called a revolution. It is merely that the people desire to get possession of the sources of wealth and can only do so by violent means. Although the revolution of society is difficult to accomplish today, the time is surely coming when it will be an accomplished fact, but by what desperate means it shall be accomplished and through what dangers the state shall pass, it is difficult to prognosticate. If we do not, in the beginning of our republic, take thought for the future, by-and-by, when capitalism is developed, its oppression may be worsed than the despotism which we have just thrown off, and we may again have to pass through a period of bloodshed. Will not that be deplorable?

There is one point to which we ought to give the greatest attention. when the new government is established it will be necessary that all land deeds shall be changed. This is a necessary corollary of the revolution. If we desire to forward the revolution of society, then when the change is made a slight alteration should be introduced into the form of the deed in order that the greatest results may be achieved. Formerly, people owning land paid taxes according to the area, making a distinction only between the best, medium and common land. In the future, taxes ought to be levied according to the value, not the area of the land. For land varies much more than in the ratio of these three degrees. I don't know by how much the land in Nanking differs in value from ⟨the⟩ land on the Bund in Shanghai, but if you rate it according to this old method of three degrees you cannot assess it justly. It would be better to tax it according to its value, the poor land paying a low tax and valuable land a high tax. The valuable land is mostly in the busy marts and is in the possession of wealthy men; to tax them heavily would be no oppression. The poor land is mostly the possession of poor people in far back districts; nothing but the lightest taxes should be levied on them. For instance, a piece of land on the Bund pays taxes at the rate of a few dollars to the acre and a piece of land of equal area in the country pays an equal tax. This is far from being just. If the tax were levied on the value of the land then this injustice would be done away with. If you compare the value of land in Shanghai today with what it was one hundred years ago, it has increased ten thousand fold. Now, industry in China is about to be developed. Commerce will be advanced, and in fifty years' time we shall see many Shanghais in China. Let us take time by the forelock and make sure that the unearned increment of wealth shall belong to the people and not to private capitalists who happen to be owners of the soil.

PLAIN SPEAKING FROM CHINA

1919

PLAIN SPEAKING FROM CHINA *

1919

* Dr. Sun Yat-Sen is recognized as a patriot even by those who hate him, and in China there are many who feel that way toward him. They can't help it. He spoils all their plans. When a small group of Chinese militarists planned with Japanese militarists for the consolidation of the country, so that Japan could more easily conquer it, Dr. Sun Yat Sen went down to Canton and pulled five of the best provinces out of the government. When northern and southern militarists had come to terms as to what they could get for themselves out of the peace between them, Dr. Sun injected the parliamentary issue into the debates and broke up the Peace Conference. Dr. Sun is spoiling things again. Just now the officials are trying to borrow money from America and Dr. Sun points out forcefully that China wants Americean machines, not loans. —Editor of *The Independent*

China does not need money. We need brains and machinery, but not money.

It is not China that has been constantly borrowing.

The Peking Government borrows. Americans must recognize that the Peking Government does not represent the country. Nor does the Canton Government represent the country. It is represented more nearly by the merchants here in

Shanghai, by the growing middle class which is carefully leaving politics alone and which is devoting itself to building up the industry of the country.

Young China, the China of the Students' Movement, of the anti-Japanese Boycott, of the encouragement of native industry, of opposition to signing the peace treaty, is the China which will have to pay any loans made today. And whether they will pay them or not depends upon the character of the loan rather than the force of the lender. One can always scuttle the ship—when it is impossible to do anything else. And Japan and the rest of the world, if it forces on us political loans, is forcing also upon itself the dangers of just such a situation.

We have plenty of raw material here... more perhaps than any other nation in the world. We don't need to import a thing and the day will come when we won't import much. But our needs are increasing and our processes of production are slow. Furthermore, we can buy your manufactured articles cheaper than we can make them, because we do not yet understand large scale production and we have not organized industry on a modern basis. But that state of affairs cannot go on forever. The day is fast approaching when China will use her own resouces and her own labor to produce what she needs. If we want to go about it slowly, stupidly, we can wait until we have made our own machinery, but that is an uneconomic method. But why should we be made either to remain backward and weak or to borrow money on the security of our sovereignty. No other nation is given that alternative. Why force it on China? Japan has been forcing it on China, but we believe that America is our friend. Therefore we want to borrow from America two things, machines and experts to teach us how to run them.

Capitalists are used to dealing with governments. They like to make loans which are secured by a government. But the downfall of Russia, Germany and the Balkans must have convinced bankers that governments are not very safe propositions. The French thought that the autocracy of Russia would live forever and that their investments in that autocracy would be safe forever. But it is not working out. The awakening of the masses in every country and the determination of the masses that their future shall not be mortgaged to finance the inefficiency and selfishness of the present has made loan-making to governments an unsafe business proposition. Do you really believe that the people of the tiny nations of Europe will ever be in a position to pay their tremendous war debts? Do you think that any nation can determine its own future when that future is mortgaged to the bankers of another nation? I should not believe so.

The capitalists have always lent money to the Chinese Government, but that won't work out either. When a genuine, people's parliament meets, we shall repudiate every loan that the Peking Government has made unconstitutionally and if, for instance, Japan wants to fight us for the money, let her come here. It will only involve the world in another war, in a banker's war. But we shall do it. Every boy in every school in China, every girl in every school in China, is pledged to that. They can destroy us for their dollars, but we are big enough to bring them down with us. Every banker lending money to the Chinese Government is paying in advance for his own financial funeral.

Your American bankers are making the mistake of imitating their British and Japanese predecessors. They are dealing with the Peking Government. Some of them insulted us of the south by suggesting that they would give us a share in the spoils. We don't want any spoils. We want to be boycotted as we want Peking boycotted. We are neither of the north nor of the south. We are Chinese without discriminating adjectives and we feel that if money is to come from America, we want it to come in the form of machinery, of engineers, of efficiency〔efficient] experts, of management.

My proposal is that American capitalists join with Chinese in the creation of national industry. The Americans put up the money for the machinery, and for the payment of the foreign experts. The Chinese will put up the money for the raw materials and human labor. That the partnership be as far as possible on a fifty-fifty basis and that the Americans be given a fairly large but not exorbitant return on their capital. This proposition ought to be worth while to American capitalists, who are hampered by so many things in their own country. I would suggest further that the Americans provide clauses in the contracts, so that the Chinese can put them out after a stated period. The underlying principle should be a short time investment with a large profit. The guarantees on this proposition would not be as gilt edged as a government loan is said to be, but how gilt edged are the Trans-Siberian bonds today? And what do you know about any government tomorrow?

There is another issue involved: China cannot forever go on buying things that she can easily manufacture at home. The thing is too absurd. China will sooner or later manufacture her own things. Your manufacturers will never be able to compete in China with China-made things. Therefore either you start plants here or sooner or later you will have to get out of the Chinese market. Why then not open plants here? Why not made[make] things here?

Shanghai

THE INTERNATIONAL DEVELOPMENT OF CHINA

July 20, 1920

This work is
affectionately dedicated
to
Sir. James and Lady Cantlie
My revered teacher and devoted friends
to whom I once owed my life

CONTENTS

PREFACE 128
A PROJECT TO ASSIST THE READJUSTMENT OF
 POST-BELLUM INDUSTRIES 130
PROGRAM Ⅰ 136
PROGRAM Ⅱ 152
PROGRAM Ⅲ 190
PROGRAM Ⅳ 233
PROGRAM Ⅴ 292
PROGRAM Ⅵ 313
CONCLUSION 320
APPENDIX Ⅰ 326
APPENDIX Ⅱ 337
APPENDIX Ⅲ 342
APPENDIX Ⅳ 344
APPENDIX Ⅴ 346
APPENDIX Ⅵ 348

MAPS

	Facing Page
FIGURE 1	352
FIGURE 2	353
MAP I	354
MAP II	355
MAP III	356
MAP IV	357
MAP V	358
MAP VI	359
MAP VII	360
MAP VIII	361
MAP IX	362
MAP X	363
MAP XI	364
MAP XII	365
MAP XIII	366
MAP XIV	367
MAP XV	368
MAP XVI	369

PREFACE

As soon as Armistice was declared in the recent World War, I began to take up the study of the International Development of China, and to form programs accordingly. I was prompted to do so by the desire to contribute my humble part in [to] the realization of world peace. China, a country possessing a territory of 4,289,000 square miles, a population of 400,000,000 people, and the richest mineral and agricultural resources in the world, is now a prey of militaristic and capitalistic powers—a greater bone of contention than the Balkan Peninsula. Unless the Chinese question could be settled peacefully, another world war greater and more terrible than the one just past will be inevitable. In order to solve the Chinese question, I suggest that the vast resources of China should be developed internationally under a socialistic scheme, for the good of the world in general and the Chinese people in particular. It is my hope that as a result of this, the present spheres of influence can be abolished; the international commercial war can be done away with; the internecine capitalistic competition can be got rid of, and last, but not least, the class struggle between capital and labor can be avoided. Thus the root of war will be forever exterminated so far as the case of China is concerned.

Each part of the different programs in this International Scheme, is but a rough sketch or a general policy produced from a layman's thought with very limited materials at his disposal. So alterations and changes will have to be made after scientific investigation and detailed survey. For instance, in regard to the projected Great Northern Port, which is to be situated between the mouths of the Tsingho and the Lwanho, the writer thought that the entrance of the harbor should be at the eastern side of the port, but from actual survey by technical engineers, it is found that the entrance of the harbor should be at the western side of the port instead. So I crave great indulgence on the part of experts and specialists.

I wish to thank Dr. Monlin Chiang, Mr. David Yui, Dr. Y. Y. Tsu, Mr. T. Z. Koo, and Dr. John Y. Lee, who have given me great assistance in reading over the manuscripts with me. Special thanks are due to Mr. T. Z. Koo, who has undertaken to see the book through the press for me.

Shanghai, July 20, 1920

Sun Yat-sen

THE INTERNATIONAL DEVELOPMENT OF CHINA

July 20, 1920

A PROJECT TO ASSIST THE READJUSTMENT OF POST-BELLUM INDUSTRIES

It is estimated that during the last year of the World War the daily expenses of the various fighting nations amounted to two hundred and forty millions of dollars gold. It is accepted by even the most conservative way, that only one half of this sum was spent on munitions and other direct war supplies, that is, one hundred and twenty millions of dollars gold. Let us consider these war supplies from a commercial point of view. The battlefield is the market for these new industries, the consumers of which are the soldiers. Various industries had to be enlisted and many new ones created for the supplies. In order to increase the production of these war commodities day by day, people of the warring countries and even those of the neutral states had to be content with the barest necessities of life and had to give up all former comforts and luxuries.

Now the war is ended and the sole market of these war supplies had closed, let us hope, forever, for the good of humanity. So, henceforth, we are concerned with the problem as to how a readjustment might be brought about. What is to be considered first is the reconstruction of the various countries, and next the supply of comforts and luxuries that will have to be resumed. We remember that one hundred and twenty million dollars were spent every day on direct war supplies. Let us then suppose that the two items mentioned will take up one half of this sum, that is, sixty millions of dollars a day which will still leave us a balance of sixty million dollars a day to be utilized. Besides, [the] many millions of soldiers who were once consumers will from now on become producers again. Furthermore, the unification and nationalization of all the industries, which I might call the Second Industrial Revolution, will be more far-reaching than that of the first one in which Manual Labor was displaced by Machinery. This second industrial revolution will increase the productive power of man many times more than the first one. Consequently, this unification and nationalization of industries on account of the World War will further complicate the readjustment of the post-war industries. Just imagine sixty million dollars a day or twenty-one billions and nine hundred millions of dollars a year of new trade created by the war suddenly have to stop when peace is concluded! Where in this world can Europe and America look for a market to consume this enormous saving from the war?

If the billions of dollars worth of war industries can find no place in the post-bellum readjustment, then they will be a pure economic waste. The result will not only disturb the economic condition of the producing countries, but will also be a great loss to the world at large.

All the commercial nations are looking to China as the only "dumping ground" for their over-production. The pre-war condition of trade was unfavorable to China. The balance of imports over exports was something over one hundred million dollars gold annually. The market of China under this condition could not expand much for soon after there will be no more money or commodities left for exchanging goods with foreign countries. Fortunately, the natural resources of China are great and their proper development would create an unlimited market for the whole world and would utilize the greater part, if not all of the billions of dollars worth of war industries soon to be turned into peace industries.

China is the land that still employs manual labor for production and has not yet entered the first stage of industrial evolution, while in Europe and America the second stage is already reached. So China has to begin the two stages of industrial evolution at once by adopting the machinery as well as the nationalization of production. In this case China will require machinery for her vast agriculture, machinery for her rich mines, machinery for the building of her innumerable factories, machinery for her extensive transportation systems and machinery for all her public utilities. Let us see how this new demand for machinery will help in the readjustment of war industries. The workshops that turn out cannon can easily be made to turn out steam rollers for the construction of roads in China. The workshops that turn out tanks can be made to turn out trucks for the transportation of the raw materials that are lying everywhere in China. And all sorts of warring machinery can be converted into peaceful tools for the general development of China's latent wealth. The Chinese people will welcome the development of our country's resources provided that it can be kept out of Mandarin corruption and ensure the mutual benefit of China and of the countries cooperating with us.

It might be feared by some people in Europe and America that the development of China by war machinery, war organization and technical experts might create unfavorable competition to foreign industries. I, therefore, propose a scheme to develop a new market in China big enough both for her own products and for 〈the〉 products from foreign countries. The scheme will be along the following lines:

Ⅰ. The Development of a Communications System.

(a) 100,000 miles of Railways.

(b) 1,000,000 miles of Macadam Roads.

(c) Improvement of Existing Canals.

    (1) Hangchow-Tientsin Canals.

    (2) Sikiang-Yangtze Canals.

(d) Construction of New Canals.

    (1) Liaoho-Sunghwakiang Canal.

    (2) Others to be projected.

(e) River Conservancy.

    (1) To regulate the Embankments and Channel of the Yangtze River from Hankow to the sea thus facilitating Ocean-going ships to reach that port at all seasons.

    (2) To regulate the Hoangho Embankments and Channel to prevent floods.

    (3) To regulate the Sikiang.

    (4) To regulate the Hwaiho.

    (5) To regulate various other rivers.

(f) The Construction of more Telegraph Lines and Telephone and Wireless System[Systems] all over the Country.

II. The Development of Commercial Harbors.

  (a) Three largest Ocean Ports with future capacity equalling New York Harbor to be constructed in North, Central and South China.

  (b) Various small Commercial and Fishing Harbors to be constructed along the Coast.

  (c) Commercial Docks to be constructed along all navigable rivers.

III. Modern Cities with public utilities to be constructed in all Railway Centers, Termini and alongside Harbors.

IV. Water Power Development.

V. Iron and Steel Works and Cement Works on the largest scale in order to supply the above needs.

Ⅵ. Mineral Development.

Ⅶ. Agricultural Development.

Ⅷ. Irrigational Work on the largest scale in Mongolia and Sinkiang.

Ⅸ. Reforestation in Central and North China.

Ⅹ. Colonization in Manchuria, Mongolia, Sinkiang, Kokonor〔Koko Nor〕, and Tibet.

If the above program could be carried out gradually, China will not only be the "Dumping Ground" for foreign goods but actually will be the "Economic Ocean" capable of absorbing all the surplus capital as quickly as the Industrial Nations can possibly produce by the coming Industrial Revolution of Nationalized Productive Machinery. Then there will be no more competition and commercial struggles in China as well as in the world.

The recent World War has proved to mankind that war is ruinous to both the Conqueror and the Conquered, and worse for the Aggressor. What is true in Military warfare is more so in trade warfare. Since President Wilson has proposed a League of Nations to end Military war in the future, I desire to propose to end the trade war by cooperation and mutual help in the Development of China. This will root out probably the greatest cause of future wars.

The world has been greatly benefited by the development of America as an industrial and a commercial nation. So a developed China with her four hundred millions of population, will be another New World in the economic sense. The nations which will take part in this development will reap immense advantages. Furthermore, international cooperation of this kind cannot but help to strengthen the Brotherhood of Man. Ultimately, I am sure, this will culminate to be the keystone in the arch of the League of Nations.

In order to carry out this project successfully I suggest that three necessary steps must be taken. First, that the various Governments of the Capital-supplying Powers must agree to joint action and a unified policy to form an International Organization with their war work organizers, administrators and experts of various lines to formulate plans and to standardize materials in order to prevent waste and to facilitate work. Second, the confidence of the Chinese people must be secured in order to gain their cooperation and enthusiastic support. If the above two steps are accomplished, then the third step is to open formal negotiation for the final contract of the project with the Chinese Government. For which I suggest that it be on the same basis as the contract I once concluded with the Pauling Company of London, for the construction of the Canton-Chungking Railway, since it was the fairest to both parties and the one most welcomed by the Chinese people, of all contracts that were ever made between China and the foreign countries.

And last but not least, a warning must be given that mistakes such as the notorious Sheng Shun Hwai's nationalized railway scheme in 1911 must not be committed again. In those days foreign bankers entirely disregarded the will of the Chinese people, and thought that they could do everything with the Chinese Government alone. But to their regret, they found that the contracts which they had concluded with the Government, by heavy bribery, were only to be blocked by the people later on. Had the foreign bankers gone in the right way of first securing the confidence of the Chinese people, and then approaching the Government for a contract, many things might have been accomplished without a hitch. Therefore, in this International Project we must pay more attention to the people's will than ever before.

If my proposition is acceptable to the Capital-supplying Powers, I will furnish further details.

PROGRAM I

The industrial development of China should be carried out along two lines: (1) by private enterprise and (2) by national undertaking. All matters that can be and are better carried out by private enterprise should be left to private hands which should be encouraged and fully protected by liberal laws. And in order to facilitate the industrial development by private enterprise in China, the hitherto suicidal internal taxes must be abolished, the cumbersome currency must he re formed, the various kinds of official obstacles must be removed, and transportation facilities must be provided. All matters that cannot be taken up by private concerns and those that possess monopolistic character should be taken up as national undertakings. It is for this latter line of development that we are here endeavoring to deal with. In this national undertaking, foreign capital have to be invited, foreign experts and organizers have to be enlisted, and gigantic methods have to be adopted. The property thus created will be state owned [state-owned] and will be managed for the benefit of the whole nation. During the construction and the operation of each of these national undertakings, before its capital and interest are fully repaid, it will be managed and supervised by foreign experts under Chinese employment. As one of their obligations, these foreign experts have to undertake the training of Chinese assistants to take their places in the future. When the capital and interest of each undertaking are paid off, the Chinese Government will have the option to employ either foreigners or Chinese to manage the concern as it thinks fit.

Before entering into the details of this International Development Scheme, four principles have to be considered:

(1) The most remunerative field must be selected in order to attract foreign capital.

(2) The most urgent needs of the nation must be met.

(3) The lines of least resistance must be followed.

(4) The most suitable positions must he chosen.

In conformity with the above principles, I formulate PROGRAM I as follows:

I. The construction of a Great Northern Port on the Gulf of Pechili.

II. The building of a system of railways from the Great Northern Port to the Northwestern extremity of China.

III. The Colonization of Mongolia and Sinkiang (Chinese Turkestan).

IV. The construction of canals to connect the inland waterway systems of North and Central China with the Great Northern Port.

V. The development of the iron and coal fields in Shansi and the construction of an iron and steel works.

These five projects will be worked out as one program, for each of them will assist and accelerate the development of the others. The Great Northern Port will serve as a base of operation of this International Development Scheme, as well as a connecting link of transportation and communication between China and the outer world. The other four projects will be centered around it.

PART I

THE GREAT NORTHERN PORT

I propose that a great deep water[deep-water] and ice free[ice-free] port be constructed on the Gulf of Pechili. The need of such a port in that part of China has been keenly felt for a long time. Several projects have been proposed such as the deepening of the Taku Bar, the construction of a harbor in the Chiho estuary, the Chinwangtao Harbor which has actually been carried out on a small scale and the Hulutao Harbor which is on the point of being constructed. But the site of my projected port is in none of these places for the first two are too far from the deep water line and too near to fresh water which freezes in winter. So it is impossible to make them into deep water[deep-water] and ice free[ice-free] ports, while the last two are too far away from the center of population and are unprofitable as commercial ports. The locality of my projected port is just at midway between Taku and Chinwangtao and at a point between the mouths of the Tsingho and Lwanho, on the cape of the coast line between Taku and Chinwangtao. This is one of the points nearest to deep water in this Gulf. With the fresh water of the Tsingho and Lwanho diverted away, it can be made a deep water [deep-water] and ice free[ice-free] port without much difficulty. Its distance to Tientsin is about seventy or eighty miles less than that of Chinwangtao to Tientsin. Moreover, this port can be connected with the inland waterway systems of North and Central China by canal, whereas in the case of Chinwangtao and Hulutao this could not be done. So this port is far superior as a commercial harbor than Hulutao or Chinwangtao which at present is the only ice free[ice-free] port in the Gulf of Pechihli.

From a commercial standpoint this port will be a paying proposition from the very beginning of its construction, owing to the fact that it is situated at the center of the greatest salt industry in China. The cheapest salt is produced here by sun evaporation only. If modern methods could be added, also utilizing the cheap coal near by [nearby], the production could increase many times more and the cost could thus be made much cheaper. Then it can supply the whole of China with much cheaper salt. By this industry alone it is quite sufficient to support a moderate sized harbor which must be the first step of this great project. Besides, there is in the immediate neighborhood the greatest coal mine that has yet been developed in China, the Kailan Mining Company. The output of its colliery is abont four million tons a year. At present the company uses its own harbor, Chinwangtao, for shipping its exports. But our projected port is much nearer to its colliery than Chinwangtao. It can be connected with the mine by canal thus providing it with a much cheaper carriage than by rail to Chinwangtao. Furthermore, our projected port will in future consume much of the Kailan coal. Thus eventually the Company must use our port as a shipping stage for its exports. Tientsin, the largest commercial center in North China, has no deep harbor and is ice bound several months a year in winter, and so has to use our projected port entirely as an outlet for its world trade. This is the local need only but for this alone it is quite sufficient to make our projected port a paying proposition.

But my idea is to develop this port as large as New York in a reasonable limit of time. Now, let us survey the hinterland to see whether the possibility justifies my ideal or not. To the southwest are the provinces of Chihli and Shansi, and the Hoangho valley with a population of nearly a hundred millions. To the northwest are the undeveloped Jehol district and the vast Mongolian Prairie with their virgin soil waiting for development, Chihli with its dense population and Shansi with its rich mineral resources have to depend upon this port as their only outlet to the sea. And if the future Dolon Nor and Urga Railway is completed with connection to the Siberian line then Central Siberia will also have to use this as its nearest seaport. Thus its contributing or rather distributing area will be larger than that of New York. Finally, this port will become the true terminus of the future Eurasian Railway System, which will connect the two continents together. The land which we select to be the site of our projected port is now almost worth next to nothing. Let us say two or three hundred square miles be taken up as national property absolutely for our future city building. If within forty years we could develop a city as large as Philadelphia, not to say New York, the land value alone will be sufficient to pay off the capital invested in its development.

The need of such a port in this part of China goes without saying. For the provinces of Chihli, Shansi, Western Shantung, Northern Honan, a part of Fengtien and the greater part of Shensi and Kansu with a population of about 100 millions are lacking of a seaport of this kind. Mongolia and Sinkiang as well as the rich coal and iron fields of Shansi will also have to depend on the Chihli coast as their only outlet to the sea. And the millions of congested population of the coast and the Yangtze valley need an entrance to the virgin soil of the Mongolian Prairie and the Tienshan Valley. The port will be the shortest doorway and the cheapest passage to these regions.

The locality of our projected port is nearest to deep water line, and far away from any large river which might carry silt to fill up the approach of the harbor like those of the Hoangho entrance and the Yangtze estuary which cause great trouble to conservancy work. So it has no great natural obstacle to be overcome. Moreover, it is situated in an arid plain with few people living on it, so it has no artificial hindrance to be overcome. We can do whatever we please in the process of construction.

As regards the planning and estimation of the work of the harbor construction and city building, I must leave them to experts who have to make extensive surveys and soundings before detailed plan and proper estimation could be made. Whereas for rough reference see Map I, and Figures 1 and 2. *

> * As soon as this first program reached the American Legation in Peking, the former Minister, Dr. Paul S. Reinsch, immediately sent an expert to survey the site which the writer indicated, and found that it is really the best site on the Chihli Coast for a world harbor, excepting that the entrance of the port should be at the west side instead of the east side as the writer proposed. Detailed plans have been made as Figures 1 and 2.

PART II

THE NORTHWESTERN RAILWAY SYSTEM

Our projected Railway will start at the Great Northern Port and follow the Lwan Valley to the prairie city of Dolon Nor, a distance of three hundred miles. This railway should be built in double tracks at the commencement. As our projected Port is a starting point to the sea, so Dolon Nor is a gate to the vast prairie which our projected Railway System is going to tap. It is from Dolon Nor our Northwestern Railway System is going to radiate. First, a line N. N. E. will run parallel to the Khingan Range to Khailar, and thence to Moho, the gold district on the right bank of the Amur River. This line is about eight hundred miles in length. Second, a line N. N. W. to Kurelun, and thence to the frontier to join the Siberian line near Chita. This line has a distance of about six hundred miles. Third, a trunk line northwest, west, and southwest, skirting off the northern edge of the desert proper, to Urumochi at the western end of China, a distance of about one thousand six hundred miles all on level land. Fourth, a line from Urumochi westward to Ili, a distance of about four hundred miles. Fifth, a line from Urumochi southeast across the Tienshan gap into the Darim basin, then turning southwest running along the fertile zone between the southern watershed of the Tienshan and the northern edge of the Darim Desert, to Kashgar, and thence turning southeast to another fertile zone between the eastern watershed of the Pamir, the northern watershed of the Kuenlum Mountain and the southern edge of the Darim Desert, to the city of Iden or Keria, a distance of about one thousand two hundred miles all on level land. Sixth, a branch from the Dolon Nor Urumochi Trunk Line, which I shall call Junction A, to Urga and thence to the frontier city Kiakata, a distance of about three hundred and fifty miles. Seventh, a branch from Junction B to Uliassutai and beyond N. N. W. up to the frontier, a distance of about six hundred miles. And eighth, a branch from Junction C northwest to the frontier, a distance of about four hundred and fifty miles. See Map II.

Regarded from the principle of "following the line of least resistance" our projected railways in this program is the [most] ideal one. For most of the seven thousand miles of lines under this project are on perfectly level land. For instance, the Trunk Line from Dolon Nor to Kashgar and beyond, about a distance of three thousand miles right along is on the most fertile plain and encounters no natural obstacles, neither high mountains nor great rivers.

Regarded from the principle of "the most suitable position", our projected railways will command the most dominating position of world importance. It will form a part of the trunk line of the Eurasian system which will connect the populous centers, Europe and China, together. It will be the shortest line from the Pacific Coast to Europe. Its branch from Ili will connect with the future Indo-European line, and through Bagdad, Damascus and Cairo, will ⟨also⟩ link up [also] with the future African system. Then there will be a through route from our projected port to Capetown. There is no existing railway commanding such a world important[important world] position as this.

Regarded from the principle of the "most urgent need of the Nation", this railway system becomes the first in importance, for the territories traversed by it are larger than the eighteen provinces of China Proper. Owing to the lack of means of transportation and communication at present these rich territories are left undeveloped and millions of laborers in the congested provinces along the coast and in the Yangtze Valley are without work. What a great waste of natural and human energies. If there is a railway connecting these vast territories, the waste labor of the congested provinces can go and develop these rich soils for the good not only of China but also of the whole commercial world. So a system of railways to the northwestern part of the country is the most urgent need both politically and econmically for China today.

I have intentionally left out the first principle — "the most remunerative field must be selected" — not because I want to neglect it but because l mean to call more attention to it and treat it more fully. It is commonly known to financiers and railway men that a railway in a densely populated country from end to end is the best paying proposition, and a railway in a thinly settled country from end to end is the least paying one. And a railway in an almost unpopulated country like our projected lines will take a long time to make it a paying business. That is why the United States Government had to grant large tracts of public lands to railway corporations to induce them to build the transcontinental lines to the Pacific Coast, half a century ago. Whenever I talked with foreign railway men and financiers about the construction of railways to Mongolia and Sinkiang, they generally got very shy of the proposition. Undoubtedly they thought that it is [was] for political and military reasons only that such a line as the Siberian Railway was built, which traversed through a thinly populated land. But they could not grasp the fact which might be entirely new to them, that a railway between a densely populated country and a sparsely settled country will pay far better than ⟨the⟩ one that runs from end to end in a densely populated land. The reason is that in economic conditions the two ends of a well populated country are not so different as that between a thickly populated country and a newly opened country. At the two ends of a well populated country, in many respects, the local people are self-supplying, excepting a few special articles which they depend upon the other end of the road to supply. So the demand and supply between the two places are not very great, thus the trade between the two ends of the railway could not be very lucrative. While the difference of the economic condition between a well populated country and an unpopulated country is very great. The workers of the new land have to depend upon the supplies of the thickly populated country almost in everything excepting foodstuffs and raw materials which they have in abundance and for disposal of which they have to depend upon the demand of the well populated district. Thus the trade between the two ends of the line will be extraordinarily great. Furthermore, a railway in a thickly populated place will not affect much the masses which consist of the majority of the population. It is only the few well-to-do and the merchants and tradesmen that make use of it. While with a railway between a thickly populated country and a sparsely settled or unsettled country, as soon as it is opened to traffic for each mile, the masses of the congested country will use it and rush into the new land in a wholesale manner. Thus the railway will be employed to its utmost capacity in passenger traffic from the beginning. The comparison between the Peking-Hankow Railway and the Peking-Mukden Railway in China is a convincing proof.

The Peking-Hankow Railway is a line of over eight hundred miles running from the capital of the country to the commercial center in the heart of China right along in an extraordinarily densely settled country from end to end. While the Peking-Mukden line is barely six hundred miles in length running from a thickly populated country to thinly populated Manchuria. The former is a well paying line put 〔but〕 the latter pays far better. The net profit of the shorter Peking-Mukden Line is sometimes three to four millions more yearly than that of the longer Peking-Hankow line.

Therefore, it is logically clear that a railway in a thickly populated country is much better than 〈the〉 one that is in a thinly populated country in remuneration. But a railway between a very thickly populated and a very thinly populated or unpopulated country is the best paying proposition. This is a law in Railway Economics which hitherto had not been discovered by railway men and financiers.

According to this new railway economic law, our projected railway will be the best remunerative project of its kind. For at the one end, we have our projected port which acts as a connecting link with the thickly populated coast of China and the Yangtze Valley and also the two existing lines, the Kinghan and the Tsinpu, as feeders to the projected port and the Dolon Nor line. And at the other end, we have a vast and rich territory, larger than China Proper, to be developed. There is no such vast fertile field so near to a center of a population of four hundred millions to be found in any other part of the world.

PART III

THE COLONIZATION OF MONGOLIA AND SINKIANG

The Colonization of Mongolia and Sinkiang is a complement of the Railway scheme. Each is dependent upon the other for its prosperity. The colonization scheme, besides benefitting the railway, is in itself a greatly profitable undertaking. The results of the United States, Canada, Australia, and Argentina are ample proofs of this. In the case of our project, it is simply a matter of applying waste Chinese labor and foreign machinery to a fertile land for production for which its remuneration is sure. The present Colonization of Manchuria, notwithstanding its topsy turvy [topsy-turvy] way which caused great waste of land and human energy, has been wonderfully prosperous. If we would adopt scientific methods in our colonization project we could certainly obtain better results than all the others. Therefore, I propose that the whole movement be directed in a systematic way by state organization with the help of foreign experts and war organizers, for the good of the colonists particularly and the nation generally.

The land should be bought up by the state in order to prevent the speculators from creating the dog-in-the-manager system, to the detriment of the public. The land should be prepared and divided into farmsteads, then leased to colonists on perpetual term. The initial capital, seeds, implements and houses should be furnished by the state at cost price on cash or on the instalment plan. For these services, big organizations should be formed and war work measures should be adopted in order to transport, to feed, to clothe and to house every colonist on credit in his first year.

As soon as a sufficient number of colonists is settled in a district, franchise should be given for self-government and the colonists should be trained to manage their own local affairs with perfect democratic spirit.

If within ten years we can transport, let us say, ten millions of the people, from the congested provinces of China, to the Northwestern territory to develop its natural resources, the benefit to the commercial world at large will be enormous. No matter how big a capital that shall have been invested in the project ⟨is,⟩ it could be repaid within a very short time. So in regard to its bearing to "the principle of remuneration" there is no question about it.

Regarded from "the principle of the need of the Nation" colonization is the most urgent need of the first magnitude. At present China has more than a million soldiers to be disbanded. Besides, the dense population will need elbow room to move in. This Colonization project is the best thing for both purpose [purposes]. The soldiers have to be disbanded at great expense and hundreds of millions of dollars may be needed for disbandment alone, in paying them off with a few months' pay. If nothing more could be done for these soldiers' welfare, they will either be left to starve or to rob for a living. Then the consequences will be unimaginable. This calamity must be prevented and prevented effectively. The best way for this is the colonization scheme. I hope that the friendly foreign financiers, who have the welfare of China at heart, when requested to float a reorganization loan for the Chinese Government in the future, will persist on the point—that the money furnished must first be used to carry out the colonization scheme for the disbanded soldiers. Otherwise, their money will only work disasters to China.

For the million or more of the soldiers to be disbanded, the district between our projected port and Dolon Nor is quite enough to accommodate them. This district is quite rich in mineral resources and is very sparsely settled. If a railway is to start at once from the projected port to Dolon Nor, these soldiers could be utilized as a pioneer party for the work of the port, of the railway, of the developing of the adjacent land beyond the Great Wall, and of preparing Dolon Nor as a jumping ground for further colonization development of the great northern plain.

PART IV

THE CONSTRUCTION OF CANALS TO CONNECT THE INLAND WATERWAY SYSTEMS OF NORTH AND CENTRAL CHINA WITH THE GREAT NORTHERN PORT

This scheme will include the regulation of the Hoangho and its branches, the Weiho in Shensi, and the Fenho in Shansi and connecting canals. The Hoangho should be deepened at its mouth in order to give a good drawing to clear its bed of silt and carry the same to the sea. For this purpose, jetties should be built far out to the deep sea, as those at the mouths of the Mississippi in America. Its embankments should be parallel in order to make the width of the channel equal right along, so as to give equal velocity to the current which will prevent the deposit of silt at the bottom. By dams and locks, it could be made navigable right up to Lanchow, in the province of Kansu, and at the same time water power could be developed. The Weiho and the Fenho can also be treated in the same manner so as to make them navigable to a great extent in the provinces of Shensi and Shansi. Thus the provinces of Kansu, Shensi, and Shansi can be connected by waterway with our projected port on the Gulf of [Pe]chihli, so that cheap carriage can be provided for the rich mineral and other products from these three hitherto secluded provinces.

The expenses of regulating the Hoangho may be very great. As a paying project, it may not be very attractive but as a flood preventive measure, it is the most important task to the whole nation. This river has been known as "China's Sorrow" for thousands of years. By its occasional overflow and bursting of its embankments, millions of lives and billions of money have been destroyed. It is a constant source of anxiety in the minds of all China's statesmen from time immemorial. A permanent safeguard must be effected, once for all, despite the expenses that will be incurred. The whole nation must bear the burden of its expenses. To deepen its mouth, to regulate its embankments and to build extra dykes are only half of the work to prevent flood. The entire reforestation of its watershed to prevent the washing off of loess in [is] another half of the work in the prevention of flood.

The Grand Canal, the former Great Waterway of China between the North and the South for centuries, and now being reconstructed in certain sections, should be wholly reconstructed from end to end, in order to restore the inland waterway traffic from the Yangtze Valley to the North. The reconstruction of this canal will be a great remunerative concern for it runs right along from Tientsin to Hangchow in an extremely rich and populous country.

Another new canal should be constructed from our projected port to Tientsin to link up all the inland waterway systems to the new port. This new canal should be built extra wide and deep, let us say, similar to the present size of the Peiho, for the use of the coasting and shallow-draft vessels which the Peiho now accommodates for other than the winter seasons. The banks of this canal should be prepared for factory sites so as to enable it to pay not only by its traffic but also from the land on both sides of its banks.

As for planning and estimating these river and canal works, the assistance of technical experts must be solicited.

PART V

THE DEVELOPMENT OF THE IRON AND COAL FIELDS IN CHIHLI AND SHANSI, AND THE CONSTRUCTION OF IRON AND STEEL WORKS

Since we have in hand in this program the work of the construction of the Great Northern Port, the work of the building of a system of railways from the Great Northern Port to the North Western Extremity of China, the work of the Colonization of Mongolia and Sinkiang, and the work of the construction of canals and improvement of rivers to connect with the Great Northern Port, the demand for materials will be very great. As the iron and coal resources of every industrial country are decreasing rapidly every year, and as all of them are contemplating the conservation of their natural resources for the use of future generations, if all the materials for the great development of China were to be drwan 〔drawn〕 from them, the draining of the natural resources of those countries will be detrimental for their future generations. Besides, the present need of the post-bellum reconstruction of Europe has already absorbed all the iron and coal that the industrial world could supply. Therefore, new resources must be opened up to meet the extraordinary demand of the development of China.

The unlimited iron and coal fields of Shansi and Chihli should be developed on a large scale. Let us say a capital of from five hundred to a thousand million dollars Mex. should be invested in this project. For as soon as the general development of China is started we would have created a vast market for iron and steel which the present industrial world will be unable to supply. Think of our railway construction, city building, harbor works, and various kinds of machineries and implements that will be needed! In fact, the development of China means the creation of a new need of various kinds of goods, for which, we must undertake to create the supply also, by utilizing the raw materials near by[nearby]. Thus a great iron and steel works is an urgent necessity as well as a greatly profitable project.

In this FIRST PROGRAM, we have followed the four principles set forth at the outset pretty closely. As needs create new needs and profits promote more profits, so our first program will be the forerunner of the other great developments, which we will deal with shortly.

PROGRAM II

As the Great Northern Port is the center of our first program, so the Great Eastern Port will be the center of our second program. I shall formulate this program as follows:

I. The Great Eastern Port.

II. The Regulating of the Yangtse Channel and Embankments.

III. The Construction of River Ports.

IV. The Improvement of Existing Waterways and Canals in connection with the Yangtze.

V. The Establishment of Large Cement Works.

PART I

THE GREAT EASTERN PORT

Although Shanghai is already the largest port in all China, as it stands it will not meet the future needs and demands of a world harbor. Therefore there is a movement at present among the foreign merchants in China to construct a world port in Shanghai. Several plans have been proposed such as to improve the existing arrangement, to build a wet dock by closing the Whangpoo, to construct a closed harbor on the right bank of the Yangtze outside of Whangpoo, and to excavate a new basin just east of Shanghai with a shipping canal to Hangchow Bay. It is estimated that a cost of over one hundred million dollars Mex. must be spent before Shanghai can be made a first-class port.

According to the four principles I set forth in Program I, Shanghai as a world port for Eastern China is not in an ideal position. The best position for a port of that kind is at a point just south of Chapu on the Hangchow Bay. This locality is far superior to Shanghai as an eastern port for China from the standpoint of our four principles as set forth in our first program. Henceforth, in our course of discussion, we shall call this the "Projected Port" so as to distinguish it from Shanghai, the existing port of Eastern China.

The Projected Port

The "Projected Port" will be on the Bay which lies between the Chapu and the Kanpu promontories, a distance of about fifteen miles. A new sea wall should be built from one promontory to the other and a gap should be left at the Chapu end, a few hundred feet from the hill as an entrance to the harbor. The sea wall should be divided into five sections of three miles each. For the present, one section of three miles in length and one and a half miles in width should be built and a harbor of three or more square miles so formed would be sufficient. With the growth of commerce one section after another could be added to meet the needs. The front sea wall should be built of stone or concrete, while the transverse wall between the sea wall and the land side should be built of sand and bush mattress as a temporary structure to be removed in case of the extension of the harbor. Once a harbor is formed there need be no trouble regarding the future conservancy work, for there is no silt-carrying water in the vicinity by which the harbor and its approaches may be silted up afterwards. The entrance of our harbor is in the deepest part of the Hangchow Bay, and from the entrance to the open sea there is an average depth of six to seven fathoms at low water. The largest ocean liner could therefore come into port at any hour. Thus as a first-class seaport in Central China our Projected Port is superior to Shanghai. See Map III.

From the viewpoint of the principle of the line of least resistance, our Projected Port will be on new land which will offer absolute freedom for city planning and industrial development. All public utilites and transportation plants can be constructed according to the most up-to-date methods. This point alone is an important factor for a future city like ours which in time is bound to grow as large as New York City. If one hundred years ago human [humans] [foresight] could have foreseen the present size and population of New York, much of the labor and money spent could have been saved and blunders due to shortsightedness avoided in meeting conditions of the ever growing population and commerce of that city. With this in view a great Eastern Port in China should be started on new ground to insure room for growth proportionate to its needs.

Moreover, all the natural advantages which Shanghai possesses as a central mart and Yangtze Port in Eastern China are also possessed by our Projected Port. Furthermore, our Projected Port in comparison with Shanghai is of shorter distance, by rail communication, to all the large cities south of the Yangtze. And if the existing waterway between this part of the country and Wuhu were improved then the water communication with the upper Yangtze would also be shorter from our Projected Port than from Shanghai. And all the artificial advantages possessed by Shanghai as a large city and a commercial center in this part of China can be easily attained by our Projected Port within a short time.

Comparing Shanghai with our Projected Port from a remunerative point of view in our development scheme, the former is much inferior in position to the latter, for valuable lands have to be bought and costly plants and existing arrangements have to be scrapped the cost of which alone is enough to construct a fine harbor on our projected site. Therefore, it is hightly [highly] advisable to construct another first-class port for Eastern China like the one I here propose, leaving Shanghai to be an inland mart and manufacturing center as Manchester is in relation to Liverpool, Osaka to Kobe, and Tokyo to Yokohama.

Our Projected Port will be a highly remunerative proposition for the cost of construction will be many times cheaper than Shanghai and the work simpler. The land between Chapu and Kanpu and farther on will not cost more than fifty to one hundred dollars a mow. The State should take up a few hundred square miles of land in this neighborhood for the scheme of our future city development. Let us say two hundred square miles of land at the price of one hundred dollars a mow be taken up. As six mows make an acre and six hundred and forty acres a square mile, two hundred square miles would cost 76,000,000 dollars Mex. An enormous sum for a project indeed! But the land could be fixed at the present price and the State could buy only that part of land which will immediately be taken up and used. The other part of the land would remain as State land unpaid for and left to the original owners' use without the right to sell. Thus the State only takes up as much land as it could use in the development scheme at a fixed price which remains permanent. The payment then would be gradual. The State could pay for the land from its unearned increment afterwards, so that only the first allotment of land has to be paid for from the capital fund; the rest will be paid for by its own future value. After the first section of the harbor is completed and the port developed, the price of land then would be bound to rise rapidly, and within ten years the land value within the city limits would rise to various grades from a thousand to a hundred thousand dollars per mow. Thus the land itself would be a source of profit. Besides there would also be the profit from the scheme itself, i.e., the harbor and the city. Because of its commanding position, the harbor has every possibility of becoming a city equal to New York. It would probably be the only deep-water seaport for the Yangtze Valley and beyond, an area peopled by two hundred million inhabitants, twice the population of the whole ⟨United⟩ States. The rate of growth of such a city would be in proportion to the rate of progress of the working out of the development scheme. If war work methods, that is, gigantic planning and efficient organization, were applied to the construction of the harbor and city, then an Oriental New York City would spring up in a very short time.

Shanghai as the Great Eastern Port

If only to provide a deep-water harbor for the future commerce in this part of China is our object then there is no question about the choice between Shanghai and our Projected Port. From every point of view Shanghai is doomed. However, in our scheme of development of China, Shanghai has certain claims for our consideration which may prove its salvation as an important city. The curse of Shanghai as a world port for future commerce is the silt of the Yangtze which fills up all its approaches rapidly every year. This silt, according to the estimation of Mr. Von Heidenstam, Engineer-in-chief of the Whangpoo Conservancy Board, is a hundred million tons a year and is sufficient to cover an area of forty square miles ten feet deep. So before Shanghai can be considered ever likely to become a world port this silt problem must first be solved. Fortunately, in our program, we have the regulation of the Yangtze Channels and Embankments, which will cooperate in solving the problem of Shanghai. Thus with this scheme in mind we might just as well consider that the silt question of Shanghai has been solved and let us go ahead, while leaving the regulation of the Yangtze Estuary to the next part, to deal with the improvement of the Shanghai Harbor.

There are many plans proposed by experts for improving the Shanghai Harbor as stated before and some of them will necessitate the scrapping of all the work which has been done by the Whangpoo Conservancy Board for the last twelve years, at the cost of eleven million taels. Here I wish to present a layman's plan for the consideration of specialists and the public.

My project for the construction of a world harbor in Shanghai is to leave the existing arrangement intact from the mouth of the Whangpoo to the junction of Kao Chiao Creek above Gough Island. Thus all the work hitherto done by the Whangpoo Conservancy Board for the last twelve years will be saved. The plan is to cut a new canal from the junction of Kao Chiao Creek right into Pootung to prolong that part of the channel which has been completed by the Conservancy Work, and to enlarge the curve along the right side of the Whangpoo River and join it again, at the second turn above Lunghwa Railway Junction, so as to make the river from that point to a point opposite Yangtzepoo Point almost in a straight line and thence a gentle curve to Woosung. This new canal would encircle nearly thirty square miles of land which would form the civic center and the New Bund of our future Shanghai. Of course the present crooked Whangpoo right in front of Shanghai would have to be filled up to form boulevards and business lots. It gose [goes] without saying that the reclaimed lots from the Whangpoo would become State property and the land between this and the new river and beyond should be taken up by the State and put at the disposal of the International Development Organization. Thus it may be possible for Shanghai to compete with our Projected Port economically in its construction and therefore to attract foreign capital, to the improvement of Shanghai as a future world port. See Map Ⅳ.

Below Yangtzepoo Point I propose to build a wet dock. This dock would [should] be laid between the left bank of the present Whangpoo, from Yangtzepoo Point to the turn above Gough Island and the left bank of the new river. The space of the dock would [should] be about six square miles. A lock entrance is to be constructed at the point above Gough Island. The wet dock would be forty feet deep and the new river can also be made the same depth by flushing with the water, not as proposed by experts, from a lock canal between the Yangtze and the Taihu, at Kiangyin, but from our improved waterway between this part of the country and Wuhu, so that a much stronger current could be obtained.

As we see that the present Whangpoo has to be reclaimed from the second turn above Lunghwa Railway Junction to Yangtzepoo Point for city planning, then the question of how to dispose of the Soochow Creek must be answered. I propose that this stream should be led alongside the right bank of the future defunct river and straight on to the upper end of the wet dock, thence joining the new canal. At the point of contact of the Creek and the wet dock a lock entrance may be provided in order to facilitate water traffic from Soochow as well as the inland water system directly with the wet dock.

As the first principle in our program was remuneration, all our plans must strictly follow this principle. To create Pootung Point, therefore, as a civic center and to build a new Bund farther on along the left bank of the new canal in order to increase the value of the new land which would result from this scheme must be kept in mind. Only by so doing [doing so] would the construction of Shanghai as a deep harbor be worth while. And only by creating some new and valuable property in this foredoomed port [that] Shanghai could [could Shanghai] be saved from the competition of our Projected Port. After all, the most important factor for the salvation of Shanghai is the solution of the 〈silt question of the⟩Yangtze Estuaries. Now let us see what effect [and] bearing the regulating of the Yangtze Channel and Embankments have [has] upon the question, and this we are going to deal with in the next part.

PART II
THE REGULATING OF THE YANGTZE RIVER

The regulating of the Yangtze River may be divided as follows:

A. From the deep-water line of the sea to Whangpoo Junction.

B. From Whangpoo Junction to Kiangyin.

C. From Kiangyin to Wuhu.

D. From Wuhu to Tungliu.

E. From Tungliu to Wusueh.

F. From Wusueh to Hankow.

A. Regulating of the Estuary from Deep-water Line up to the Junction of Whangpoo

It is a natural law that the obstruction to navigation in all rivers is begun at their mouths, therefore the improvement of any river for navigation must start from the estuary. The Yangtze River is no exception to this rule, therefore to regulate the Yangtze, we must begin by dealing with its estuaries.

The Yangtze has three estuaries, namely, the North Branch lying between the left bank and the Island of Tsungming, the North Channel lying between the Tsungming Island and the Tungsha Banks and the South Channel lying between the Tungsha Banks and the right bank. Henceforth for the sake of convenience I shall call them the North, Middle, and South Channels.

The silting up of a river's mouth is due to the loss of velocity in its current when the water gets into the wide opening at its junction with the sea and causes the silt to deposit there. The remedy is to maintain the velocity of the current by narrowing the mouth of the river so that it equals that of the upper part. In this way the silt is suspended in the water moving on into the deep sea. The narrowing process may be accomplished by walls or training jetties. And thus the silt may be carried by the water into the deepest part of the open sea and before it settles down upon the bottom a returning tide will carry it from the approach into the shallow parts on both sides of the river's mouth. The mouth of a river can be kept clear from deposit of silt by the action and reaction of the ebb and flow tide. The conservancy of an estuary of any river is accomplished by utilizing these natural forces.

In order to regulate the estuary of the Yangtze we have to study the three channels which form its mouth and to find out which of these channels is to be selected as the regulated entrance into the sea. In Mr. Von Heidenstam's proposal for the improvement of the approach of Shanghai Harbor, he recommends two alternatives, viz., either to block up the North and Middle Channels and to leave the South Channel only for the mouth of the Yangtze, or to train the South Channel only and leave the other two alone. For the present, he thinks, perhaps for the sake of economy, the latter scheme would be enough. But the training of the South Channel alone as the approach to Shanghai would leave it in a state of perpetual anxiety as has been apprehended by Mr. Von Heidenstam and other experts, for the main volume of the water of the Yangtze may be diverted into either of the other two channels and leave the Southern one to be silted up at any time. Therefore to make the approach of Shanghai once for all safe and permanent, it is necessary to block up two of the three channels, leaving only one as an approach to the port. This is also the only feasible way of regulating the estuary of the Yangtze.

In our scheme of regulating the Yangtze Estuary I should recommend using the North Channel only and to block the other two. Because the North Channel is the shortest way to the deep-sea line and by using it as the only mouth of the Yangtze, we have on both sides of it more shallow banks to be reclaimed by its silt. Thus the expenditure would be less and the results greater. But this would leave Shanghai in the lurch. Therefore in a cooperative scheme like this I would apply the theory of killing two birds with one stone by using the Middle Channel, since it would suit both of our purposes. The reason for this is because [that] the regulating of the Yangtze Estuary and the securing of a Shanghai approach have different purposes, hence we must consider them differently.

In my project of regulating the Yangtze Estuary I have two aims, namely, to secure a deep channel to the open sea and to save as much silt as possible for the purpose of reclamation of land. The Middle Channel provides three ready receptacles for the deposit of the silt for the formation of new land: the Haimen, the Tsungming, and the Tungsha Banks. Besides these banks there are many hundreds of square miles of shallow bottom which in the course of ten or twenty years will also form land. As remuneration is our first principle we must consider it in every step of our progress. The reclamation of about a thousand square miles of land even in forty not to say twenty years would be ample profit. At the lowest estimate the reclaimed land would be worth twenty dollars per mow. If after ten years five hundred square miles would be ready for cultivation purposes then we would gain a profit of 38,000,000 dollars. Whereas to make an approach by the South Channel the receptacle ground will be on one side only, that is, the Tungsha Banks, while on the right of the approach is the deep Hangchow Bay which would take hundreds of years to fill up, and in the meanwhile half of the silt would be wasted. To Shanghai as a seaport the silt is a curse but to the shallow banks the silt would be a blessing.

Since it is a profitable undertaking to reclaim the above mentioned banks and the neighboring shallows, we can quite well afford to build a double stone wall from the shore end of the Yangtze right out into the deep sea far beyond Shaweishan Island which has a distance of about forty miles. A stone wall from one fathom to five fathoms in height at low-water level would likely not exceed an average cost of two hundred thousand dollars a mile as cheap stone can easily be obtained from the granite islands nearby, in the Chusan Archipelago. A wall of forty miles on each side that is eighty miles in all will cost sixteen million dollars or thereabouts. And considering that 200 or 300 square miles of Haimen, Tsungming, and the Tungsha Banks would be converted into arable land within a short time, the expense of building the wall is well justified. Furthermore, the construction of this wall means that there will be a safe and permanent approach for a world port in Shanghai as well as a deep outlet for the Yangtze. See Map V.

The regulating wall on the right side should be built from the junction of the Whangpoo by prolongation of its right jetty describing a gentle curve into the depths of the South Channel and turning toward the opposite side and cutting through the Blockhouse Island into the Middle Channel, then running eastward right into the five-fathom line southeast of Shaweishan Island. The left wall would be a continuation from that of Tsungming at Tsungpao Sha Island parallel with the right wall by a distance of about two miles. This wall should curve to a point at or near Drinkwater Point at Tsungming Island, then project into the five-fathom line at the open sea passing by just at the south side of the Shaweishan Island. A glance at the map here attached (Map V) would be sufficient to show how the future outlet of the Yangtze as well as the future approach of Shanghai should be. The two regulating submerged walls on both sides would be as high as low-water level so as to give a free passage of the water over the top at flood tide. This will serve the purpose of carrying back the silt from the sea when the tide comes in, thus to reclaim the shallow spaces inclosed behind the walls on both sides of the river more quickly than otherwise. The new channel formed by these two parallel walls would likely be deeper than the present South Channel outside the Whangpoo, which is forty to fifty feet deep because the velocity of the current will be greater than the present one, due to the concentration of three channels into one. Furthermore, the depth would be more uniform and stable than at present. Although the regulating walls end at the five-fathom line, the momentum of the current would continue beyond that point, and so would cut into the deep water outside. This would serve the double purpose [purposes] of draining the Yangtze Estuary as well as keeping open the approach to Shanghai.

B. From Whangpoo Junction to Kiangyin

This part of the channel of the Yangtze River is most irregular and changeable. The widest part is over ten miles while the Kiangyin Narrow is only but three-quarters of a mile. The depth of the channel at the open part is from five to ten fathoms while that of Kiangyin Narrow is twenty fathoms. Judging by the depth of the water at this point a width of one and a half miles must be provided for the channel in order to slow down the current and to give a uniform velocity right along the river. So the two-mile wide channel at Whangpoo Junction has to be tabulated into one mile and a half at Kiangyin. See Map VI.

The north or left embankment commencing at Tsungpao Sha continues with the sea wall and makes a convex curve up to Tsungming Island at a point about six miles northwest from Tsungming city. Then it follows along the shore of Tsungming right up to Mason Point and transversing 〔transverses〕 across the north channel parallel to the north shore at a distance of three or four miles right up to Kinshan Point. Thence it cuts across the deep channel which was formed in recent years and curves southwestward to join the shore northeast of Tsingkiang and follows the shore line for a distance of about seven or eight miles, then cuts into the land side to give this part of the river a width of one and a half miles from the fort at the Kiangyin side. This embankment from Tsungpao Sha to Tsingkiang Point oppostie Kiangyin fort is about one hundred miles in length.

South of Tsungming Island a part of this embankment and a part of the wall that projects into the sea together inclose a shallow space of about 160 square miles good for reclamation purposes. The other part of the embankment, which runs from Mason Point at the head of Tsungming Island to Tsingkiang shore, incloses another space of about 130 square miles.

The right embankment starts at the end of the left jetty of Whangpoo Junction and, skirting along the Paoshan shore and passing the Blonde Shoal into the deep, crosses the Confucius Channel on into Actaon Shoal and follows the right side of Harvey Channel on to Plover Point. Then it turns northwest across the deep channel into Langshan Flats, thence recrosses the deep channel at Langshan Crossing into Johnson Flats, then joins the Pitman King Island, and thence skirts along the shore right into the foot of the hills at Kiangyin forts. This embankment incloses two shallow spaces: one above and the other below Plover Point, together about 160 square miles. Alongside of both of these embankments there are [are there] shallow spaces amounting to about 450 square miles, a great part of which having already formed land and a part already appearing in low water. When these spaces are cut off from the moving current the process of reclamation would be made to work more rapidly, so it is not extravagant to hope that within the course of twenty years the whole of these 450 square miles would be completely reclaimed and ready for cultivation. The profits from the new lands thus reclaimed would amount to about $29,760,000 if only taken at $20 per mow. The profits from the new lands will be netted from the beginning of the work and will increase every year up to the completion of the reclamation process.

With a profit of $30,000,000 in the course of twenty years before us, it is a worth-while proposition to take up. Now let us see what amount of capital should be invested before the whole project of our reclamation work could be completed. In order to reclaim this 450 square miles of land two hundred miles of embankments have to be built. Part of these projected embankments will be along the shore line, a greater part will be in midstream, and a small part in deep channel. Those along the shore line need not be bothered with except that the concave surface must be protected with stone or concrete work. Those in midstream should be filled up with stone ten feet or less below low-water level just enough to give a resistance to the undercurrent in order to prevent it from running sideward. Thus the main current would follow the line of least resistance and cut the channel, as directed by the rudimental embankment, by its own force. This rudimental embankment would cost less than the sea wall which I estimated at $200,000 per mile. Except at one point, that is, the junction of the North

Channel at Mason Point, which has to be blocked up entirely, the cost for which, as has been estimated by experts, would amount to over a million dollars for a distance of two or three miles. Thus the profits accuring [accruing] from the reclaimed lands would be quite sufficient to pay for the embankments. So far we see that the regulating of the Yangtze from the sea to Kiangyin is a self-paying proposition from the reclamation of land alone, aside from the improvement of the navigation of the Yangtze River.

C. From Kiangyin to Wuhu

This part of the river is quite different in nature from that below Kiangyin. Its channel is more stable and only in a few places ⟨do⟩ sharp curves occur and the water has cut into the concave sides of the land, thus occasionally making new channels along the sides of the two shores. This section of the river is about 180 miles in length. See Map Ⅶ.

The regulating works here would be more complicated than those below Kiangyin. For besides the dilated parts which have to be reclaimed in the same manner as those of the lower part of the river, the sharp curves have to be straightened and side channels have to be blocked, and midstream islands have to be removed, and narrows have to be widened to give uniform width to the river. However, most of the existing embankments in this part could be left as they are except some of the concave surfaces of the shores have to be protected by either stone or concrete work. The regulating works of the channel and the embankments can be done by artificial means as well as by natural processes so as to economize as much as possible. The cost of the whole works of this part of the river cannot be accurately estimated until a detail survey is made; but in a rough guess $400,000 per mile may not be very far from the mark. Thus 180 miles will cost $72,000,000 exclusive of the expenses for the widening of the point between Nanking and Pukow, in which case valuable properties will have to ⟨be⟩ removed.

The Kwachow cut is to straighten the three sharp curves in front of and above Chinkiang by converting them into one. Two and a half miles of the land in the northern shore opposite Chinkiang will have to be cut into in order to form a new channel of a mile or more in width. The part of the river in front of, and above and below Chinkiang has to be reclaimed. The new land thus reclaimed would form the water ⟨in⟩ front of Chinkiang city, the value of which may be sufficient to defray the cost of the work and compensate for the land taken away on the northern shore, to form the new channel. So the works of this part will be at least a self-paying proposition.

The narrow between Pukow and Hsiakwan from pier to pier is barely six cables wide. The depth of the water in this narrow from the shallowest to the deepest is six to twenty-two fathoms. The land of the Hsiakwan side had occasionally sunk away on account of the too rapid current and the depth of the water. This indicates that this part is too narrow for the volume of the Yangtze water to pass. Therefore a wider passage must be provided [for]. In order to do so, the whole town of Hsiakwan must be sacrificed as the river must be widened right up to the foot of the Lion Hill, so as to provide a passage of a mile wide at this point. What the cost for the compensation of this valuable property of Hsiakwan [will be] will have to be submitted to the experts for a careful investigation before it can be determined. This will be the most costly part of the whole project for the regulating of the Yangtze. But undoubtedly some equally valuable property can be created along the riverside near by [nearby] in place of Hsiakwan, so that a balance may be realized by the work itself.

The channel below the Nanking Pukow Narrow will follow the short passage alongside of the foot of the Mofushan to Wulungshan. The loop around the island north of Nanking will have to be blocked up in order to straighten the course of the river.

The section of the river from Nanking to Wuhu is almost in a straight line with three dilatations along its course: one just above Nanking, the other two just above and below the East and West Pillars. To regulate the first dilatation the channel above Metsechow should be blocked up and the island outside of it should be partly cut to widen the proper channel. To regulate the other two dilatations the river should be made to curve toward Taiping Fu to follow the deep channel on the right bank. The left channel should be blocked up. The islands along this curve should be partly or wholly removed. To regulate the dilatation above the Pillars, the Friends Channel should be blocked up and Friends Island be partly cut away. And the left bank below Wuhu should also be cut to give the channel a uniform width.

D. From Wuhu to Tungliu

This part of the river is about 130 miles in length. Along its course there are six dilatations, the most prominent of which is the one that lies immediately below Tungling, which extends over ten miles from side to side. In each of these dilatations there are usually two or three channels with newly formed islands between them. The deep passage often changes from one side to the other, and it is not uncommon that all of the channels are filled up at the same time, thus stopping navigation altogether for a considerable period. See Map VIII.

In regulating the part of the river from ten miles above Wuhu to ten miles below Tatung, I propose to cut a new channel through the midstream islands formed by the three dilatations and the sharp corners of the shore, in order to straighten as well as to shorten the river, as marked by the dotted lines in the map attached here. The cost of the cut could not be estimated until a detail [detailed] survey is made. But as soon as the embankments are laid out the natural force of the river's own current will do a great part of the dredging work, so that the expenses of the cutting for the new channel will be much less than usual. Above Tatung there are two sharp turns of the left shore to be cut. One is on the left shore at the point where the beacon now stands about twelve miles from Tatung. In this place a few miles of the left shore will have to be cut away. The other cut is just below the city of Anking hence to Kianglung beacon, a distance of about six miles. By this cut we do away with the sharp turns of the river at Chuan Kiang Kau. These cuttings would cost much more than the piling of stone at the lower reach of the river. It is quite certain that the reclamation of the side channels of this part will not cover the cost of the cuttings. Therefore this part of the regulating work will not be self-paying, but the navigation of the Yangtze, the protection it gives to both sides to the land, and the prevention of floods in the future will amply compensate for such work.

E. From Tungliu to Wusueh

This part of the river is about eighty miles in length. The land along the right bank is generally hilly while that along the left is low. Along its course there are four dilatations. In three of these dilatations the current has cut into the left or northern bank of the river and then turns back into its main course again almost at right angles. At such points the bank is very unstable. Between the channels of these dilatations islands are being formed. See Map IX.

The regulating works of this part are much easier to construct than those of the lower part. The three diverting semicircular channels have to be blocked up at the upper ends, and the lower openings left open for silt to go into at flood seasons in order to reclaim them by the natural process. The other dilatations should be narrowed in from both sides by jetties. A few places will have to be cut, the most important being the Pigeon Island and the turn above Siau Ku Shan. Some of the midstream islands will have to be removed, and a few wide places filled up in order to make the channel uniform, so as to give a regular minimum depth of six fathoms right along the whole course.

F. From Wusueh to Hankow

The part of the river is about one hundred miles long. Above Wusueh we enter into the hilly country on both sides. The river here is generally about half a mile wide, with a depth of from five to twelve fathoms or sometimes more in certain places. See Map X.

To regulate this part of the river a few wide spaces have to be reclaimed to give a uniform channel, and the side channels at three or four palces〔places〕 closed up. Then we can make a channel with a uniform depth of from six to eight fathoms at all seasons. At Collison Island section of the river the Ayres Channel has to be closed up, leaving the winter channel alone so as to give a gentle curve above and below this island. At Willes Island and Gravenor Island point the round channel and the channel between these two islands must be blocked up. The river must be made to cut through Willes Island to make a shorter curve. At Bouncer Island the South channel must be blocked up and above this the Low Point turn must be cut away to form a gentler curve. From this point to Hankow the river should be made narrower first by reclaiming the right side as far as the meeting of the southwest curve with the right bank then the reclamation should start at the opposite side of the left bank and right up along the front of Hankow Settlement until the Han River Mouth is reached. Thus a depth of six to eight fathoms can be secured right up to the Bund of Hankow.

To sum up, the whole length of the regulating course of the river from the deep sea to Hankow is about 630 miles. The embankments will be twice this length; that is, 1,260 miles. I have estimated that the sea wall at the mouth of the river could be built at $200,000 a mile, thus for both sides $400,000 a mile will be sufficient for the 140 miles from the deep sea to Kiangyin. For, in this part we have only the two embankments to deal with, which merely requires the tumbling of stones into the water until the pile is strong enough to hold the current to a directed course. As soon as these stone ridges on both sides of the river are formed, nature will do the rest to make the channel deep. The work for this part, therefore, is simple.

But the work for certain sections of the upper part of the river is more complicated as about fifty or sixty miles of solid land [of] from ten to twenty feet above water level and thirty to forty feet below have to be cut in order to straighten the river's course. Of this cutting and removing work, how much will have to be done artificially and how much can be done by nature, I leave to the experts to estimate. Excepting this, the other parts of this work, I think, cannot cost much more than $400,000 a mile. So that the whole work from the sea to Hankow, a distance of 630 miles will cost about $252,000,000, or let us say, including the unknown part, $300,000,000 for the completion of the entire project for the regulating of the Yangtze River. By this regulating of the Yangtze River, we secure an approach of 600 miles inland for ocean-going vessels into the very center of a continent of two hundred millions of people of which half or one hundred million is located immediately along 600 miles of the great water highway. As regards remuneration for the work, this project will be more profitable than either the Suez or Panama Canal.

Although we could not find means whereby the works above Kiangyin may be made self-paying as those of the sections below by the reclamation of land, ⟨the⟩ profit from city building along the course of the river can be realized after regulating work is completed.

In conclusion, I must say that the figures given concerning the harbor works and the Yangtze regulation are merely rough estimates which must be in the nature of the case. As regards the costs of building the rudimental dikes at the estuary of the Yangtze as well as along the dilating parts of the river, the estimation may seem too low. But the data on which I base my estimate are as follows: first, my own observation of the private enterprise of reclamation by building dikes at the Canton delta around my native village; second, the cheap stone that can be obtained at the Chusan Archipelago; third, the estimation of Mr. Tyler, Coast Inspector of the Maritime Customes for the blocking up of the North Channel at the upper end of Tsungming Island, where the narrowest part is about three miles. He says that a million tales or more is necessary for the work. Or, let us say, in round figures, five hundred thousand dollars(Mex.) a mile. This is two and a half times my estimate. Now, let us compare the difference. The three-mile channel at the upper end of Tsungming has an average depth of twenty feet of water, while in my project the sea wall or dikes will be built in water having an average of less than two thirds of this depth. Moreover, the work of blocking up the North Channel entirely at a right angle is many times more costly than that of building a rudimental dike of the same length in a parallel line with the current. Since five hundred thousand dollars are enough to block up crosswise a mile of river twenty feet deep, two fifths of that sum should be quite sufficient to finance the work that I have projected. While writing this, I came across an article in the *Chicago Railway Review*, May 17, 1919, dealing with the same subject, which states that steel skeleton is a better and cheaper substitute for stone or other materials for building dikes and jetties in a muddy river like ours. Thus, by this new method, we may be able to construct embankments, with cheaper material than I have hitherto known. So, although the estimate which I have made may be somewhat low, yet it is not so far from correct as it seems at first sight.

PART III

THE CONSTRUCTION OF RIVER PORTS

The construction of river ports along the Yangtze between Hankow and the sea will be one of the most remunerative propositions in our development scheme. For this part of the Yangtze Valley is richest in agricultural and mineral products in China and is very densely populated. With the cheap water transportation provided by the completion of the regulating work both side [sides] of this water highway will surely become industrial beehives. And with cheap labor nearby, it will not be a surprise if in the near future both banks will become two continuous cities, as it were, right along the whole extent of the river from Hankow to the sea. In the meantime a few suitable spots should be chosen for profitable city development. For this purpose I will start from the lower part of the river as follows:

A. Chinkiang and North Side.

B. Nanking and Pukow.

C. Wuhu.

D. Anking and South Side.

E. ⟨The⟩ Poyang Port.

F. Wuhan.

A. Chinkiang and North Side

Chinkiang is situated at the junction of the Grand Canal and the Yangtze. It was an important center of inland water traffic between the north and the south before the steam age [Steam Age]. But it will resume its former grandeur and become more important when the old inland waterway is improved, and new ones are constructed. For it is the gateway between the Hoangho and Yangtze Valleys. Besides, by the southern portion of the Grand Canal, Chinkiang is connected with the Tsientang Valley—the richest part of China. Thus, this city is bound to grow into a great commercial center in the near future.

In our regulation work of the Yangtze, we shall add a piece of new land, over six square miles, in front of Chinkiang. This land on the south side of the river will be utilized for city-planning for our new Chinkiang. On the north side, land should also be taken up by the state to build another city. The north side will be bound to outgrow that of the south for the whole of Hoangho Valley could only emerge into the Yangtze by waterway through this point. Docks should be built between here and Yangchow for accommodation of inland vessels, and modern facilities should be provided for transhipment between inland vessels and ocean-going steamers. This port should be made as a distributing center as well as a collecting center for the salt of the eastern coast. This, with the help of modern methods, will reduce transportation expenses. Stone or concrete bands or quays should be built on both sides of the river and tidal jetties should be provided for train ferries. In time, when commerce grows, tunnels or bridges may be added to facilitate traffic of the two sides. The streets should be wide so as to meet modern demands. The water front and its neighborhood should be planned for industrial and commercial uses and the land beyond should be planned for residential purpose. Every modern public utility should be provided. In regard to the details of planning the city, I most leave them to the expert.

B. Nanking and Pukow

Nanking was the old capital of China before Peking, and is situated in a fine locality which comprises high mountains, deep water and a vast level plain—a rare site to be found in any part of the world. It also lies at the center of a very rich country on both sides of the lower Yangtze. At present, although ruined and desolate, it still has a population of over a quarter of a million. Once it was the home of many industries especially silk and now the finest satin and velvet are still produced here, Nanking has yet a greater future before her when the resources of the lower Yangtze Valley are properly developed.

In the regulation of the Yangtze I propose to cut away the town of Hsiakwan, so that the wharf of Nanking could be removed into the deep channel between Metsechow and the outskirts of Nanking. This channel should be blocked up, thereby a wet dock could be formed to accommodate all ocean-going vessels. This point is much nearer the inhabited parts of the city than Hsiakwan. And the land between this projected wet dock and the city could form a new commercial and industrial quarter which will be many times larger than Hsiakwan. Metsechow in time, when commerce grows, may also be developed into city lots and business quarters. For the future development of Nanking the land within and without the city should be taken up at the present price under the same principle which I have proposed for the Projected Port at Chapu.

Pukow, opposite Nanking, on the other side of the river, will be the great terminus of all the railways of the great northern plain to the Yangtze. It will be the nearest river port for the rich coal and iron fields of Shansi and Honan, giving access to the lower Yangtze district and hence to the sea. As the great transcontinental trunk line to the sea whether terminating at Shanghai or at our Projected Port, would pass through this point, the construction of a tunnel under the Yangtze to connect Nanking and Pukow by rail at the same time when the cities are being constructed, will not be at all premature. This will at once make possible a through train journey from Shanghai to Peking.

Concrete or stone embankment should be built along the shore above and below the present Pukow point many miles in each direction. Modern streets should be laid out on the land within the embankment so as to be ready for various building purposes. The land on the north side of the river should be taken up by the state for public uses of this international development scheme 〔International Development Scheme〕 on the same basis as at our Projected Ports.

C. Wuhu

Wuhu is a town of 120,000 inhabitants and is the center of the rice trade in the lower part of the Yangtze. It is at this point that I propose to make an intake of the water which will go to flush the Whangpoo River at Shanghai, and which will form the upper end of a canal to the sea at Chapu. In the regulating work of the Yangtze the concave part above the junction of the Yangki Ho has to be filled up and the convex part of the opposite side has to be cut away. The junction of the projected canal and the river will be at about a mile or so below the Lukiang junction. The projected canal will run northeast to a point between the southeast corner of Wuhu city and the foot of the hill. There it joins the Yangki Ho and, following the course as far as Paichiatien, branches off in the northeastern direction. This gives Wuhu a southeast waterfront along the left side of the canal. New bunds should be built along both sides of the canal as well as alongside the Yangtze and at the junction of the canal docks for inland vessels should be constructed with modern plants for transhipment of goods. Wide streets should be laid out from the Bund of the Yangtze far into the inland following the direction of the canal. The bund alongside the Yangtze should be reserved for commercial purposes and those alongside the canal for factories. Wuhu is in the midst of a rich iron and coal field, so it will surely become an industrial center when this iron and coal field is properly developed. Cheap materials, cheap labor, and cheap foodstuffs are abundant at the spot waiting for modern science and machinery to turn them into greater wealth for the benefit of mankind.

D. Anking and South Side

Anking, the capital of Anhwei, was once a very important city but since its destruction by the Taiping war [War] it has never recovered its former greatness. Its present population is about 40,000 only. Its immediate neighborhood is very rich in mineral and agricultural products. The great tea district of Liuan and the rich mineral district in the southeastern corner of Honan province will have to make Anking their shipping port when railways are developed. In the Yangtze

Conservancy work, the concave turn of the river in front and west of the city has to be filled up. This reclaimed land should be for the extension of a new city, where modern transportation plants should be built.

Eagle Point, on the south side opposite Anking should be cut away to make the river curve more gently and to give the channel a uniform width. A new city should be laid out at this point, for from here we command the vast tea districts of southern Anhwei and western Chekiang. The rich inland city of Hweichow, with the highly productive country around it, will have to make this port its shipping station. As Wuhu is the center of the rice trade these twin cities of Anking will be the centers of the tea trade. Like Wuhu, these twin cities are also situated in the midst of rich iron and coal fields which will assist them to become important industrial centers in the near future. So to build twin cities at this point of the river will be a very profitable undertaking.

E. The Poyang Port

I propose to construct a port at a point between the Poyang Lake and the Yangtze River. This will be the sole port of the Kiangsi province. Every city of this province is connected by natural waterways which, if improved, will become a splendid water transportation system. The province of Kiangsi has a population of 30,000,000 and is extremely rich in mineral resources. A modern port acting as a commercial and industrial center for the development of this resourceful province would be a most remunerative proposition in our project.

The site of the port will be on the west side of the entrance to the Poyang Lake and the right bank of the Yangtze. It will be an entirely new city built on new ground, part of which will be reclaimed from the shallow side of the lake. In the regulating work of the Poyang Channel, a training wall should be built from the foot of the Taku Tang Hill to Swain Point opposite to Stone Bell Hill of Hukow. A closed dock should be constructed within this training wall for the accommodation of inland water vessels. The city should be laid out on the triangular space formed by the right bank of the Yangtze, the left side of the Poyang Lake and the foot hill of the Lushan Mountain. This triangle is about 10 miles on each side, excellent for city development. The porcelain industry should be established here instead of at Kingteh Chen, for great damages often occur owing to the lack of transportation facilites, and to the necessity of transhipment for the export of the finished articles from the latter place. Modern plants on a large scale should be adopted for the manufacturing of cheap wares as well as fine articles in our projected Poyang Port, for here we shall have the greater advantage of collecting raw materials than at Kingteh Chen. Thus the concentrating of the various manufactures in an advantageous center will result in quickening the growth of our new city. This Poyang Port is bound to grow into one of the great commercial and manufacturing centers in China, judging from the possibilities of Kiangsi alone. It will not only be a great shipping port of the Yangtze but will also be a railway center between North and South China. Thus to develop this port on a large scale is quite justifiable from an economic point of view.

F. Wuhan

Wuhan signifies the three cities of Wuchang, Hankow, and Hanyang. This point is the headwater of our projected ocean passage, the pivot of the railway system of China Proper, and will become the most important commercial metropolis in the country. The population of these three cities is over a million and could be easily doubled or trebled, if improvements would be made. At present, Hanyang possesses the largest iron works in China, and Hankow, many modern industries, while Wuchang is becoming a great cotton manufacturing city. Besides, Hankow is the trade center of Central and West China, and the greatest tea market we have. The provinces of Hupeh, Hunan, Szechwan, and Kweichow and a part of Honan, Shensi, and Kansu all depend upon Hankow as their only port to the outside world. When railways are developed in China, Wuhan will be still more important and will surely become one of the greatest cities in the world. So in planning the future city of Wuhan we must adopt for its development a scale as large as that of New York or London.

In the regulation of the Yangtze embankments, we have to reclaim the front of Hankow from the jetty of Lungwangmiao at the junction of the Han River fight along the left bank to the point where the Yangtze turns eastward. This reclaimed space will be at an average of about 500 to 600 yards wide. This will narrow down the river at this part to give a uniform channel of 5 to 6 cables in width and to give the Hankow settlement a strip of valuable land along its waterfront. This will also help to pay a part of the expenses for city construction. The sharp bend of the Han River just before it joins the Yangtze should be straightened so as to make a gentler curve around Lungwangmiao Point and thus enable the currents of both rivers to flow in the same direction at their junction. The Hanyang embankment will follow pretty closely the present shore line but not beyond the iron works jetty. The wide space of the river above Wuchang city should be walled in to make a closed dock for inland water as well as oceangoing vessels. Below Wuchang, an embankment parallel to that of the left side should be built so as to make the future city extend far below the present one. A tunnel should be constructed to connect both embankments at a point where the Kinghan railway makes its first turn when it comes to the Yangtze River. And another tunnel or bridge should be constructed between Hankow and Hanyang on one side and Wuchang on the other at the junction of the Han River and the Yangtze. Additional tunnels or bridges may be constructed at different points when the city grows larger in the future. All the outlying land of these trio-cities should be taken up on the same basis as at our projected seaports, so that private monopoly and speculation in land may be prevented, and that the unearned increment will go to the State to help the payment of capital and interest on the foreign loans which are to be made in this international development scheme.

PART IV

THE IMPROVEMENT OF THE EXISTING WATERWAYS AND CANALS

The existing waterways and canals in connection with the Yangtze may be enumerated as follows:

A. The Grand Canal.

B. The Hwaiho.

C. The Kiangnan Waterway System.

D. The Poyang Waterway System.

E. The Han River.

F. The Tungting System.

G. The Upper Yangtze.

A. The Grand Canal

The Grand Canal connects with the Yangtze at a point opposite Chinkiang and runs northward right up to Tientsin, a distance of over 600 miles. We understand that a detailed survey of the Kiangpeh part of the canal has begun and the work of improving it will commence soon. In our project, I propose to substitute the Kiangpeh portion of the Grand Canal by the Yangtze outlet of the Hwaiho.

B. The Hwaiho

The Hwaiho rises in the northwest corner of Honan and runs southeast and east to the north of Anhwei and Kiangsu. Its outlets have been sealed up in recent years so its water has accumulated in the Hungtse Lake and it depends upon evaporation as its only means of disposing the water. Thus in the heavy rainy season, it floods a vast extent of the country surrounding the lake and causes great misery to millions of people. So the conservancy of the Hwaiho is a very urgent question of China today. Recently, many investigations have been made and many plans proposed. Mr. Jameson, chief engineer for the American Red Cross Society, has proposed two outlets for the Hwaiho: one following the old course of the Yellow River to the sea and another [the other] through Paoying and Kaoyu Lakes to the Yangtze. In this project I propose to follow Mr. Jameson's plan for the sea outlet only as far as the old Yellow River and for the Yangtze outlet only as far as Yangchow. When the sea outlet or north branch reaches the old Yellow River I will lead it across into the Yenho and follow the Yenho to its northern turn. From there, we cut across the narrow strip of land into the Kuanho which enters the sea at the nearest deep water line. This saves a great deal of work of excavating the old course of the Hoangho. When the southern branch reaches

Yangchow, I propose to make the canal pass east of that city instead of west as Mr. Jameson proposed, so that its current will join the Yangtze in the same direction at the new curve below Chinkiang city.

Both of these outlets or branches of the Hwaiho should be made at least twenty feet deep right along, so that coastal vessels from the north to the Yangtze could use them as passage [passages] instead of going round the Yangtze estuary, thus shortening the distance by about 300 miles. And with twenty feet depth for both outlets, the Hwaiho and the Hungtse Lake would be well drained and the present bottom of the lake, which is sixteen feet above sea level would be converted into agricultural land at once. Thus 6,000,000 mow of land could be reclaimed according to the estimate of Mr. Jameson, from the Hungtse and the neighboring lakes. If twenty dollars a mow be taken for its value, a sum of $120,000,000 could be netted. Besides this direct profit to the Government there is an area of some 17,000 square miles of occasionally flooded land which would be made flood-proof so that normally we shall have two crops a year instead of two only in five years. That is to say, the 17,000 square miles or 10,880,000 acres will be made to produce five times more than at present. For instance, if the value of the gross production be estimated at fifty dollars an acre, then the total value would be $544,000,000 Mex. and five times ⟨of⟩ this sum would amount to $2,720,000,000 Mex. What an enormous profit to the country!

C. The Kiangnan Waterway System

This system comprises the South Grand Canal, the Whangpoo, the Taihu, and its connections. The most important improvement I intend to make here is to widen and deepen the Wuhu-Ihsing Waterway between the Yangtze and the

Taihu, and from there to dredge a deep channel right through the Taihu to a point midway of the Grand Canal between Sochow [Soochow] and Kashing. At Kashing, divide it [it can be divided] into two branches:—one following the Kashing Sunkiang Canal to Whangpoo, and the other, to the Projected Port at Chapu. This waterway between the Yangtze and the Whangpoo before it reaches Shanghai, should be made as wide and deep as possible so as to make it carry sufficient water to flush the Shanghai harbor as well as to provide a shorter passage for inland water vessels between the Yangtze and the seaports. This waterway will act as silt carrier by which the Taihu and the various lakes alongside of it may be reclaimed in the future. Besides the main object for which this canal is assigned, the reclamation scheme and the local traffic would also add profit to it. This makes its remuneration doubly sure. As no accurate surveys of the shallow Taihu and other lakes and swamps could be obtained, the exact number of mow to be reclaimed could not be given here. But in a rough estimate I should say that the reclaimed space of the Kiangnan Lakes would be about the same in extent as those of Kiangpeh (the North of the Yangtze).

D. The Poyang Waterway System

This system drains the entire area of Kiangsi province. Every hsien, city, and important town is reached by waterway. Waterways are the only means of communication in this province as well as in all the porvinces of Southeastern China, before the advent of railways. The lower part of the Kiangsi waterway system suffers the same irregularities as those of the lower Yangtze as both are on low land. So, to regulate it, a similar work as that for the Yangtze should be applied. The Poyang Lake should be divided by deep channels from the junction of each river, and these should join together to form larger channels and finally unite into one main channel at a point near Chuki and, running through the narrow part of the lake, join the Yangtze at Hukow. The sides of the deep channels should be lined with submerged stone ridges as high as the shallow part of the lake, whereby the channels would serve the purpose of draining as well as of navigation.

The shallow space beside those channels will be reclaimed into arable land in due time. So the work of regulating the Poyang channels will be well paid by reclamation.

E. The Han River

This river is navigable for small crafts through its main body up to Hanchung in the southwest corner of Shensi; and through its branches up to Nanyang and Shekichen in the southwest corner of Honan. This navigable stream commands quite a large area of watershed. The upper part, that is above Siangyang, is in mountainous country. From Siangyang to Shayang it is in a wide, open valley and below Shayang it runs into the Hupeh swamp.

To improve this river dams should be built above Siangyang in order to utilize water power as well as to make locks for larger crafts to ascend to the navigable point now navigable only for small crafts. Below Siangyang, where the river is very wide and shallow, rudimental dikes should be constructed of stones or piles in order to restrict its channel and to reclaim the shallow space on both sides by natural process. In the swamp, the river should be straightened and deepened. A new canal between the Han and the Yangtze at Shasi should be constructed to provide a shorter passage between Hankow and Shasi and beyond. This canal in the swamp should be open to the lakes along its course so as to let the silt-carrying water enter into them in the flood season, thus filling them up quicker.

F. The Tungting System

This system of waterway [waterways] drains the whole province of Hunan and beyond. The most important branches are the Siangkiang and the Yuankiang. The former runs through Hunan into the northeast corner of Kwangsi province and connects with the Sikiang system by a canal near Kweilin. The latter runs across the west border of Hunan into the eastern part of Kweichow province. Both could be improved for the navigation of large crafts. The canal between the Yangtze and the Sikiang watersheds should be reconstructed and modern locks should be provided in it as well as along the two waterways. Thus, vessels of ten feet draught may freely pass between the Yangtze and the Sikiang. The Tungting Lake should be drained by deep channels in the same manner as the Poyang Lake, and its shallow space reclaimed by natural process.

G. The Upper Yangtze

I include the part from Hankow to Ichang also in the upper [Upper] Yangtze, because it is at Hankow that the ocean navigation ends, and the inland water communication begins. So, in dealing with the improvement of the Upper Yangtze, I will begin at Hankow. At present the Upper Yangtze is navigable for shallow draught steamers up to Kiating, a point about 1,100 miles above Hankow by river. If improvement be made farther on, then shallow draught steamers could navigate right up to Chengtu, the capital of Szechwan province, and the center of the richest plain in West China, about sixty miles up the Min River.

To improve the Upper Yangtze from Hankow to Yochow, the work is much similar to that of the lower part. The channel should be regulated by rudimental dikes. The concave embankments in sharp bends should be protected by stone or concrete; obstacles in midstream should be removed. The great loop, called the Farmer Bend, above Kinkow, should be cut through at the neck of Paichow, and the sharp point of Houchin Kwang should be cut away to make the curve of the river more gentle.

The tortuous part of the Yangtze, north of the Tungting Lake, between Kinho Kow and Skipper Point, should be blocked up altogether and a new channel made through Tungting Lake, returning to the Yangtze by the Yochow Channel. This avoids the crooked passage and shortens the river course considerably. From Skipper Point to Ichang the dilatation should be restricted by dikes of stone or piling, and some sharp points of the shores should be cut away to make the curves more gentle.

The Yangtze River above Ichang enters the Gorges which run about a hundred miles up to the Szechwan depression, known as the Red Basin. This part of the river from Ichang right along to its source is confined by rocky banks, very narrow and deep, having an average depth of six fathoms and at some particular points even thirty fathoms. Many rapids and obstructions occur along its course.

To improve the Upper Yangtze, the rapids should be dammed up to form locks to enable crafts to ascend the river as well as to generate water power. Obstructions should be blasted and boulders removed. Thus, a ten-foot channel right along from Hankow to Chungking could be obtained so that through inland water transportation could be established from Chungking to Peking in the north and to Canton in the south, as well as to all navigable points in China Proper all the year round. In this way, transportation expenses to the richest emporium in West China could be reduced hundredfold. The benefit to the people will be enormous and the encouragement to commerce will indeed be great.

PART V

THE ESTABLISHMENT OF LARGE CEMENT WORKS

Steel and cement are the basis of modern construction, and the most important factors of the material civilization of the present age. In the various projects of our development scheme, the demand for steel and cement will be so enormous that all manufacturing countries combined will not be able to supply the needs. Therefore, in our first program, I have proposed to establish large steel works in the rich iron and coal fields in the provinces of Shansi and Chihli; so in this second program I propose to establish large cement works along the shores of the Yangtze River. The Yangtze Valley is exceptionally rich in materials for cement, limestone and coal lying side by side at the water edge along the navigable channel from Chinkiang upward. Thus, local supplies could be created for local needs.

At present, there is one cement works at Shihuiyau near Hoangshikang at the upper reach. It is situated between a deep water wharf and a limestone hill. The limestone is so near by that it can be cut and shoveled into the kilns immediately. Between Hankow and Kiukiang there are many places possessing the same advantage. Below Kiukiang, there are also many such advantageous positions as Matang, Wushiki and many others between Kiukiang and Anking. Between Anking and Nanking there are exceptionally good locations for putting up cement works scuh as Tatung, Tikang, and Tsaishisze, all these places being provided abundantly with limestone and coal and iron, lying side by side.

With the huge harbor works, city building, and embankment construction, the market for cement will be so great that a capital of one to two hundred million dollars should be invested for the supply. This work should be started gradually in accord with the acceleration of the other works [work] of the general development so that one project will further the other, and over-production and waste of capital individually in any of the parts of the general scheme will be guarded against. This will help make each of them a profitable business by itself.

PROGRAM III

The main feature of the third program will be the construction of a great southern port which will complete the plan for three first-class seaports in China as proposed in the preliminary part of this International Development Scheme. Our Great Southern Port will naturally be Canton, which is not only the center of commerce in South China but also the largest city in all China. Until recent time it was the largest city on the coasts of the Pacific, and the center of commerce of Asia. With the development of China, Canton will surely resume its former importance. Around this southern metropolis I formulate the third program as follows:

I. The Improvement of Canton as a World Port.

II. The Improvement of the Waterway System of Canton.

III. The Construction of the Southwestern Railway System of China.

IV. The Construction of Coast Ports and Fishing Harbors.

V. The Establishment of Shipbuilding Yards.

PART I

THE IMPROVEMENT OF CANTON AS A WORLD PORT

Canton's position as a seaport has been taken away by Hongkong since its cession to England after the Opium War. But as a commercial center of South China, Canton still holds its own, despite the advantages of deep-water harbor, the artificial improvements of Hongkong, and the political dominance of England. The loss of its position as a seaport is entirely due to the ignorance of the Chinese people who never made any combined effort to improve the welfare of the country, and also to the corrupt government and officials of the Manchu Dynasty. Since the establishment of the Republic, the people have begun to awake very rapidly and many schemes have been suggested to make Canton a seaport. This awakening of the millions of Chinese has caused much apprehension to the Hongkong Government. The authorities of that colony have been doing their utmost to hinder every move to restore Canton as a seaport and try to nip every scheme in the bud. Of course, if Canton is improved and made into a world port, then all the services that Hongkong performs for her as a shipping stage would be dispensed with altogether. But a developed Canton and a prosperous China will recompense Hongkong in various ways a hundred times more than its present position as the monopolized ocean port of a backward and poor China. Just look at the port of Victoria in British Columbia, which was once the only seaport of West Canada as well as the Northwestern region of the United States, but it prospered very little then with an undeveloped hinterland despite its monopolistic character. Whereas as soon as the rival ports arose, Vancouver on its own side, and Seattle and Tacoma on the American side, all within the same distance as Hongkong is to Canton, all of them because of a developed hinterland prospered wonderfully, despite the keen competition between them as seaports. Thus, we see that competitive seaports like Vancouver, Seattle, and Tacoma instead of killing Victoria, as was one supposed by shortsighted people, have made it more prosperous than ever. Then, why doubt that a prosperous Canton and a developed China would not give the same result to Hongkong? This is but a natural outcome. Therefore, there should be no fear that a prosperous Canton and a developed China would be harmful to Hongkong as a free port. So, instead of doing the utmost as hitherto to hinder the development of Canton as a seaport, the Hongkong authorities should do their utmost to encourage such a project. Besides, the development of Canton and South China will benefit the English as a whole commercially a hundred times more than Hongkong can do at present. Although the local authorities of that crown colony do not see far enough to realize it, [however,] I believe that the great statesmen and captains of industries in the now mightiest empire of the world would surely see it. With this belief in my mind I feel quite safe in giving publicity [to] the scheme of my international development of Canton as a world port in South China.

Canton is situated at the head of the Canton Delta, which is formed by the junction of three rivers—the Sikiang or West River, the Peikiang or North River, and the Tungkiang or East River. The area of this delta is about 3,000 square miles and it has the most fertile alluvial soil known in China. The land yields three crops a year—two crops of rice and one crop of other products such as potatoes or beets. In silk culture, it gives eight crops every year. The most delicious fruits of many varieties are produced in this delta. This is the most thickly populated district of all China. Within this delta and its immediate neighborhood, more than half of the population of Kwangtung province is found. This is the reason why, despite the great productivity of this fertile delta, large quantities of foods have to be supplied by the surrounding country as well as by foreign imports. Before the age of machinery, Canton for centuries was well known as an industrial center of Eastern Asia. The workmanship and handicraft of its people are still unequaled in many parts of the world. If machinery will be introduced in its industries under our international development scheme [International Development Scheme], Canton will soon recover its former grandeur as a great manufacturing center.

As a world port, Canton is in a most advantageous position. Being situated at the junction of three navigable rivers and at the head of the ocean navigation, it is a pivot of inland water as well as ocean communication in South China. If the Southwestern railway system is completed, then Canton will be equal in importance to the two great ports in North and East China, in regard to transportation facilities. The ocean approach of Canton is generally deep excepting at two points which can be easily trained and dredged to enable modern liners to pass in and out at any hour. The deep water line of the ocean reaches up to Lingting Island, where the depth is from 8 to 10 fathoms. Above Lingting, the channel get shallower(about 3 or 4 fathoms) and runs about 15 miles up to the Fumen Entrance. From this point the water becomes deep again(between 6 and 10 fathoms) right up to the Second Bar—a distance of 20 miles. At the Second Bar, the water is about 18 to 20 feet deep for only a few hundred yards. After crossing the Second Bar, the water becomes deep again for a distance of 10 miles averaging about 30 feet deep up to the First Bar which will be the city limit of our future Canton.

To improve the Approach to Canton, I suggest that two submerged training walls be built at the left side of Canton Estuary above Lingting Island—one from the shore to the head of the Kongsu Bank, and another [the other] from the end of the same bank to the head of the Lingting Bank. The first training wall will be 3 to 4 feet under water just at the same level of the bank. The second wall will be from 4 feet at one end to 16 feet at the other, which are the levels of the respective banks which it connects. (See(1) (3) Map XI.)It will cross a channel of 24 feet deep between them. These two walls together with the four-foot Kongsu Bank will act as one continuous wall and will direct the undercurrent which now runs between the left shore and Lingting Bank, into the middle part of the estuary, thus cutting a channel between the bar and the bank of the same name to meet the deep water on the west side of Lingting Island. On the right side of the Canton Estuary, a training wall should be built from the lower part of Fraser Bank in a southeasterly direction across the 24-foot channel into the Lingting Bar ending at the east edge of that bar. (See (2) Map XI.) Thus, with these submerged walls on both sides of the estuary to confine the undercurrent in the middle, a very deep channel can be formed to connect with the Fumen Entrance at one end and the Lingting trough at the other both of which are about 50 feet deep so that a thoroughfare from deep sea right up to the Second Bar of the Pearl River will be created.

These submerged sea walls taken together are about 8 miles in length and will be built only 6 to 12 feet from the bottom of the sea. The expenses will not be much while the acceleration of the natural reclamation process will be very great. Thus, the lands that will be formed on both sides by these walls will far more than repay the expenses of the work of building these walls.

To regulate the Approach of Canton, in that part of the Pearl River from the Fumen Entrance to Whangpoo [Whampoa], I suggest that the East River Estuaries be concentrated in a single outlet by using the uppermost channel which joins the Pearl River at the lower point of Davids Island. The other outlets of the East River, which joins [join] the Pearl River below the Second Bar, should be closed up by dams built to the height of the normal water level so as to permit them to serve as flood channels in the rainy season. By concentrating the whole volume of water of the East River above the Second Bar, a stronger current could be obtained to flush the upper part of this section of the river.

In the training works [work] of this section, I propose that several jetties should be built as follows: First, a jetty from Elliot Island at point (A) to the farther side of Calcutta Shoal opposite the lower point of Parker Island. This will block the current between Elliot Island and Calcutta Shoal and divert it into the present 36-foot channel thus making it deeper by its natural force. Second, another jetty from Bolton Island, at point (B) to midstream terminating at the lower side of the Second Bar, on the right side of the river. Third, a jetty from the lower point of Pattinger Island at (C) to midstream terminating at the lower side of the same bar on the left side of the river. Thus the Second Bar would be flushed by the concentrated current created by these two jetties. The shallow bottom above these jetties should be dredged to the required depth. If a rocky bottom is found at this bar it should be blasted and removed, so as to give a uniform depth to the whole approach. Fourth, the channel between the right bank of the river and Bolton Island should be blocked up at (D). Fifth, a jetty from Pattinger Island at (E) to the head of the Second Bar Bank in midstream so as to cut off the current at the left side of the river and to increase the velocity in the middle channel. Sixth, a jetty from the right shore at (F) about midway between Danes Island and the Second Bar, should be built to the head of the Midstream Shoal so as to cut off the current at the right side of the river. And seventh, another jetty from the lower point of Davids Island at (G) to midstream opposite to the end of jetty (F). Jetties (G) and (F) will concentrate the current of the upper Pearl River while at the same time jetty (G) will also turn the East River current into the same direction as that of the Pearl River. (See Map XII.)

By these seven jetties, the current between Whangpoo [Whampoa] and Fumen could be controlled and the bottom of the river flushed to a depth of 40 feet or more, thus creating a thoroughfare for ocean-going steamers from the open sea right up to the city of Canton. These jetties taken together will be not more than 5 miles in length and mostly in very shallow water. After the building of these jetties, land will be rapidly formed between jetties along both sides of the channel by natural process. The reclaimed land alone will be quite enough to pay the expenses of consturcting[constructing] these jetties, aside from the fact that the main object of regulating the river and opening up a deep channel for ocean transportation will have been realized.

Having dealt with the approach to Canton, we may now take up the improvement of Canton City itself as a world port. The harbor limit of Canton will be at the First Bar. From there, the harbor will follow the deep water of Cambridge Reach and the water between Whampoa and Danes Island into American Reach. At this point it will cut through Actason Island to the south of Honam Island and follow the Elliot Passage to Mariners Island. From Mariners Island following the Fatshan Creek, a straight channel should be cut in a southwesterly direction to the Tamchow Channel. Thus, a new waterway will be made from the First Bar to Tamchow Channel, a distance of about 25 miles. This waterway will be the main outlet of the North River as well as a thoroughfare for the West River, and will also serve as the harbor of Canton. By conveying all the water of the North River and a part of that of the West River through this waterway, the current will be strong enough to flush the harbor to a depth of 40 feet or more. (See Map XIII.)

The new city of Canton will be extended from Whangpoo [Whampoa] to Fatshan, separated by the Macao Fort and Shameen Reaches. The section that lies east of this water should be developed into commercial quarters and that west of it into factory quarters. The factory section should be transected by canals connecting with the Fati and Fatshan Creeks so as to give cheap transportation facilities to every factory. In the commercial section, tidal wharves with modern plants and warehouses should be provided. A bund should be built from the First

Bar Island along the north side of the new waterway, the west side of Honam Island to connect with the bund of Shameen, and the northwestern side of Canton city. Another bund should be built from above Fati along the east side of Fati Island to Mariners Island thence turning southwest along the left bank of the new waterway. The Front Reach, that is, the river between the present Canton city and Honam Island should be filled up from the upper point of Honam to Whampoa for city building.

In regard to the question of remuneration, the development of Canton as a world port will be the most profitable undertaking of the kind in the International Development Scheme. Because, besides its commanding position as a commercial metropolis and its possession of advantageous facilities as a manufacturing center of South China, a modern residential city is in great demand in this part of the country. The well-to-do people and merchants of this rich delta as well as those retired Chinese merchants and millionaires abroad all over the world are very eager to spend their remaining days at home. But owing to the lack of modern conveniences and comforts they reluctantly remain in foreign countries. Thus to build a new city with modern equipments for residential purposes alone, in Canton, would pay splendidly. The land outside of Canton is at present about 200 dollars a mow. If the land marked off for the future city of Canton should be taken up by the State on the same basis as elsewhere in this International Development Scheme, immediately after the streets are laid out and improvements made, the price of land would rise from ten to fifty times its original value.

The landscape of the environment of Canton is exceptionally beautiful and charming. It is an ideal place for planning a garden city with attractive parks. The location of the city of Canton resembles that of Nanking but is of greater magnitude and beauty. It possesses three natural elements—deep water, high mountains, and vast extent of level land which furnish facilities for an industrial and commercial center and provide as well natural scenery for the enjoyment of man. The beautiful valleys and hills of the northern shore of the Pearl River could be laid out for ideal winter resorts and the high mountain tops could be utilized for summer resorts.

Within the city limits at the northwest corner, a rich coal field has been found. When the coal is mined and modern plants for generating electricity and producing gas are provided, then cheap electricity and gas could be had for transportation, for manufacturing, for lighting, heating, and cooking purposes. And so the present wasteful methods of transportation, and expensive fuels for manufacturing and cooking for the populous city of Canton can be done away with entirely. Thus great economic wonders could be wrought by such improvements. The present population of Canton is over a million and if our development plan is carried out, this city would grow in leaps and bounds within a very short time. The population will become greater than any other city and the profit of our undertaking will become correspondingly large.

PART II

THE IMPROVEMENT OF THE WATERWAY SYSTEM OF CANTON

The most important waterway system in South China is the Canton system. Besides this the others are not of much importance and will be dealt with elsewhere with their ports. In dealing with the Canton system of waterways, I have to divide it as follows:

A. The Canton Delta.

B. The West River.

C. The North River.

D. The East River.

A. The Canton Delta

To improve the Canton Delta we have to consider the proposition from three points of view: first, the problem of flood prevention; second, the problem of navigation; and third, the problem of reclamation. Each of these problems affects the others so the solution of one will help that of the others.

First, the problem of flood prevention. The frequent repetition of floods in recent years has wrought great disasters to the people in the neighborhood of Canton. It has destroyed lives by the thousands and property by the millions. The part which suffers most is the country between Canton and Lupao, lying just immediately north of the Canton Delta. This fatal spot is, I think, created by the silting up of the main outlet of the North River immediately below Sainam. On account of this, the North River has to find its outlets through the West River by the short canal at Samshui and through two small streams—one from Sainam, and another [the other] from Lupao. The former runs in a northeasterly direction and the latter in a southeasterly direction and they join at Kuanyao. From this point, the river takes a northeasterly course as far as Kamli, thence, turning southeast, passes the west suburb of Canton. Since the North River is silted up below Sainam, its channel above that spot is also getting shallower every year. At present the river above Samshui city is only about four or five feet deep.

When the North River rises its water generally finds its way into the West River through the Kongkun Canal. But if the West River should rise at the same time, then there would be no outlet for the North River and its water would accumulate until it overflowed its dikes above and below Lupao. This would naturally cause the dikes to break at some point and allow the water to rush out and flood the whole country that is meant to be protected by these dikes. The remedy for the North River is to reopen the main outlet below Sainam and have the whole channel dredged deep from Tsingyuen to the sea. Fortunately, in our improvement of the navigation of the Canton Delta, we have to do the same thing; so this [one] work will serve two purposes.

The remedy for the West River is that the shallow part just at its junction with the sea between Wangkum and Sanchoo Islands should be trained by walls on both sides—a long one on the left, and a short one on the right—so as to concentrate the current to cut the river bed here to a depth of twenty feet or more. In this way, a uniform depth is secured, for after passing the Moto Entrance the West River has an average depth of 20 to 30 feet right along its whole course through this delta. With a uniform depth all the way to the sea, the undercurrent will run quickly and drain off the flood water more rapidly. Besides the deepening process, both shores should be regulated so as to give a uniform width to the channel. Mid-stream shoals and islands should be removed.

The East River Valley does not suffer so severely from floods as those of the other two rivers, the West and the North, and its remedy will be provided in the regulation of the river for navigation. This will be dealt with in that connection.

Second, the problem of navigation in the Canton Delta in connection with the three rivers. In dealing with this question we commence with the West River. In former days the traffic between the West River Valley and Canton always passed through Fatshan and Samshui, a distance of about 35 miles. But since the silting up of the Fatshan Channel below Sainam, the traffic has to take a great detour by descending the Pearl River south eastward as far as Fumen, then turn northwest into the Shawan Channel, then southeast into the Tamchow Channel, and then west into the Tailiang Channel and south into the Junction Channel and Maning Reach. Here it enters into the West River and runs a northwesterly direction up to Samshui Junction on this river. The whole journey covers a distance of about 95 miles, which compared with the old route is longer by 60 miles. The traffic between Canton and the West River Valley is very great. At present there are many thousands of steam lanches [launches] plying between Canton City and the outlying districts, and more than half of that number are carrying traffic to and fro on the West River. Every boat has to run 95 miles on each trip whereas if the channel between Samshui and Canton is improved, the distance would be only 35 miles. What a great saving it will be!

In our project to improve the Canton Approach and Harbor, I suggested the draining of a deep channel from the sea to Whangpoo [Whampoa] and from Whampoa to Tamchow Channel. We now have to prolong this channel from its Tamchow Junction up to Samshui Junction on the West River. This Channel should be made at least 20 feet deep so as to join the deeper water of the West River above the Samshui Junction. And the same depth should be maintained in the North River itself some distance above Samshui, so as to give facility for the navigation of larger vessels up the river when the whole waterway is improved.

To improve the East River for navigation in the Canton Delta we should concentrate the current of its estuaries into one single outlet by using the right channel which joins the Pearl River at Davids Island, thus deepening the channel as well as shortening the distance between Canton and the East River districts when the upper part of the river is improved.

Another improvement in the Canton Delta for navigation is the opening of a straight canal between Canton City and Kongmoon so as to shorten the passage of the heavy traffic between this metropolis and the Szeyap districts. This canal should begin by straightening the Chanchun Creek south of Canton as far as Tsznai. Then crossing the Tamchow Channel it should enter into the Shuntuck Creek and follow this creek to its end emerging into the Shuntuck Branch at right angles. From there, a new canal must be cut straight to the turn of the Tailiang Channel near Yungki, then the canal should follow this channel through Yellow Reach as far as the Junction Bend. Here another new canal must be cut through to the Hoichow Creek, then it should follow Kuchan Channel to the main channel of the West River, and crossing it enter into the Kongmoon Branch. Thus, a straight canal can be formed between Canton and Kongmoon. In order to understand the improvement of the Canton Delta more clearly see Maps XIV and XV.

Third, the problem of reclamation. A very profitable undertaking in the Canton Delta is the reclamation of new land. This process has been going on for centuries. Many thousands of acres of new land are thus being added to cultivation from year to year. But hitherto all the reclamation has been effected by private enterprise only, and there are no regulations for it. So sometimes this private enterprise causes great detriment to public welfare such as blocking up navigable channels and causing floods. A glaring case is the reclamation work just above the Moto Islands, which blocks more than half of the Main Channel of the West River. In the regulation of the West River, I propose to cut this new land away. In order to protect the public welfare, the reclamation work in this Delta must be taken up by the State and the profits must go to defray the expenses of improving this waterway system for navigation, as well as for the prevention of floods. At present, the area that can be gradually reclaimed is large in extent. On the left side of the Canton Estuary, the available area is about 40 square miles, and on the right side, about 140 square miles. On the estuaries of the West River from Macao to Tongkwa Island, there is an available area of about 200 square miles. Of the 380 square miles, about one fourth would be ready for reclamation within the next ten years. That is to say about 95 square miles could be reclaimed and put to cultivation within a decade. As one square mile contains 640 acres and one acre six mow, so 95 square miles will be equal to 364,800 mow. As cultivated land in this part of China generally costs more than fifty dollars a mow, so, if fifty dollars be taken as the average rate, the value of these 364,800 mow would amount to $18,240,000. This will help a great deal to defray the expenses of improving the waterway for navigation and for preventing floods in this Delta.

B. The West River

The West River is at present navigable for comparatively large river steamers up to Wuchow, a distance of 220 miles by water from Canton, and for small steamers up to Nanning, a distance of 500 miles from Canton, at all seasons. As for small crafts, the West River is navigable in most of its branches, west to the Yunnan frontier, north to Kweichow, northeast to Hunan and the Yangtze Valley by the Shingan Canal.

In improving the West River for navigation I shall divide the work into subsections as follows:

(1) From Samshui to Wuchow.

(2) From Wuchow to the junction of the Liukiang.

(3) Kweikiang or the North Branch of the West River from Wuchow to Kweilin and beyond.

(4) The South Branch from Shunchow to Nanning.

(1) From Samshui to Wuchow. This part of the West River is generally deep and does not need much improvement for vessels up to ten-foot draught excepting at a few points. The midstream rocks should be blasted and removed, and sand banks and dilating parts should be regulated by submerged dikes to secure a uniform channel and to make the velocity of the current even, so that a stable fairway could be maintained all the year round. The traffic of this river would be sufficiently great to pay for all the improvements which we propose to make.

(2) From Wuchow to the Junction of the Liukiang. At this junction, a river port should be built to connect the deep navigation from the sea and the shallow navigation of Hungshui Kiang and the Liukiang which penetrate the rich mineral districts of Northwest Kwangsi and Southwest Kweichow. This port will be about fifty miles from Shunchow which is the junction of the Nanning branch of the river. So here we have only to improve a distance of fifty miles, for the improvement of the river between Shunchow and Wuchow will be included in the plan for the Nanning Port. Dams and locks would be necessary to make this part of the river navigable for ten-foot draught vessels. But these dams at the same time would serve the purpose of producing water power.

(3) Kweikiang or the North Branch of the West River from Wuchow to Kweilin and beyond. As Kweikiang is smaller, shallower and has more rapids along its course, so its improvement will be more difficult than that of the other

parts of the waterway. But this will be a very profitable proposition in this Southern waterway project, for this river not only serves the purpose of transportation in this rich territory but will also serve as a passage for through traffic between the Yangtze and the West River valleys. The improvement should commence from the junction at Wuchow up to Kweilin, and thence upward to the Shingan Canal, then downward to the Siang River, and thereby connecting with the Yangtze River. A series of dams and locks should be built for vessels to ascend to the inter-watershed canal and another series should descend on the other side. The expenses of building these two series of dams and locks could not be estimated until accurate surveys are made. But I am sure this project will be a paying one.

(4) From Shunchow to Nanning. This portion of the Yukiang is navigable for small steamers up to Nanning, the center of commerce in South Kwangsi. From Nanning small crafts can navigate through the Yukiang as far as the east border of Yunnan, and through Tsokiang as far as the north border of Tongking. If this waterway be improved up to Nanning, then it would be the nearest deep river port for the rich mineral districts of the whole southwest corner of China, which includes the whole province of Yunnan, a greater part of Kweichow and half of Kwangsi. The immediate neighborhood of Nanning is also very rich in minerals, such as antimony, tin, iron, coal and also in agricultural products. So to make Nanning the head of a deep water communication system will be a paying proposition. To improve the waterway up to Nanning, a few dams and locks along its course will have to be built for vessels of ten-foot draught to go up as well as for water power. The expense for this work cannot be estimated without detailed surveys but it would probably be much less than the improvement of Kweikiang from Wuchow to the Shingan Canal.

C. The North River

The North River from Samshui to Siuchow is about 140 miles long. The greater part of its course is confined in the hilly districts, but after it emerges from the Tsingyuen Gorge it comes into a wide, open country, which connects with the plain of Canton. Here the dangerous floods occur most often. Since the silting up of its proper outlet below Sainam, the North River from that point up to the gorge has become shallower every year, so the dikes at the left side, that is, on the side of the plain, often break thus causing the inundation of the whole plain above Canton. Thus the regulation of the river at this part has two aspects to be considered: first, the prevention of flood and second, the improvement of navigation. In dealing with the first aspect nothing could be better than deepening the river by dredging. In the improvement of the Canton Approach and Harbor and also of the Canton Delta, we have to cut a deep channel right from the deep sea up to Sainam. In the improvement of the lower part of the North River, we have simply to continue the cutting process higher up until we have a deep channel, say 15 to 20 feet as far as the Tsingyuen Gorge, either by artificial or natural means. By this deepening of the bottom of the river, the present height of the dikes will be quite enough to protect the plains from being flooded.

In dealing with the second aspect, as we have already deepened the part of the river from Sainam to the Tsingyuen Gorge for flood prevention, we have at the same time solved the navigation question. It has now only the upper part to be dealt with. I propose to make this river navigable up to Siuchow, the center of commerce as well as the center of the coal and iron fields of Northern Kwangtung. To improve the part above the gorge for navigation, dams and locks should be built in one or two places before a ten-foot draught vessel can ascend up to that point. Although this river is parallel with the Canton-Hankow Railway, yet if the coal and iron fields of Siuchow are properly developed, a deep waterway will still be needed for cheap transportation of such heavy freight as iron and coal to the coast. So to build dams for water power and to construct locks for navigation in this river will be a profitable undertaking as well as a necessary condition for the development of this part of the country.

D. The East River

The East River is navigable for shallow crafts up to Laolung Sze, a distance of about 170 miles from the estuary at the lower point of Davids Island near Whangpoo [Whampoa]. Along its upper course, rich iron and coal deposits are found. Iron has been mined here since time immemorial. At present most of the utensils used in this province are manufactured from the iron mined. So to make a deep navigable waterway up to these iron and coal fields will be most remunerative.

To improve the East River for navigation as well as for flood prevention, I propose to start the work at the lower point of Davids Island as stated in the improvement of the Canton Approach. From here, a deep channel should be dredged up to Suntang, and a mile above that point a new channel should be opened in the direction of Tungkun city, by connecting the various arms of water between these two places and joining the left branch of the East River immediately above Tungkun city. All other channels leading from this new channel to the Pearl River should be closed up to normal water level so as to make these colsed-up [closed-up] channels serve as flood outlets in rainy seasons. Thus by blocking up the rest of the estuaries of the East River, all the water would form one strong current which will dredge the river bottom deeper, and maintain the depth permanently. The body of the river should be trained to a uniform width right along its course up to tidal point, and above this point, the river should be narrowed in proportion to its volume of water. Thus the whole river would dredge itself deep far up above Waichow city. The railway bridge at the south side of Shelung should be made a turning bridge so as to permit large steamers to pass through it. Some sharp turns of the river should be reduced to gentle curves and midstream obstacles should be removed. The portion of the river above Waichow should be provided with dams and locks so as to enable ten-foot draught vessels to ascend as near as possible to the iron and coal fields in the valley.

PART III

THE CONSTRUCTION OF THE SOUTHWESTERN RAILWAY SYSTEM OF CHINA

The southwestern part of China comprises Szechwan, the largest and richest province of China Proper, Yunnan, the second largest province, Kwangsi and Kweichow which are rich in mineral resources, and a part of Hunan and Kwangtung. It has an area of 600,000 square miles, and a population of over 100,000,000. This large and populous part of China is almost untouched by railways, except a French line of narrow gauge from Laokay to Yunnanfu, covering a distance of 290 miles.

There are great possibilities for railway development in this part of the country. A network of lines should radiate fan-like from Canton as pivot to connect every important city and rich mineral field with the Great Southern Port. The construction of railways in this part of China is not only needed for the development of Canton but also is essential for the prosperity of all the southwestern provinces. With the construction of railways rich mines of various kinds could be developed and cities and towns could be built along the lines. Developed lands are still very cheap and undeveloped lands and those with mining possibilities cost almost next to nothing even though not State-owned. So if all the future city sites and mining lands be taken up by the government before railways construction is started, the profit would be enormous. Thus no matter how large a sum is invested in railway construction, the payment of its interest and principal will be assured. Besides, the development of Canton as a world port is entirely dependent upon this system of railways. If there be no such network of railway traversing the length and breadth of the southwestern section of China, Canton could not be developed up to our expectations.

The southwestern section of China is very mountainous, except the Canton and Chengtu plains, which have an area of from 3,000 to 4,000 square miles each. The rest of the country is made up almost entirely of hills and valleys with more or less open space here and there. The mountains in the eastern part of this section are seldom over 3,000 feet high but those near the Tibetan frontier generally have an altitude of 10,000 feet or more. The engineering difficulties in building these railways are much greater than those of the northwestern plain. Many tunnels and loops will have to be constructed and so the construction costs of the railway per mile will be greater than ⟨those⟩ in other parts of China.

With Canton as the terminus of this system of railroads, I propose that the following lines be constructed:

A. The Canton-Chungking line via Hunan.

B. The Canton-Chungking line via Hunan and Kweichow.

C. The Canton-Chengtu line via Kweilin and Luchow.

D. The Canton-Chengtu line via Wuchow and Suifu.

E. The Canton-Yunnanfu-Tali-Tengyueh line ending at the Burma border.

F. The Canton-Szemao line.

G. The Canton-Yamchow line ending at Tunghing, on the Annam border.

A. The Canton-Chungking Line via Hunan

This line will start from Canton and follow the same direction as the Canton-Hankow line as far as the junction of the Linkiang with the North River. From that point the railroad turns into the valley of Linkiang, and follows the course of the river upward above the city of Linchow. There it crosses the watershed between the Linkiang and the Taokiang and proceeds to Taochow, Hunan. Thence it follows the Taokiang to Yungchow, Paoking, Sinhwa, and Shenchow, and up to Peiho across the boundary of Hunan into Szechwan by Yuyang. From Yuyang the line proceeds across the mountain to Nanchuen, thence to Chungking after crossing the Yangtze. This railway which has a total length of about 900 miles passes through a rich mineral and agricultural country. In the Linchow district north of Kwangtung, rich coal, antimony, and wolfram deposits are found; in southwestern Hunan, tin, antimony, coal, iron, copper and silver; and at Yuyang, east of Szechwan, antimony and quicksilver. Among agricultural products found along this line we may mention sugar, groundnuts, hemp, tung oil, tea, cotton, tobacco, silk, grains, etc. There is also an abundance of timber, bamboo and various kinds of forest products.

B. The Canton-Chungking Line via Hunan and Kweichow

This line is about 800 miles in length, but as it runs in the same track with line (a) from Canton to Taochow, a distance of about 250 miles, it leaves only 550 miles to be accounted for. This line, therefore, actually begins at Taochow, Hunan, and goes through the northeastern corner of Kwangsi passing by Chuanchow, and then through the southwestern corner of Hunan passing by Chengpu and Tsingchow. Thence it enters into Kweichow by Sankiang and Tsingkiang and crosses a range of hill to Chengyuan. From Chengyuan this line has to cross the watershed between Yuankiang and Wukiang to Tsunyi. From Tsunyi it will follow the trade route which leads to Kikiang and then crosses the Yangtze by the same bridge as line (a) to Chungking. This railway will also pass through rich mineral and timber districts.

C. The Canton-Chengtu line via Kweilin and Luchow

This line is about 1,000 miles long. It runs from Canton directly west to Samshui, where it crosses the North River to the mouth of Suikiang. Then, it ascends the valley of the same name to Szewui and Kwangning. Next, it enters into Kwangsi at Waisap, thence to Hohsien and Pinglo. From there it follows the course of the Kweikiang up to Kweilin. Thus the rich iron and coal fields that lie between these two provincial capitals, Canton and Kweilin, will be tapped. From Kweilin the road turns west to Yungning and then proceeds to follow the Liukiang valley into Kweichow province at Kuchow. From Kuchow it goes to Tukiang and Pachai and following the same valley it crosses a range of hills into Pingyueh, thence it goes across the Yuankiang watershed into the Wukiang valley at Wengan and Yosejen. From Yosejen it follows the trade route through Luipien Hills to Jenhwai, Chishui, and Nachi. Then it crosses the Yangtze to Luchow. From Luchow, it runs through Lungchang, Neikiang, Tzechow, Tzeyang and Kienchow to Chengtu. The last part of the line traverses very rich and populous districts of the famous Red Basin of Szechwan province. The middle portion of this line between Kweilin and Luchow lies in a very rich mineral country which possesses great possibilities for further development. This line will open up a thinly populated part for the crowded districts at both ends of the line.

D. The Canton-Chengtu Line via Wuchow and Suifu

This line is about 1,200 miles in distance, it commences at the west end of the Samshui bridge which crosses the North River at that point for line (c), and following the left bank of the West River enters the Shiuhing Gorge to the Shiuhing city. It passes Takhing, Wuchow, and Tahwang along the same bank. While the river here turns southwestwards the line turns northwestwards to Siangchow and then crosses Liukiang to Liuchow and Kingyuan. Then it goes to Szegenhsien and across the Kwangsi and Kweichow border to Tushan and Tuyun. From Tuyun the line turns more westerly to Kweiyang, the capital of Kweichow province. Next, it proceeds to Kiensi and Tating and then leaving the Kweichow border at Pichieh it enters Yunan at Chenhiung. Turning northward to Lohsintu and crossing the Szechwan border at that point, it proceeds to Suifu. From Suifu the road follows the course of the Minkiang, passes by Kiating and enters the Chengtu plain to Chengtu, the capital of Szechwan. This line runs from one densely populated district to another and passes through a wide strip of thinly populated and undeveloped country in the middle. Along its course many rich iron and coal fields, silver, tin, antimony, and other valuable metal deposits are found.

E. The Canton-Yunnanfu-Tali-Tengyueh Line

This line is about 1,300 miles in length from Canton to the Burma border at Tengyueh. The first 300 miles of the line from Canton to Tahwang will be the same as line (d). From the Tahwang junction this line branches off to Wusuan and following in a general way the course of the Hungshui Kiang passes through Tsienkiang and Tunglan. Then it cuts across the southwestern corner of Kweichow province passing by Sinyihsien and thence enters Yunnan province at Loping and by way of Luliang to Yunnanfu, the capital of the province. From Yunnanfu this line runs through Tsuyung to Tali, then turns southwestwards to Yungchang and Tengyueh ending at the Burma border.

At Tunglan, near the Kweichow border in Kwangsi, a branch line of about 400 miles should be projected. This line should follow the Pepan Kiang valley, up to Kotuho, and Weining. Thence it enters Yunnan at Chaotung, and crosses the Yangtze River at Hokeow, where it enters Szechwan. Crossing the Taliang mountain, it goes to Ningyuan. This branch line taps the famous copper field between Chaotung and Ningyuan, the richest of its kind in China.

The main line running through the length of Kwangsi and Yunnan from east to west, will be of international importance, for at the frontier it will join the Rangoon Bhamo line of the Burmese Railway System. It will be the shortest road from India to China. It will bring the two populous countries nearer to each other than now. By the new way the journey can be made in a few days, whereas by the present sea-route it takes [as] many weeks.

F. The Canton-Szemao Line

This line to the border of Burma is about 1,100 miles long. It starts from south of Canton, passes Fatshan, Runshan, and crosses the West River from Taipinghu to Samchowhu. Thence it proceeds to Koming, Sinhing and Loting. After passing Loting it crosses the Kwangsi border at Pingho, and proceeds to Junghsien and then westward, crossing the Yukiang branch of the West River, to Kweihsien. Thence it runs north of Yukiang to Nanning. At Nanning a branch line of 120 miles should be projected. Following the course of the Tsokiang it goes to Lungchow where it turns southward to Chennankwan on the Tongking border to join the French line at that point. The main line from Nanning proceeds in the same course as the upper Yukiang to Poseh. Then it crosses the border into Yunnan at Poyai, and by way of Pamen, Koukan, Tungtu and Putsitang to Amichow, where it crosses the French Laokay-Yunnan line. From Amichow it proceeds to Linanfu, Shihping and Yuankiang where it crosses the river of the same name. Thence it passes through Talang, Puerhfu and Szemao and finally ends at the border of Burma near the Mekong River. This line taps the rich tin, silver, and antimony deposits of south Yunnan and Kwangsi, while rich iron and coal fields are found right along the whole line. Gold, copper, mercury, and lead are also found in many places. As regards agricultural products, rice and groundnuts are found in great abundance, also camphor, cassia, sugar, tobacco, and various kind [kinds] of fruits.

G. The Canton-Yamchow Line

This line is about 400 miles long measuring from the west end of the Sikiang bridge. Starting from Canton it runs on the tracks of line (f) as far as the farther side of the bridge over the West River. Thence it branches off to the southwest to Hoiping and Yanping, and by way of Yeungchun to Kochow and Fachow. At Fachow, a branch line of 100 miles should be projected to Suikai, Luichow and Haian on the Hainan Straits where, by means of a ferry, it connects with Hainan Island. The mainline continues from Fachow westward to Sheshing, Limchow, Yamchow and ends on the Annam border at Tunghing, where it may connect with a French line to Haiphong. This line is entirely within the Kwangtung province. It passes through a very populous and productive country. Coal and iron are found along the whole line, while gold and antimony, in some parts. Agricultural products, as sugar, silk, camphor, ramie, indigo, groundnuts, and various kinds of fruits are raised here.

The total length of this system as outlined above is about 6,700 miles. In addition, there will be two connecting lines between Chengtu and Chungking; another from cast of Tsunyi on line (b) southward to Wengan on line (e); another from Pingyueh on line (c) to Tuyun on line (d); another from the border of Kweichow on line (d) through Nantan and Noti to Tunglan on line (e), thence through Szecheng to Poseh on line (f). These connecting lines total about 600 miles. So the grand total will be about 7,300 miles.

This system will be intersected by three lines. First, the existing French line from Laokay to Yunnanfu with a projected line from Yunnanfu to Chungking crosses line (f) at Amichow, line (e) at Weining, line (d) at Suifu, line (c) at Luchow, and meets lines (a) and (b) at Chungking. Second, the projected British line from Shasi to Sinyi crosses line (a) at Shenchow, line (b) at Chengyuan, line (c) at Pingyueh, line (d) at Kweiyang and a branch of line (e) at a point west of Yungting. Third, the projected American line from Chuchow to Yamchow crosses line (a) at Yungchow, line (b) at Chuanchow, line

(c) at Kweilin, line (d) at Liuchow, line (e) at Tsienkiang, line (f) at Nanning, and meets line (g) at Yamchow. Thus, if this system and the three projected French, British, and American lines are completed, Southwestern China would be well provided with railway communications.

All these lines will run through the length and breadth of a vast mineral country, in which most of the essential and valuable metals of the world are found. There is no place in the world which possesses as here so many varieties of rare metals, such as wolfram, tin, antimony, silver, gold, and platinum and at the same time so richly provided with the common but essential metals, such as copper, lead, and iron. Furthermore, almost every district in this region is abundantly provided with coal, so much so that there is a common saying: "*Mu mei pu lih cheng*," that is, "Nobody would build a city where there is no coal underneath." The idea was that in case of a siege those within the city might obtain fuel from under the ground. In Szechwan, petroleum and natural gas are also found in abundance.

Thus, we see that this Southwestern Railway System for the development of mineral resources in the mountainous regions of Southwestern China is just as important as the Northwestern Railway System is for the development of agricultural resources in the vast prairies of Mongolia and Turkestan. These railway systems are a necessity to the Chinese people and a very profitable undertaking to foreign capitalists. They are of about equal length, viz. —about 7,000 miles. The cost per mile of the Southwestern System will be at least twice that of the Northwestern System, but the remuneration from the development of mineral resources will be many times that from the development of agricultural resources.

PART IV

THE CONSTRUCTION OF COAST PORTS AND FISHING HARBORS

After planning the three world ports on the coast of China, it is time for me to go on and deal with the development of second- and third-class seaports and fishing harbors along the whole coast in order to complete a system of seaports for China. Recently, my projected plan of the Great Northern Port was so enthusiastically received by the people of Chihli Province that the Provincial Assembly has approved the project and decided to carry it out at once as a provincial undertaking. For this object, a loan of $40,000,000 has been voted. This is an encouraging sign and doubtless the other projects will be taken up sooner or later by either the provinces or the Central Government, when the people begin to realize their necessity. I propose that four second-class seaports and nine third-class seaports and numerous fishing harbors should be constructed.

The four second-class seaports will be arranged so as to be placed in the following manner: one on the extreme north, one on the extreme south, and the other two midway between the three great world ports.

I shall deal with them according to the order of their future importance as follows:

A. Yingkow.

B. Haichow.

C. Foochow.

D. Yamchow.

A. Yingkow

Yingkow is situated at the head of the Liaotung Gulf and was once the only seaport of Manchuria. Since the improvement of Talien as a seaport, the trade of Yingkow has dwindled and lost half of its former business. As a seaport, Yingkow has two disadvantages, first, the shallowness of its approach from the sea and second, the blocking up by ice for several months in winter. Its only advantages over Talien is that it is situated at the mouth of the Liaoho and has inland water communication throughout the Liao valley in south Manchuria. The half of the former trade that it still holds at present against Talien is entirely due to the inland water facility. To make Yingkow outmatch Talien again in the future and become first in importance after the three great world ports, we must improve its inland water communication, as well as deepen its approach from the sea. In regard to the improvement of the approach 〈, the〉 work similar to the improvement of the Canton Approach should be adopted. Besides the construction of a deep channel, about twenty feet in depth, reclamation work should be carried out at the same time. For, the shallow and extensive swamp at the head of the Liaotung Gulf could be turned into rice-producing land from which great profit could be derived. Regarding the inland water communication, not only the water system in the Liao valley but also the Sungari and the Amur Systems have to be improved. The most important work is the construction of a canal to connect these systems and this I shall now discuss in the next paragraph.

The Liaoho-Sungari Canal is the most important factor in the future prosperity of Yingkow. It is by this canal only that this port can be made the most important of the second-class seaports in China and further the vast forest lands, the virgin soil and the rich mineral resources of North Manchuria can be connected by water communication with Yingkow. So this canal is all important for Yingkow, without which Yingkow as a seaport could at most hold her present position, a town of 60,000 to 70,000 inhabitants and an annual trade of $30,000,000 to $40,000,000 only and could never gain a place as the first of the second-class seaports in China. This canal can be cut either south of Hwaiteh in a line parallel to the South Manchurian Railway between Fan Kia Tun and Sze Tung Shan, a distance of less than ten miles, or north of Hwaiteh in a line between Tsing-shan-pao and Kaw-shan-tun, a distance of about fifteen miles. In the former case the canal is shorter but it makes the waterway as a whole longer, while in the latter case, the canal is about twice as long but it makes the waterway as a whole shorter between the two systems. In either line, there are no impassable physical obstacles. Both lines are on the plain but the elevation of the one may be higher than that of the other, which is the only factor that will determine the choice between the two. If this canal is constructed, then the rich provinces of Kirin and Heilungkiang and a portion of Outer Mongolia will be brought within direct water communication with China Proper. At present, all water traffic has to go by way of the Russian Lower Amur, then round a great detour of the Japan Sea before reaching China Proper. This canal will not only be a great necessity to Yingkow as a seaport, but will also have a great bearing on the whole Chinese nation economically and politically. With the Liaoho-Sungari Canal completed Yingkow will be the grand terminus of the inland waterway system of all Manchuria and Northeastern Mongolia; and with the approach from the sea deepened it will also be a seaport next in importance only to the three first-class world ports.

B. Haichow

Haichow is situated on the eastern edge of the central plain of China. This plain is one of the most extensive and fertile areas on earth. As a seaport, Haichow is midway between the two great world ports along the coast line, namely the Great Northern and the Great Eastern Ports.

It has been made as the terminus of the Hailan railway, the trunk line of central China from east to west. Haichow also possesses the facility of inland water communication. If the Grand Canal and the other waterway systems are improved, it will be connected with the Hoangho Valley in North China, the Yangtze Valley in Central China, and the Sikiang Valley in South China. Its deep sea approach is comparatively good, being the only spot along the 250 miles of the North Kiangsu coast that could be reached by ocean steamers to within a few miles of the shore. To make Haichow a seaport for 20 feet draught vessels, the approach has to be dredged for many miles from the mouth of the river before the four fathoms [fathom] line could be reached. Although possessing better advantages than Yingkow, in being ice free, Haichow, as a second-class seaport, has ⟨to⟩ be content to take a second place after Yingkow, because she does not have as vast a hinterland as Yingkow, nor such a monopolistic position in regard to inland water communication.

C. Foochow

Foochow, the capital of Fukien province, ranks third among our second-class seaports. Foochow is already a very large city, its inhabitants being nearly a million. It is situated at the lower reach of the Min River, about 30 miles from the sea. The hinterland of this port is confined to the Min Valley with an area of about 30,000 square miles. The territory beyond this valley will be commanded by other coast or river ports, so the area commanded by this port is much smaller than that by Haichow. Consequently, it could be given only the third place in the category of second-class seaports. The Foochow approach from the Outer Bar to Kinpei Entrance is very shallow. After this Entrance is passed, the river is confined on both sides by high hills and becomes narrow and deep right up to Pagoda Anchorage.

I propose that a new port should be constructed at the lower part of Nantai Island. For here land is cheap and there will be plenty of room for modern improvement. A locked basin for shipping could be constructed at the lower point of Nantai Island, just above Pagoda Anchorage. The left branch of the Min River above Foochow City should be blocked up so as to concentrate the current to flush the harbor at the south side of Nantai. The blocked-up channel on the north side of that island should be left to be reclaimed by natural process or may be used as a tidal basin to flush the channel below Pagoda Anchorage, if it is found necessary. The upper Min River must be improved as far as possible for inland water traffic. Its lower reach from Pagoda Anchorage to the sea must be trained and regulated to secure a through channel of 30 feet or more to the open sea. Thus Foochow could also be made a calling port for ocean liners that ply between the world ports.

D. Yamchow

Yamchow is situated at the head of Tongking Gulf in the extreme south of the China coast. This city is about 400 miles west of Canton—the Great Southern Port. All the districts lying west of Yamchow will find their way to the sea by this port 400 miles shorter than by Canton. As sea transportation is commonly known to be twenty times cheaper than rail transportation, the shortening of a distance or 400 miles to the sea means a great deal economically to the provinces of Szechwan, Yunnan, Kweichow, and a part of Kwangsi. Although Nanning, an inland water port, lying northwest of Yamchow, is much nearer to the hinterland than Yamchow, yet it could not serve this hinterland as a seaport. So all the direct import and export trade will find Yamchow the cheapest shipping stage.

To improve Yamchow as a seaport the Lungmen River should be regulated in order to secure a deep channel to the city, and the estuary should be deepened by dredging and training to provide a good approach to the port. This port has been selected as the terminus of the Chuchow Yamchow Railway (Chu-Kin line) which will run from Hunan through Kwangsi into Kwangtung. Although the hinterland of this port is much larger than that of Foochow, yet I still rank it after that city because the area commanded by it is also commanded by Canton, the southern world port, and by Nanning, the river port, and so all internal as well as indirect import and export trade must go to the other two ports. It is only the direct foreign trade that will use Yamchow. Thus, in spite of its extensive hinterland it is very improbable that it could outmatch Foochow in the future as a second-class port.

Besides the three great world ports, and the four second-class ports, I propose to construct nine third-class ports along the China coast, from north to south, as follows:

A. Hulutao.

B. ⟨The⟩ Hoangho Port.

C. Chefoo.

D. Ningpo.

E. Wenchow.

F. Amoy.

G. Swatow.

H. Tienpak.

I. Hoihou.

A. Hulutao

Hulutao is an ice-free and deep-water port, situated on the west side of the head of Liaotung Gulf, about 60 miles from Yingkow. As a winter port for Manchuria, it is in a more advantageous position than Talien for it is about 200 miles shorter by rail to the sea than the latter and is on the edge of a rich coal field. When this coal field and the surrounding mineral resources are developed, Hulutao will become the first of the third-class ports and a good outlet for Jehol and Eastern Mongolia. This port may be projected as an alternative to Yingkow, as the sole port of Manchuria and Eastern Mongolia, if a canal could be constructed to connect it with the Liaoho. It is only by inland water communication that Yingkow could be made the important port of Manchuria in the future and it will be the same in the case of Hulutao. So if inland water communication could be secured for Hulutao it will entirely displace Yingkow. If it is found to be economically cheaper in the long run to construct a Hulutao-Liaoho Canal than to construct a deep harbor at Yingkow, the Hulutao harbor will have to be placed on the northwest side of the peninsula instead of on the southwest as at present projected, for the present site has not enough room for anchorage without building an extensive breakwater into the deep sea, which will be [a] very expensive work. Furthermore, there would not be room enough for city planning on the narrow peninsula, whereas on the other side, the city could be built on the mainland with unlimited space for its development.

I suggest that a sea wall be built from the northern point of Lienshanwan to the northern point of Hulutao to close up the Lienshan Bay and make it into a closed harbor, and an entrance be opened in the neck of Hulutao to the south side where deep water is found. This closed harbor will be over 10 square miles in extent but only some parts need to be dredged to the required depth at present. On the north side of the harbor, another entrance into the neighboring bay should be left open between the sea wall and the shore, and another breakwater should be built across the next bay. From there, a canal should be constructed either by cutting into the shore or by building a wall parallel with the coast line until it reaches the lowland from where a canal should be cut to connect with the Liaoho. If a canal is thus constructed for Hulutao, then it will at once take the place of Yingkow and become the first of the second-class ports.

B. The Hoangho Port

The Hoangho Port will be situated at the estuary of the Hoangho on the southern side of the Gulf of Pechihli, about 80 miles from our Great Northern Port. When the Hoangho regulation is completed its estuary will be approachable by ocean steamers, and a seaport will naturally spring up there. As it commands a considerable part of the northern plain in the provinces of Shantung, Chihli, and Honan and possesses the facility of inland water communication, this port is bound to become an important third-class port.

C. Chefoo

Chefoo is an old treaty port situated on the northern side of the Shantung Peninsula. Once it was the only ice-free port in the whole of North China. Since the development of Talien in the north and the development of Tsingtau in the south its trade has dwindled considerably. As a seaport, it will undoubtedly hold its own when the railroads in the Shantung Peninsula are developed, and the artificial harbor is completed.

D. Ningpo

Ningpo is also an old treaty port, situated on a small river, the Yungkiang, in the eastern part of Chekiang province. It has a good approach, deep water reaching right up to the estuary of the river. The harbor can be easily improved by simply training and straightening two bends along its course up to the city. Ningpo commands a very small but rich hinterland. Its people are very enterprising, and are famed for their workmanship and handicrafts second only to those of Canton. Thus Ningpo is bound to become a manufacturing city when China is industrially developed. But owing to the proximity of the Great Eastern Port, Ningpo will not likely have much import and export trade directly with foreign countries. Most of its trade will be carried on with the Great Eastern Port. So a moderate harbor for local and coast-wise traffic will be quite sufficient for Ningpo.

E. Wenchow

Wenchow is situated near the mouth of the Wukiang in south Chekiang. This seaport has a wider hinterland than Ningpo, its surrounding districts being very productive. If railroads are developed it will undoubtedly command considerable local trade. At present the harbor is very shallow, unapproachable by even moderate-sized coastal steamers. I suggest that a new harbor at Panshiwei, north of Wenchow Island be constructed. For this purpose, a dike should be built between the northern bank and the head of Wenchow Island to block up the river entirely on the northern side of that island leaving only a lock entrance. The Wukiang should be led through the channel on the south side of the island for the purpose of reclaiming the vast expanse of the near-by shallows as well as for draining the upper stream. The approach from the southern side of Hutau Island to the port should be dredged. On the right side of the approach, a wall should be built in the shallow between Wenchow Island and Miau Island and in the shallows between Miau Island and Sanpam Island so as to form a continuous wall to prevent the silt of Wukiang from entering into the approach. Thus a permanent deep channel will be secured for the new port of Wenchow.

F. Amoy

Amoy, an old treaty port, is situated on the island of Siming. It has a great, deep, and fine harbor, commanding a considerable hinterland in southern Fukien and Kiangsi, very rich in coal and iron deposits. This port carries on a busy trade with the Malay Archipelago and the Southeastern Asian Peninsula. Most of the Chinese residents in the southern islands, Annam, Burma, Siam, and the Malay States are from the neighborhood of Amoy. So the passenger traffic between Amoy and the southern colonies is very great. If railways are developed to tap the rich iron and coal fields in the hinterland, Amoy is bound to develop into a much larger seaport than it is at present. I suggest that a modern port be constructed on the west side of the harbor to act as an outlet for the rich mineral fields of southern Fukien and Kiangsi. This port should be equipped with modern plants in order to connect land and sea transportation together.

G. Swatow

Swatow is situated at the mouth of the Hankiang at the extreme east of Kwangtung. In relation to emigration, Swatow is much similar to Amoy, for it also supplies a great number of colonists to southeastern Asia and the Malay Archipelago. So its passenger traffic with the south is just as busy as Amoy. As a seaport Swatow is far inferior to Amoy, on account of its shallow approach. But is [in] regard to inland water communication, Swatow is in a better position as the Hankiang is navigable for many hundreds of miles inland by shallow crafts. The country around Swatow is very productive agriculturally, being second only to the Canton Delta along the Southern seaboard. In the upper reaches of the Hankiang there are very rich iron and coal deposits. The approach to the port of Swatow can be improved easily by a little training and dredging, thus making it a fine local port.

H. Tienpak

Tienpak is situated at a point in the coast of Kwangtung province between the estuary of the West River and the island of Hainan. Its surrounding districts are rich in agricultural products and mineral deposits. So a shipping port in this part is quite necessary. Tienpak can be made into a fine harbor by entirely walling in the bay from its west side and by opening a new entrance into the deep water in the neck of the peninsula southeast of the bay. Thus a good approach could be secured. The harbor is very wide but only a part need be dredged for large vessels and the rest of the space could be used by fishing boats and other shallow crafts.

I. Hoihou

Hoihou is situated on the north side of Hainan Island on the strait of the same name, opposite Haian on the Luichow Peninsula. Hoihou is a treaty port, similar to Amoy and Swatow, supplying a great number of colonists to the south; Hainan is a very rich but undeveloped island. Only the land along the coast is cultivated, the central part being still covered by thick forests and inhabited by aborigines, and it is very rich in mineral deposits. When the whole island is fully developed, the port of Hoihou will be a busy harbor for export and import traffic. The harbor of Hoihou is very shallow, and so even small vessels have to anchor miles away in the roadstead outside. This is very inconvenient for passengers and cargoes, so the improvement of the Hoihou harbor is a necessity. Furthermore this harbor will be the ferry point between this island and the mainland for railway traffic when the railway systems of the mainland and the island are completed.

FISHING HARBORS

As regards fishing harbors all out first-, second-, and third-class ports must also furnish facilities and accommodations for fishery. Thus all of these, i. e., three first-class ports, four second-class ports, and nine third-class ports, will be fishing harbors as well. But besides these sixteen ports there is still room and need to construct more fishing harbors along the coast of China. I propose, therefore, that five fishing harbors be constructed along the northern coast, that is, along the coast of Fengtien, Chihli, and Shantung, as follows:

(1) Antung, on Yalu River, on the border of Korea.

(2) Haiyangtao, on the Yalu Bay, south of Liaotung Peninsula.

(3) Chinwangtao, on the coast of Chihli, between the Liaotung and Pechihli gulfs, the present ice-free port of Chihli province.

(4) Lungkau, on the northwestern side of Shantung Peninsula.

(5) Shitauwan, at the southeastern point of the Shantung Peninsula.

Six fishing harbors should be constructed along the eastern coast, that is, along the coasts of Kiangsu, Chekiang, and Fukien, as follows:

(6) Shinyangkang, on the eastern coast of Kiangsu, south of the old mouth of the Hoangho.

(7) Luszekang, at the northern point of the Yangtze Estuary.

(8) Changtukang, in the midst of Chusan Archipelago.

(9) Shipu, north of Sammen Bay, east of Chekiang.

(10) Funing, between Foochow and Wenchow, east of Fukien.

(11) Meichow Harbor, north of Meichow Island, between Foochow and Amoy.

Four fishing harbors should be constructed on the southern coast, that is, along the seaboard of Kwangtung and Hainan Island, as follows:

(12) Sanwei, on the eastern coast of Kwangtung, between Hongkong and Swatow.

(13) Sikiang Mouth, This harbor should be on the northern side of Wangkum Island. When the Sikiang Mouth is regulated, the Wangkum Island will be connected with the mainland by a sea wall, so a good harbor site could thus be provided.

(14) Haian, situated at the end of the Luichow Peninsula opposite to Hoihou, on the other side of Hainan Strait.

(15) Yulinkang, a fine natural harbor at the extreme south of the Hainan Island.

These fifteen fishing harbors with the greater ports, numbering 31 in all, will link up the whole coast line of China from Antung, on the Korean border to Yamchow, near the Annam border, providing, on an average, a port for every 100 miles of coast line. This completes my project of seaports and fishing harbors for China.

At first sight objections might be raised that too many seaports and fishing harbors are provided for one country. But I must remind my readers that this one country, China, is as big as Europe and has a population larger than that of Europe. If we take a similar length of the coast line of western Europe we would see that there are many more ports in Europe than in China. Besides, the coast line of Europe is many times longer than that of China, and in every hundred miles of the European coast line there are more than one considerable sized port. Take Holland, for instance. Its whole area is not larger than the hinterland of Swatow, one of our third-class seaports, yet it possesses two first-class ports, Amsterdam and Rotterdam, and numerous small fishing ports. Let us also compare our country with the United States of America in regard to seaports. America has only one fourth the population of China yet the number of ports on her Atlantic coast alone is many times more than the number provided in my plan. Thus, this number of ports for China for the future is but a bare necessity. And I have considered only those that will pay from the beginning so as to adhere strictly to the principle of remuneration that was laid down at the outset of my first program. See Map XVI.

PART V

THE ESTABLISHMENT OF SHIPBUILDING YARDS

When China is well developed according to my programs, the possession of an oversea mercantile fleet, of ships for coastal and inland water transportation, and of a large fishing fleet will be an urgent necessity. Before the outbreak of the late World War, the world's seagoing tonnage was 45,000,000 tons. If China is equally developed industrially, according to the proportion of her population, she would need at least 10,000,000 tons of oversea and coastal shipping for her transportation service. The building of this tonnage must be a part of our industrial development scheme; for cheap materials and labor can be obtained in the country, and so we could build ships for ourselves much cheaper than any foreign country could do for us. And besides the building of a seagoing fleet, we have to build our inland water crafts and fishing fleets. Foreign shipping yards could not do this service for us on account of the impracticability of transporting such numerous small crafts across the ocean. Thus, in any case, China has to put up her own yards to build her inland water crafts and fishing fleets. So the establishment of ship building yards is necessary as well as a profitable undertaking from the beginning. The shipping yards should be established at such river and coastal ports that have the facility of supplying materials and labor. All the yards should be under one central management. Large capital should be invested in the project so as to procure a yearly output of 2,000,000 tons of various kinds of vessels.

All types of vessels should be standardized both in design and equipment. The old and wasteful types of inland water crafts and fishing boats should be replaced by modern efficient designs. The inland water crafts should be designed on the basis of certain standard draughts such as the 2-foot, 5-foot, and 10-foot classes. The fishing trawlers should be standardized into the one-day, the five-day, and the ten-day service classes. The coastal transports should be standardized into the 2,000-, the 4,000-, and the 6,000-ton classes, and for oversea transports we should have standardized ships of 12,000-, 24,000-, and 36,000-ton classes. Thus, the many thousands, of inland water crafts and fishing junks that now ply the rivers, lakes, and coasts of China may be displaced by new and cheaper crafts of a few standard types which could perform better services at less expense.

Int. Development of China, July 20, 1920

PROGRAM IV

In my first and third programs, I have described my plans for the Northwestern Railway System and the Southwestern Railway System. The former is for the purpose of relieving the congestion of population in the coast [coastal] districts and the Yangtze Valley by opening up for colonization the vast unpopulated territory in Mongolia and Sinkiang, as well as of developing the Great Northern Port. The latter is for the purpose of exploiting the mineral resources of Southwestern China, as well as of developing the Great Southern Port—Canton. More railroads will be needed for the adequate development of the whole country. So in this fourth program, I shall deal entirely with railroads which will complete the 100,000 miles proposed in my introductory part of this International Development Scheme. The program will be as follows:

I. The Central Railway System.

II. The Southeastern Railway System.

III. The Northeastern Railway System.

IV. The Extension of the Northwestern Railway System.

V. The Highland Railway System.

VI. The Establishment of Locomotive and Car Factories.

PART I

THE CENTRAL RAILWAY SYSTEM

This will be the most important railway system in China. The area which it serves comprises all of China Proper north of the Yangtze and a part of Mongolia and Sinkiang. The economic nature of this vast region is that the southeastern part is densely populated while the northwestern part is thinly populated, and that the southeastern part possesses great mineral wealth while the northwestern part possesses great potential agricultural resources. So every line of this system will surely pay as the Peking-Mukden line has proved.

With the Great Eastern Port and the Great Northern Port as termini of this system of railroads, I propose that, besides the existing and projected lines in this region, the following be constructed, all of which shall constitute the Central Railway System.

A. The Great Eastern Port-Tarbogotai line.

B. The Great Eastern Port-Urga line.

C. The Great Eastern Port-Uliassutai line.

D. The Nanking-Loyang line.

E. The Nanking-Hankow line.

F. The Sian-Tatung line.

G. The Sian-Ninghsia line.

H. The Sian-Hankow line.

I. The Sian-Chungking line.

J. The Lanchow-Chungking line.

K. The Ansichow-Iden line.

L. The Chochiang-Koria line.

M. The Great Northern Port-Hami line.

N. The Great Northern Port-Sian line.

O. The Great Northern Port-Hankow line.

P. The Hoangho Port-Hankow line.

Q. The Chefoo-Hankow line.

R. The Haichow-Tsinan line.

S. The Haichow-Hankow line.

T. The Haichow-Nanking line.

U. The Sinyangkang-Hankow line.

V. The Luszekang-Nanking line.

W. The Coast line.

X. The Hwoshan-Kashing line.

A. The Great Eastern Port-Tarbogotai Line

This line begins at the Great Eastern Port on the seaboard, and runs in a northwesterly direction to Tarbogotai on the Russian frontier, covering a distance of about 3,000 miles. If Shanghai be the Great Eastern Port, the Shanghai-Nanking Railway will form its first section. But if Chapu be chosen, then this line should skirt the Taihu Lake on the southwest through the cities of Huchow, Changhing, and Liyang to Nanking, then crossing the Yangtze at a point south of Nanking, to Chiautsiao and Tingyuen. Thence, the line turns westward to Show-chow and Yingshang, and enters Honan province at Sintsai. After crossing the Peking-Hankow line at Kioshan and passing Piyang, Tanghsien, and Tengchow, it turns northwestward to Sichwan and Kingtsekwan, and enters the province of Shensi. Ascending the Tan Kiang Valley, it passes through Lungkucha and Shangchow, and crosses the Tsinling Pass to Lantien and Sian, the capital of Shensi, formerly the capital of China. From Sian, it goes westward, following the valley of the Weiho. It passes through Chowchih, Meihsien, and Paoki and enters the province of Kansu at Sancha, thence proceeding to Tsinchow, Kungchang, Titao, and Lanchow, the capital of Kansu. From Lanchow it follows the old highway which leads into Liangchow, Kanchow, Suchow, Yumen, and

Ansichow. Thence it crosses the desert in a northwesterly direction to Hami, where it turns westward to Turfan. At Turfan this line meets the Northwestern Railway System and runs on the latter's track to Urumochi and Manass where it leaves that track and proceeds northwesterly to Tarbogotai on the frontier, crossing the Shair Mountain on the way. This line runs from one end of the country to the other encountering in its entire length of 3,000 miles only four mountain passes, all of which are not impassable for they have been used from time immemorial, as trade highways of Asia.

B. The Great Eastern Port-Urga Line

The line starts from the Great Eastern Port and uses the same track as line (a) as far as Tingyuen, the second city after crossing the Yangtze River at Nanking. From Tingyuen, its own track begins and the line proceeds in a northwesterly direction to Hwaiyuan, on the Hwai River, thence to Mongcheng, Kwoyang, and Pochow. Turning more northward, it crosses the Anhwei border into Honan, and passing through Kweiteh it crosses the Honan border into Shantung. After passing through Tsaohsien, Tingtao, and Tsaochow, it crosses the Hoangho and enters Chihli province. Passing through Kaichow it re-enters Honan to Changteh, thence it follows the Tsingchangho valley, in a northwesterly direction, across the Honan border into Shansi. Here the line enters the northern corner of the vast iron and coal field of Shansi. After entering Shansi, the line follows the river valley to Liaochow and Yicheng, and crosses the watershed into the Tungkwoshui Valley to Yutse and Taiyuan. From Taiyuan, it proceeds northwestward through another rich iron and coal field of Shansi to Kolan. Thence, it turns westward to Poate, where it crosses the Hoangho to Fuku, in the northeastern corner of Shensi. From Fuku, the line proceeds northward, cuts through the Great Wall into the Suiyuan District and crosses the Hoangho to Saratsi. From

Saratsi, the line runs in a northwesterly direction across the vast prairie to Junction A of the Northwestern Trunk Line, where it joins the common track of the Dolon Nor-Urga line to Urga. This line runs from a thickly populated country at one end in Central China to the vast thinly populated but fertile regions of Central Mongolia, having a distance of about 1,300 miles from Tingyuen to Junction A.

C. The Great Eastern Port-Uliassutai Line

Starting from the Great Eastern Port, this line follows line (a) as far as Tingyuen, and line (b) as far as Pochow. At Pochow, it branches off on its own track and proceeds westward across the border to Luye, in Honan. Thence it turns northwestward to Taikang, Tungsu, and Chungmow where it meets the Hailan line and runs in the same direction with it to Chengchow, Jungyang, and Szeshui. From Szeshui it crosses the Hoangho to Wenhsien, thence to Hwaiking and over the Honan border into Shansi. It now passes through Yancheng, Chinshui, and Fowshan to Pingyang where it crosses the Fen River and proceeds to Puhsien and Taning, then westward to the border where it crosses the Hoangho into Shensi. Thence it proceeds to Yenchang, and follows the Yenshui Valley to Yenan, Siaokwan, and Tsingpien. Then running along the south side of the Great Wall, it enters Kansu, and crosses the Hoangho to Ninghsia. From Ninghsia, it proceeds northwestward across the Alashan Mountain to Tingyuanying at the edge of the desert. Thence it proceeds in a straight line northwestward to Junction B of the Northwestern Railway System, where it joins that system and runs to Uliassutai. This part of the line passes through desert and grassland both of which could be improved by irrigation. The distance of this line from Pochow to Junction B is 1,800 miles.

D. The Nanking-Loyang Line

This line runs between two former capitals of China, passes through a very populous and fertile country, and taps a very rich coal field at the Loyang end. It starts from Nanking, running on the common track of lines (a) and (b) and branches off at Hwaiyuan westward to Taiho. After passing Taiho, it crosses the Anhwei border into Honan. Thence it runs alongside the left bank of the Tashaho to Chowkiakow, a large commercial town. From Chowkiakow, it proceeds to Linying where it crosses the Peking-Hankow line thence to Hiangcheng and Yuchow where the rich coal field of Honan lies. After Yuchow it crosses the Sungshan watershed to Loyang where it meets the Hailan line running from east to west. This line is about 300 miles from Hwaiyuan to Loyang.

E. The Nanking-Hankow Line

This line will run alongside the left bank of the Yangtze River, connecting with Kiukiang by a branch line. It starts on the opposite side of Nanking and goes southwest to Hochow, Wuweichow and Anking, the capital of Anhwei province. After Anking, it continues in the same direction to Susung and Hwangmei, where a branch should be projected to Siaochikow, thence across the Yangtze River to Kiukiang. After Hwangmei, the line turns westward to Kwangchi, then northwestward to Kishui, and finally westward to Hankow. It covers a distance of about 350 miles through a comparatively level country.

F. The Sian-Tatung Line

This line starts from Sian and runs northward to Sanyuan, Yaochow, Tungkwan, Yichun, Chungpu, Foochow, Kanchuan, and Yenan, where it meets the Great Eastern Port-Uliassutai line. From Yenan, it turns northeastward to Suiteh, Michih, and Kiachow on the right bank of the Hoangho. Thence it runs along the same bank to the junction of the Weifen River with the Hoangho (on the opposite side), where it crosses the Hoangho to the Weifen Valley and proceeds to Singhsien and Kolan, there crossing the Great Eastern Port-Urga line. From Kolan it proceeds to Wuchai and Yangfang, where it crosses the Great Wall to Sochow and then Tatung there meeting the Peking-Suiyuan line. This line is about 600 miles long. It passes through the famous oil field in Shensi, and the northern border of the northwestern Shansi coal field. At Tatung, where it ends, it joins the Peking-Suiyuan line and through the section from Tatung to Kalgan it will connect with the future Northwestern System which will link Kalgan and Dolon Nor together.

G. The Sian-Ninghsia Line

This line will start from Sian in a northwesterly direction to Kingyanghsien, Shunhwa, and Samshui. After Samshui, it crosses the Shensi border into Kansu at Chengning and then turns west to Ningchow. From Ningchow, it follows the Hwan Valley along the left bank of the river up to Kingyangfu and Hwanhsien, where it leaves the bank and proceeds to Tsingping and Pingyuan, where it meets the Hwan River again and follows that valley up to the watershed. After crossing the watershed, it proceeds to Lingchow, then across the Hoangho to Ninghsia. This line covers a distance of about 400 miles and passes through a rich mineral and petroleum country.

H. The Sian-Hankow Line

This is a very important line connecting the richest portion of the Hoangho Valley with the richest portion of the central section of the Yangtze Valley. It starts from Sian on the track of line (a), crosses the Tsingling and descends the Tankiang Valley as far as Sichwan. At this point, it branches off southward across the border into Hupeh, and following the left bank of the Han River, passes Laohokow to Fencheng, opposite Siangyang. After Fencheng, it follows continuously the same bank of the Han River to Anlu, thence proceeding in a direct line southeastward to Hanchwan and Hankow. This line is about 300 miles long.

I. The Sian-Chungking Line

This line starts from Sian almost directly southward, crosses the Tsingling Mountain into the Han Valley, passes through Ningshen, Shihchuan, and Tzeyang, ascends the Jenho Valley across the southern border of Shensi into the province of Szechwan at Tachuho. Then crossing the watershed of the Tapashan into the Tapingho Valley, it follows that valley down to Suiting and Chuhsien. Thence it turns to the left side of the valley to Linshui and follows the trade road to Kiangpeh and Chungking. The entire distance of this line is about 450 miles through a very productive region and rich timber land.

J. The Lanchow-Chungking Line

Thin [This] line starts from Lanchow southwestward and follows the same route as line (a) as far as Titao. Thence, it branches off and ascends the Taoho Valley across the Minshan watershed into the Heishui Valley following it down to

Kiaichow and Pikow. After Pikow, it crosses the Kansu border into Szechwan and proceeds to Chaohwa, where the Heishuiho joins the Kialing. From Chaohwa, it follows the course of the Kialing River down to Paoning, Shunking, Hochow, and Chungking. The line is about 600 miles long, running through a very productive and rich mineral land.

K. The Ansichow-Iden Line

This line passes through the fertile belt of land between the Gobi Desert and the Altyntagh Mountain. Although this strip of land is well watered by numerous mountain streams yet it is very sparsely populated, owing to the lack of means of communication. When this line is completed, this strip of land will be most valuable to Chinese colonists. The line starts from Ansichow westward to Tunhwang, and skirts the southern edge of the Lobnor Swamp to Chochiang. From Chochiang, it proceeds in the same direction via Cherchen to Iden where it connects with the terminus of the Northwestern System. With this System, it forms a continuous and direct line from the Great Eastern Port to Kashgar at the extreme west end of China. This line from Ansichow to Iden is about 800 miles in length.

L. The Chochiang-Koria Line

This line runs across the desert alongside the lower part of the Tarim River. The land on both sides of the line is well watered and will be valuable for colonization as soon as the railroad is completed. This line is about 250 miles in length and connects with the line that runs along the northern edge of the desert. It is a short cut between fertile lands on the two sides of the desert.

M. The Great Northern Port-Hami Line

This line runs from the Great Northern Port in a northwesterly direction by way of Paoti and Siangho to Peking. From Peking it runs on the same track with the Peking-Kalgan Railway to Kalgan, where it ascends the Mongolian Plateau. Then it follows the caravan road northwestward to Chintai, Bolutai, Sessy, and Tolibulyk. From Tolibulyk, it takes a straight line westward crossing the prairie and desert of both the Inner and Outer Mongolia to Hami where it connects with the Great Eastern Port-Tarbogotai line which runs almost directly west to Urumochi, the capital of Sinkiang. Thus, it will be the direct line from Urumochi to Peking and the Great Northern Port. This line is about 1,500 miles in length, the greater part of which will run through arable land and so when it is completed it will form one of the most valuable railways for colonization.

N. The Great Northern Port-Sian Line

This line will run westward from the Great Northern Port to Tientsin. From here it runs southwestward to Hokien, passing through Tsinghai and Tachen. From Hokien, it runs more westerly to Shentseh, Wuki, and Chengting where it joins the Chengtai line as well as crosses the Kinhan line. From Chengting it takes the same road as the narrow gauge Chengtai line which has to be reconstructed into standard gauge so as to facilitate through trains to Taiyuan and farther on. From Taiyuan it runs southwestward to Kiaocheng, Wenshui, Fenchow, Sichow, and Taning. After Taning it turns westward and crossing the Hoangho, it turns southwestward to Yichwan, Lochwan, and Chungpu where it joins the Sian-Tatung line and runs on the same tracks to Sian. Its length is about 700 miles over very rich and extensive iron, coal, and petroleum fields, as well as productive agricultural lands.

O. The Great Northern Port-Hankow Line

This line starts from the Great Northern Port skirting the coast to Petang, Taku, and Chikow, thence to Yenshan and crosses the Chihli border into Shantung at Loling. From Loling, it goes to Tehping, Linyi and Yucheng where it crosses the Tiestsin〔Tientsin〕-Pukow line, proceeds to Tungchang and Fanhsien, and then crosses the Hoangho to Tsaochow. After Tsaochow it passes the Shantung border into Honan, crossing the Hailan line to Suichow. From Suichow it proceeds to Taikang where it crosses line (c), then to Chenchow and Chowkiakow where it crosses line (d) and thence to Siangcheng, Sintsai, Kwangchow, and Kwangshan. After Kwangshan it crosses the boundary mountain into Hupeh, passing through Hwangan to Hankow. This line is about 700 miles long, running from the Great Northern Port to the commercial center of central China.

P. The Hoangho Port-Hankow Line

This line starts from the Hoangho Port in a southwesterly direction to Pohsing, Sincheng, and Changshan, then across the Kiauchow-Tsinan line to Poshan. Thence it ascends the watershed into the Wen Valley to Taian where it crosses the Tientsin-Pukow line to Ningyang and Tsining. From Tsining it proceeds in a straight line southwestward to Pochow in Anhwei, and Sintsai in Honan. At Sintsai it joins the Great Northern Port-Hankow line to Hankow. The distance of this line from the Hoangho Port to Sintsai is about 400 miles.

Q. The Chefoo-Hankow Line

This line starts at Chefoo of the northern side of the Shantung Peninsula and crosses that Peninsula to Tsimo, on the southern side, via Laiyang and Kinkiakow. From Tsimo it proceeds southwestward across the shallow mud flat at the head of Kiauchow Bay in a straight line to Chucheng. After Chucheng it crosses the watershed into the Shuho Valley to Chuchow and Ichow, then proceeds to Hsuchow where it meets the Tientsin-Pukow line and the Hailan line. From Hsuchow it runs on the same track with the Tientsin-Pukow line as far as Suchow in Anhwei, then branches off to Mongcheng and Yinchow, and crosses the border into Honan at Kwangchow, where it meets the Great Northern Port-Hankow line and proceeds together to Hankow. This line from Chefoo to Kwangchow is about 550 miles in length.

R. The Haichow-Tsinan Line

This line starts from Haichow following the Linhung River to Kwantunpu, then turns westward to Ichow. From Ichow it turns first northward then northwestward, passing by Mongyin and Sintai to Taian. At Taian it joins the Tsinpu line and proceeds in the same track to Tsinan. This line covers a distance, from Haichow to Taian, of about 110 miles, tapping the coal and iron fields of southern Shantung.

S. The Haichow-Hankow Line

This line starts at Haichow in a southwesterly direction, goes to Shuyang and Sutsien, probably in the same route as the projected Hailan line. From

Sutsien it proceeds to Szechow and Hwaiyuan, where it crosses the Great Eastern Port-Urga and Uliassutai lines. After Hwaiyuan it goes to Showchow and Chenyangkwan, thence continuing in the same direction across the southeastern corner of Honan and the boundary mountain into Hupeh, proceeds to Macheng and Hankow, covering a distance of about 400 miles.

T. The Haichow-Nanking Line

This line goes from Haichow southward to Antung then including [inclining] a little south to Hwaian. After Hwaian it crosses the Paoying Lake (which will be reclaimed according to the regulation of the Hwaiho in Part IV, Program II) to Tienchang and Luho, thence to Nanking. Distance, about 180 miles.

U. The Sinyangkang-Hankow Line

This line starts from Sinyangkang to Yencheng, then crossing the Tasung Lake (which will be reclaimed) to Hwaian. From Hwaian it turns southwestward passing over the southeastern corner of the Hungtse Lake (which will also be reclaimed) to Suyi, in Anhwei. After Suyi, it crosses the Tientsin-Pukow line near Mingkwang, to Tingyuen, where it meets lines (b) and (c). After Tingyuen, it proceeds to Liuan and Hwoshan, then crosses the boundary mountain into Hupeh passing through Lotien to Hankow, a distance of about 420 miles.

V. The Luszekang-Nanking Line

This line starts at Luszekang, a fishing harbor to be constructed at the extremity of the northern point of the Yangtze Estuary. From Luszekang it proceeds westward to Tungchow where it turns northwestward to Jukao, and then westward to Taichow, Yangchow, Luho, and Nanking. This line is about 200 miles long.

W. The Coast Line

This line starts at the Great Northern Port, and follows the Great Northern Port-Hankow line as far as Chikow, where it begins its own line. Keeping along the coast, it crosses the Chihli border to the Hoangho Port, in Shantung, then proceeds to Laichow where it takes a straight cut away from the coast to Chaoyuan and Chefoo, thus avoiding the projected Chefoo-Weihsien line. From Chefoo it proceeds southeastward through Ninghai to Wenteng, where one branch runs to Jungcheng and another to Shihtao. The main line turns southwestward to Haiyang and Kinkiakow, where it joins the Chefoo-Hankow line, and follows it as far as the western side of Kiauchow Bay, thence southward to Lingshanwei. From Lingshanwei the line proceeds southwestward along the coast to Jichao, and crosses the Shantung border into Kiangsu, passing Kanyu to Haichow. Thence it proceeds southeastward to Yencheng, Tungtai, Tungchow, Haimen, and Tsungming Island which will be connected with the mainland by the regulation works of Yangtze embankment. From Tsungming trains can be ferried over to Shanghai. This line from Chikow to Tsungming is about 1,000 miles in length.

X. The Hwoshan-Wuhu-Soochow-Kashing Line

This line starts from Hwoshan to Shucheng and Wuwei, then across the Yangtze River to Wuhu. After Wuhu it goes to Kaoshun, Liyang, and Ihing, then crosses over the northern end of Taihu (which will be reclaimed) to Soochow, where it meets the Shanghai-Nanking line. From Soochow it turns southward to Kashing on the Shanghai-Hangchow line. This line runs over very populous and rich districts of Anhwei and Kiangsu provinces, covering a distance of about 300 miles, which will form the greater part of the shortest line from Shanghai to Hankow.

PART II

THE SOUTHEASTERN RAILWAY SYSTEM

This system covers the irregular triangle which is formed by the Coast [coast] line between the Great Eastern and the Great Southern Ports, as the base, by the Yangtze River from Chungking to Shanghai, as one side, and by line (a) of the Canton-Chungking Railway as the other side, with Chungking as the apex. This triangle comprises the provinces of Chekiang, Fukien, and Kiangsi, and a part respectively of Kiangsu, Anhwei, Hupeh, Hunan, and Kwangtung. This region is very rich in mineral and agricultural products, especially iron and coal deposits which are found everywhere. And the whole region is thickly populated. So railway construction will be very remunerative.

With the Great Eastern Port and the Great Southern Port and the second- and third-class ports that lie between the two as termini of this system of railroads, I propose that the following lines be constructed:

A. The Great Eastern Port-Chungking Line.

B. The Great Eastern Port-Canton Line.

C. The Foochow-Chinkiang Line.

D. The Foochow-Wuchang Line.

E. The Foochow-Kweilin Line.

F. The Wenchow-Shenchow Line.

G. The Amoy-Kienchang Line.

H. The Amoy-Canton Line.

I. The Swatow-Changteh Line.

J. The Nanking-Siuchow Line.

K. The Nanking-Kaying Line.

L. The Coast Line Between the Great Eastern and the Great Southern Ports.

M. The Kienchang-Yuanchow Line.

A. The Great Eastern Port-Chungking Line

This line connects the commercial center of western China—Chungking—with the Great Eastern Port in almost a straight route south of the Yangtze River. It starts from the Great Eastern Port and goes to Hangchow, then through Linan, Changhwa, to Hweichow, in Anhwei. From Hweichow it proceeds to Siuning and Kimen, then crosses the border into Kiangsi and passing Hukow reaches Kiukiang. From Kiukiang it follows the right bank of the Yangtze, crosses the Hupeh border to Hingkwochow and then proceeds to Tungshan and Tsungyang, where it passes over the border to Yochow in Hunan. From Yochow it takes a straight line across the Tungting Lake (which will be reclaimed) to Changteh. From Changteh it proceeds up the Liu Shui Valley, passing through Tzeli, and crossing the Hunan border to Hofeng, in Hupeh and then to Shinan and Lichwan. At Shinan a branch should be projected northeastward to Ichang, and at Lichwan another branch should be projected northwestward to Wanhsien, both on the left side of the Yangtze River. After Lichwan it crosses the Hupeh border into Szechwan, passing Shihchu to Foochow, then passes the Wukiang and proceeds along the right side of the Yangtze River as far as lines (a) and (b) of the Canton-Chungking Railway and then crosses together on the same bridge to Chungking on the other side of the river. The length of this line including branches, is about 1,200 miles.

B. The Great Eastern Port-Canton Line

This is a straight line from one first-class seaport to another. It starts from the Great Eastern Port and goes to Hangchow, then turning southwestward, follows the left bank of the Tsien Tang River through Fuyang, Tunglu to Yenchow and Chuchow. Then it proceeds across the Chekiang-Kiangsi border to Kwangsin. From Kwangsin it goes through Shangtsing and Kinki to Kienchang, then proceeds to Nanfeng, Kwangchang, and Ningtu. After Ningtu it proceeds to Yutu, Sinfeng, Lungnan, and crossing the boundary mountain of Kiangsi and Kwangtung, to Changning. Thence via Tsungfa it goes to Canton, covering a distance of about 900 miles.

C. The Foochow-Chinkiang Line

This line starts from Foochow, goes by way of Loyuan and Ningteh to Fuan, and then proceeds across the Fukien-Chekiang border to Taishun, Kingning,

Yunho, and Chuchow. Thence it proceeds to Wuyi, Yiwu, Chukih, and Hangchow. After Hangchow it goes to Tehtsing and Huchow and then crosses the Chekiang border into Kiangsu. Then it proceeds by way of Ihing, Kintan, and Tanyang to Chinkiang. This line is about 550 miles in length.

D. The Foochow-Wuchang Line

This line starts from Foochow and following the left bank of the Min River and passing Shuikow and Yenping reaches Shaowu. After Shaowu, it proceeds across the Fukien border into Kiangsi and then passes through Kienchang and Fuchow to Nanchang, the capital of Kiangsi. From Nanchang it proceeds to Hingkwo, in Hupeh, and passes on to Wuchang, the capital of Hupeh. It covers a distance of about 550 miles.

E. The Foochow-Kweilin Line

This line starts from Foochow, crosses the Min River and proceeds by way of Yungfu, Tatien, Ningyang, and Liencheng to Tingchow. Thence it crosses the Fukien-Kiangsi border to Shuikin. From Shuikin it proceeds to Yutu and Kanchow and then to Shangyiu and Chungyi. After Chungyi it crosses the Kiangsi-Hunan border to Kweiyanghsien and Chenchow, where it crosses the Canton-Hankow line to Kweiyangchow. Thence it continues to Sintien, Ningyuan, and Taochow, where it meets lines (a) and (b) of the Canton-Chungking Railway. After Taochow it turns southward following the Taoho Valley to the Kwangsi border and then crossing it, proceeds to Kweilin. This line covers a distance of about 750 miles.

F. The Wenchow-Shenchow Line

This line begins from the new Wenchow Port and follows the left bank of the Wukiang as far as Tsingtien. From Tsingtien it proceeds to Chuchow and Suenping and turns westward across the Chekiang border to Yushan in Kiangsi. After Yushan it goes to Tehsing, Loping, and then skirting the southern shore of Poyang Lake, goes through Yukan to Nanchang, the capital of Kiangsi. From Nanchang it proceeds to Juichow, Shangkao, and Wantsai, then crosses the Kiangsi border to Liuyang in Hunan, and Changsha, the capital of Hunan. After Changsha it goes to Ningsiang, Anhwa, and Shenchow where it connects with line (a) of the Canton-Chungking Railway, and with the Shasi-Singyi line. This line covers a distance of about 850 miles.

G. The Amoy-Kienchang Line

This line starts from the new port of Amoy and goes to Changtai, then following the Kiulungkiang to Changping, Ningyang, Tsingliu, and Kienning. After Kienning it proceeds across the Kiangsi border to Kienchang, where it connects with the Great Eastern Port—Canton line, the Foochow-Wuchang line, and the Kienchang-Yuanchow line. This line covers a distance of about 250 miles.

H. The Amoy-Canton Line

This line starts at the new port of Amoy, and proceeds to Changchow, Nantsing, and Siayang, where it crosses the Fukien border to Tapu, in Kwangtung. From Tapu it goes to Tsungkow, Kaying, Hinning, and Wuhwa. After Wuhwa it crosses the watershed between the Hankiang and the Tungkiang rivers to Lungchun [lungchuan], then following the Tungkiang down to Hoyun, it crosses another watershed to Lungmoon, Tsengshin and Canton. This line covers a distance of about 400 miles.

I. The Swatow-Changteh Line

This line starts from Swatow, proceeds to Chaochow, Kaying, and then crosses the Kwangtung border to Changning in Kiangsi. From Changning it crosses the watershed into Kungkiang Valley and follows that river down to Hweichang and Kanchow. From Kanchow it proceeds to Lungchuan, Yungning, and Lienhwa, where it crosses the Kiangsi border into Hunan. After that, it proceeds to Chuchow and Changsha, the capital of Hunan. From Changsha it goes to Ningsiang, Yiyang, and Changteh where it ends, connecting with the Great Eastern Port—Chungking line, and the Shasi-Singyi line. This line covers a distance of about 650 miles.

J. The Nanking-Siuchow Line

This line starts from Nanking and runs along the right bank of the Yangtze to Taiping, Wuhu, Tungling, Chichow, and Tungliu. After Tungliu it passes over the Anhwei border into Kiangsi, at Pengtseh, and goes to Hukow. At Hukow it meets the Great Eastern Port—Chungking line and crosses the bridge together with that line to the projected Poyang Port. From the Poyang Port it runs along the west shore of the Poyang Lake through Nankang and Wucheng to Nanchang, where it meets the Wenchow-Shenchow and Foochow-Wuchang lines. From Nanchang it proceeds up the Kan Kiang Valley, via Linkiang to Kian, where it crosses the projected Kienchang-Yuanchow line. After Kian, it proceeds to Kanchow where it crosses the Foochow-Kweilin line. Thence it goes to Nankanghsien and Nanan. After Nanan it crosses the boundary mountain, Tayuling, into Kwangtung at Nanyung, thence passes through Chihing to Siuchow, where it meets the Canton-Hankow line. This line covers a distance of about 800 miles.

K. The Nanking-Kaying Line

This line starts from Nanking, proceeds to Lishui and Kaoshun and then crosses the Kiangsu border into Anhwei at Suencheng. From Suencheng it proceeds to Ningkwo and Hweichow. After Hweicbow it crosses the Anhwei border into Chekiang, passing through Kaihwa, Changshan, and Kiangshan, and leaving Chekiang enters Fukien at Pucheng. From Pucheng it proceeds via Kienningfu to Yenping where it crosses the Foochow-Wuchang line and then goes through Shahsien and Yungan to Ningyang, where it meets the Foochow-Kweilin and Amoy-Kienchang lines. From Ningyang it proceeds to Lungyen and Yungting, then joining the Amoy-Canton line at Tsungkow proceeds together to Kaying, its terminus. This line runs over a distance of about 750 miles.

L. The Coast Line Between the Great Eastern and the Great Southern Ports

This line starts from the Great Southern Port—Canton— proceeds in the same direction as the Canton-Kowloon line as far as Shelung and then goes its own way following the course of the Tungkiang River to Waichow. From Waichow it proceeds to Samtochuck, Haifung, and Lukfung, then turning northeastward goes to Kityang and Chaochow. After Chaochow it goes to Jaoping, then crossing the Kwangtung-Fukien border to Chaoan. Thence it proceeds to Yunsiao, Changpu, Changchow, and Amoy. From Amoy it proceeds to Chuanchow, Hinghwa, and Foochow, the capital of Fukien. After Foochow it proceeds in the same direction as the Foochow-Chinkiang line, as far as Fuan, then turns eastward to Funing, and northward to Futing. After Futing it crosses the Fukien border into Chekiang and proceeds through Pingyang to Wenchow. At Wenchow it crosses the Wukiang and proceeds to Lotsing, Hwangyen, and Taichow. Thence, it proceeds through Ninghai to Ningpo, its own terminus, where it connects with the Ningpo-Hangchow line, thus linking it up with the Great Eastern Port via Hangchow. This line covers a distance from Canton to Ningpo of about 1,100 miles.

M. The Kienchang-Yuanchow Line

This line starts from Kienchang and runs through Yihwang, Loan, Yungfeng, and Kishui to Kian, where it crosses the Nanking-Siuchow line. After Kian it proceeds to Yungsin and Lienhwa where it meets the Swatow-Changteh line. Thence it crosses the Kiangsi border into Hunan, at Chaling, then through Anjen to Hengchow where it crosses the Canton-Hankow line. From Hengchow the line proceeds to Paoking where it crosses line (a) of the Canton-Chungking Railway then westward to Yuanchow, its terminus, where it joins with the Shasi-Singyi line. This line covers a distance of about 550 miles.

The total length of this Southeastern Railway System is about 9,000 miles.

PART III

THE NORTHEASTERN RAILWAY SYSTEM

This system will cover the whole of Manchuria, a part of Mongolia, and a part of Chihli province—an area of nearly 500,000 square miles, with a population of 25,000,000. This region is surrounded by mountains on three sides and opens on the south to the Liaotung Gulf. Amidst these three mountain ranges lies a vast and fertile plain drained by three rivers—the Nonni on the north, the Sungari on the northeast, and the Liaoho on the south. This part of China was once regarded as a desert, but since the completion of the Chinese Eastern Railway it has been found to be the most productive soil in China. It supplies the whole of Japan and a part of China with nitrogenous food in the form of soya bean. This bean, the wonderful properties of which were early discovered by the Chinese, contains the richest nitrogenous substance among vegetables and has been used as a meat substitute for many thousand years. Vegetable milk is extracted from this bean, and from this milk various kinds of preparations are made. The extraction from this bean has been proved by modern chemists to be richer than any kind of meat. The Chinese and the Japanese have used this kind of artificial meat and milk from time immemorial. Recently food administrators in Europe and America have paid great attention to this meat substitute, while the export of soya bean to Europe and America has steadily increased. This Manchu Mongolian plain is destined to be the source of the world's supply of soya bean. Besides soya bean, this plain also produces a great quantity of various kinds of grains, and supplies the entire Eastern Siberia with wheat. The Manchurian mountains are exceedingly rich in timber and minerals—gold being especially found in great quantities in many localities.

Railway construction in this region has proved to be a most profitable undertaking. At present there are already three railway systems tapping this rich country, viz., the Peking-Mukden line, the best paying railroad in China, the Japanese South-Manchurian Railway, also a very remunerative line, and the Chinese Eastern Railway, the best paying portion of the whole Siberian system. Besides these, there are many lines projected by the Japanese. In order to develop this rich region properly a network of railways should be projected.

Before dealing with the separate lines of this network of railways, I should like to propose a center for them, just as the spider's nest is to a cobweb. I shall name this central city "Tungchin", the Eastern Mart, which should be situated at a point southwest of the junction of the Sungari and Nonni rivers, about 110 miles west by south from Harbin, and will be in a more advantageous position than the latter. This new city will be the center not only of the railway system but also of the inland water communication when the Liaoho-Sungari Canal is completed. With the projected city of Tungchin as a center, I propose the following lines:

A. The Tungchin-Hulutao line.

B. The Tungchin-Great Northern Port line.

C. The Tungchin-Dolon Nor line.

D. The Tungchin-Kerulen line.

E. The Tungchin-Moho line.

F. The Tungchin-Korfen line.

G. The Tungchin-Yaoho line.

H. The Tungchin-Yenchi line.

I. The Tungchin-Changpeh line.

J. The Hulutao-Jehol-Peking line.

K. The Hulutao-Kerulen line.

L. The Hulutao-Hailar line.

M. The Hulutao-Antung line.

N. The Moho-Suiyuan line.

O. The Huma-Chilalin or Shihwei line.

P. The Ussuri-Tumen-Yalu-Coast line.

Q. The Linkiang-Dolon Nor line.

R. The Chikatobo-Sansing or Ilan line.

S. The Sansing or Ilan-Kirin line.

T. The Kirin-Dolon Nor line.

A. The Tungchin-Hulutao Line.

This is the first line that radiates from this projected Manchurian railway center, and is the shorter of the two direct lines that lead to the ice-flee ports on the Liaotung-Chihli Gulf. It runs almost parallel to the South Manchurian Railway, the distance between the two lines being about 80 miles at the northern end, converging to 40 miles at Sinmin, and diverging again after that point. According to the original agreement with the former Russian Government, no parallel line within 100 miles was allowed to be built. But such restriction must be abolished under this new International Development Scheme for the benefit of all concerned. This line starts from Tungchin, and proceeds southward across the vast Manchurian plain by Changling, Shuangshan, Liaoyuan, and Kangping, to Sinmin in a straight line covering a distance of about 270 miles. After Sinmin, the line joins the Peking-Mukden Railway and runs on the same track for a distance of about 130 miles to Hulutao.

B. The Tungchin-Great Northern Port Line

This line is the second that radiates from this railway center direct to a deep water ice-free seaport. It starts from Tungchin, proceeding in a southwesterly direction, passes Kwangan, midway between Tungchin and the West Liaoho, and many other small settlements before it crosses the Liaoho. After crossing the Liaoho, it enters the mountainous regions of the Jehol district by a valley to Fowsin, a hsien city, and crosses the watershed into the Talingho Valley. After passing through the Talingho Valley, the line crosses another watershed into the Luan Valley by a branch of the same river. Then it penetrates the Great Wall and proceeds to the Great Northern Port by way of Yungping and Loting. The whole length of this line is about 550 miles, the first half of which is on level land and the second half in mountainous country.

C. The Tungchin-Dolon Nor Line

This is the third line that radiates from the railway center and proceeds nearly in a westerly direction across the plain to Taonan where it crosses the projected Aigun-Jehol line (Japanese), and also meets the termini of two other projected lines, the Changchun-Taonan and the Tsengkiatun-Taonan (Japanese). After Taonan, the line turns more southward by skirting along the foothills of the southeastern side of the Great Khingan range where vast virgin forests and rich minerals are found. Then it passes through the upper Liaoho Valley formed by the Great Khingan Mountain on the north, and the Jehol Mountain on the south and through the towns of Linsi and Kingpang to Dolon Nor, where it meets the trunk line of the Northwestern Railway system. This line covers a distance of about 480 miles, a great part of which is on level land.

D. The Tungchin-Kerulen Line

This is the fourth line that radiates from the Tungchin Railway center. It runs in a northwesterly direction almost parallel with the Harbin-Manchuli line of the Chinese Eastern Railway, the distance between the two lines varying from 100 to 130 miles. The line starts from Tungchin on the north side of the junction of the Nonni and Sungari rivers and proceeds westward across the Nonni River to Talai, and then turns northwestward across the plain into the valley of the north branch of the Guileli River. After entering the valley, it follows the stream up to its source, then crosses the Great Khingan Mountain watershed into the Mongolian Plain by the Khalka River, and follows the right bank of this river to the north end of Bor Nor Lake. Thence it turns directly westward to the Kerulen River, and follows the south bank of the river to Kerulen. This line covers a distance of about 630 miles.

E. The Tungchin-Moho Line

This is the fifth line that radiates from this railway center. It starts from the north side of the junction of the Nonni and Sungari rivers, and proceeds northwestward across the northern end of the Great Manchurian Plain to Tsitsiha. At Tsitsiha, it joins the projected Chinchow-Aigun line and proceeds together northwestward alongside the left bank of the Nonni River as far as Nunkiang where it separates from the other. Thence it resumes the northwesterly direction and proceeds into the upper Nonni Valley until the headwater is reached. Then it crosses the northern extremity of the Great Khingan Range to Moho, where it joins the terminus of the Dolon Nor-Moho line. This line is about 600 miles long. About a quarter of this length runs on the plain, the second quarter runs along the lower Nonni Valley, the third along the Upper Valley, and the fourth runs in mountainous but gold-bearing regions, where only physical difficulties are to be expected.

F. The Tungchin-Korfen Line

This is the sixth line from the railway center. It also starts on the northern side of the Nonni-Sungari junction, and proceeds across the plain by the cities Chaotung and Tsingkang. After Tsingkang it crosses the Tungkun River, proceeds to Hailun, and then, ascending the Tungkun Valley, crosses the watershed of the Little Khingan Mountain. Thence it descends into the Korfen Valley and proceeds by Chelu to Korfen on the right bank of the Amur River. This line covers a distance of 350 miles, two thirds of which run on comparatively level land and one third in mountainous district. This is the shortest line from Tungchin to the Amur River and the Russian territory on yonder side.

G. The Tungchin-Yaoho Line

This is the seventh line that radiates from this railway center. It starts from the northern side of the Nonni-Sungari junction and traverses the plain on the left of the Sungari River by Chaochow, then crosses the Chinese Eastern Railway, and the Hulan River to Hulan. After Hulan, it proceeds to Payen, Mulan, and Tungho, then crosses the Sungari River to Sansing, now called Ilan. Thence it proceeds into the Wokan Valley and crosses the watershed by Chihsingshitse and Takokai into the Noloho Valley and passing by various villages and towns along this river to Yaohohsien, ends at the junction of the Noloho and the Ussuri River. This line covers a distance of 500 miles in very fertile country.

H. The Tungchin-Yenchi Line

This is the eighth line that radiates from this railway center. It starts from the eastern side of the Nonni-Sungari junction and proceeds in a southeasterly direction on the right side of the Sungari River to Fuyu or Petunai and various towns along the road on the same side of the river until it comes across the Harbin-Talien Railway, then turns away from the road and proceeds eastward to Yushu and Wuchang. After Wuchang, the line turning more southward, proceeds to Fengtechang and then follows the same direction to Omu. At Omu, it crosses the Mutan River, then proceeds to Liangshuichuan and Shehtauho, where it joins the Japanese Hweining-Kirin line and proceeds together to Yenchi. This line covers a length of about 330 miles through very rich agricultural and mineral country.

I. The Tungchin-Changpeh Line

This is the ninth line that radiates from the Tungchin railway center. It starts from the south side of the Nonni-Sungari junction and proceeds in a southeasterly direction across the plain to Nungan. After Nungan, it crosses the Itung River and proceeds continuously in the same direction across several branches of the same river to Kiudaichan, where it joins the Changchun-Kirin line and proceeds together as far as Kirin. After Kirin, it goes its own way following the right bank of the Sungari River in a southeasterly direction to the junction of Lafaho River and turns southward along the same bank of the Sungari to Huatien. After Huatien, it continues in the same course up to Toutaokiang, as far as Fusung, then turns southeastward into the Sunghsiangho Valley and proceeds upward to the Changpeh Shan watershed by skirting the south side of the Celestial Lake, then turns southward following the Aikiang River to Changpeh on the Korean frontier. This line covers a distance of about 330 miles. Some great difficulties are to be overcome in the last portion of the line where it crosses the Changpeh watershed.

J. The Hulutao-Jehol-Peking Line

With this line I shall begin to deal with a new group of the Northeastern Railway System which will make Hulutao, the ice-free port on the Liaotung Gulf as their center and terminus. This, the first line, starts from Hulutao and proceeds westward up the Shaho Valley to Sintaipienmen. Thence it crosses the mountainous district through Haiting, Mangniuyingtse, and Sanshihkiatse to Pingchuan, and continues in the same direction to Jehol or Chengteh. After Jehol, it proceeds by the old imperial highway to Lwanping, then turns southwestward to Kupehkow where it penetrates the Great Wall. Thence it follows the same highway through Miyun and Shunyi to Peking. This line covers a distance of about 270 miles.

K. The Hulutao-Kerulen Line

This is the second line of the Hulutao radiation. It starts from this seaport and proceeds northward through the mountainous region of Jehol by Kienping and Chihfeng. Thence, the line follows the highway across the Upper Valley of Liaoho to Chianchang, Sitoo, Takinkou, and Linsi. After Linsi, it proceeds up the Lukiako Valley and crosses the watershed at the southern extremity of the Great Khingan Mountain, through Kanchumiao and Yufuchih. Then it proceeds to Payenbolak, Uniket, and Khombukure where it joins with the Dolon Nor-Kerulen line and proceeds together to Kerulen. This line up to Khombukure covers a distance of about 450 miles, tapping a very rich mineral, timber, and agricultural country.

L. The Hulutao-Hailar Line

This, the third line, starts from Hulutao and proceeds by way of Chinchow along the west side on the Talingho River to Yichow, where it crosses the Talingho to Chinghopienmen and Fowsin. After Fowsin, the line goes northward to Suitung, thence, crossing the Siliaoho to Kailu, it proceeds between the Great and Little Fish Lakes to Kinpan and Tachuan. Then it proceeds across the Great Khingan Mountain into the Oman Valley and follows the same river to Hailar. This line covers a distance of about 600 miles passing through rich mineral and agricultural land and virgin forests.

M. The Hulutao-Antung Line

This, the fourth line, starts from Hulutao and proceeding northeastward, follows the course of the projected Liaoho-Hulutao Canal, and then goes eastward to Newchwang and Haicheng. From there it proceeds southeastward to Simuchen, where it joins the Antung-Mukden line and proceeds together to Antung on the Korean border. This line covers a distance of about 220 miles. This together with the Hulutao-Jehol-Peking line will make the shortest line from Antung and beyond, i. e., Korea, to Peking.

N. The Moho-Suiyuan Line

With this as the first I am going to deal with another group of lines in this system. These will be the circumferential lines which link up the radii from the Tungchin center in two semicircles, the outer and the inner. This Moho-Suiyuan line starts from Moho and proceeds along the right bank of the Amur River to Ussuri, Omurh, Panga, Kaikukang, Anlo, and Woshimen. After this point, the river bends more southward and the line follows the same bend to Ankan, Chahayen, Wanghata, and Huma. From Huma, it proceeds to Sierhkenchi, Chila, Manchutun, Heiho, and Aigun where it meets the terminus of the Chinchow-Aigun line. After Aigun, the line turns more eastward to Homolerhchin, Chilirh, and Korfen where it meets the terminus of the Tungchin-Korfen line. Thence it proceeds to Wuyun, Foshan, and Lopeh. After Lopeh, it goes to Hokang at the junction of the Amur and Sungari. At this point, the line crosses the Sungari River to Tungkiang and proceeds to Kaitsingkow, Otu and Suiyuan where it ends. This line covers a distance of 900 miles running all its way through the gold-producing region.

O. The Huma-Chilalin or Shihwei Line

This is merely a branch of the Moho-Suiyuan line. It starts from Huma and follows the Kumara River passing by the Taleitse Gold Mine and Wapalakow Gold Mine. Then it proceeds up the Kumara River in a westerly and southwesterly direction to its southern source and there it crosses the watershed into the Halarh Valley, thence descending the valley to Chilalin or Shihwei. This line covers a distance of about 320 miles running in an extremely rich gold district.

P. The Ussuri-Tumen-Yalu-Coast Line

This, the second line of the outer semicircle, starts by continuing the first line at Suiyuan, and proceeds along the left bank of the Ussuri River, passing Kaulan, Fuyeu, and Minkang, to Yaoho, where it meets the terminus of the Tungchin-Yaoho line. From Yaoho, it runs parallel to the Russian Ussuri Railway on the east side of the river as far as Fulin. After Fulin, it parts from the Russian line by turning westward following the Mulingho River to Mishan on the northwestern corner of the Hanka Lake. Thence it goes to Pinganchin, turns southward alongside the boundary line and crosses the Harbin-Vladivostok line at Siusuifen Station to Tungning. After Tungning, it continues the same southward course alongside the boundary line to a point between Szetaukow and Wutaukow, then turns westward to Hunchun, and northwestward to Yenchi where it meets the projected Japanese Hweining-Kirin line. From Yenchi, it follows the Japanese line to Holung, and proceeds southwestward by the left side of the Tumen River across the watershed into the Yalu Valley, where it meets the Tungchin-Changpeh line. After Changpeh it turns westward and northwestward following the right bank of the Yalu to Linkiang, thence southwestward, still following the right bank of the Yalu, to Tsianhsien and then continues in the same direction, along the Yalu bank, to Antung, where it meets the Antung-Mukden Railway. After Antung, it proceeds to Tatungkow at the mouth of the Yalu, thence along the coast to Takushan and Chwangho, then westward through Situn and Pingfangtien to join the South Manchurian Railway at Wukiatun. This line covers a distance of 1,100 miles, which runs from end to end right along the southeastern boundary of Manchuria.

Q. The Linkiang-Dolon Nor Line

This is the third line of the outer semicircle of the Tungchin railway center, and connects the radiating lines south of the center. It starts from Linkiang at the southwestward turn of the Yalu River, and proceeds across the mountainous region passing by Tunghwa, Hingking, and Fushun, to Mukden, where it crosses the South Manchurian Railway. From Mukden, it goes together with the Peking-Mukden line as far as Sinmin, where it crosses the Tungchin-Hulutao line and proceeds northwestward through Sinlihtun to Fowsin. After Fowsin the line enters the hilly district of the upper Liaoho Valley, and proceeds to Chihfeng, after passing through numerous small villages and camping places in this vast pasture. After Chihfeng the line proceeds through the Yinho Valley by Sanchotien, Kungchuling, and Tachientse, to Famuku, thence follows the Tulakanho to Dolon Nor, covering a distance of about 500 miles.

R. The Chikatobo-Sansing or Ilan Line

This is the first line of the inner semicircle which connects the radiating lines from the Tungchin railway center on the northeast. It starts from Chikatobo on the upper reach of the Amur, and proceeds eastward and southeastward through many valleys and mountains of the Great Khingan Range to Nunkiang. After Nunkiang, it goes in a more southerly direction to Keshan, thence to Hailun, and then crosses the Sungari to Sansing or Ilan. This line covers a distance of about 700 miles, passing through an agricultural and gold-producing country.

S. The Sansing or Ilan-Kirin Line

This is the second line of the inner semicircle. It starts from Sansing and proceeds southwestward along the right bank of the Mutan River through Tauchan, Erchan, Sanchan, and Szuchan, to Chengtse where it crosses the Harbin-Vladivostok line. Then it goes to Ninguta, after crossing over the Mutan River from right to the left bank. After Ninguta it proceeds southwestward passing through Wungcheng, Lanchichan, Talachan, and Fungwangtien, to Omu. From Omu it joins the Japanese Hweining-Kirin line and proceeds westward to Kirin. This line covers a distance of about 200 miles, along the fertile Mutan Valley.

T. The Kirin-Dolon Nor Line

This is the third line of the inner semicircle in the Tungchin system. It starts from Kirin and follows the old highway westward to Changchun where it meets the termini of the Chinese Eastern Railway from the north and the Japanese South Manchurisn [Manchurian] Railway from the south. After Changchun, it proceeds across the plain to Shuangshan where it meets the Tungchin-Hulutao line and the Japanese Szupingkai-Chengkiatun-Taonan line. From Shuangshan, it crosses the Liao River to Liaoyuan, thence it traverses the vast plain, crossing the Tungchin-Great Northern Port line and goes to Suitung where it meets the Hulutao-Hailar line. After Suitung, it proceeds up the Liao Valley where it comes across the Hulutao-Kerulen line and then crosses the watershed to

Dolon Nor where it ends. This line covers a distance of 500 miles.

This completes the cobweb system of the projected North-Eastern Railway. The total length of this entire system is about 9,000 miles.

PART IV

THE EXTENSION OF
THE NORTHWESTERN RAILWAY SYSTEM

The Northwestern Railway System covers the region of Mongolia, Sinkiang, and a part of Kansu, an area of 1,700,000 square miles. This territory exceeds the area of the Argentine Republic by 600,000 square miles. Argentina is now the greatest source of the world's meat supply, while the Mongolian pasture is not yet developed, owing to the lack of transportation facilities. As Argentina has superseded the United States in supplying the world with meat, so the Mongolian pasture will some day take the place of Argentina, when railways are developed and cattle raising is scientifically improved. Thus the construction of railroads in this vast food-producing region is an urgent necessity as a means of relieving the world from food shortage. In the first program of this International Development Scheme, I proposed 7,000 miles of railways for this vast and fertile region, for the purpose of developing the Great Northern Port, and relieving the congested population of southeastern China. But this 7,000 miles of railways form merely a pioneer line. In order to develop this virgin continent properly, more railways have to be constructed. Therefore in this plan, namely, the Extension of the Northwestern Railway System, I propose the following lines:

A. The Dolon Nor-Kiakata line.

B. The Kalgan-Urga-Tannu Ola line.

C. The Suiyuan-Uliassutai-Kobdo line.

D. The Tsingpien-Tannu Ola line.

E. The Suchow-Kobdo line.

F. The Northwestern Frontier line.

G. The Tihwa or Urumochi-Ulankom line.

H. The Gaskhiun-Tannu Ola line.

I. the Uliassutai-Kiakata line.

J. The Chensi or Barkul-Urga line.

K. The Suchow-Urga line.

L. The Desert Junction-Kerulen line.

M. The Khobor-Kerulen-Chikatobo line.

N. The Wuyuan-Taonan line.

O. The Wuyuan-Dolon Nor line.

P. The Yenki-Ili line.

Q. The Ili-Hotien line.

R. The Chensi-Kashgar line and its branches.

A. The Dolon Nor-Kiakata Line

This line starts from Dolon Nor and proceeds in a northwesterly direction, following the caravan road across the vast pasture to Khorkho, Kuoto, and Suliehto. After Suliehto, it crosses the boundary line into Outer Mongolia by the same road to Khoshentun, Lukuchelu, and Yangto. Thence it crosses the Kerulen River to Otukunkholato, and enters the hilly region where it crosses the Kerulen watershed and the Chikoi watershed. The water from the Kerulen watershed flows into the Amur, and thence into the Pacific Ocean, while the water from the Chikoi watershed flows into Lake Baikal, and thence to the Arctic Ocean. After crossing the Chikoi watershed, it follows a branch of the Chikoi River to Kiakata. This line covers a distance of about 800 miles.

B. The Kalgan-Urga-Tannu Ola Line

This line starts from Kalgan at the Great Wall, and proceeds northwestward up the plateau, crosses a range of hills into the Mongolian prairie, and goes to Mingan, Boroldshi, Ude, and Khobor, where it crosses the Dolon Nor-Urumochi trunk line. After Khobor, it proceeds across the vast and rich pasture of Mubulan, then proceeds in a straight line through Mukata and Nalaiha to Urga. From Urga, it goes into the hilly district crossing Selenga Valley to a point opposite the southern end of Lake Kos Gol, and then turns northward across a range of mountains to Khatkhyl on the southern shore of Kos Gol. After Khatkhyl, it skirts Kos Gol Lake along the western shore for some distance, then turns northwestward and westward, following the course of the Khua Kem River to a point near its exit at the frontier line, then turns southwestward up the Kemtshik Valley to its headwater, passes through Pakuoshwo, and ends at the boundary line between the Russian and Chinese territories. This line covers a distance of about 1,700 miles.

C. The Suiyuan-Uliassutai-Kobdo Line

This line starts from Suiyuan in the northwestern corner of Shansi, and proceeds in a northwesterly direction across the hilly country into the Mongolian pasture to Tolibulyk, where it crosses the Great Northern Port-Hami line, and the Great Eastern Port-Urga line. After Tolibulyk, it proceeds in a straight line in the same direction passing through Barunsudshi to the capital of Tuchetu. Thence it continues in the same straight line northwestward to Gorida. After Gorida, it follows the caravan road to Kolitikolik where it crosses the Great Northern Port-Urumochi trunk line. From Kolitikolik, the line turns northwestward, then westward and proceeds across many streams and valleys and passes by many small towns to Uliassutai. At Uliassutai, it crosses the B Junction-Frontier branch of the Great Eastern Port-Urumochi line. After Uliassutai, the line proceeds westward following the trade road, passes through Khuduku, Bogu, Durganor, and Sakhibuluk to Kobdo. Thence the line turns northwestward to Khonga, Ukha, and Clegei, then westward to Beleu and ends at the frontier. This line is about 1,500 miles long.

D. The Tsingpien-Tannu Ola line

This line starts from Tsingpien at the Great Wall, on the northern border of Shensi, proceeds through the Ordos country by Bonobalgasun, Orto, and Shinchao, and then crosses the Hoangho to Santaoho. From Santaoho, it proceeds across Charanarinula Mountain into Mongolian prairie in a northwesterly direction to Kurbansihata where it crosses the Peking-Hami line, then it goes to Unikuto and Enkin, where it crosses the Great Northern Port-Urumochi line. After Enkin, the line enters into a valley and watered district, proceeds northward to Karakorum, and then turns northwestward across various streams and valleys of the tributary of the Selenga River by Sabokatai and Tsulimiau. After Tsulimiau, it proceeds in the same direction across the Selenga River, follows its branch, the Telgir Morin River, up to its source and crosses the watershed into Lake Teri Nor. Then it follows the outlet of the Teri Nor to the Khua Kem River, where it ends by joining the Kalgan-Urga-Tannu Ola line. This line covers a distance of about 1,200 miles.

E. The Suchow-Kobdo Line

This line starts from Suchow in a northwesterly direction penetrating the Great Wall at Chiennew, and proceeds to the coal field, about 150 miles from Suchow. Then it goes to Habirhaubuluk and Ihatoli. A short way from this place the line comes across the Peking-Hami line and then proceeds to Balaktai. After this the line passes a bit of pure desert to Timenchi. After entering the hilly and watered country it proceeds to Gaskhiun where it crosses the Great Northern Port-Urumochi trunk line. After Gaskhiun, it proceeds to Wolanhutok, Tabateng, and Tabutu where it joins the Kucheng and Kobdo highway and following it, proceeds to Kobdo, through Batokuntai and Sutai. Here the line ends, covering a distance of about 700 miles.

F. The Northwestern Frontier Line

This line starts from Ili following the Urumochi-Ili line to Santai, on the eastern side of Zairam Lake, then proceeds northeastward by itself to Tuszusai on the west side of Ebi Lake. After Tuszusai it proceeds to Toli where it crosses the Central Trunk line, that is, the Great Eastern Port-Tarbogotai line. Thence it goes to Nanlukotai and Stolokaitai by passing through a vast forest and a rich coal field. From Stolokaitai, the line follows the highway and proceeds to Chenghwaszu, the capital of Altai province. Thence it crosses a mountain range by the Urmocaitu Pass into the Kobdo Valley, and follows the course of the Kobdo River to Beleu where it joins the Suiyuan-Kobdo line and proceeds to Clegei. From Clegei, it proceeds by itself to Tabtu via Usungola and Ulankom. At Tabtu, it joins the other line again and proceeds together to the Khua Kem River in the Tannu Ola district. It then turns eastward ascending the river to the junction of the Bei Kem and Khua Kem Rivers, then starts again on its own course, following the former river and proceeds up to its source in a northeasterly direction ending at the frontier. This line covers a distance of about 900 miles.

G. The Tihwa or Urumochi-Ulankom Line

This line starts from Tihwa following the Dolon Nor trunk line to Fowkang, then proceeds by its own route almost northward through Chipichuan to Khorchute. From Khorchute, it turns northeastward and proceeds across a hilly district to Kaiche, then to Turhuta, where it crosses a branch line from Junction C of the Great Northern Port-Urumochi line. After Turhuta, it turns northward, proceeds up the Pakaningale Valley to Zehoshita, and then crosses the Tilikta Pass. Thence it turns northeastward proceeding across the newly cultivated country to Kobdo. After Kobdo, it proceeds through a fertile plateau, by crossing many rivers and skirting many lakes to Ulankom, where it ends by joining the Northwestern Frontier line. It covers a distance of about 550 miles.

H. The Gaskhiun-Tannu Ola Line

This line starts from Gaskhiun and proceeds northeastward across a hilly and watered country through Hatonhutuk and Talangjoleu, to Pornulu. After Pornulu, the line proceeds across the Sapkhyn Valley by Huchirtu and Porkho to Uliassutai where it meets the Suiyuan-Kobdo, and the Great Eastern Port-Uliassutai lines. After Uliassutai, the line proceeds northward to a quite new country by first crossing the headwaters of Selenga, then the headwaters of the Tess River. In the Tess Valley the line crosses a vast virgin forest. After emerging from this forest it proceeds northwestward across the watershed into the Khua Kem Valley in Tannu Ola and ends by joining the Northwestern Frontier line. This line covers a distance of about 650 miles.

I. The Uliassutai-Kiakata Line

This line starts from Uliassutai and runs on the track of the Gaskhiun-Tannu Ola line, until it reaches the Eder River, a branch of the Selenga. Then, turning off eastward, it begins its own course and proceeds downward following the course of the Eder River, crossing the Tsingpien-Tannu Ola line, to the junction of this river with the Selenga. There it joins the Kalgan-Urga-Tannu Ola line and proceeds together eastward in the common track for some distance until the other line turns southeastward, when this line turns northeastward following the Selenga down to Kiakata. This line covers a distance of about 550 miles, running through a fertile valley.

J. The Chensi or Barkul-Urga Line

This line starts from Chensi or Barkul and proceeds northeastward across a cultivated region through Tutaku to Urkesiat. After Urkesiat, it crosses the Suchow-Kobdo line, then traverses the vast pasture on the north side of the Gobi Desert to Suchi and Dalantura. Thence it turns more northward across the Great Eastern Port-Uliassutai line, and the Dolon Nor-Urumochi line to Tashunhutuk. After this point the line crosses the Suiyuan-Uliassutai line at Ologai and proceeds over the watershed into the Selenga Valley where it crosses the Tsingpien-Tannu Ola line at Sabokatai. From here it turns eastward across a hilly and watered region to Urga. This line covers a distance of about 800 miles.

K. The Suchow-Urga Line

This line starts from Suchow and proceeds by Kinta to Maumu, and then follows the Taoho or Edsina River, which waters this strip of oasis, to the lakes. Thence it crosses the Gobi Desert, where it meets the crossing lines of the Peking-Hami and the Great Eastern Port-Uliassutai railways and with them forms a common junction. From this junction it proceeds across desert and pasture lands to another railway crossing which is formed by the Suiyuan-Kobdo and Tsingpien-Tannu Ola lines, also forming a common junction together. Thence it proceeds into pasture land through Hatengtu and Tolik to Sanintalai, where it crosses the Dolon Nor-Urumochi line. After Sanintalai, the line proceeds through Ulanhoshin and many other small towns an [and] encampments to Urga. This line covers a distance of about 700 miles. One thirds of this length is through the desert and the other two thirds through watered pasture land.

L. The Desert Junction-Kerulen Line

This line starts from the Desert Junction, proceeds northeastward to the pastural land and crosses the Tsingpien-Tannu Ola line south of Ulan Nor Lake. Thence it proceeds to the Tuchetu Capital where it crosses the Suiyuan-Kobdo line. After the Tuchetu Capital it goes across a pasture to Junction A. From Junction A, it proceeds to Ulanhutuk and Chientingche, then crosses the Kalgan-Tannu Ola line to Zesenkhana. From Zesenkhana, the line follows the course of the Kerulen River down in a northeasterly direction to the city of Kerulen, where it crosses the Dolon Nor-Kerulen line, and meets the Kerulen-Tungchin line. This line covers a distance of about 800 miles.

M. The Khobor-Kerulen-Chikatobo Line

This line starts from Khobor, the crossing junction of the Dolon Nor-Urumochi, and the Kalgan-Urga-Tannu Ola lines, and proceeds northeastward across a vast pasture to Khoshentun, where it crosses the Dolon Nor-Kiakata line. After Khoshentun, it proceeds in the same direction across a similar pasture to Kerulen, where it crosses the Dolon Nor-Kerulen line. Then it proceeds first along the right bank of the Kerulen River, then crosses to the left side, and passes along the northwestern side of Hulan Lake. After Hulan Lake, the line crosses the Chinese Eastern Railway, and the Arguna River, then proceeds along the right bank of the river to Chikatobo, where the line ends by joining the Dolon Nor-Moho and the Chikatobo-Sansing lines. This line covers a distance of about 600 miles. The first half of it runs on dry land and the second half on watered land.

N. The Wuyuan-Taonan Line

This line starts from Wuyuan at the northwest bend of the Hoangho and proceeds northeastward across the Sheiten Ula Mountain and pasture to Tolibulyk, where it meets the crossing junction of three lines—the Peking-Hami line, the Suiyuan-Kobdo line, and the Great Eastern Port-Urga line. From Tolibulyk the line proceeds continuously in the same direction across a pasture to Khobor where it meets the crossing junction of the Dolon Nor-Urumochi and the Peking-Urga lines, and also the terminus of the Khobor-Kerulen line. After Khobor the line turns more eastward and runs across the Dolon Nor-Kiakata line midway to Khombukure, where it crosses the Dolon Nor-Kerulen and the Hulutao-Kerulen lines. From Khombukure the line proceeds to Dakmusuma, where it crosses the Dolon Nor-Moho line. Thence it goes eastward across the Great Khingan Mountain to Tuchuan, then turns southeastward to Taonan, where it ends. This line covers a distance of about 900 miles.

O. The Wuyuan-Dolon Nor Line

This line starts from Wuyuan and proceeds northeastward across the Sheiten Ula Mountain to Maomingan, where it crosses the Great Eastern Port-Urga line. Then it proceeds across the vast pasture and the Suiyuan-Kobdo line to Bombotu, where it passes over the Peking-Hami line. After Bombotu, the line turns eastward and proceeds across the Kalgan-Urga-Tannu Ola line, then goes to Dolon Nor, where it ends by joining the Dolon Nor-Mukden-Linkiang line, which forms a direct route from the upper Hoangho Valley to the rich Liaoho Valley. This line covers a distance of about 500 miles.

P. The Yenki-Ili Line

This line starts from Yenki or Karashar, and proceeds northwestward across the mountain pass into the Ili Valley. It then follows the Kunges River downward, in a westerly direction, traversing a most fertile valley, to Ining and Kuldja or Ili, the principal city of the Ili district near the Russian border, where it joins the Ili-Urumochi line. This line covers a distance of about 400 miles.

Q. The Ili-Hotien Line

This line starts from Ili or Kuldja, proceeds southward across the Ili River, then eastward along the left side of the river and then southeastward and southward to Bordai. From here it turns southwestward into Tekes Valley and proceeding upward crosses the Tekes River to Tienchiao and then ascends the mountain pass. After the mountain pass the line turns southeastward, traverses a vast coal field and then turns southwestward to Shamudai, where it crosses the Turfan-Kashgar line. From Shamudai it turns southward across the fertile zone of the north side of the Tarim Valley, to Bastutakelak. Then it proceeds southwestward to Hotien passing by on the way many small settlements in the fertile zone of the Hotien River which flows across the desert. At Hotien the line meets the Kashgar-Iden line. After Hotien the line proceeds upward to the highland south of the city and ends at the frontier. This line covers a distance of about 700 miles.

R. The Chensi-Kashgar Line and Its Branches

This line starts from Chensi and proceeds southwestward along the Tienshan pasture through Yenanpao, Shihkialoong, and Taolaitse to Chikoching, then along the Tienshan forest through Wutungkwo, Tungyenchi, Siyenchi, and Olong to Sensien, where it crosses the Central Trunk line. After Sensien it proceeds along the northern edge of the Tarim Desert through Lakesun City and Shehchuan to Hora, where it crosses the Cherchen-Koria line. From Hora the line proceeds along the course of the Tarim River, passing by many new settlements, fertile regions, and virgin forests, to Bastutakelak, where it crosses the Ili-Hotien line. Thence it goes through Pachu to Kashgar where it meets the Urumochi-Iden line. After Kashgar it proceeds northwestward to the frontier where it ends. Attached to this line are two branches. The first branch proceeds from Hora southwestward through many oases to Cherchen. The second proceeds from Pachu southwestward along the Yarkand River to Sache and then westward to Puli near the frontier. This line including the branches covers a distance of about 1,600 miles. The total length of this entire system is about 16,000 miles. See general map.

PART V

THE HIGHLAND RAILWAY SYSTEM

This, the last part of my railway program, is the most difficult and most expensive undertaking of its kind; consequently, it must be the least remunerative of all the railway enterprises in China. So no work should be attempted in this part until all the other parts are fully developed. But when all the other parts are well equipped with railways then railway construction in this highland region will also be remunerative, despite the difficulties and the highly expensive work in construction.

The highland region consists of Tibet, Kokonor, and a part of Sinkiang, Kansu, Szechwan, and Yunnan, an area of a about 1,000,000 square miles. Tibet is known to be the richest country in the world for gold deposits. Furthermore the adjacent territories possess rich agricultural and pastoral lands. This vast region is little known to the outside world. The Chinese call Tibet "the Western Treasury", for, besides gold, there are other kinds of metals especially copper, in great quantities. Indeed the name of the Western Treasury is most appropriately applied to this unknown region. When the world's supply of precious metals are exhausted, we have to resort to this vast mineral bearing region for supply. So railways will be necessary at least for mining purposes. I therefore propose the following lines:

A. The Lhasa-Lanchow line.

B. The Lhasa-Chengtu line.

C. The Lhasa-Tali-Cheli line.

D. The Lhasa-Taklongshong line.

E. The Lhasa-Yatung line.

F. The Lhasa-Laichiyaling line.

G. The Lhasa-Nohho line.

H. The Lhasa-Iden line.

I. The Lanchow-Chochiang line.

J. The Chengtu-Dzunsasak line.

K. The Ningyuan-Cherchen line.

L. The Chengtu-Menkong line.

M. The Chengtu-Yuankiang line.

N. The Suifu-Tali line.

O. The Suifu-Mengting line.

P. The Iden-Gortok line.

A. The Lhasa-Lanchow Line

This is the most important line of this system for it connects the capital city of Tibet—a vast secluded region with several millions of people—with the central trunk line of the country. The route which it passes through is inhabitable and is already slightly inhabited in the region between the ends of the proposed line. So it will probably be a paying line from the beginning. This line starts from Lhasa, following the old imperial highway in a northward direction and porceeds〔proceed〕 by Talong to Yarh, which lies on the southeastern side of Tengri Nor Lake. After Yarh, the line turns more eastward and proceeds across the watershed from the Sanpo Valley to the Lukiang Valley by the Shuangtsu Pass. Thence turning more eastward the line proceeds across the headwater of the Lukiang to that of the Yangtze by passing many valleys, streams, and mountain passes. Then it crosses the main body of the Upper Yangtze, which is here known as the Kinshakiang, over the Huhusair Bridge. After crossing the bridge, it turns southeastward, then eastward across the Yangtze Valley into the Hoangho Valley, where it passes through many small towns and encampments into the Starry Sea region. At the Starry Sea, the line passes between the lakes of Oring Nor and Tsaring Nor. Thence it turns northeastward across the southeast valley of the Zaidam region, and returns into the Hoangho Valley again. Then it proceeds through Katolapo and various towns to Dangar, now called Hwangyuan, situated near the border between Kansu and Kokonor. After Dangar, the line turns southeastward following the course of the Sining River, proceeds downward through a very rich valley and passes through Sining, Nienpai, and hundreds of small towns and villages to Lanchow. This line covers a distance of 1,100 miles.

B. The Lhasa-Chengtu Line

This line starts from Lhasa and proceeds northeastward on the former imperial highway by Teking and Nanmo to Motsukungchia. Thence it turns southeastward and northeastward to Giamda. From Giamda, the line turns northward, then northeastward where it proceeds through the Tolala Pass to Lhari. After Lhari the line goes in an easterly direction and passes Pianpa, Shihtuh, and many small towns to Lolongchong. Thence it crosses the Lukiang by the Kayu Bridge and then turns northeastward to Kinda and Chiamdo. After Chiamdo the line instead of following the imperial high way southeastward to Batang, turns northeastward, following another trade route, and proceeds to Payung at the northwestern corner of Szechwan. From Payung, it proceeds across the Kinshakiang over the bridge near Sawusantusze. The line then turns southeastward, enters the Ichu Valley and proceeds downward to Kantzu on the Yalung River. Thence it proceeds to Chango and Yinker, to Badi on the Great Golden River, and Mongan on the Little Golden River. After Mongan, the line goes through the Balan Pass to Kwanhsien, and entering the Chengtu Plain, reaches Chengtu by

Pihsien. This line covers a distance of about 1,000 miles.

C. The Lhasa-Tali-Cheli Line

This line starts from Lhasa by the same track as the Lhasa-Chengtu line as far as Giamda. From Giamda, it proceeds by its own track southeastward, following a branch of the Sanpo River to Yulu, where this branch joins its main stream. After Yulu, it follows the left bank of the Sanpo River passing by Kongposaga to Timchao. From Timchao, the line truns away from the Sanpo River and proceeds in an eastward direction to Timchong city, Ikung, Kuba, and Shuachong. After Shuachong, the line proceeds southeastward to Lima, thence eastward to Menkong on the Lukiang. From Menkong, the line turns southward and goes along the right bank of the Lukiang passing Samotung to Tantau. Then crossing the Lukiang, it proceeds across the watershed through Gaiwa village to the Lantsang (or Mekong) River, and to Hsiaoweisi beyond it. After Hsiaoweisi, it follows the river bank to the Chenghsin Copper Mine, thence it turns away from the river and proceeds by Hosi, Erhyuan, Tengchow, and Shangkwang to Tali. From Tali, the line proceeds to Hsiakwan, Fengyi, Menghwa, and then meets the Lantsang River again at Paotien. Thence it follows the left bank southward right through to Cheli, where it ends. This line covers a distance of 900 miles.

D. The Lhasa-Taklongshong Line

This line starts from Lhasa and proceeds southward by way of Teking to the Sanpo River where turning eastward it follows the left bank of the river to Sakorshong. After crossing the Sanpo River to Chetang, it proceeds southward by Chikablung, Menchona, Tawang, Dhirangjong to Taklongshong and continues farther on until it reaches the Assam frontier. This line covers a distance of 200 miles.

E. The Lhasa-Yatung Line

This line starts from Lhasa and proceeds southwestward by Chashih following the former imperial highway by Yitang and Kiangli to Chushui. At Chushui, it crosses to Sanpo River over the Mulih Bridge to Chakamo on the south side, thence to Tamalung, Paiti, Tabolung, and Nagartse. After Nagartse, the line turns westward to Jungku, Lhalung, and Shachia. At Shachia, the line leaves the former imperial highway and turns southwestward again and proceeds via Kula to Yatung at the Sikkim border. This line covers a distance of 250 miles.

F. The Lhasa-Laichiyaling Line and Branches

This line starts from Lhasa and proceeds northwestward by Chashih following the former imperial road to Little Taking, and westward to Yangpachin and Sangtolohai. Thence turning southwestward, it proceeds to Namaling and Tangto, and crosses the Sanpo River at Lhaku. After Lhaku, the line turns westward to Shigatse, the second important city in Tibet whence it proceeds in the same direction to Chashihkang, Pangcholing, and Lhatse all on the right side of the Sanpo River. From Lhatse, a branch line starts southwestward via Chayakor and Dingri to Niehlamuh on the Nepal border. The main line, however, crosses to the left side of the Sanpo River and proceeds on the same highway via Nabringtaka to Tadum where another branch line proceeds southwestward to the Nepal border. The main line continues northwestward via Tamusa and Choshan to Gortok, thence turning westward it proceeds to Laichiyaling on the Sutlej River and ends on the Indian border. This line, including the two branches, covers a distance of

850 miles.

G. The Lhasa-Nohho Line

This line starts from Lhasa and runs in the same track as line (f) to Sangtolohai where it proceeds by its own line northwestward to Teching, Sangchashong, and Taktung. Thence, it enters into the richest gold field in Tibet and through Wengpo, Tulakpa, Kwangkwei, and Ikar reaches Nohho, where the line ends. It covers a distance of 700 miles.

H. The Lhasa-Iden Line

This line starts from Lhasa, following the common track of lines (f) and (g) to the southwestern corner of Tengri Lake, whence it proceeds by its own track northwestward by Lungmajing, Tipoktolo and four or five other small places to Sari. After sari, the line penetrates a vast tract of uninhabited land to Pakar and Suketi. Thence crossing the mountain passes and descending from the highland to the Tarim Basin through sorkek to Yasulakun, the line joins the Cherchen-Iden railway of the Northwestern System and proceeds on the same track to Iden. This line covers a distance of 700 miles.

I. The Lanchow-Chochiang Line

This line starts from Lanchow, on the same track of the Lhasa-Lanchow line as far as the southeastern corner of the Lake Kokonor. Thence it proceeds on its own track by skirting along the southern shore of Lake Kokonor to Dulankit, where it turns southwestward to Dzunsasak. From Dzunsasak, the line proceeds in a westerly course along the southern side of the Zaidam Swamp, and passes

Tunyueh, Halori, and Golmot to Hatikair. After Hatikair, the line turns northwestward by Baipa, Nolinjoha, to Orsinte. Thence turning more northward, it proceeds across the mountain range by Tsesinvitusuik and Tuntunomik to Chochiang, where it ends by joining the Ansi-Iden and Chochiang-Koria lines, covering a distance of 700 miles.

J. The Chengtu-Dzunsasak Line

This line starts from Chengtu and proceeds to Kwanhsien on the track of the Lhasa-Chengtu line, thence northward on its own track by Wenchuan, to Mauchow. Then, it proceeds northwestward following the course of the Minkiang to Sungpan. After Sungpan, it ascends the Min Valley passing Tungpi to Shangleyao, where it crosses the watershed from the Yangtze River side to that of the Hoangho. Thence the line proceeds to Orguseri, and following a branch of the Hoangho to the northwestern turn of its main stream, it proceeds along its right bank via Chahuntsin to Peilelachabu. There it crosses the Hoangho to the northwest turn of the old imperial road, where it joins the Lhasa-Lanchow line and proceeds as far as Lanipar. Then turning northwestward, it proceeds by its own line to Dzunsasak, where it ends by joining the Lanchow-Chochiang line. This line covers a distance of 650 miles.

K. The Ningyuan-Cherchen Line

This line starts from Ningyuan and proceeds in a northwestward direction via Hwaiyuanchen to the Yalungkiang. Then it ascends along the left side of that river to Yakiang, and crossing to the right side of that river it proceeds by the old post road to Siolo, where it turns away from the river and follows the same post road to Litang. From Litang it proceeds in the same direction but follows another road to Kangtu, on the left side of the Kinshakiang. Following the same side of the river, it proceeds to Sawusantusze, where it crosses the Lhasa-Chengtu line. After Sawusantusze, the line continues in the same direction and follows the same side of the Kinshakiang via Tashigompa, to the Huhusair Bridge, where it crosses the Lhasa-Lanchow line. Then following a northern branch of the Kinshakiang to its source and crossing the watershed, it proceeds along the caravan road by Hsinszukiang and Olokung to Cherchen, where it ends, covering a distance of about 1,350 miles. This is the longest line of this system.

L. The Chengtu-Menkong Line

This line starts from Chengtu and proceeds southwestward by Shuangliu, Hsintsin, Mingshan, to Yachow. From Yachow, it turns northwestward and proceeds to Tienchuan, then westward to Tatsienlu, Tunyolo, and Litang. After Litang, the line proceeds southwestward through Batang and Yakalo, to Menkong, covering a distance of about 400 miles of very mountainous country.

M. The Chengtu-Yuankiang Line

This line starts from Chengtu on the same track of the Chengtu-Menkong line, proceeds to Yachow and thence by its own track in the same direction via Jungching, to Tsingliu. After Tsingliu, the line proceeds southward through Yuehsi to Ningyuan, where it meets the head of the Ningyuan-Cherchen line. After Ningyuan, it goes to Kwaili, then crosses the Kinshakiang to Yunnanfu where it crosses the Canton-Tali line. From Yunnanfu, it proceeds along the west side of the Kunming Lake to Kunyang, and through Hsinshing, Hsingo, to Yuankiang, where the line ends by joining the Canton-Szemao line. It covers a distance of about 600 miles.

N. The Suifu-Tali Line

This line starts from Suifu and proceeds along the left bank of the Yangtze River to Pingshan and Lupo. After Lupo, it turns away from the river in a southwesterly direction and scale [scales] the Taliangshah Mountains to Ningyuan, where it crosses the Chengtu-Yuankiang line and meets the termini of the Canton-Ningyuan line and the Ningyuan-Cherchen line. Thence continuing in the same direction, it crosses the Yalungkiang to Yenyuan and Yungpeh. After Yungpeh, the line turns more southward, across the Kinshakiang to Sincheng and thence to Tali, where it ends by meeting the Canton-Tali line and the Lhasa-Tali line. It covers a distance of about 400 miles.

O. The Suifu-Mengting Line

This line starts from Suifu on the same track as the Suifu-Tali line as far as Lupo. From Lupo, it goes on its own track across the Yangtze River here known as the Kinshakiang, and follows the right side of that river upward to its southward bend where it crosses the Chengtu-Yuankiang line, to Yuanmow. From Yuanmow, it proceeds to Tsuyung, where it crosses the Canton-Tali line, thence to Kingtung. After Kingtung, it proceeds southwestard [southwestward] across the Lantsangkiang or Mekong River, to Yunchow, thence turning southwestward, it follows a branch of the Lukiang River to Mengting and ends on the frontier. This line covers a distance of about 500 miles.

P. The Iden-Gortok Line

This line starts from Iden, and proceeds southward along the Keriya River to Polu, thence following the caravan road up the highland to Kuluk. From Kuluk, it proceeds south westward via Alasa and Tunglong to Nohho, it skirts aroung the eastern end of the Nohtso-Lake to Rudok and proceeds southwestward to Demchok, on the Indus River. From Demchok, it proceeds southeastward following the Indus River up to Gortok, where it ends by joining the Lhasa-Laichiyaling line. This line covers a distance of about 500 miles. This highland system totals about 11,000 miles.

PART VI

THE ESTABLISHMENT OF LOCOMOTIVE AND CAR FACTORIES

The railways projected in the Fourth Program will total 62,000 miles; and those in the First and the Third Programs about 14,000 miles. Besides these, there will be double tracks in the various trunk lines, which will make up a grand total of no less than 100,000 miles, as stated in the preliminary part of these programs. With this 100,000 miles of railways to be constructed in the coming ten years, the demands for locomotives and cars will be tremendous. The factories of the world will be unable to supply them, especially at this juncture of reconstruction after the great World War. So the establishment of locomotive and car factories in China to supply our own demands of railway equipment will be a necessary as well as a profitable undertaking. China possesses unlimited supplies of raw materials and cheap labor. What we need for establishing such factories is foreign capital and experts. What amount of capital should be invested in this project I have to leave to experts to decide.

I suggest that four large factories should be started simultaneously at the beginning—two on the coast and two on the Yangtze. Of those on the coast, one should be at the Great Northern Port, and the other at the Great Southern Port—Canton. Of those on the Yangtze, one should be at Nanking and the other at Hankow. All ⟨the⟩ four are in centers of both land and water communication, where skilled labor can easily be obtained. They are also near our iron and coal fields. Besides these four great factories, others should be established at suitable centers of iron and coal fields when our railways will be more developed.

All the factories should be under one central control. The locomotives and cars of our future railways should be standardized so as make possible the interchange of parts of machinery and equipment. We should also adopt the standard gauge, that is, the 4 feet $8\frac{1}{2}$ inch gauge which has been adopted by most of the railways of the world. In fact, almost all the railways hitherto built in China are of this gauge. The purpose of the propsoed standardization is to secure the highest efficiency as well as the great [greatest] economy.

PROGRAM V

In the preceeding [preceding] four programs, I dealt exclusively with the development of the key and basic industries. In this one, I am going to deal with the development of the *main* group of industries which need foreign help. By the main group of industries, I mean those industries which provide every individual and family with the necessaries and comforts of life. Of course, when the key and basic industries are developed, the various other industries will spontaneously spring up all over the country, in a very short time. This had been the ease [case] in Europe and America after the industrial revolution. The development of the key and the basic industries will give plenty of work to the people and will raise their wages as well as their standard of living. When wages are high, the price for necessaries and comforts of life will also be increased. So the rise in wages will be accompanied by the rise in the cost of living. Therefore, the aim of the development of some of the main group of industries is to help reduce the high cost of living when China is in the process of international development, by giving to the majority of the people plenty of the essentials and comforts of life as well as higher wages.

It is commonly thought that China is the cheapest country to live in. This is a misconception owing to the common notion of measuring everything by the value of money. If we measure the cost of living by the value of labor then it will be found that China is the most expensive country for a common worker to live in. A Chinese coolie, a muscular worker, has to work 14 to 16 hours a day in order to earn a bare subsistence. A clerk in a shop, or a teacher in a village school cannot earn more than a hundred dollars a year. And the farmers after paying their rents and exchanging for a few articles of need with their produce have to live from hand to mouth. Labor is very cheap and plentiful but food and commodities of life are just enough to go round for the great multitude of the four hundred millions in China in an ordinary good year. In a bad year, a great number succumb to want and starvation. This miserable condition among the Chinese proletariat is due to the non-development of the country, the crude methods of production and the wastefulness of labor. The radical cure for all this is industrial development by foreign capital and experts for the benefit of the whole nation. Europe and America are a hundred years ahead of us in industrial development; so, in order to catch up in a very short time we have to use their capital, mainly their machinery. If foreign capital cannot be gotten, we will have to get at least their experts and inventors to make for us our own machinery. In any case, we must use machinery to assist our enormous man-power to develop our unlimited resources.

In modern civilization, the material essentials of life are five, namely, food, clothing, shelter, means of locomotion, and the printed page. Accordingly I will formulate this program as follows:

I. The Food Industry.

II. The Clothing Industry.

III. The Housing Industry.

IV. The Motoring Industry.

V. The Printing Industry.

PART I

THE FOOD INDUSTRY

The food industry should be treated under the following headings:

A. The Production of Food.

B. The Storage and Transportation of Food.

C. The Preparation and Preservation of Food.

D. The Distribution and Exportation of Food.

A. The Production of Food

Human foods are drived from three sources: the land, the sea and the air. By far the most important and greatest in quantity consumed is aerial food of which oxygen is the most vital element. But this aerial food is abundantly provided by nature, and no human labor is needed for its production except that which is occasionally needed for the airman and the submariner. So this food is free to all. It is not necessary for us to discuss it here. The production of food from the sea which I have already touched upon when I dealt with the construction of fishing harbors and the building of fishing crafts, will also be left out here. It is the specific industries in the production of food from land, which need foreign help that are to be discussed here.

China is an agricultural country. More than half of its population is occupied in the work of producing foot [food]. The Chinese farmer is very skillful in intensive cultivation. He can make the land yield to its utmost capacity. But vast tracts of arable lands are lying waste in thickly populated districts for one cause or other. Some are due to lack of water, some to too much of it and some to the "dog in the manager" system—the holding up of arable land by speculators and land sharks for higher rents and prices.

The land of the eighteen provinces alone is at present supporting population of four hundred millions. Yet there is still room for development which can make this same area of land yield more food if the waste land be brought under cultivation, and the already cultivated land be improved by modern machinery and scientific methods. The farmers must be protected and encouraged by liberal land laws by which they can duly reap the fruits of their own labor.

In regard to the production of food in our international development scheme [International Development Scheme], two necessary undertakings should be carried out which will be profitable at the same time:

(1) A scientific survey of the land.

(2) The establishment of factories for manufacturing agricultural machinery and implements.

(1) A scientific survey of the land. China has never been scientifically surveyed and mapped out. The administration of land is in the most chaotic state and the taxation of land is in great confusion, thus causing great hardships on the poor peasants and farmers. So, under any circumstance, the survey of land is the first duty of the government to execute. But this could not be done without

foreign help, owing to lack of funds and experts. Therefore, I suggest that this work be taken up by an international organization. This organization should provide the expenses of the work by a loan, and should carry out the work with the required number of experts and equipmen [equipment]. How much will be the expenses for the survery and what is the amount of time required and how large on[an] organization is sufficient to carry on the work, and whether aerial survey by aeroplanes be practical for this work are questions which I shall leave to experts to decide.

When the topographical survey is going on a geological survey may be carried out at the same time so as to economize expenses. When the survey work is done and the land of each province is minutely mapped out, we shall be able to readjust the taxation of the already cultivated and improved land. As regards the waste and uncultivated lands we shall be able to determine whether they are suitable for agriculture, for pasture, for forestry, or for mining. In this way, we can estimate their value and lease them out to the users for whatever production that is most suitable. The surplus tax of the cultivated land and the proceeds of waste land will be for the payment of the interest and principal of the foreign loan. Besides the eighteen provinces, we have a vast extent of agricultural and pastoral lands in Manchuria, Mongolia, and Sinkiang, and a vast extent of pastural land in Tibet and Kokonor. They will have to be developed by extensive cultivation under the colonization scheme, which is alluded to in the first program.

(2) The establishment of factories for manufacturing agricultural machinery and implements. When the waste land is rechaimed [reclaimed], cultivated land improved and waste labor set to work on the land, the demands for agricultural machinery and implements will be very great. As we have cheap labor and plenty of iron and coal, it is better and cheaper for us to manufacture than to im-

port the implements and machinery. For this purpose, much capital should be invested, and factories should be put up in industrial centers or in the neighborhood of iron and coal fields, where labor and material could be easily found.

B. The Storage and Transportation of Food

The most important foodstuff to be stored and transported is grain. Under the present Chinese method, the storage of grain is most wasteful for if kept in large quantities it is often destroyed by insects or damaged by weather. It is only in small quantities and by great and constant care that grains can be preserved for a certain period of time. And the transportation of grains is also most expensive for the work is mostly done on man's shoulders. When the grains reach the waterway it is [they are] carried in a most makeshift way without the least semblance of ⟨a⟩ system. If the method of storing and transporting of grain be improved, a great economic saving could be accomplished. I propose that a chain of grain elevators be built all over the country and a special transport fleet be equipped all along the waterways by this International Development Organization. What will be the capital for this project and where the elevators should be situated have yet to be investigated by experts.

C. The Preparation and Preservation of Food

Hitherto the preparation of food is entirely by hand with a few primitive implements. The preservation of food is either by salt or sun heat. Mills and cannery method are scarely [scarcely] known. I suggest that a system of rice mills should be constructed in all the large cities and towns in the Yangtze Valley and South China where rice is the staple food. Flour mills should be put up in all large cities and towns north of the Yangtze Valley, where wheat, oats, and cereals other than rice are the staple food. All these mills should be under one central management so as to produce the best economic results. What amount of capital should be invested in this mill system by this international development scheme 〔International Development Scheme〕 should be subjected to detailed investigation.

In regard to the preservation of food, fruits, meats and fishes should be preserved by canning or by refrigeration. If the canning industry is developed there will be created a great demand for tinplates. Therefore the establishment of tinplate factories will be necessary and also profitable. Such factories should be situated near the iron and tin fields. There are many localities in South China where tin, iron, and coal are situated near each other, thus providing ready materials for the factories. The tinplate factories and the canneries should be combined into the one enterprise so as to secure ⟨the⟩ best economic results.

D. The Distribution and Exportation of Food

In ordinary good years, China never lacks food. There is a common saying in China that "One year's tilling will provide three year's wants". In the richer sections of the country, the people generally reserve three or four years 〔years'〕 food supply in order to combat a bad year. But when China is developed and organized as an economic whole, one year's food reserve should be kept in the country for the use of the local people and the surplus should be sent out to the industrial centers. As the storage and transportation of food will be under a central management so the distribution and exportation of food should be under the same charge. All surplus grains of a country district should be sent to the nearest town for storage and each town or city should store one year's food. All the staple food should be sold only at cost price to the inhabitants according to their number, by the distributing department. And the surplus food should be exported to foreign countries where it is wanted and where the highest price can be obtained by the export department under the central management. Thus the surplus food will not be wasted as hitherto under the prohibition law. The proceeds of this export will surely amount to a huge sum which will be used in the payment of the interest and principal of the foreign loan invested in this undertaking.

We cannot complete this part of the food industry without giving special consideration to the Tea and Soya indurstries. The former, as a heverage [beverage], is well known throughout and used by the civilized world and the latter is just beginning to be realized as an importnt [important] foodstuff by the scientists and food administrators. Tea, the most healthy and delicious beverage of mankind, is produced in China. Its cultivation and preparation form one of the most important industries of the country. Once China was the only country that supplied the world with tea. Now China's trade has been wrested away from her by India and Japan. But the quality of the Chinese tea is still unequalled. The Indian tea contains too much tannic acid, and the Japanese tea lacks the flavor which the Chinese tea possesses. The best tea is only obtainable in China—the native land of tea. China lost her tea trade owing to the high cost of its production. The high cost of production is caused by the inland tax as well as the export duty and by the old methods of cultivation and preparation. If the tax and duty are done away with and new methods introduced, China can recover her former position in this trade easily. In this International Development Scheme, I suggest that a system of modern factories for the preparation of tea should be established in all the tea districts, so that the tea should be prepared by machinery instead of, as hitherto, by hand. Thus the cost of production can be greatly reduced and the quality improved. As the world's demand for tea is daily increasing and will be more so by a dry United States of America, a project to supply cheaper and better tea will surely be a profitable one.

Soya bean as a meat substitute was discovered by the Chinese and used by the Chinese and the Japanese as a staple food for many thousands of years. As meat shortage has been keenly felt in carnivorous countries at present, a solution must be found to relieve it. For this reason I suggest that in this International Development Scheme we should introduce this artificial meat, milk, butter and cheese to Europe and America, by establishing a system of soya been [bean] factories in all the large cities of those countries, so as to provide cheap nitrogenous food to the western people. Modern factories should also be established in China to replace those old and expensive methods of production by hand, so as to procure better economic results as well as to produce better commodities.

PART II

THE CLOTHING INDUSTRY

The principal materials for clothes are silk, linen, cotton, wool and animal skins. I shall accordingly deal with them under the following headings:

A. The Silk Industry.

B. The Linen Industry.

C. The Cotton Industry.

D. The Woolen Industry.

E. The Leather Industry.

F. The Manufacturing of Clothing Machinery.

A. The Silk Industry

Silk is a Chinese discovery and was used as a material for clothes for many thousands of years before the Christian Era. It is one of the important national industries of China. Up to recent time, China was the only country that supplied silk to the world. But now this dominant trade has been taken away from China by Japan, Italy and France, because those countries have adopted scientific methods for silk culture and manufacture, while China still uses the same old methods ⟨as those⟩ of many thousands [thousand] years ago. As the world's demand for silk is increasing daily, the improvement of the culture and manufacture of silk will be a very profitable undertaking. In this International Development Scheme, I suggest first that scientific bureaus be established in every silk district to give directions to the farmers and to provide healthy silk-worm eggs. These bureaus should be under central control. At the same time, they will act as collecting stations for cocoons so as to secure a fair price for the farmers. Secondly, silk filiatures [filatures] with up-to-date machinery should be established in suitable districts to reel the silk for home as well as for foreign consumption. And lastly, modern factories should be put up for manufacturing silk for both home and foreign markets. All silk filiatures [filatures] and factories should be under a single national control and will be financed with foreign capital and supervised by experts to secure the best economic results and to produce better and cheaper commodities.

B. The Linen Industry

This is an old Chinese industry. In southern China there is produced a kind of very fine linen in the form of ramie, known as China-grass. This fiber if treated by modern methods and machinery becomes almost as fine and glossy as silk. But in China, so far as I know, there is not yet such new method [methods] and machinery for the manufacturing of this linen. The famous Chinese grass-cloth is manufactured by the old method of handlooms. I propose that new methods and machinery be introduced into China by this International Development Organization to manufacture this linen. A system of modern factories should be established all over the ramie-producing districts in South China where raw materials and labor are obtainable.

C. The Cotton Industry

Cotton is a foreign product which was introduced into China centuries ago. It became a very important Chinese industry during the handloom age. But after the import of foreign cotton goods into China, this native handicraft industry was gradually killed by the foreign trade. So, great quantities of raw cotton are exported and finished cotton goods are imported in large quantities into China. What an anomaly when we consider the enormous, cheap labor in China. However a few cotton mills have been started recently in treaty ports which have made enormous profits. It is reported that during the last two or three years most of the Shanghai cotton mills declared a dividend of 100 per cent [percent] and some even 200 per cent [percent]! The demand for cotton goods in China is very great but the supply falls short. It is necessary to put up more mills in China for cotton manufacturing. Therefore, I suggest in this International Development Scheme to put up a system of large cotton mills all over the cotton-producing districts under one central national control. Thus the best economic results will be obtained and cotton goods can be supplied to the people at a lower cost.

D. The Woolen Industry

Although the whole of Northwestern China—about two-thirds of the entire country is a pastural land yet the woolen industry has never been developed. Every year, plenty of raw materials are exported from China on the one hand and plenty of finished woolen goods imported on the other. Judging by the import and export of the woolen trade the development of woolen industry in China will surely be a profitable business. I suggest that scientific methods be applied to the raising of sheep and to the treatment of wool so as to improve the quality and increase the quantity. Modern factories should be established all over northwestern China for manufacturing all kinds of finished woolen goods. Here we have the raw materials, cheap labor and unlimited market. What we want for the development of this industry is foreign capital and experts. This will be one of the most remunerative projects in our International Development Scheme, for the industry, will be a new one and there will be no private competitors on the field.

E. The Leather Industry

This will also be a new industry in China, despite the fact that there are a few tanneries in the treaty ports. The export of hides from and the import of leather goods into China are increasing every year. So, to establish a system of tanneries and factories for leather goods and footgear will be a lucrative undertaking.

F. The Manufacturing of Clothing Machinery

The machinery for the manufacturing of various kinds of clothing materials is in great demand in China. It is reported that the orders for cotton mill machinery have been filled up for the next three years from manufacturers in Europe and America. If China is developed according to my programs, the demand for machinery will be many times greater than at present and the supply in Europe and America will be too short to meet it. Therefore to establish factories for the manufacturing of clothing machinery is a necessary as well as a profitable undertaking. Such factories should be established in the neighborhood of iron and steel factories, so as to save expenses for transportation of heavy materials. What will be the capital for this undertaking should be decided by experts.

PART III

THE HOUSING INDUSTRY

Among the four hundred millions in China the poor still live in huts and hovels, and in caves in the loess region of north China while the middle and the rich classes live in temples. All the so-called houses in China, excepting a few after western style and those in treaty ports are built after the models of a temple. When a Chinese builds a house he has more regard for the dead than for the living. The first consideration of the owner is his ancestral shrine. This must be placed at the center of the house, and all the other parts must be complement and secondary to it. The house is planned not for comfort but for ceremonies, that is, for "the red and white affairs", as they are called in China. The "red affair" is the marriage or other felicitous celebrations of any member of the family, and the "white affair" is the funeral ceremonies. Besides the ancestral shrine there are the shrines of the various household gods[goods]. All these are of more importance than man and must be considered before him. There is not a home in old China that is planned for the comfort and convenience of man alone. So now when we plan the housing industry in China in our International Development Scheme, we must take the houses of the entire population of China into consideration. "To build houses for four hundred millions, it is impossible!" some may exclaim. This is the largest job ever conceived by man. But if China is going to give up her foolish traditions and useless habits and customs of the last three thousand years and begin to adopt modern civilization, as our industrial development scheme [Industrial Development Scheme] is going to introduce, the remodelling of all the houses according to modern comforts and conveniences is bound to come, either unconsciously by social evolution or consciously by artificial construction. The modern civilization so far attained by western nations is entirely an unconscious progress, for social and economic sciences are but recent discoveries. But henceforth all human progress will be more or less based upon knowledge, that is upon [which is] scientific planning. As we can forsee now, within half a century under our industrial development, the house of all China will be renewed according to modern comfort and convenience. Is it not far better and cheaper to rebuild the houses of all China by a preconceived scientific plan than by none? I have no doubt that if we plan to build a thousand houses at one time it would be ten time cheaper than to plan and build one at a time, and the more we build the cheaper terms we would get. This is a positive economic law. The only danger in this is over-production. That is the only obstacle for all production on a large scale. Since the industrial revolution in Europe and America, every financial panic before the world war was caused by over-production. In the case of our housing industry in China, there are four hundred million customers. At least fifty million houses will be needed in the coming fifty years. Thus a million houses a year will be the normal demand of the country.

Houses are a great factor in civilization. They give men more enjoyment and happiness than food and clothes. More than half of the human industries are contributing to household needs. The housing industry will be the greatest undertaking of our International Development Scheme, and also will be the most profitable part of it. My object of the housing industry is to provide cheap houses to the masses. A ten thousand dollar house now built in the treaty port can be produced for less than a thousand dollars and yet a high margin of profit can be made. In order to accomplish this we have to produce transport, and distribute the materials for construction. After the house is finished, all household equipment must be furnished. Both of [the] these will be comprised in the housing industry which I shall formulate as follows:

A. The Production and Transportation of Building Materials.

B. The Construction of Houses.

C. The Manufacturing of Furniture.

D. The Supply of Household Utilities.

A. The Production and Transportation of Building Materials

The building materials are bricks, tiles, timber, skeleton iron, stone, cement and mortar. Each of these materials must be manufactured or cut out from raw materials. So kilns for the manufacture of tiles and bricks must be put up. Mills for timers [timbers] must be established, also factories for skeleton irons. Quarries must be opened and factories for cement and mortar must be started.

All these establishments must be put up at suitable districts where materials and markets are near one another. All should be under one central control so as to regulate the output of each of these materials in proportion to the demand. After the materials are ready they must be transported to the places where they are wanted by special bottoms on waterways, and by special cars on railways so as to reduce the cost as low as possible. For this purpose special boats and cars must be built by the shipbuilding department and the car factory.

B. The Construction of Houses

The houses to be built in China will comprise public building [buildings] and private residences. As the public buildings are to be built with public funds for public uses which will not be a profitable undertaking, a special Government Department should therefore be created to take charge ⟨of⟩. The houses that are to be built under this International Development Scheme will be private residences only with the object to provide cheap houses for the people, as well as to make profit for this international concern. The houses will be built on standardized types. In cities and towns the houses should be constructed on two lines: the single family and the group faimly houses. The former should again be subdivided into eight-roomed, ten-roomed and tweleve [twelve]-roomed houses, and the latter into ten-family, hundred-family and thousand-family houses, with four or six rooms for each family. In the country districts the houses should be classified according to the occupation of the people, and special annexes such as barns and dairies should be provided for the farmers. All houses should be designed and built according to the needs and comfort [comforts] of man; so a special architectual department should be established to study the habits, occupations and needs of different people and make improvements from time to time. The construction should be performed as much as possible by labor-saving machinery so as to accelerate work and save expenses.

C. The Manufacturing of Furniture

As all houses in China should be remodelled all furniture should be replaced by up-to-date ones, which are made for the comforts and needs of man. Furniture of the following kinds should be manufactured: the library, the parlor, the bedroom, the kitchen, the bathroom and the toilet. Each kind should be manufactured in a special factory under the management of the International Development Organization.

D. The Supply of Household Utilities

The household utilities are water, light, heat, fuel and telephones. Except in treaty ports, there is no water-supply system in any of the cities and towns of China. Even many treaty ports possess none as yet. In all the large cities, the people obtain their water from rivers which at the same time act as sewage. The water supply of the large cities and towns in China is most unsanitary. (1) It is an urgent necessity that water supply systems should be installed in all cities and towns in China without delay. Therefore special factories for equipping the water system should be established in order to meet the needs. (2) Lighting plants should be installed in all the cities and towns in China. So factories for the manufacture of the machinery lighting plants should be established. (3) Modern heating plants should be installed in every household, using either electricity, gas, or steam. So the manufacturing of heating equipment is a necessity. Factories should be established for this purpose. (4) Cooking fuel is one of the most costly items in the daily needs of the Chinese people. In the country the people generally devote ten per cent [percent] of their working time to gathering fire-woods [firewood]. In town the people spend about twenty per cent [percent] of their living expenses for firewood alone. Thus this firewood question accumulates into a great national waste. The firewood and grass as a cooking fuel must be substituted by coal in the country districts, and by gas or electricity in towns and cities. In order to use coal gas and electricity, proper equipment must be provided. So factories for the manufacturing of coal gas, and electricity, stoves for every family must be established by this International Development Organization. (5) Telephones must also be supplied to every family in the cities as well as in the country. So factories for manufacturing the equipment must be put up in China, in order to render them as cheap as possible.

PART IV

THE MOTORING INDUSTRY

The Chinese are a stagnant race. From time immemorial a man is praised for staying at home and caring for his immediate surroundings only. Laotse—a contemporary of Confucius—says: "The good people are those who live in countries so near to each other that they can hear each other's cock crow and dog bark and yet they never have had intercourse with each other during their lifetime." This is often quoted as the Golden Age of the Chinese people. But in modern civilization the condition is entirely changed. Moving about occupies a great part of a man's life time. It is the movement of man that makes civilization progress. China, in order to catch up with modern civilization, must move. And the movement of the individual forms an important part of the national activity. A man must move whenever and wherever he pleases with ease and rapidity. However, China, at present, lacks the means of facility for individual movement, for all the old great highways were ruined and have disappeared, and the automobile has not yet been introduced into the interior of the country. The motor car, a recent invention, is a necessity for rapid movement. If we wish to move quickly and do more work, we must adopt the motor car as a vehicle. But before we can use the motor car, we have to build our roads. In the preliminary part of this International Development Scheme, I proposed to construct one million miles of roads. These should be apportioned according to the ratio of population in each district for construction. In the eighteen provinces of China Proper, there are nearly 2,000 hsiens. If all parts of China are to adopt the hsien administration, there will be nearly 4,000 hsiens in all. Thus the construction of roads for each hsien will be on an average of 250 miles. But some of the hsiens have more people and some have less. If we divide the million miles of roads by the four hundred million people, we shall have one mile to every four hundred. For one hundred people to build one mile of road is not a very difficult task to accomplish, if my scheme of making road-building as a condition for granting local autonomy is adopted by the nation, we shall see one million miles of road built in a very short time as if by a magic wand.

As soon as the people of China decide to build roads, this International Development Organization can begin to put up factories for manufacturing motor cars. First ⟨it⟩ start [starts] on a small scale and gradually expand [expands] the plants to build more and more until they are sufficient to supply the needs of the four hundred million people. The cars should be manufactured to suit different purposes, such as the farmer's car, the artisan's car, the businessman's car, the tourists' [tourist's] car, the truck car, etc. All these cars, if turned out on a large scale, can be made much cheaper than at present, so that everybody who wishes it, may have one.

Besides supplying cheap cars, we must also supply cheap fuel, otherwise the people will still be unable to use them. So the development of the oil fields in

China should follow the motor car industry. This will be dealt with in more detail under the mining industry.

PART V

THE PRINTING INDUSTRY

This industry provides man with intellectual food. It is a necessity of modern society, without which mankind cannot progress. All human activities are recorded, and all human knowledge is stored in printing. It is a great factor of civilization. The progress and civilization of different nations of the world are measured largely by the quantity of printed matter they turn out annually. China, though ⟨as⟩ the nation that invented printing, is very backward in the development of its printing industry. In our International Development Scheme, the printing industry must also be given a place. If China is developed industrially according to the lines which I suggested, the demand for printed matter by the four hundred millions will be exceedingly great. In order to meet this demand efficiently, a system of large printing houses must be established in all large cities in the country, to undertake printing of all kinds from newspapers to encyclopaedia. The best modern books on various subjects in different countries should be translated into Chinese and published in cheap edition form for the general public in China. All the publishing houses should be organized under one common management, so as to secure the best economic results.

In order to make printed matter cheap, other subsidiary industries must be developed at the same time. The most important of these is the paper industry. At present all the paper used by newspapers in China is imported. And the demand for paper is increasing every day. China has plenty of raw materials for making paper, such as the vast virgin forests of the northwestern part of the country, and the wild reeds of the Yangtze and its neighboring swamps which would furnish the best pulps. So, large plants for manufacturing papers should be put up in suitable locations. Besides the paper factories, ink factories, type foundries, printing machine factories, etc., should be established under a central management to produce everything that is needed in the printing industry.

PROGRAM VI

THE MINING INDUSTRY

Mining and farming are the two most important means of producing raw materials for industries. As farming is to produce food for man, so mining is to produce food for machinery. Machinery is the tree of modern industries, and the mining industry is the root of machinery. Thus, without the mining industry there would be no machinery, and without machinery there would be no modern industries which have revolutionized the economic conditions of mankind. The mining industry, after all, is the greatest factor of material civilization and economic progress. Although in the fifth part of the first program I suggested the development of the iron and coal fields in Chihli and Shansi as an auxiliary project for the development of the Great Northern Port, still, a special program should be devoted to mining in general. The mineral lands of China belong to the state, and mining in China is still in its infancy. So to develop the mining industry from the outset as a state enterprise would be sound economic measure. But mining in general is very risky and to enlist foreign capital in its development in a wholesale manner is unadvisable. Therefore, only such mining projects which are sure to be profitable will be brought under the International Development Scheme. I shall formulate this mining program as follows:

I. The Mining of Iron.

II. The Minign [Mining] of Coal.

Ⅲ. The Mining of Oil.

Ⅳ. The Mining of Copper.

Ⅴ. The Working of Some Particular Mines.

Ⅵ. The Manufacture of Mining Machinery.

Ⅶ. The Establishment of Smelting Plants.

PART Ⅰ

THE MINING OF IRON

Iron is the most important element in modern industries. Its deposits are found in great quantities in certain areas and ⟨can⟩ be easily mined. The iron mines should be worked absolutely as a state property. Besides the Chihli and Shansi iron mines, the other iron fields must also be developed. There are very rich deposits in the southwestern provinces, the Yangtze Valley and the northwestern provinces in China Proper. Sinkiang, Mongolia, Manchuria, Kokonor, and Tibet also possess large deposits of iron. We have the Han Yeh Ping Iron and Steel Works in the Yangtze Valley and the Pen Chi Hu Iron and Steel Works in South Manchuria, both of which are largely capitalized by Japan and are working very profitable lately. There should be similar works in the vicinity of Canton, The [the] Great Southern Port, and also in Szechwan, and Yunnan, where iron and coal are found side by side. The iron deposits in Sinkiang, Kansu, Mongolia, etc. , must also be developed one after the other, according to the needs of the locality. Iron and Steel Works must be put up in each of these regions to supply the local demand for manufactured iron. What amount of capital should be invested in these additional iron and steel works must be thoroughly investigated by experts. But I should say that a sum equal to or double the amount to be invested in the Chili [Chihli] and Shansi iron and steel works will not be too much, because of the great demand which will result in the development of China.

PART II

THE MINING OF COAL

China is known to be the country most rich in coal deposits, yet her coal fields are scarcely scratched. The output of coal in the United States is about six hundred million tons a year. If China is equally developed she should, according to the proportion of her population, have an output of four times as much coal as the United States. This will be the possibility of coal mining in China which the International Development Organization is to undertake. As coal deposits are found in great quantities in certain areas so its output can be estimated quite accurately beforehand. Thus, the risk is of no consideration and the profit is sure. But as coal is a necessity of civilized community and the sinews of modern industries, the principal object for mining should not be for profit alone, but for supplying the needs of mankind. After the payment of interest and capital of the foreign loans for its development, and the securing of high wages for the miners, the price of coal should be reduced as low as possible so as to meet the demands of the public as well as to give impetus to the development of various industries. I suggest that besides the mining of coal for the iron and steel works, a plan for producing two hundred million tons of coal a year for other uses should be formed at the start. Mines should be opened along the seaboard and navigable rivers. As Europe is now seeking coal from China this amount will not be over-production from the beginning. A few years later when the industries of China will be more developed more coal will be needed. How much capital will be required and what mines are to be worked, have to be submitted to scientific investigation under expert direction.

Besides coal mining, the coal products industry must be developed under the same management. This is a new industry without any competition and has an unlimited market in China. Great profits will be assured on the capital invested.

PART III

THE MINING OF OIL

It is well-known that the richest company in the world is the Standard Oil Company of New York, and that the richest man in the world is Rockefeller, organizer of this conmpany. This proves that oil mining is a most profitable business. China is known to be a very rich oil-bearing country. Oil springs are found in the provinces of Szechwan, Kansu, Sinkiang, and Shensi. How vast is the underground reservoir of oil in China is not yet known. But the already kown oil springs have never been worked and made use of, while the import of kerosene, gasoline, and crude oil from abroad is increasing every year. When China is developed as a motoring country, the use of gasoline will be increased a thousand-fold, then the supply from the foreign fields will not be able to meet the demands, as shortage of oil is already felt in Europe and America. The mining of oil in China will soon become a necessity. This enterprise should be taken up by the International Development Organization for the state. Production on a large scale should be started at once. Pipe line systems should be installed between oil districts and populous and industrial centers in the interior and also river and sea ports. What amount of capital should be invested in the project will have to be investigated by experts.

PART IV

THE MINING OF COPPER

The copper deposits, like iron ores, are found in great quantities in different places. So the quantity of ores in each mine can be accurately estimated before it is opened and its working generally runs no risk. Thus, the mining of copper should be taken up as government enterprise, as was always the case in China, and financed and worked by the International Development Organization. The richest copper deposits in China are found along the border of Szechwan and Yunnan on the Yangtze River. The government copper mine in Chaotung, in the northeastern corner of Yunnan, has been working for many centuries. Cash, the standard currency of China, was made mostly of the copper from Yunnan province. The currency still absorbs an enormous quantity of copper. Owing to the difficulty of transporting the Yunnan copper, most of the metal for currency is being imported from foreign countries. Besides currency, copper is very commonly used for many other purposes and when the industries in China are developed the demand will increase a hundred times. So the demand for this metal will be very great in the market of China alone. I suggest that production on a large scale should be adopted and modern plants should be installed in copper mines. How much capital to be invested in this enterprise should be decided by experts after careful investigation.

PART V

THE WORKING OF SOME PARTICULAR MINES

In regard to the mining of various kinds of metal, some particular mines should be taken up by the International Development Organization. There are many famous mines in China which have been worked for many centuries by hand, such as the Kochui tin mine in Yunnan, the Moho gold mine in Heilungkiang, and the Hotien jade mine in Sinkiang. All these mines are known, to have very rich deposits — the deeper the richer. Hitherto only the surface parts of those mines have been worked and the larger deposits are still untouched, owing to the lack of means of getting ride of the water. Some of the mines are still in the hands of the Government, while others have been given up to private concerns. If modem machinery is adopted the mines should revert to the Government so as to secure economy in working. Many discarded mines of this kind should be thoroughly investigated, and if found profitable, work should be resumed under the International Development Scheme. All future mining, other than government enterprise, should be leased to private concerns on contract, and when the term is up, the government has the option to take them over, if found profitable as a state property. Thus all profitable mines will be socialized in time and the profit will be equally shared by all the people in the coutry[country].

PART VI

THE MANUFACTURE OF MINING MACHINERY

Most of the metal deposits of the earth are in small quantities and scattered far and wide in various places. Most of the mining enterprises resemble farming in that it is more profitable to work by individuals and small parties. As such is the case, most of the mining enterprises have to be worked out by private concerns. In order to accelerate the development of mining, more liberal laws should be adopted; education and information should be given freely by experts employed by the state; and encouragement and financial assistance should be given by the state and private banks. The part that the International Development Organization should take in general mining enterprises is to manufacture all kinds of mining tools and machinery, and to supply them to the miners at low cost, either on cash or on credit. By distributing tools and machinery to the surplus workers in China, the mining industry would be developed by leaps and bounds. And the more the mining industry is developed the more will be the demand for tools and machinery. Thus the profits for the manufacturing concerns would be limitless, so to speak. Of course, the factories should be started on a small scale and be extended gradually according to the ratio of the development of the mining industry. I suggest that the first factory of this kind should be established at Canton, the seaport of the southwestern mining region, where raw materials and skilled labor can be easily obtained. The other factories should be established in Hankow and the Great Northern Port afterwards.

PART VII

THE ESTABLISHMENT OF SMELTING PLANTS

Smelting plants for various kinds of metals should be put up in all mining districts to turn ore into metals. These smelting plants should be conducted under the cooperative system. At first, a reasonable price should he paid to the miner when the ore is collected. Afterwards, when the metal is sold, either at home or in foreign markets, the smelting works will take a share of the profit to cover the expenses, the interest, the sinking fund, etc. The surplus profit should be divided among the workers according to their wages, and among the capitalists according to the proportion of ore they contribute to the furnace. In this way we can encourage private mining enterprise which forms the root of other industries. All smelting works should be put up according to local needs and their scale should be determined by experts and managed under a central control.

CONCLUSION

In this International Development Scheme, I venture to present a practical solution for the three great world questions which are the International War, the Commercial War and the Class War. As it has been discovered by post-Darwin philosophers that the primary force of human evolution is cooperation and not struggle as that of the animal world, so the fighting nature, a residue of the animal instinct in man, must be eliminated from man, the sooner the better.

International war is nothing more than pure and simple organized robbery on a grand scale, which all right-minded people deplore. When the United States of America turned the recent European conflict into a world war by taking part in it, the American people to a man determined to make this war end[war] forever. And the hope of the peace-loving nations in the world was raised so high that we Chinese thought that the "Tatung" or the Great Harmony Age was at hand. But unfortunately, the United States has completely failed in peace, in spite of her great success in war. Thus, the world has been thrown back to the pre-war condition again. The scrambling for territories, the struggle for food, and the fighting for raw materials will begin anew. So instead of disarmament there is going to be a greater increase in the armies and navies of the once allied powers for the next war. China, the most rich and populous country in the world, will be the prize. Some years ago there was great inclination among the Powers to divide China and Imperial Russia actually took steps to colonize Manchuria. But the then chivalrous Japan went to war with Russia and thus saved China from partition. Now the militaristic policy of Japan is to swallow China alone. So long as China is left to the tender mercy of the militaristic powers she must either succumb to partition by several powers or be swallowed up by one power.

However, the tide of the world seems to be turning. After centuries of sound slumber, the Chinese people at last are waking up and realizing that we must get up and follow in the world's progress. Now we are at the parting of the ways. Shall we organize for war or shall we organize for peace? Our militarists and reactionaries desire the former, and they are going to Japanize China, so that when the time comes they will start another Boxer Movement once more to defy the civilized world. But as the founder of the Chung Hwa Min Kuo—the Chinese Republic—I desire to have China organized for peace. I, therefore, begin to utilize my pen, which I hope will prove even mightier than the sword that I used to destroy the Manchu Dynasty, to write out these programs for organizing China for peace.

During the course of my writing, these programs have been published in various magazines and newspapers time after time and are being spread all over China. They are welcomed everywhere and by everyone in the country. So far there is not a word expressed in disfavor of my proposition. The only anxiety ever expressed regarding my scheme is where we can obtain such huge sums of money to carry out even a small part of this comprehensive project. Fortunately, however, soon after the preliminary part of my programs had been sent out to the different governments and the Peace Conference, a new Consortium was formed in Paris for the purpose of assisting China in developing her natural resources. This was initiated by the American Government. Thus we need not fear the lack of capital to start work in our industrial development. If the Powers are sincere in their motive to cooperate for mutual benefit, then the military struggle for material gain in China could eventually be averted. For by cooperation, they can secure more benefits and advantages than by struggle. The Japanese militarists still think that war is the most profitable national pursuit, and their General Staff keeps on planning a war once in a decade. This Japanese illusion was encouraged and strengthened by the campaign of 1894 against China, a cheap and short one but rich in remuneration for Japan; also by the campaign of 1904 against Russia which was a great success to the Japanese, and its fruit of victory was no less in value; finally by the campaign of 1914 against Germany which formed her part in the world war Japan took. Although Japan took the smallest part in the world war and expended the least in men and money, yet the fruit of her victory was Shantung, a territory as large as Roumania before the war, with a population as numerous as that of France. With such crowning results in every was﹝war﹞ during the last thirty years no wonder the Japanese militarists think that the most profitable business in this world is War.

The effect of the last war in Europe proves, however, just the contrary. An aggresive Germany lost entirely her capital and interests, plus something more, while victorious France gained practically nothing. Since China is awake now, the next aggression from Japan will surely be met by a resolute resistance from the Chinese people. Even granted that Japan could conquer China, it would be an impossibility for Japan to govern China profitably for any period of time. The Japanese financiers possess better foresight than their militarists as was proved during the dispute of the Manchurian and the Mongolian reservations when the former prevailed over the latter thus causing the Japanese Government to give up her monopoly of these territories to the new Consortium, in order to cooperate with the other powers. We, the Chinese people, who desire to organize China for peace will welcome heartily this new Consortium provided it will carry out the principles which are outlined in these programs. Thus, cooperation of various nations can be secured and the military struggle for individual and national gain will cease forever.

Commercial war, or competition, is a struggle between the capitalists themselves. This war has no national distinction. It is fought just as furiously and mercilessly between countries as well as within the country. The method of fighting is to undersell each other, in order to exhaust the weaker rivals so that the victor may control the market alone and dictate terms to the consuming public as long as possible. The result of the commercial war is no less harmful and cruel to the vanquished foes than an armed conflict. This war has become more and more furious every day since the adoption of machinery for production. It was once thought by the economists of the Adam Smith school that competition was a beneficent factor and a sound economic system, but modern economists discovered that it is [was] a very wasteful and ruinous system. As a matter of fact, modern economic tendencies work in a contrary direction, that is, towards concentration instead of competition. That is the reason why the trusts in America flourish in spite of the anti-trust law and the public opinion which aim at suppressing them. For trusts, by eliminating waste and cutting down expenses can produce much cheaper than individual producers. Whenever a trust enters into a certain field of industry, it always sweeps that field clean of rivals, by supplying cheap articles to the public. This would prove a blessing to the public but for the unfortunate fact that the trust is a private concern, and its object is to make as much profit as possible. As soon as all rivals are swept clean from the field of competition, the trust would raise the price of its articles as high as possible. Thus the public is oppressed by it. The trust is a result of economic evolution, therefore it is out of human power to suppress it. The proper remedy is to have it owned by all the people of the country. In my International Development Scheme, I intend to make all the national industries of China into a Great Trust owned by the Chinese people, and financed with international capital for mutual benefit. Thus once for all, commercial war will be done away with in the largest market of the world.

Class war is a struggle between labor and captial. The war is at present raging at its full height in all the highly developed industrial countries. Labor feels sure of its final victory while capitalists are determined to resist to the bitter end. When will it end and what will be the decision, no one dares to predict. China, however, owing to the backwardness of her industrial development, which is a blessing in disguise, in this respect, has not yet entered into the class war. Our laboring class, commonly known as coolies, are living from hand to mouth and will therefore only be too glad to welcome any capitalist who would even put up a sweat shop to exploit them. The capitalist is a rare specimen in China and is only beginning to make his appearance in the treaty ports.

However, China must develop her industries by all means. Shall we follow the old path of western civilization? This old path resembles the sea route of Columbus' first trip to America. He set out from Europe by a southwesterly direction through the Canary Islands to San Salvador, in the Bahama Group. But nowadays navigators take a different direction to America and find that the destination can be reached by a distance many times shorter. The path of western civilization was an unknown one and those who went before groped in the dark as Columbus did on his first voyage to America. As a late comer [corner], China can greatly profit in covering the space by following the direction already charted by western pioneers. Thus we can foresee that the final goal of the westwardly in the Atlantic is not India but the New World. So is the case in the economic ocean. The goal of material civilization is not private profit but public profit. And the shortest route to it is not competition but cooperation. In my International Development Scheme, I propose that the profits of this industrial development go first to pay the interest and principal of foreign capital invested in it; second to give high wages to labor; and third to improve or extend the machinery of production.

Besides these provisions the rest of the profit should go to the public in the form of reduced prices in all commodities and public services. Thus, all will enjoy, in the same degree, the fruits of modern civilization. This industrial development scheme [Industrial Development Scheme] which is roughly sketched in the above six programs is a part of my general plan for constructing a New China. In a nutshell, it is my idea to make capitalism create socialism in China so that these two economic forces of human evolution will work side by side in future civilization.

APPENDIX I

PRELIMINARY AGREEMENT PROVIDING FOR THE FINANCING AND CONSTRUCTION OF THE RAILWAY FROM CANTON TO CHUNGKING WITH EXTENSION TO LANCHOW

This Agreement is made at Shanghai on the fourth day of the seventh month of the second year of the Republic of China being the fourth day of July, 1913, and the contracting parties are: the Chinese National Railway Corporation (hereinafter termed "the Corporation") duly authorized in virtue of the Presidential Mandate of the ninth day of the ninth month of the Republic of China being the ninth day of September, 1912, and in virtue of the Charter of th [the] Corporation duly promulgated by a Presidential Mandate of the thirty-first day of the third month of the second year of the Republic of China being the thirty-first day of March, 1913, on the one part and Messrs. Pauling and Company, Limited, of 26 Victoria Street, London, S. W. (hereinafter termed "the Contractors") on the other part.

Now it is hereby agreed by and between the parties hereto as follows:

ARTICLE I

The Contractors, or their Assigns, agree to issue on behalf of the Government of the Republic of China a sterling Loan, bearing interest at the rate of five per cent [percent] per annum, (hereinafter referred to as "the Loan") for such an amount as may be mutually estimated to be necessary for the completion of the Railway from Canton to Chungking.

The Loan shall be of the date on which the first series of Bonds are issued and shall be called "The Chinese National Railways Government five per cent [percent] Gold Loan of 1912 for the Canton-Chungking Railway".

ARTICLE II

The proceeds of the Loan are designed for the construction and equipment of the Railway from Canton to Chungking (hereinafter called "the Railway") and for all necessary expenditure appertaining thereto as may be arranged in the Detailed Agreement, referred to in Article 17.

ARTICLE III

The payment of the interest and the redemption of the Capital of the Loan are guaranteed by the Government of the Republic of China and by a special lien upon the Canton-Chungking Railway.

This special lien constitutes a first mortgage in favour of the Contractors, acting on behalf of the Bondholders, upon the Railway itself, as and when constructed, and on the revenue of all descriptions derivable therefrom, and upon all materials, rolling stock and buildings of every description purchased or to be purchased for the Railway.

Should there be default in payments on the dates fixed of all or part of the half yearly interest or amortization payments, the Contractors shall have the right to exercise on behalf of the Bondholders all the rights of action which accrue to them from the special mortgage.

ARTICLE IV

During the time of construction of the Railway the interest on the Bonds and on any advances made by the Contractors shall be paid from the proceeds of the Loan. The accruing interest from any proceeds of the Loan not used during the period of construction, and the earnings derived by the Corporation from the working of any sections of the Railway as they are built, are to be used to make up the amount required for the payment of the said interest, and if any deficiency remains it is to be met from the proceeds of the Loan.

When the construction of the Railway is wholly completed, the interest on the Bonds is to be paid from the income or earnings of the Railway received by the Corporation, in such manner and on such dates as may be provided for in the Detailed Agreement provided for in Article 17 of this Agreement.

If, at any time, the earnings of the Railway, together with the funds available from the proceeds of the Loan, are not sufficient to meet the interest on the Bonds and the repayment of the capital in accordance with the Amortization Schedule to be attached to the Detailed Agreement, the Government of the Republic of China, in approving of this Agreement, unconditionally undertakes and promises to pay the principal of the Loan and the interest of the Loan on the due dates to be fixed therefore in the Detailed Agreement provided for in Article 17 of this Agreement.

ARTICLE V

The Bonds shall be Bonds of the Government of the Republic of China.

ARTICLE VI

The Loan shall be issued to the public in two or more series of Bonds, the first issue to be made to the amount of from one to two million pounds sterling as soon as possible after the signature of the Detailed Agreement referred to in Article 17 of this Agreement. The issue price of the Bonds shall be fixed by the Corporation and the Contractors sometime before the issue, taking the last price of similar Bonds as a basis for fixing the market price. The price payable to the Corporation shall be the actual rate of issue to the public less a sufficient amount to cover the cost of stamps on the Bonds in the various countries of issue, provided always that at least fifty per cent [percent] of the Bonds shall be issued in England, plus floatation charges of four per cent [percent] retainable by the Contractors (that is to say, a charge of four pounds for every one hundred pound Bond issued).

After the Detailed Agreement referred to in Article 17 is settled, and pending the issue of the Loan, the Contractors shall deposit the sum of fifty thousand pounds with the issuing Bank to the Canton-Chungking Railway account, and this amount can be drawn on by the Corporation for survey and other necessary expenses authorized by the Managing Director against certificates signed by the Chief Accountant and Chief Engineer. This sum of fifty thousand pounds shall bear interest at the rate of five per cent [percent] per annum and shall be refunded out of the proceeds of the Loan.

ARTICLE VII

The proceeds of the Loan shall be deposited with the issuing Bank, to be nominated and guaranteed by the Contractors, to the credit of a Canton-Chungking Railway Account on such terms as may be mutually arranged in the Detailed Agreement referred to in Article 17.

When the work of construction is ready to begin, a sum equal to the estimated expenditure in China for six months shall be transferred to a Bank in China to be mutually agreed upon and there placed to the credit of a Canton-Chungking Railway Account to be operated upon by the Corporation under certificates signed by the Chief Accountant and the Chief Engineer. This amount of estimated expenditure for six months shall be maintained by subsequent monthly transfers so that, as far as possible, there shall always be six months [months'] estimated expenditure in China on deposit in a Bank in China to be mutually agreed upon.

ARTICLE VIII

Immediately after the signing of the Detailed Agreement, the Corporation will establish a Head Office at Canton for the Canton-Chungking Railway. This Office will be under the direction of a Chinese Managing Director to be appointed by the Corporation, with whom will be associated a British Engineer-in-Chief and a British Firm of Public Accountants, of recognized standing, whose representative shall be Chief Accountant (hereinafter called "the Chief Accountant"). These British Employes [employees] shall be nominated by the Corporation and the Contractors, jointly, and shall be appointed by the Corporation. Their dismissal shall take place, only, with the joint approval of the Corporation and the Contractors.

It is understood that the duties to be performed by these employes [employees] are intended to promote the mutual interests of the Corporation and the Bondholders respectively, and it is therefore agreed that all cases of difference arising therefrom shall be referred for amicable adjustment between the Corporation and the Representative of the Contractors. The salaries and other terms of Agreement of the Engineer-in-Chief and the Chief Accountant shall be arranged between the Corporation and the Contractors; and the amount of their salaries, etc., shall be paid out of the general accounts of the Railway.

For all important technical appointments for the operation of the Railway, Europeans of experience and ability shall be engaged and wherever competent Chinese are available, they shall be employed. All such appointments shall be made, and their functions defined, by the Managing Director and the Engineer-in-Chief in consultation, and shall be submitted for the approval of the Corporation; similar procedure shall be followed in the case of Europeans employed in the Chief Accountant's department. In the event of the misconduct, or the incompetency of these European employes [employees], their services may be dispensed with by the Managing Director, after consultation with the Engineer-in-Chief, and subject to the sanction of the Corporation. The form of Agreements made with these European Employes [employees] shall conform to the usual practice.

The accounts of the receipts and the disbursements of the Railway's construction and operation, shall be in Chinese and English in the department of the Chief Accountant, whose duty it shall be to organize and supervise the same, and to report thereon for the information of the Corporation through the Managing Director, and of the Contractors as representing the Bondholders. All receipts and payments shall be certified by the Chief Accountant and authorized by the Managing Director.

For the general technical staff of the Railway, after completion of construction, the necessary arrangements shall be made by the Managing. Director in consultation with the Engineer-in-Chief, and reported to the Corporation in due course.

The duties of the Engineer-in-Chief shall consist in the efficient and economical maintenance of the Railway, and the general supervision thereof in consultation with the Managing Director. The duties of the Chief Engineer during construction shall be set forth in the Detailed Agreement, referred to in Article 17 of this Agreement.

The Engineer-in-Chief shall always give courteous consideration to the wishes and instructions of the Corporation, whether conveyed directly or through the Managing Director, and shall always comply therewith, having at the same time due regard to the efficient construction and maintenance of the Railway.

A school for the education of Chinese in Railway matters shall be established by the Managing Director subject to the approval of the Corporation.

ARTICLE IX

The Contractors shall construct and equip the Railway and shall receive as remuneration a sum equal to seven per cent [percent] on the actual cost of the construction and equipment of the Railway. The term "Equipment" shall be held to include in its meaning all requirements necessary for the operation of the Railway and shall therefore include Rolling Stock and Locomotives sufficient for operation.

It is clearly understood that the term "Equipment" does not include any purchases made for the Railway after it has been completely constructed and equipped and handed over ready for operation.

It is further clearly understood that the cost of land purchased for the Railway, the salaries of the Managing Director, Chief Accountants, Chief Engineer, and the cost of their offices and staff shall not be included in the meaning of the terms "construction and equipment".

The Contractors shall have the option of constructing on the same terms the proposed extension of the Railway to Lanchow in the Province of Kansu, or a Railway of similar milage in some other part of China to be mutually agreed upon, and this option shall be for seven years from the commencement of construction.

All other arrangements in connection with the construction and equipment of the Railway shall be settled in the Detailed Agreement referred to in Article 17.

ARTICLE X

All land that may be required along the whole course of the Railway within survey limits, and for the necessary sidings, stations, repairing shops and car sheds, to be provided for in accordance with the detailed plans, shall be acquired by the Corporation at the actual cost of the land, and shall be paid for out of the proceeds of the Loan.

ARTICLE XI

The Contractors shall hand over to the Corporation each section of the Railway, when completed, for operation in accordance with the provisions of the Detailed Agreement.

ARTICLE XII

The Contractors shall be appointed Trustees for the Bondholders and shall receive such remuneration as may be fixed in the Detailed Agreement.

ARTICLE XIII

The Government of the Republic of China, whenever necessary, will provide protection for the Railway while under construction or when in operation, and all the properties of the Railway as well as Chinese and foreigners employed thereon, are to enjoy protection from the local officials.

The Railway may maintain a force of Chinese Police with Chinese officers, their wages and maintenance to be wholly defrayed as part of the cost of the construction and maintenance of the Railway. In the event of the Railway requiring further protection by the military forces of the Government, the same shall be duly applied for by the Head Office and promptly afforded, it being understood that such military forces shall be maintained at the expense of the Government.

ARTICLE XIV

All materials of any kind that are required for the construction and working of the Railway, whether imported from abroad or from the Provinces to the scene of work, shall be exempted from Likin or other duties so long as such exemption remains in force in respect of other Chinese Railways. The Bonds of the Loan, together with their coupons and the income of the Railway shall be free from imposts of any kind by the Government of the Republic of China.

ARTICLE XV

With a view to encouraging Chinese industries, Chinese materials are to be preferred, provided price and quality are suitable.

At equal rates and qualities, goods of British manufacture shall be given preference over other goods of foreign origin.

ARTICLE XVI

The Contractors may, with the approval of the Corporation, and subject to all their obligations, transfer or delegate all or any of their rights, powers and discretions, to their sucessors or assigns.

ARTICLE XVII

As soon as this Preliminary Agreement is signed it shall be forwarded to the Government of the Republic of China for approval. When it has met with the approval of the Government of the Republic of China, a necessary Detailed Agreement shall be made embodying the principles of this Agreement with such amplifications and additions as may be mutually agreed upon between the parties hereto.

ARTICLE XVIII

On its approval of this Agreement, and acceptance of the obligations set forth herein, the Government of the Republic of China shall officially notify the British Minister at Peking of the fact, and this approval shall be taken as covering the Detailed Agreement referred to in Article 17.

ARTICLE XIX

This Agreemnt is executed in quadruplicate in English and Chinese, one copy to be retained by the Corporation, one to be forwarded to the Government of the Republic of China, one to be forwarded to the British Minister at Peking, and one to be retained by the Contractors, and should any doubt arise as to the interpretation of the Agreement, the English text shall be accepted as the standard.

Signed at Shanghai by the contracting parties on this fourth day of the seventh month of the second year of the Republic of China being the fourth day of July nineteen hundred and thirteen.

APPENDIX II

LEGATION OF THE UNITED STATES OF AMERICA

Peking, March 17, 1919

Dr. Sun Yat-sen,
29 Rue Moliere,
Shanghai, Kiangsu

Dear Dr. Sun

I have read with great interest your sketch project for the international development of China as embodied in your letter of February first to me. I congratulate you upon the broad and statesmanlike attitude with which you treat this very important subject. Your suggestion of united international participation in the development of China's resources deserves the support of all friends of China. It would be unfortunate indeed if the old regime of spheres of influence, struggles for concessions and activities flavoring of selfish exploitation should not, with the conclusion of the war, be relegated to the past. You are right in recognizing the necessity of a substitute for the old order and your proposal of a unified policy under international organization with Chinese participation for the larger development in China, natually assuming that the inalienable rights of the Chinese people are to be amply safeguarded, meets this demand admirably.

We are hopeful that conditions in China may become such that the Chinese people themselves may be encouraged to put their money into productive enterprise and participate in the larger developments. We are hopeful that the day is not far distant when the Chinese Government may be able actively to interest itself in the encouragement of native industry to the end that native capital of which there is a very considerable quantity, may be induced to lend itself to productive enterprises, because of a confidence in constructive policy on the part of the government.

If you will permit a suggestion, I would be inclined to reduce your admirable program to one which would be in closer keeping with the limits of the present world's resources in capital. As we all know devastated Europe is calling for capital for rehabilitation and other nations want capital for development programs of considerable proportions. Thus it would seem that China's program of development must of necessity take cognizance of her most immediate and most pressing needs. We are all united in that transportation occupies a prominent place in such a program. 50,000 miles of railway and 100,000 miles of good roads would seem to be sufficient to engage our attention for any plans for the immediate future. This would allow ample opportunity to penetrate the great rich unoccupied regions in the north and west, which should be opened to colonization and development as soon as possible in order to relieve the economic pressure of over population [overpopulation] in sections along the coasts and waterways, and to accord opportunities to bring the rich regions of West China into contact with the trade of the rest of China and the world at large.

Along with transportation, China needs to develop its resources in iron and coal, the two great essentials to modern industralism. Arrangements should be made whereby foreign capital can come to China's assitance in these two important industries, but care should be exercised so as to preserve to China the iron and coal necessary for its own uses, and prevent China's steel industry being mortgaged to foreign interests, in a way so as to jeopardize China's future in this important industry.

The reform of the currency and reforms in internal tax administrations are questions of immediate importance to China's economic and industrial development.

One of the greatest fields of potentiality in the immediate demands of the New China, is agriculture. The country depends in its final analysis upon the prosperity of its agriculture. At present probably as much as 80% of China's population is agricultural. China's greatest problem is the proper feeding and clothing of its vast population. Improved conditions in agriculture, opening of new lands to cultivation, irrigation and conservancy works, the encouragement of the cattle and sheep industries, the developemnt of the cotton industry and the improvement of tea, silk and the seed crops of China, are timely subjects in any program of developments. There is a vast work to be done in agriculture in China, which will lead to prosperity generally, and make possible developments with native capital in other fields of activity, whereas if agricultural improvements are neglected, it will be difficult to insure prosperity in other directions.

Thus for the present, I hope the main thought may be centered on improvements in transporation, in currency and tax administrations, in the development of coal and iron industries, and in agriculture. Many of the suggested activities included in your very extensive program will follow as a corollary to the above.

In thinking of all these developments, I believe that we should always give thought to the fact that we are not dealing with a new country but with one in which social arrangements are exceedingly intricate and in which a long-tested system of agricultural and industrial organization exists. It is to my mind most important that the transition to new methods of industry and labor should not be sudden but that the old abilites and values should be gradually transmuted. It is important that the artistic ability existing in the silk and porcelain manufacture, etc. should be maintained and fostered, and not superseded by cheaper processes. It is also highly important that no export of food should be permitted, except as to clearly ascertained surpluses of production. It would produce enormous suffering were the food prices in China suddenly to be raised to the world market level. The one factor in modern organization which the Chinese must learn better to understand is the corporation, and the fiduciary relationship which the officers of the corporation ought to occupy with respect to the stockholders. If the Chinese cannot learn to use the corporation properly, the organization of the national credit cannot be effected. Here, too, it is necessary that the capital of personal honesty which was accumulated under the old system should not be lost but transferred to the new methods of doing business. So at every point where we are planning for a better and more efficient organization, it seems necessary to hold on to the values created in the past and not to disturb the entire balance of society by too sudden changes.

I wish again to congratulate you upon the statesmanlike view with which you consider the whole question of the development of your country, and the very timely suggestions you have to make in regard to a united policy of international participation in these developments. I am glad to note that the minds of the leaders among the Chinese people today are being centered more and more upon the constructive needs of the country and efforts are being made to meet these needs, in full appreciation of China's relations with the people of other nations, to the end that China's developments in the future may work in harmony with the world developments generally.

I should be glad to hear from you further and more in detail concerning development plans.

Believe me, with the highest regard,

                                      Sincerely yours,
                                      (Signed)
                                      PAUL S. REINSCH

APPENDIX III

DEPARTMENT OF COMMERCE
OFFICE OF THE SECRETARY, WASHINGTON

May 12, 1919

Hon. Sun Yat-sen,
29 Rue Moliere,
Shanghai, China

Your Excellency:

I have read with the greatest interest the project for the International Development of China enclosed in your letter of March 17th, and agree with you that the economic development of China would be of the greatest advantage, not only to China, but to the whole of mankind.

The plans you propose, however, are so complex and extensive that it will take many years to work them out in detail. You doubtless are fully aware that it would take billions of dollars to carry out even a small portion of your proposals and that most of them would not be able to pay interest charges and expenses of operation for some years. The first question to be decided, therefore, is how the interest charges on the necessary loans could be met. The revenues of the Chinese Republic are already too heavily burdened with the interest charges on existing Government loans to warrant further charges, and hence it would seem necessary for the present to limit the projects for development to those which seem sufficiently remunerative to attract private capital. The government of the United States has consistently endeavored to manifest its disinterested friendship for the people of China and will undoubtedly cooperate in every proper way in proposals to advance their best interests.

Please accept my thanks for your kindness in submitting your proposals.

            Respectfully,
            (Signed)
            WILLIAM C. REDFIELD
            Secretary

APPENDIX IV

IL MINISTRO DELLA GUERRA

Rome, 17 Maggio, 1919

Most Honorable Sun Yat-sen,
29 Rue Moliere,
Shanghai, China

Honorable Sir:

I thank you for having so kindly communicated to me the interesting project regarding how to employ through an International Organization the exuberant industrial activities created by the war, in order to exploit the great hidden riches of China.

Though aware of the practical difficulties which present themselves in the accomplishment of this project, it meets with my utmost appreciation, I assure you, for the modern spirit by which it is animated and for the depth of its conception.

Accept my best wishes for complete success, in the advantage of your noble country and for the interest of humanity.

Believe Me,

                                  Faithfully yours,
                                  (Signed)
                                  GENERAL CAVIGLIA

APPENDIX V

Peking, June 17, 1919

Hon. Sun Yat-sen,
c/o Far Eastern Review,
Shanghai

Dear Sir:

Permit me as a professional railway man to express my pleasure with your article appearing in the *Far Eastern Review* for June.

I will not at this time express approval or disapproval of the route which you have chosen, but the idea of a line to connect up the great agricultural interior with the densely populated coast appeals to me strongly. I feel that you are making a definite contribution to railway economic theory in this respect, whereas the line itself would relieve congestion, open up a production area which would lower food costs, furnish employment to large numbers of soldiers to be disbanded, and put in circulation a large amount of hard money which would go far to correct the currency situation.

I am especially pleased to have your article appear at this time for I had already written one at the request of the publishers of the forthcoming *Trans-Pacific* magazine in which I touched upon the same line of thought. This will not appear until July and your opinions will have done much to prepare the minds of sceptics upon the subject by that time.

I trust that this intrusion of an entire stranger may be pardoned, and that you will continue to support the thought which you have so ably presented.

                                                     Very truly yours,

                                                    (Signed)

                                                   J. E. BAKER

APPENDIX VI

3, PIAZZA DEL POPOLO, ROMA

August 30, 1919

Dr. Sun Yat-sen,
29 Rue Moliere,
Shanghai, China

My Dear Dr. Sun Yat-sen:

I thank you for your very kind letter of June 19th which has just been forwarded to me from my office in Rome, also for your kindness in sending me your splendid project "To assist the Readjustment of Post-bellum Industries", and the program for "The International Development of China".

I assure you I read your proposals and studied the maps in connection with your able and logical argument with the deepest interest. And I beg you to accept my hearty congratulations.

I am entirely convinced that your noble *ideals will be* realised, not only for the benefit of China and the welfare of your own people, but for the benefit and prosperity of the whole human race.

The Nations cannot continue to deny in the future as they have in the past, the unlimited natural resources of your rich fertile country, in foods, minerals, coal and iron, etc. ; and your plans for development and activity, as well as your methods of communication for expanding and cultivating almost untouched miles of virgin soil, and bringing these products to the doors of the "World Market" by a practical and economic plan, scientifically studied out, places you at once among the very rare few unselfish humanitarian benefactors, and reveals so clearly your profound international sympathies.

The development of China's natural resources will give a new impetus and vitality to industry and commerce in your country and will not only be of incalculable benefit to your own people, but offer undeniable and unlimited advantages to all people in all nations. Therefore Governments and foreign financiers should not hesitate in giving your plans their most careful consideration and support, and come to your assistance in the realisation of your grand humanitarian project.

The construction of a great "Northern Port" on the Gulf of Pechili, and the building of a system of railways from this great Northern Port to the northwestern extremity of China, as well as the construction of canals to connect the inland waterways systems of North and Central China with the great "Northern Port", and the development of coal and iron fields in Shansi which would necessitate the construction of iron and steel works would not only offer employment to millions of your country people, but [would] open wider, and advantageously, the doors of thousands of well-organised industries in many nations.

It is very encouraging to me, dear Dr. Sun Yat-sen, to know that you look upon my plans of an "International World Centre of Communication" with favor, and that you will further the idea among your countrymen by writing about it in your magazine *The Construction*.

This city, erected upon neutral grounds would offer at once the practical framework for the essential needs of a League of Nations and could become its dignified "Administrative Centre" crowned by an International Court of Justice.

I have presented the plans and proposals of this World Centre to the rulers and governments of all nations, and hope to be able to go to Washington in October to exhibit the large original drawings and personally explain the project from a practical and economic point of view before the foreign delegates who may meet there to assist in the formation of [a] League of Nations, and I have written to President Wilson, who after receiving the volumes containing the proposals and plans, wrote that "he valued them very highly".

I hope that in the very near future this International World Centre of Communication may become a reality. It would be the means of clearly defining and bringing into focus the highest natural products as well as the most important industrial achievements of all countries. This accomplishment would be one of the first definite steps toward more friendly social and economic relations, and the practicability of establishing such cooperation cannot be disputed.

This City of Peace should rise and stand as an International Monument, erected by international contribution to commemorate the heroic struggle and noble sacrifice of millions who gave their lives on the battle fields, in the air and on the sea, that justice should triumph and open the ways for humanity to progress in peace, and free from tyranny in the future.

With the assurance, dear Dr. Sun Yat-sen, of my most profound sympathies for your noble project, and with my deep gratitude for your keen interest in my plans.

    I beg to remain, with high esteem.

                      Faithfully yours,
                        (Signed)
                        HENDRICK CHRISTIAN ANDERSEN

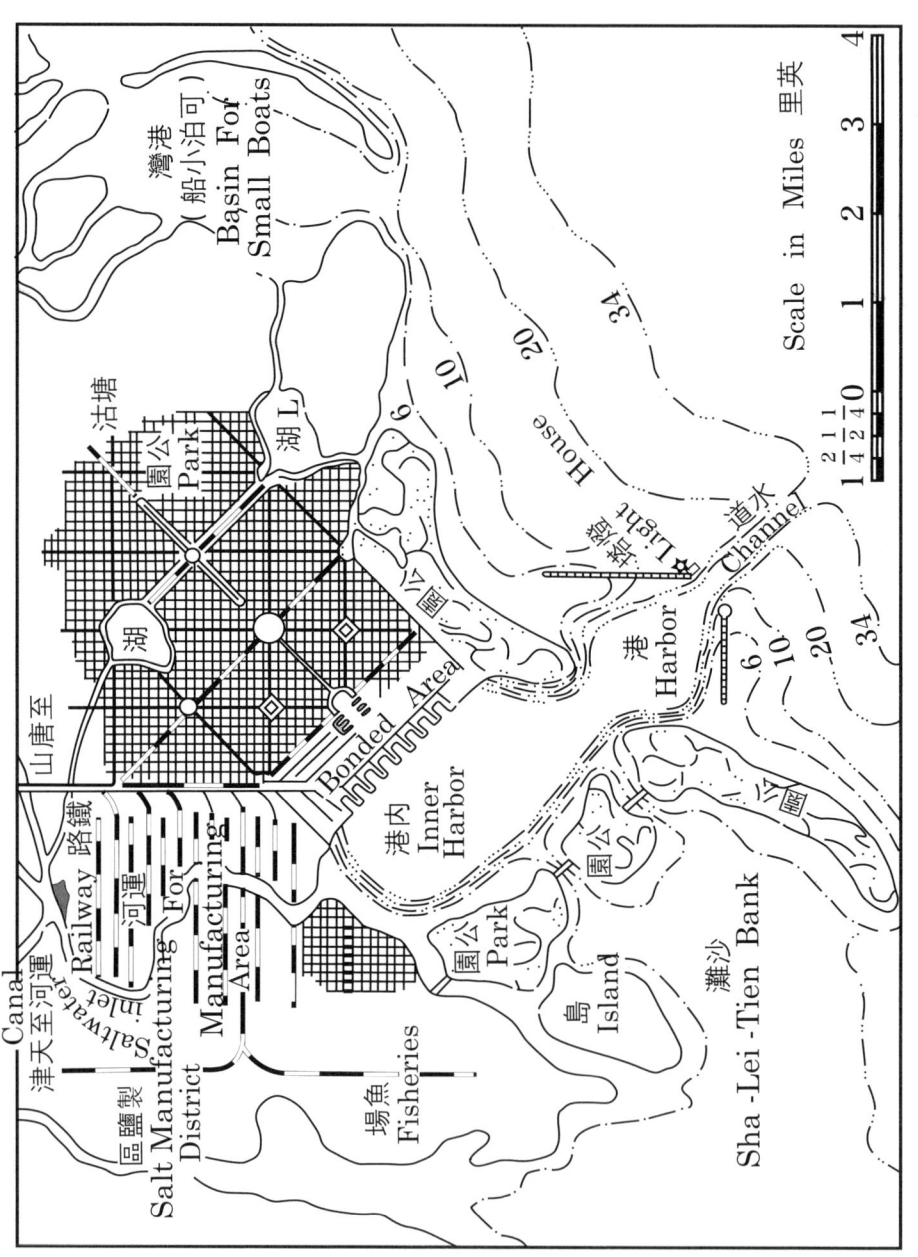

FIGURE 1

FIGURE 2

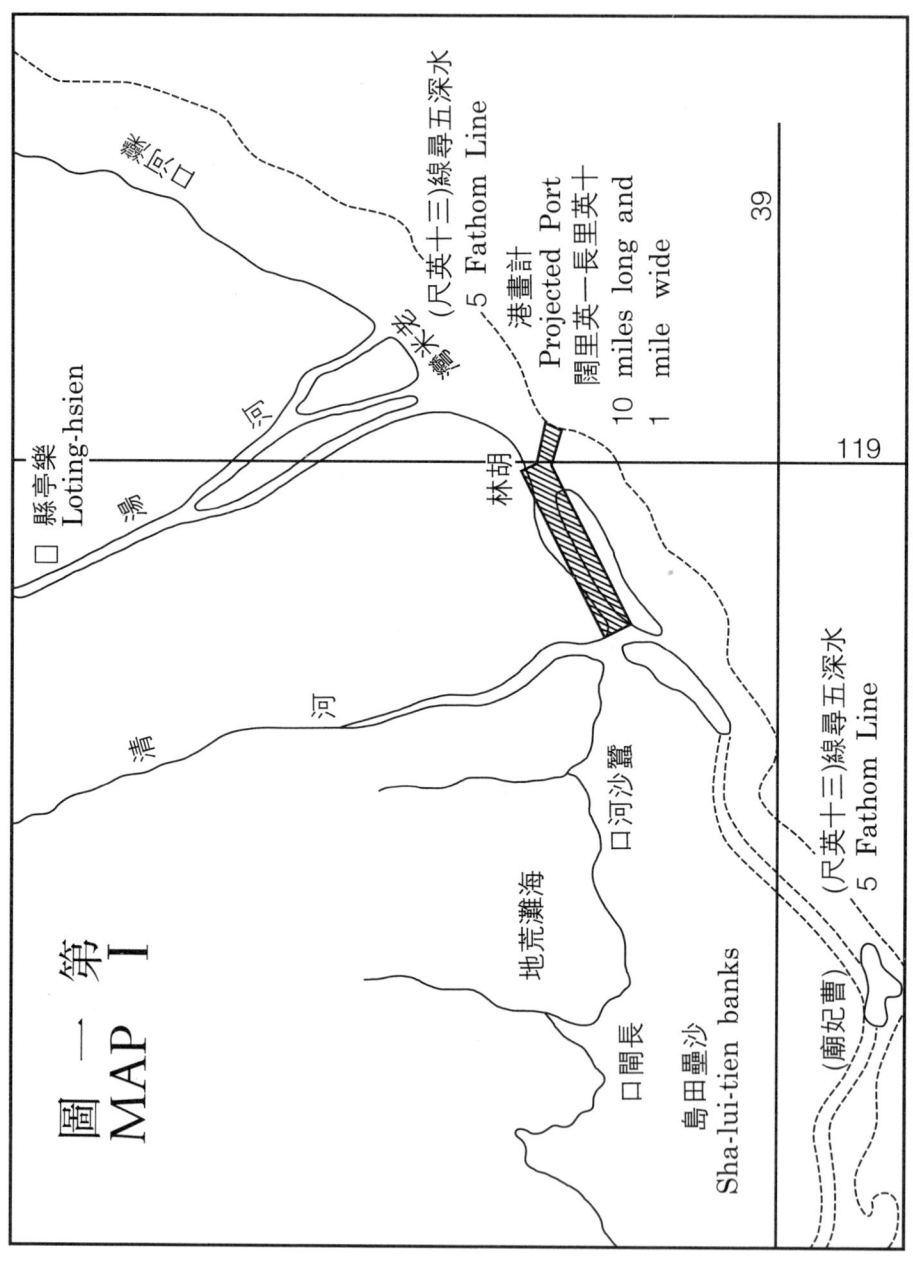

Int. Development of China, July 20, 1920

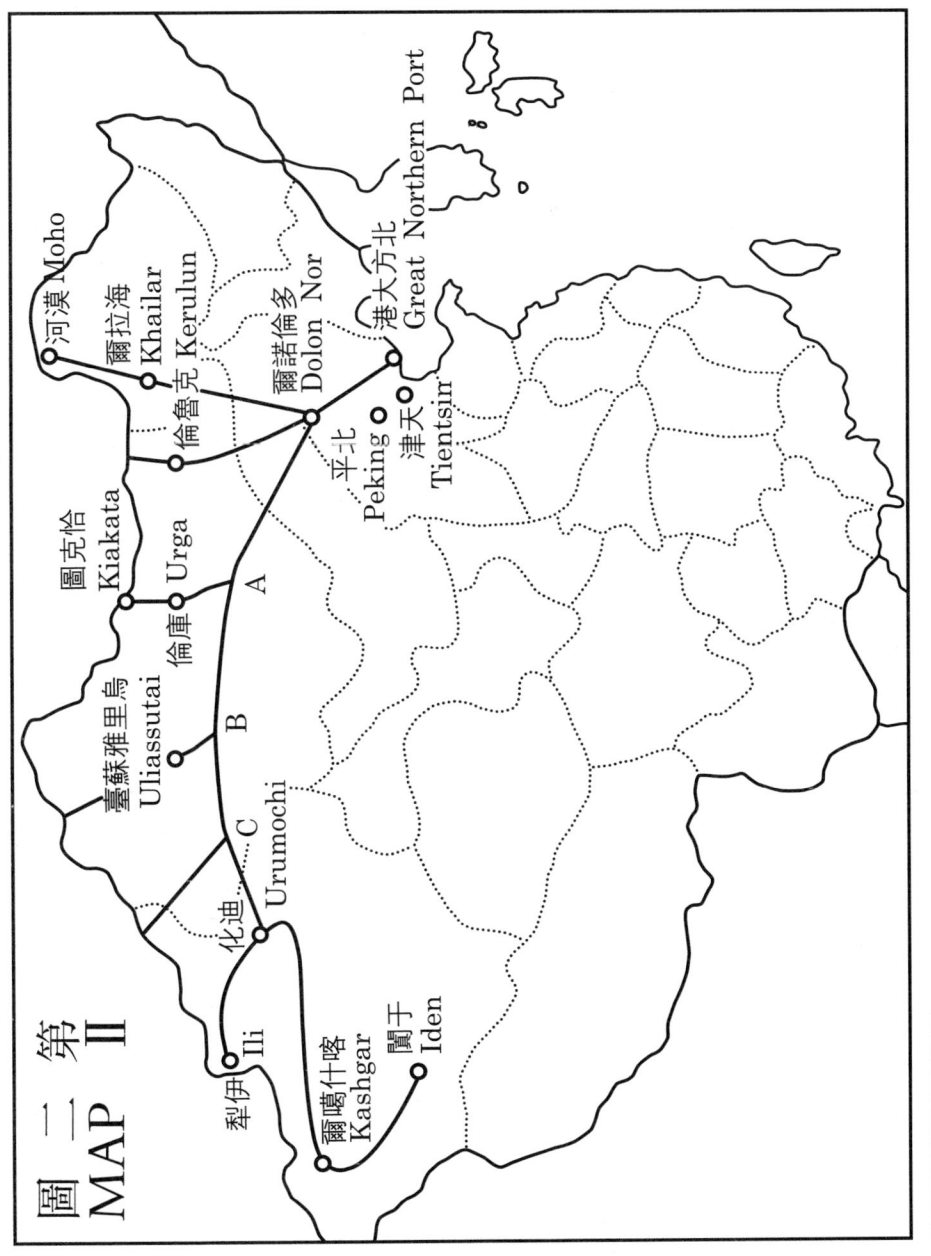

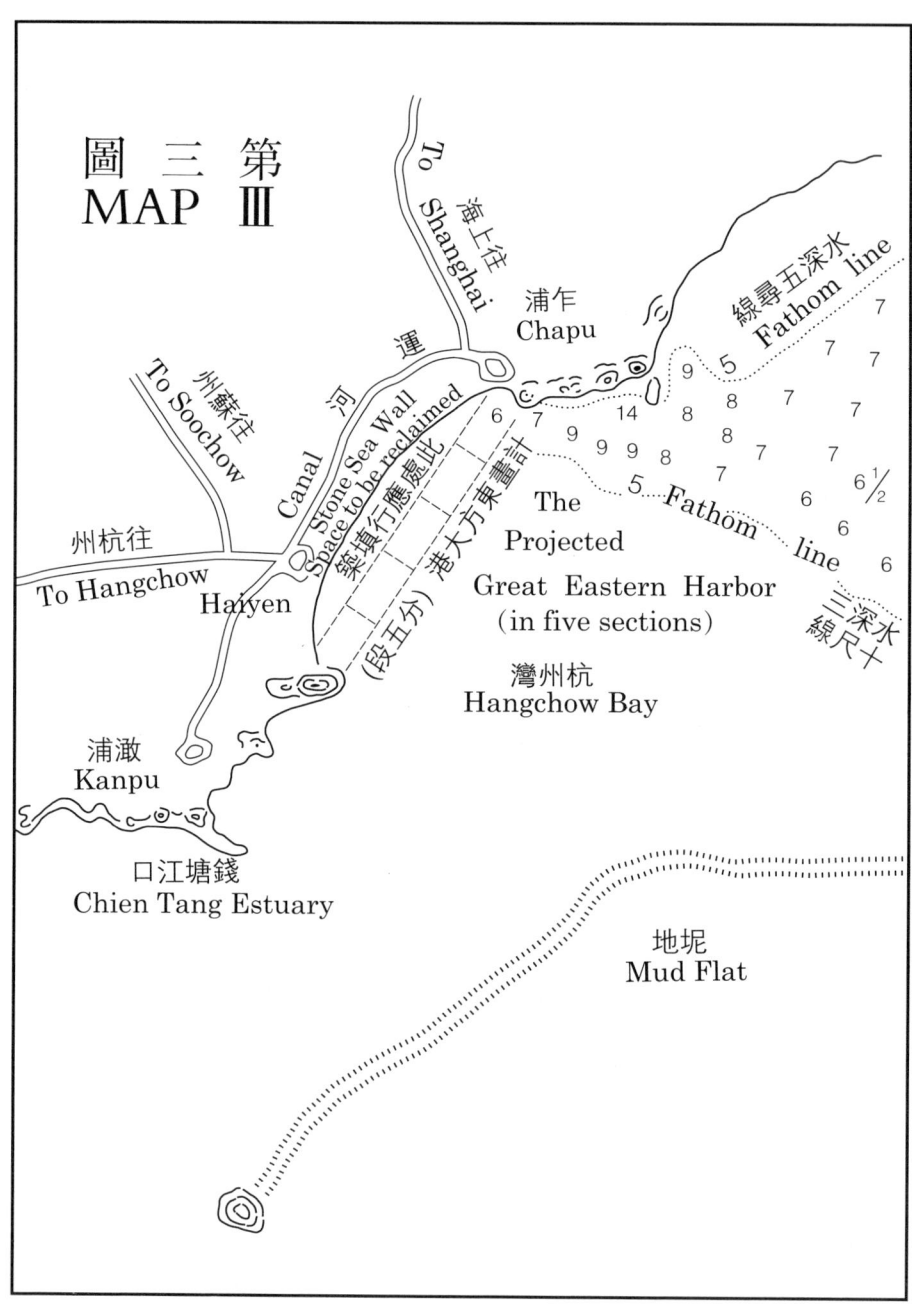

Int. Development of China, July 20, 1920

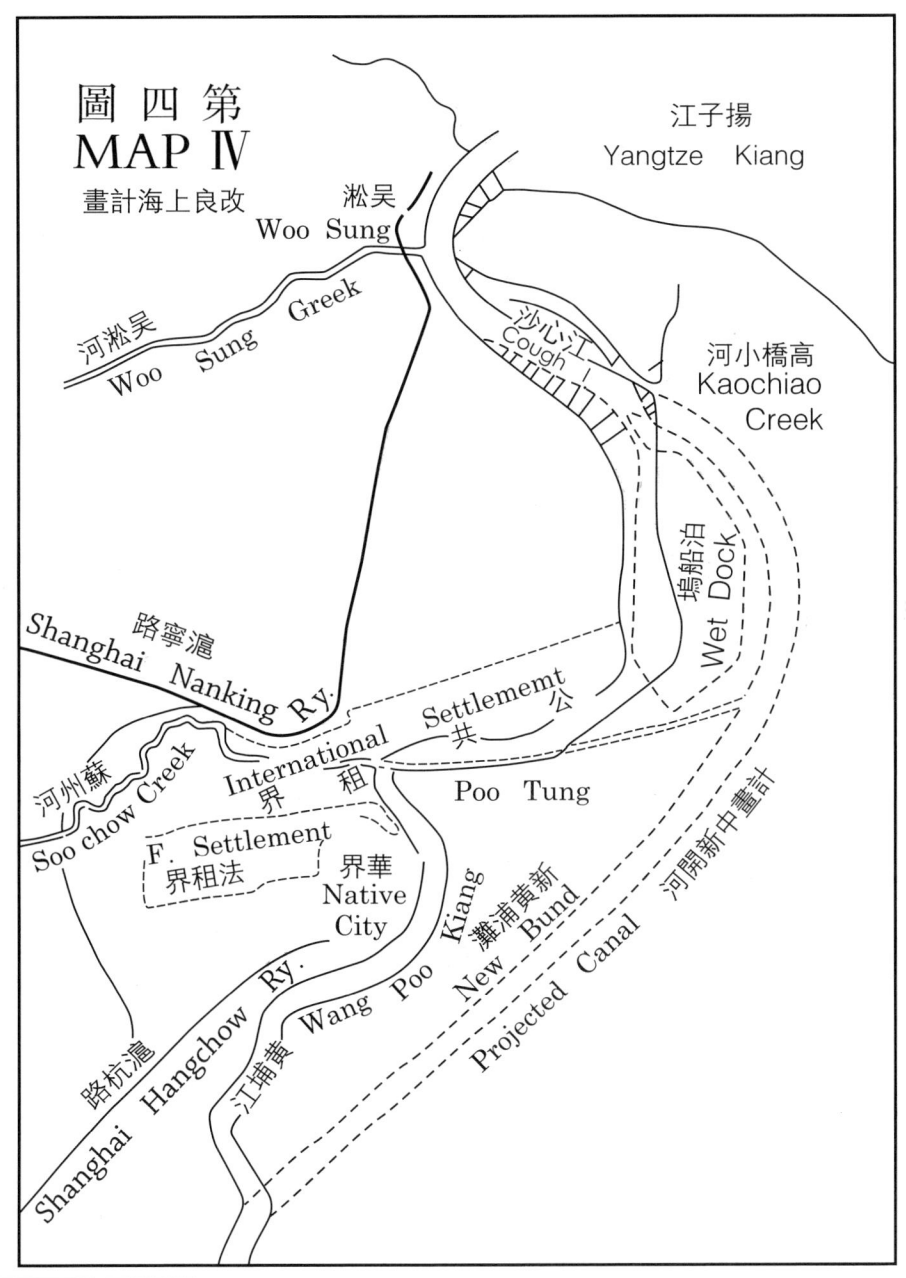

"吴淞河"拼写 Woo Sung Greek 应为 Woo Sung Creek;"公共租界"英文拼写 International Settlememt 应为 International Settlement;"黄埔江"应为"黄浦江",其拼写 Wang Poo Kiang 应为 Whang Poo Kiang。——编者

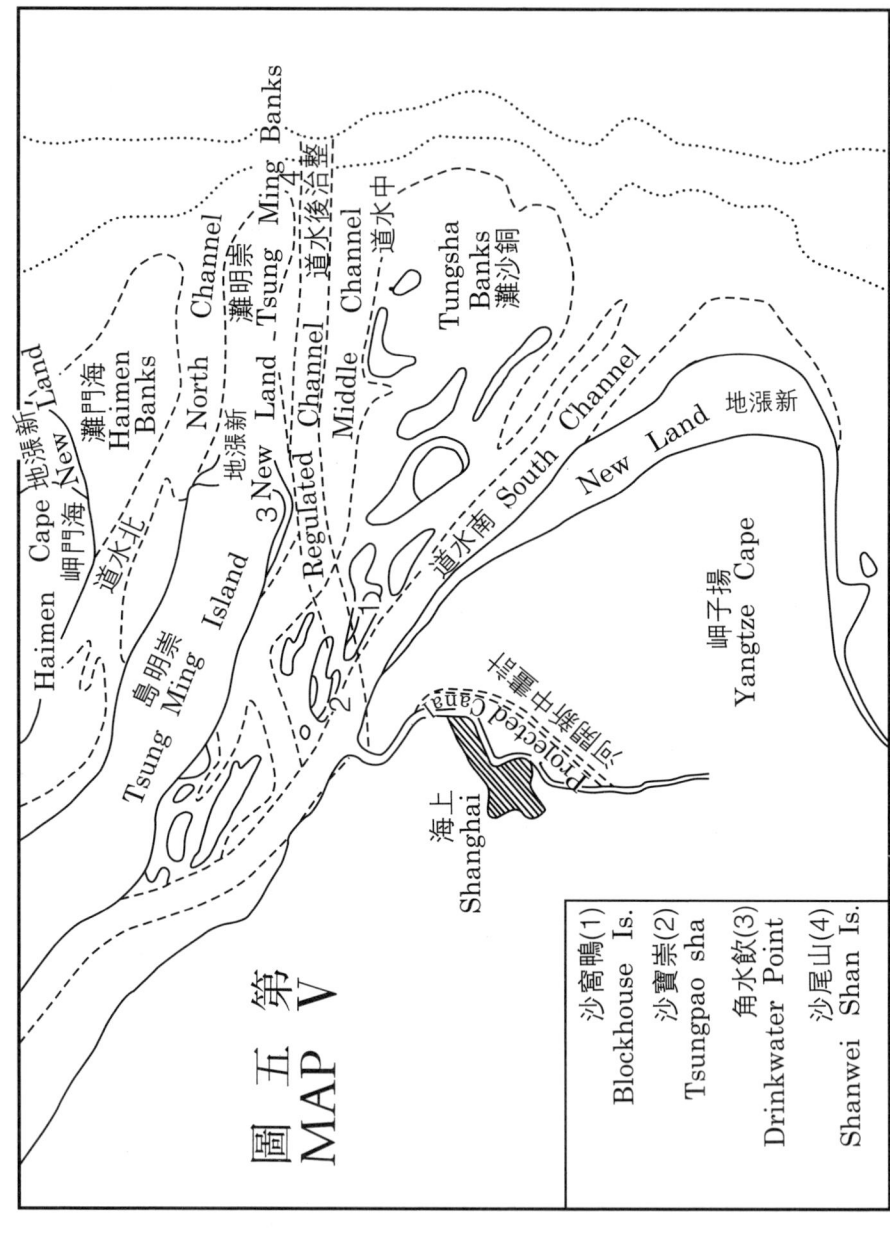

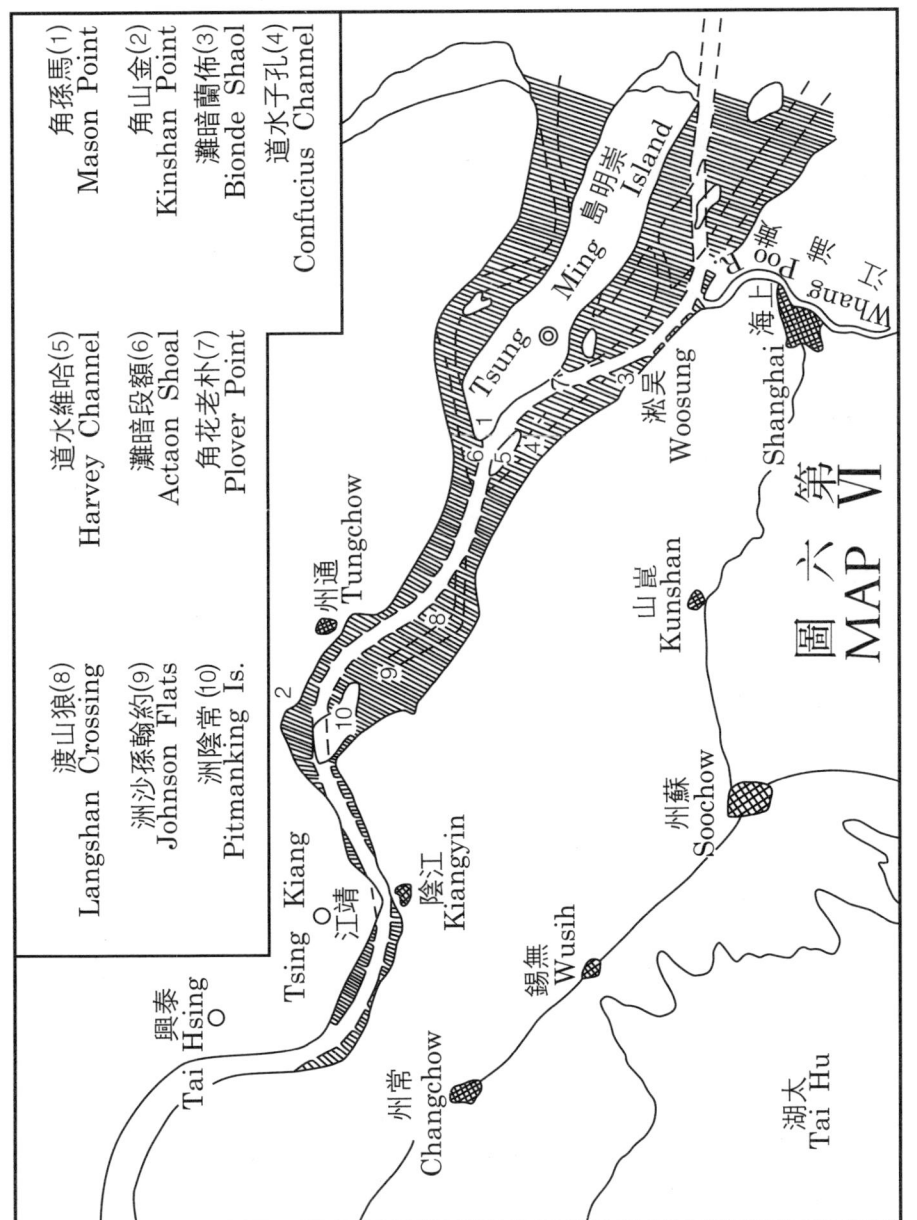

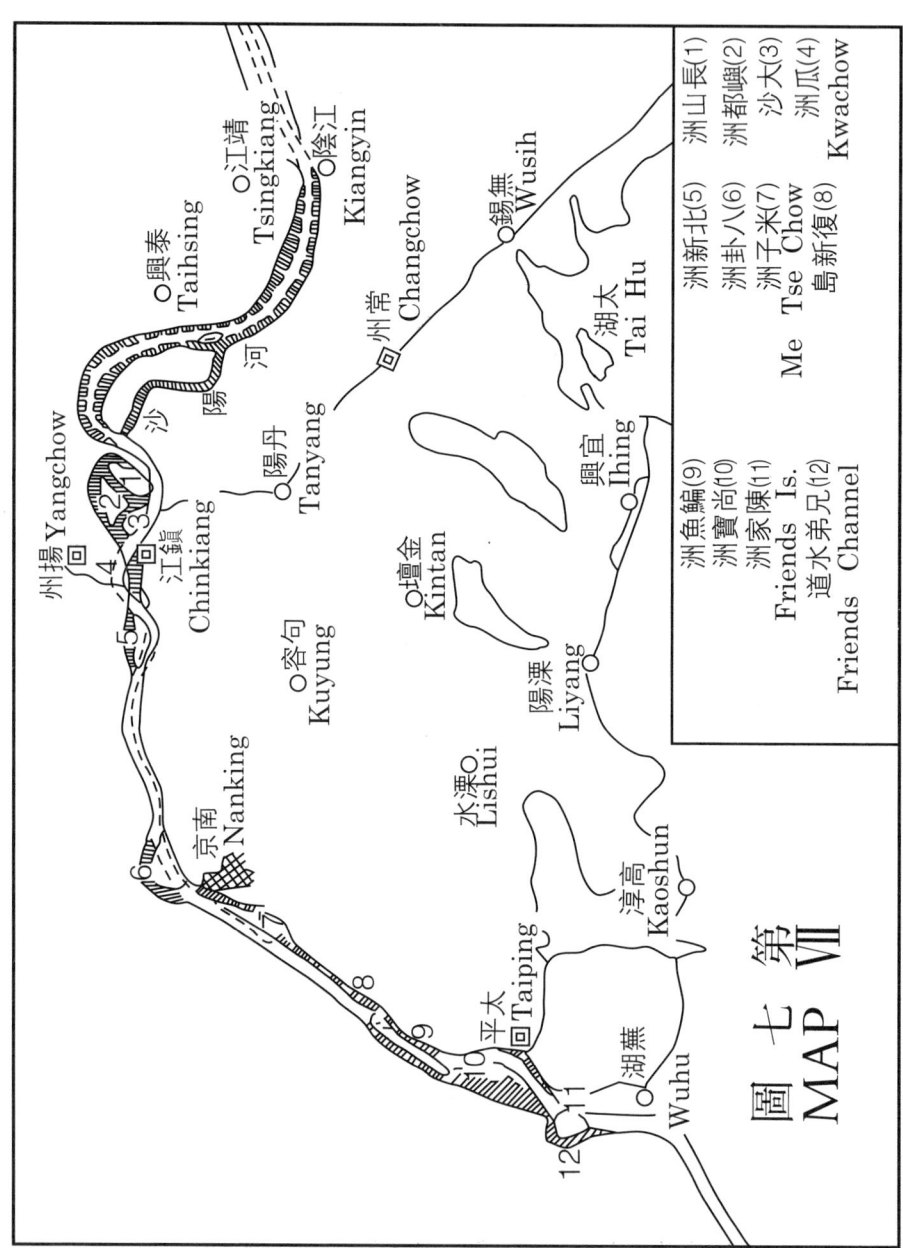

Int. Development of China, July 20, 1920

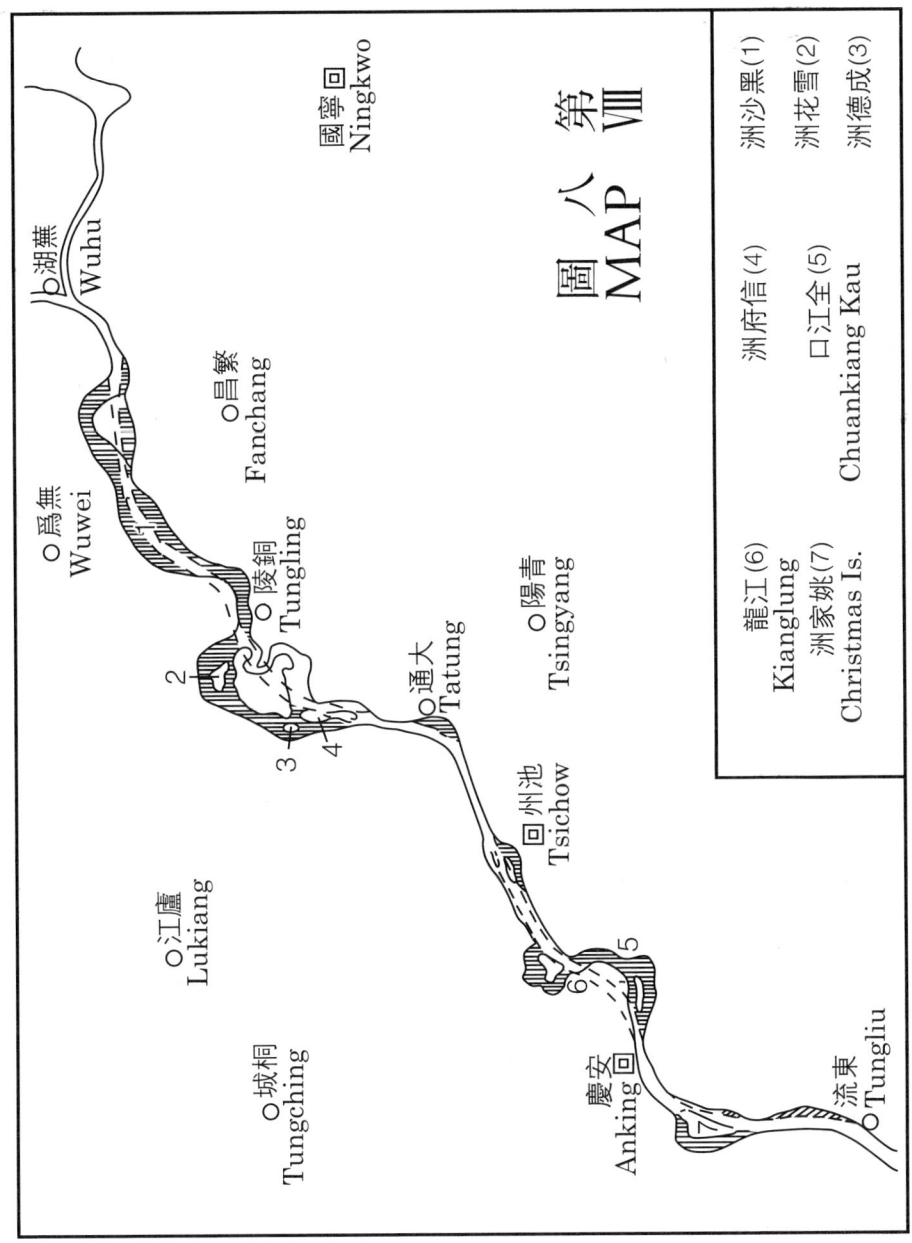

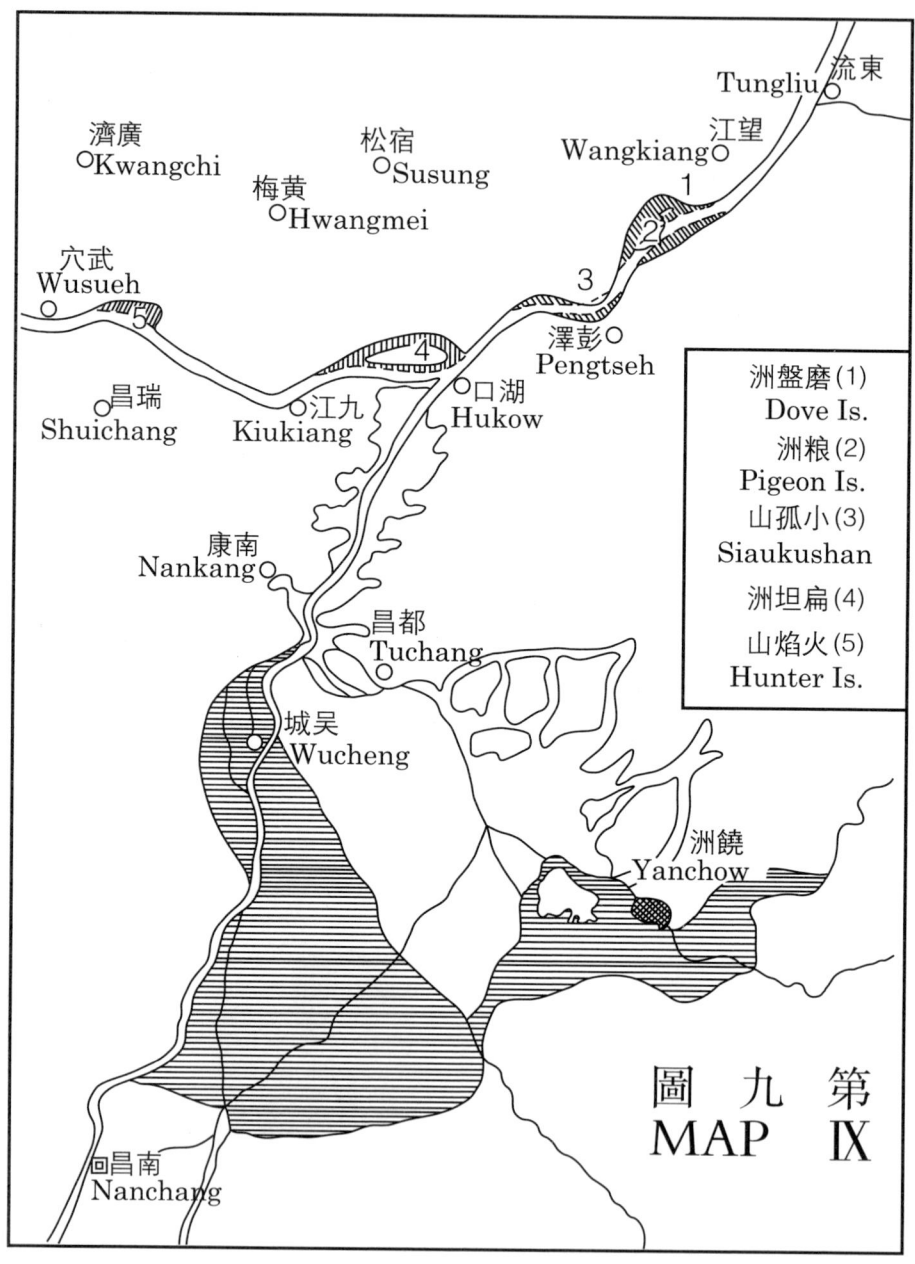

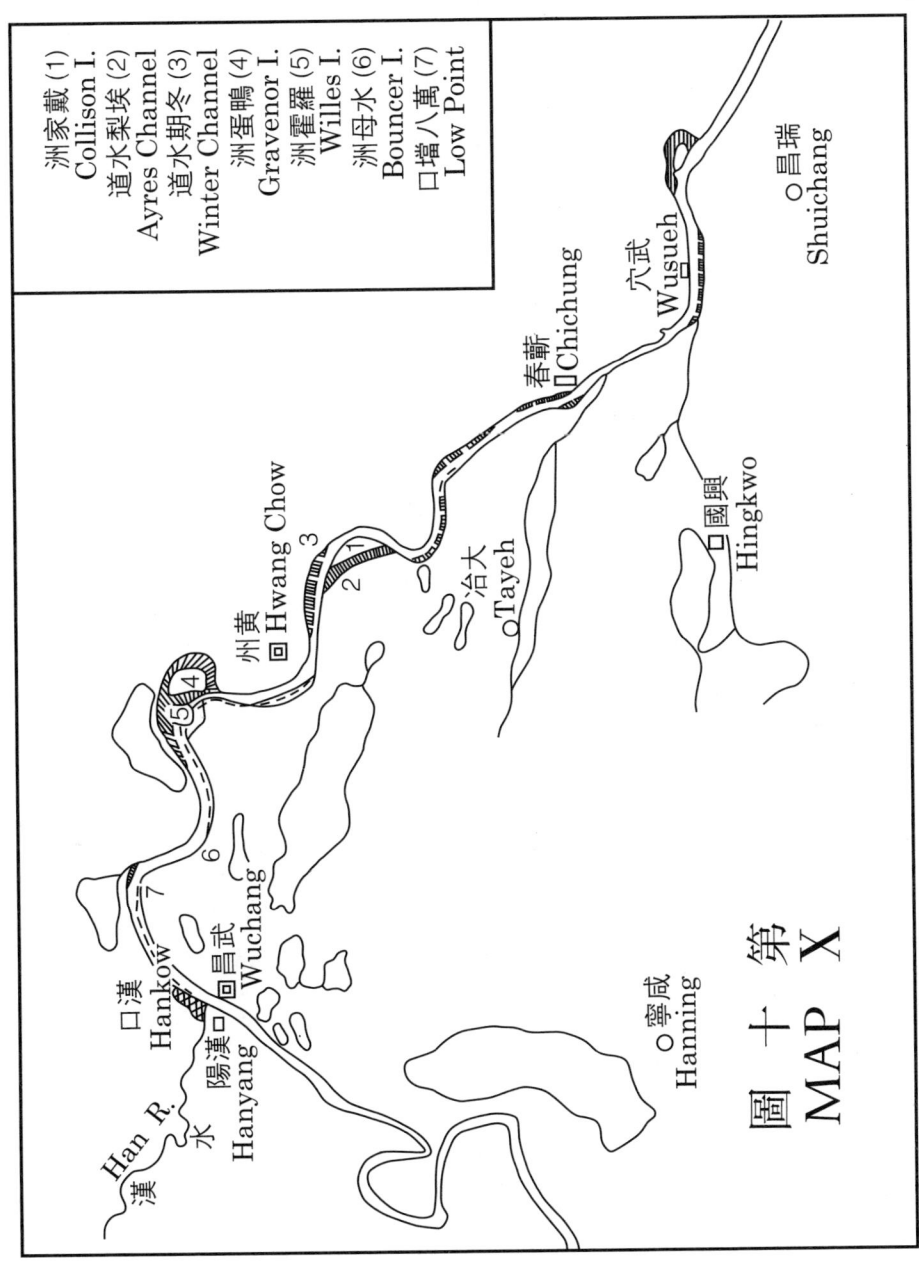

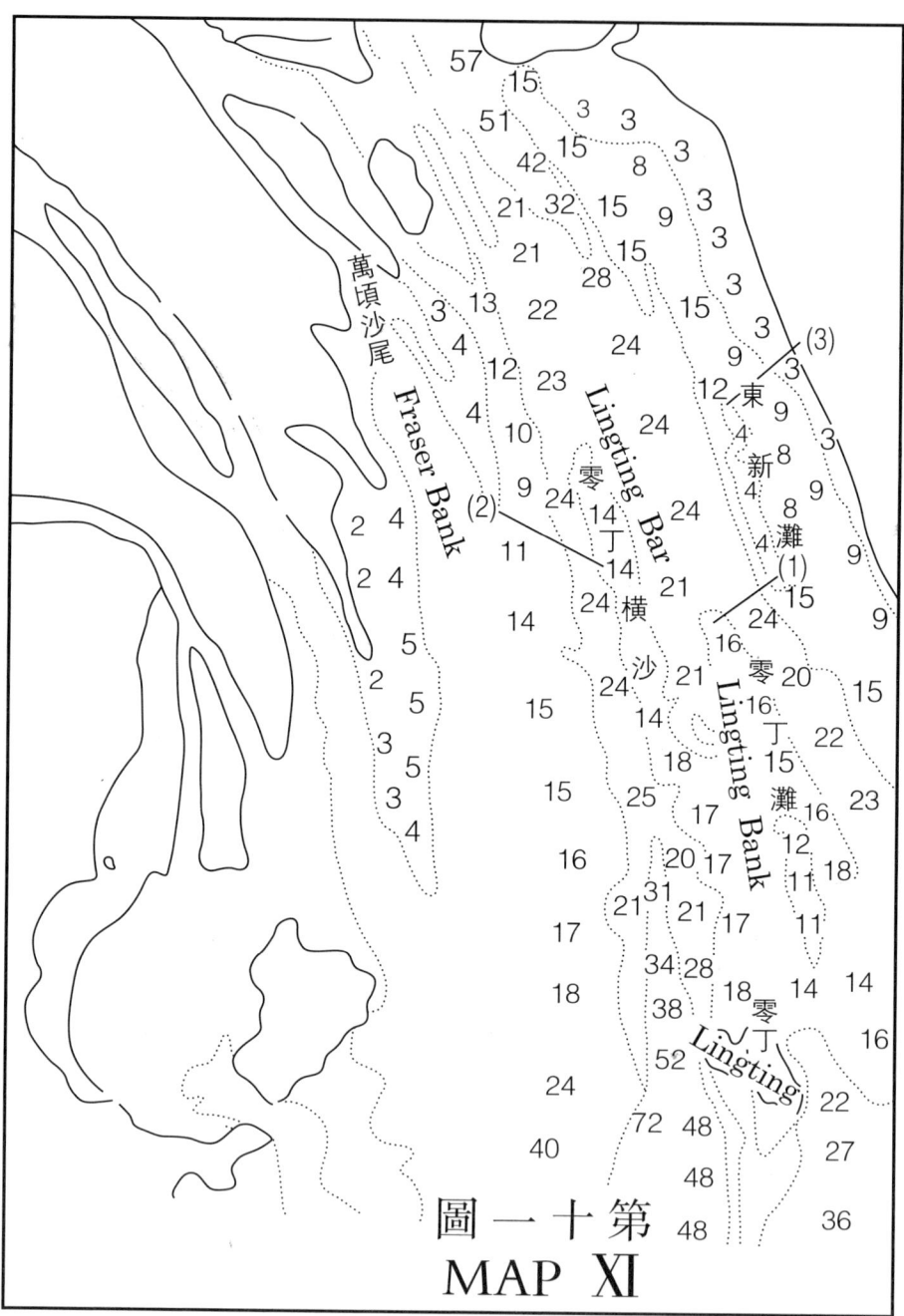

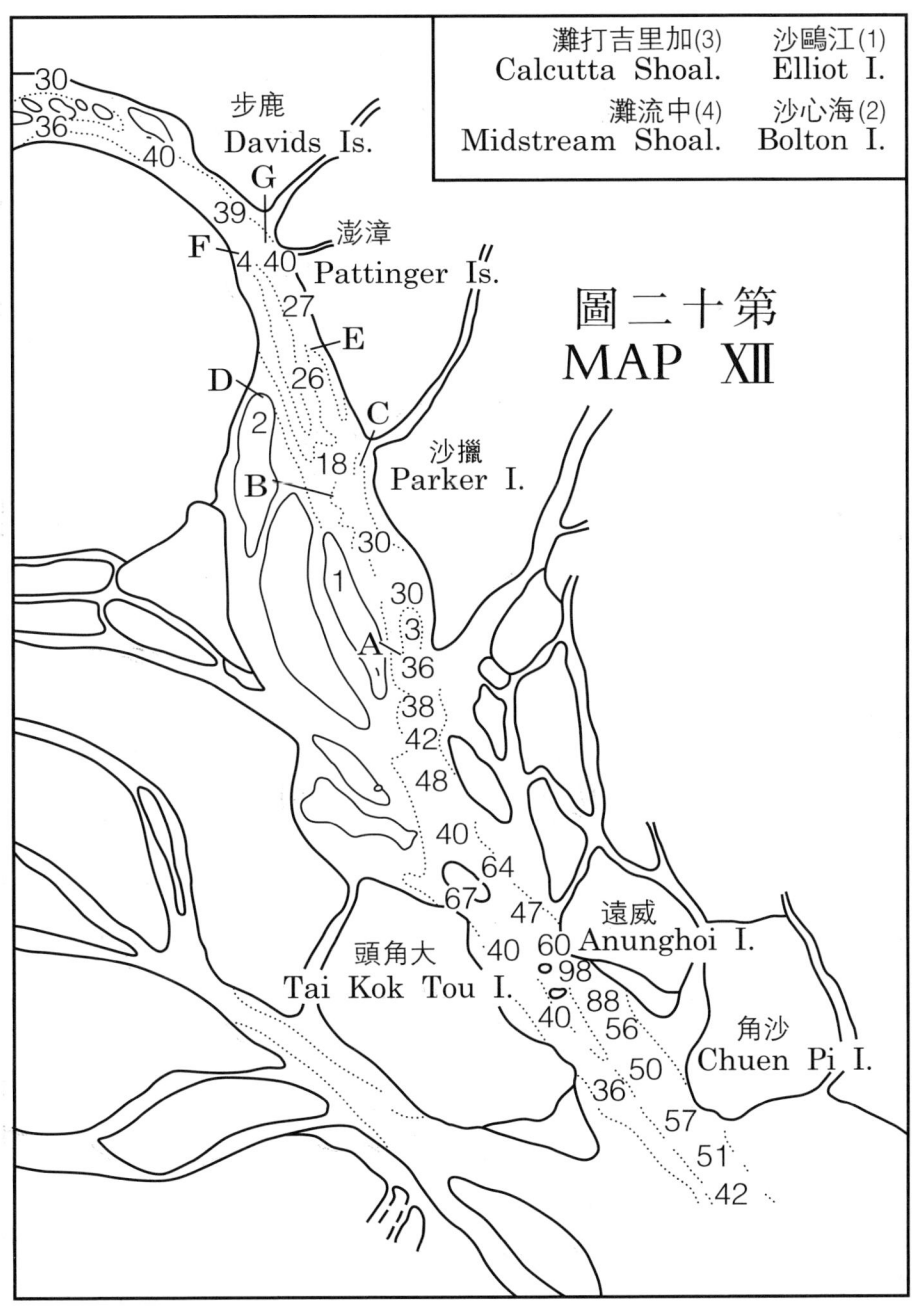

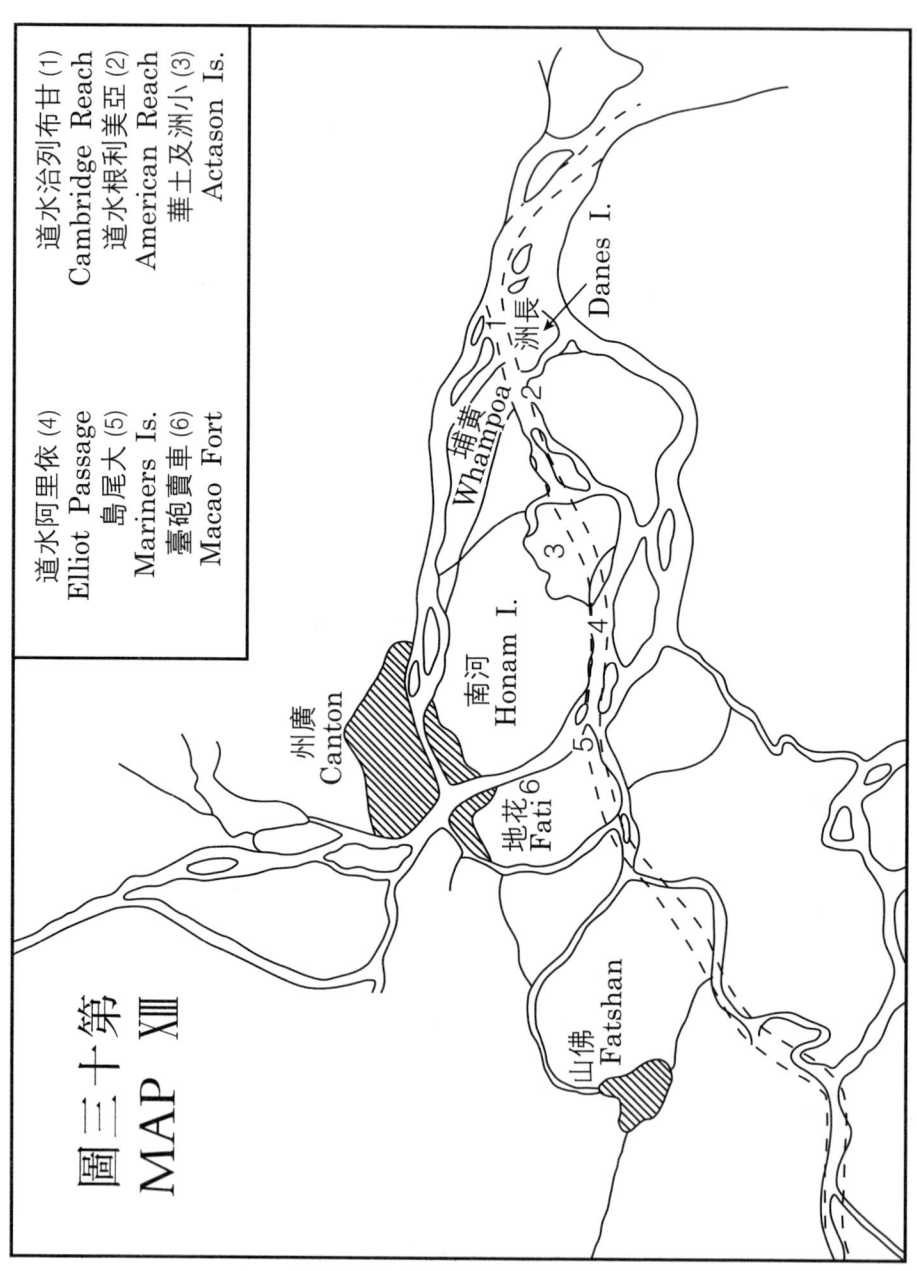

Int. Development of China, July 20, 1920

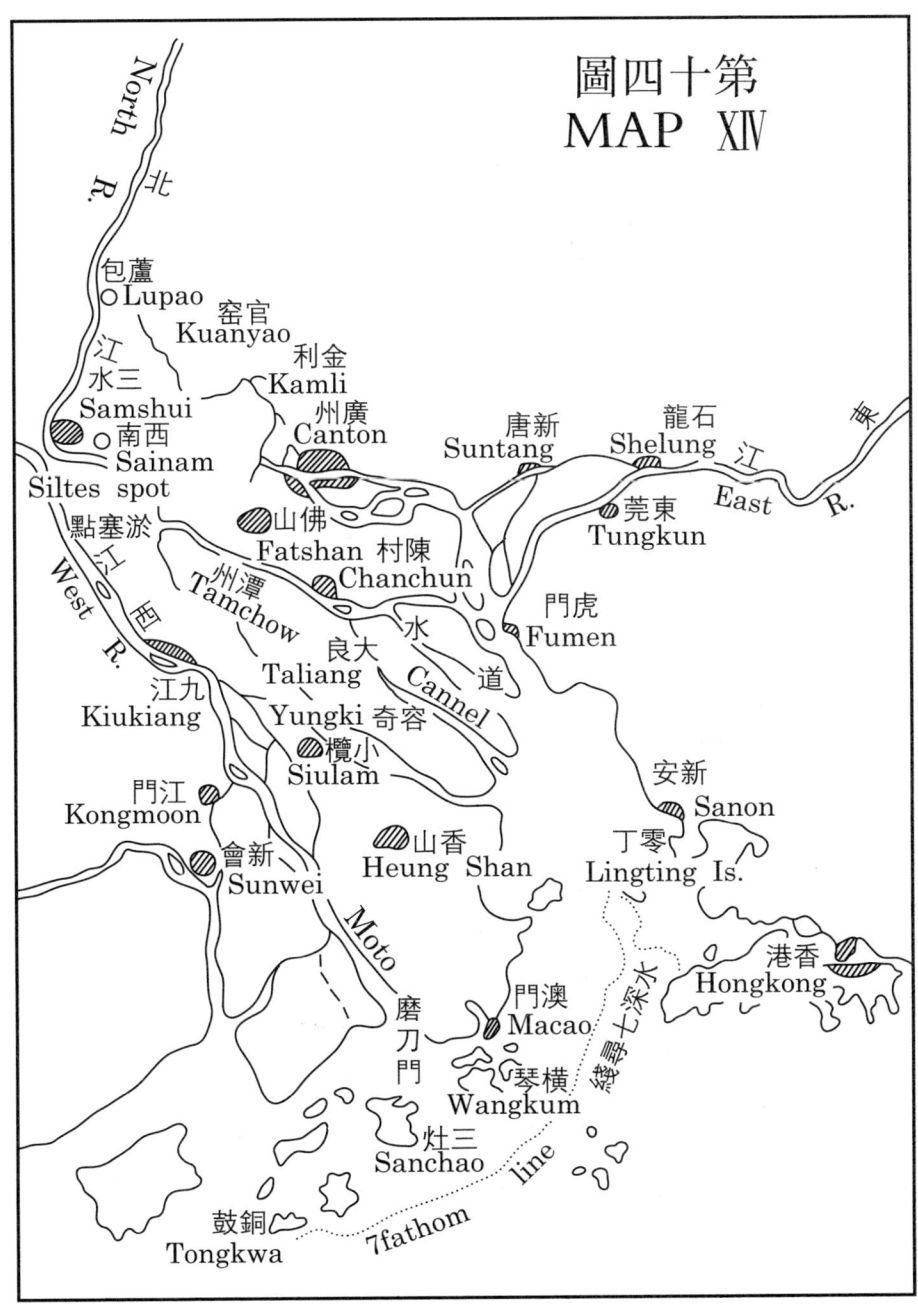

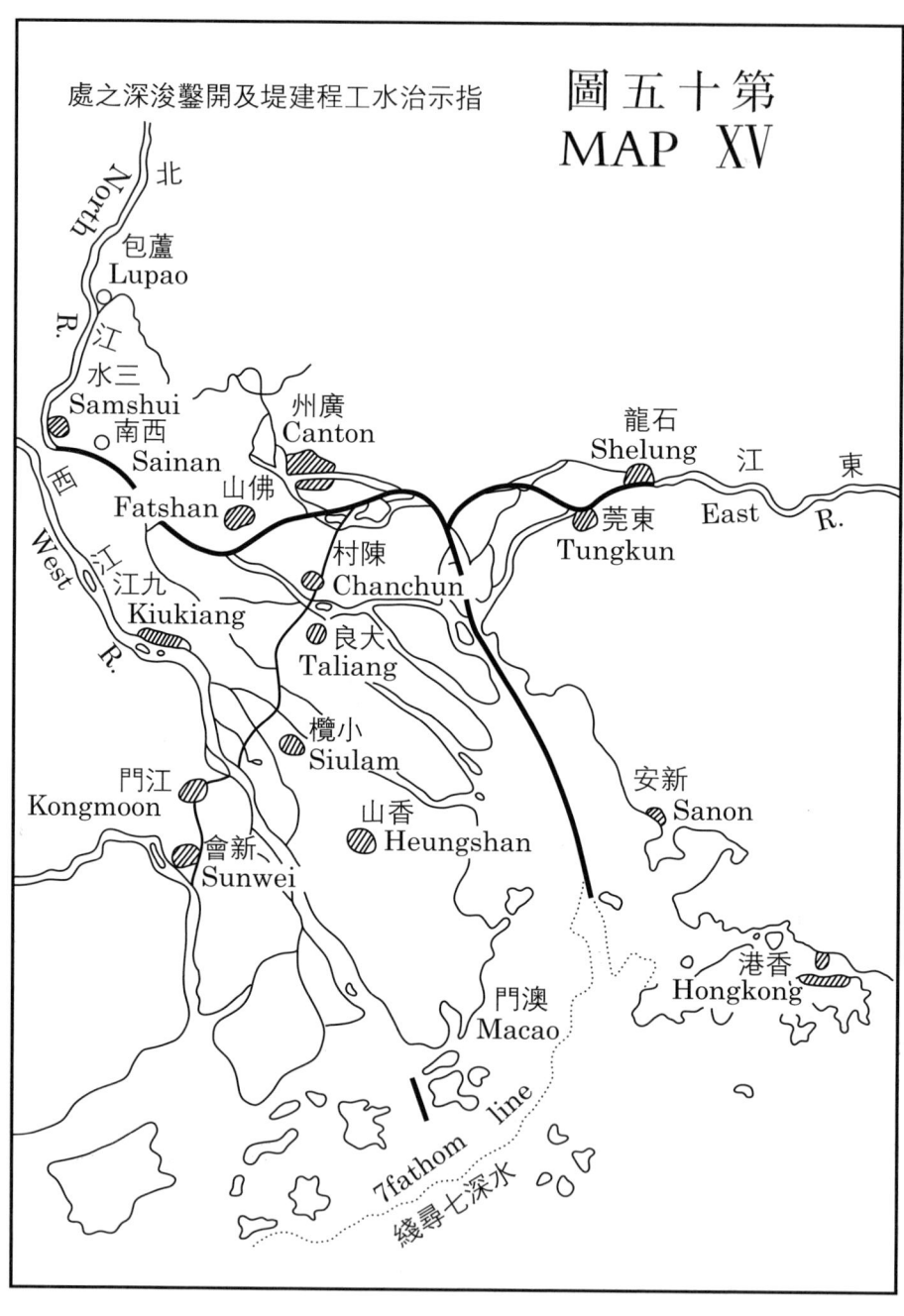

"西南"拼写 Sainan 应为 Sainam。——编者

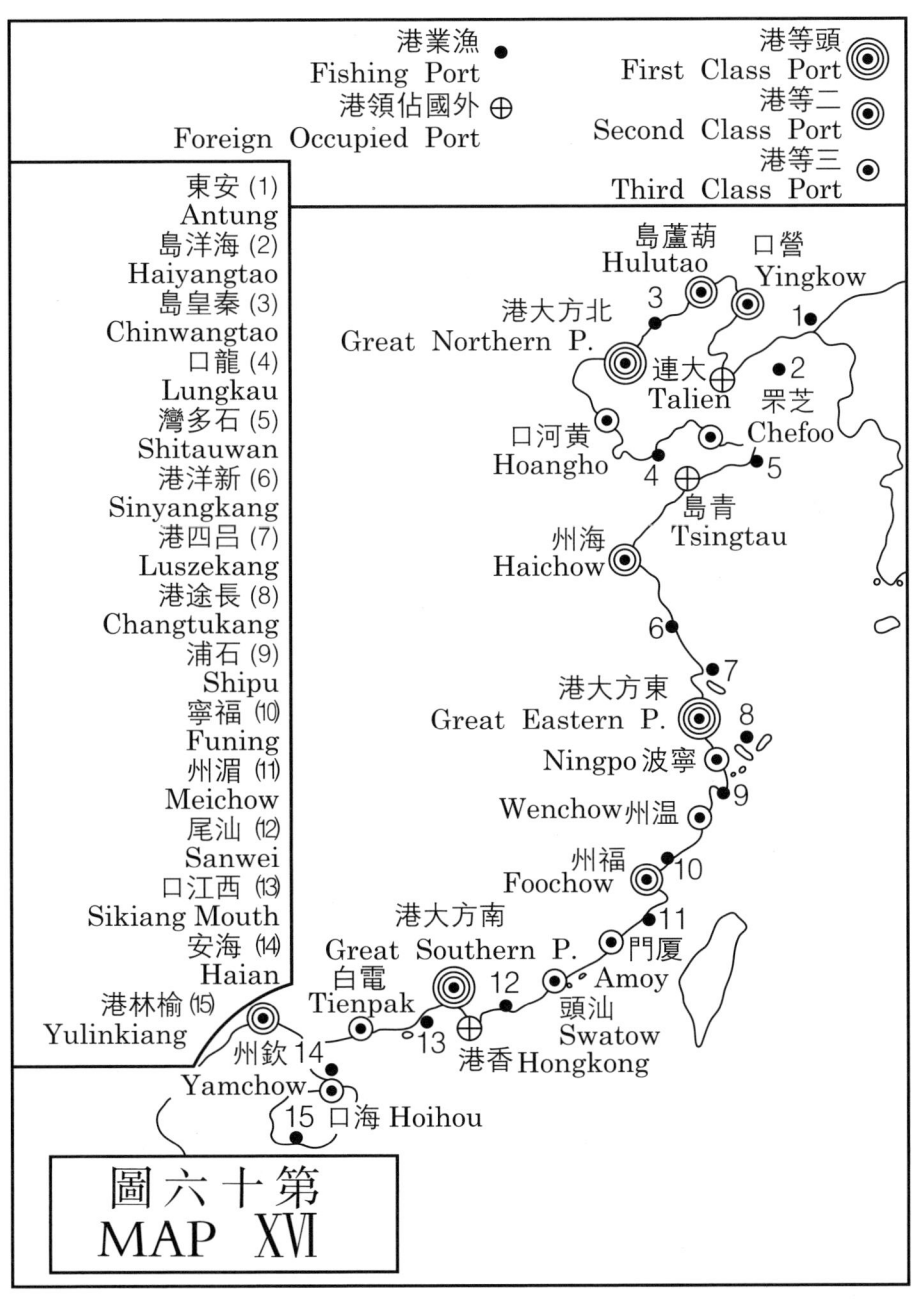

MAP XVI

"石多湾"疑为"石岛湾"之误。——编者

LETTERS, MESSAGES AND TELEGRAMS

To James Cantlie *
Oct. 1896

46 Devonshire St.

Please take care of the messenger for me at present, he is very poor and will lost [lose] his work by doing for me.

I was kidnapped into the Chinese Legation on Sunday and shall be smuggled out from England to China for death. Pray ⟨to⟩ rescue me quick?

Dr. Y. S. Sun

* The first messange [message] to Dr. James Cantlie scribbled on the two sides of a card by Dr. Sun Yat-sen.

To James Cantlie *

Oct. 1896

46 Devonshire St.

A ship is already charter [chartered] by the C. L. for the service to take me to China and I shall be locked up all the way without communication to any body. O! Woe to me!

Dr. Y. S. Sun

* 〈The〉second message from Dr. Sun Yat-sen to Dr. Cantlie.

To Felix Volkhovzky

Mar. 15, 1897

> Gray's Inn Place
> Holborn W. C.

Dear Mr. Volkhovzky:

In respond to your request I must confess to say that I cannot write anything in perfect English without a friend's help. The one who help [helped] me in my literal works happen to be absent in town in the last few days. So in regard to the article on Future and Present in China I cannot finish you with a criticism on the subject with my own pen. But as far as my opinion concern [concerned] I quite agree with its author. All its statements are perfectly correct. If I should have anything to say about it, I am only to repeat emphatically the same as ⟨what has been given in⟩ the article [has been given].

> Yours truly,
> Sun Yat Sen

To Chew

July 12, 1897

Montreal

My dear Chew:

I arrived here this morning on my way to Vancouver and the Far East. Our movement ⟨is⟩ progressing wonderfully. I am called by the members to join them in the East to plan ⟨for⟩ the future affair 〔affairs〕, How are you getting on? Can you do anything in Boston and New York with our patricts 〔patriots〕 to help us in China?

I shall stay in Vancouver until 2nd August, so I hope to hear from you before that time.

I cannot give you my address now and you can post them in care of Mr. Walter N. Fong, 916 Washington St., San Francisco.

He will forward to me when he gets my address in Vancouver. I cannot tell you anything definite about our future movement at present but will tell you when the matter is decided by the party.

Yours truly,
Sun Yat Sen

To Walter N. Fung

July 12, 1897

Montreal

My dear Walter:

I arrived here this morning from England on route for [to] Vancouver and the Far East. I did not accomplish anything of importance during my sojourn in England but our members in China have done a good deal for the cause and call to join them there to plan ⟨for⟩ the future movement.

How are you getting on with the members in San Francisco? Can you do anything to help us in China?

I should like to hear from you. I shall start early tomorrow morning for Vancouver and there I shall stay until the 2nd August then take the S. S. "Empress of India" for Yokohama.

When I get to Vancouver I shall send you my address so that we can exchange a few messages during my staying there.

Yours truly,
Sun Yat Sen

To. J. H. Stewart Lockhart *

Sept. 1897

I was told by some good authority that the HongKong Government have outlawed me on account of my attempt to emancipate my miserable countrymen from the cruelty of the Tartar Yoke. I had asked many of my English friends in London whether this is [was] the case. They said that such is [was] not an English law and usage. But my Chinese friends in Hong Kong answered the question in the affirmative. Will you be kind enough to tell me whether it is true or not? If it is the case, I will appeal [it] to the English public and the civilized world. **

Sun Yat Sen

  * Harold Z. Schiffrin, *Sun Yat-sen and the Origins of the Chinese Revolution*, pp. 144-145.

** Sun's letter to the Hong Kong Colonial Secretary, J. H. S. Lockhart, is undated, but was probably sent in September 1897. Lockhart's reply was sent to Sun in care of Feng Chingju's address in Yokohama. Both letters are enclosed in Black to Chamberlain (who was administering the government) May 18, 1898 in FO 129/283 [46].

To Kamagusu Minakata

Dec. 11, 1900

Tokyo

Dear Mr. Minakata:

Your letter reached me at Yokohama yesterday. I am very glad to hear that you have come back to your own land again. I am looking forward to see [seeing] you soon and talk [talking] over our faring to each other of the last few years.

I have only return [returned] from Formosa last month and may leave here again before long, but before my departure I will call upon you if you cannot come up ⟨to⟩ Tokyo by that time.

Many regards and wishes to you.

Yours very sincerely,
Sun Yat-sen

To Kamagusu Minakata

July 1, 1901

Dear Mr. Minakata:

Your letter of the 1st inst. was received many days ago. I was so busy that I could not answer you sooner. At present I cannot tell you when I shall start my journey by way of Kobe for I have to wait in here for some time yet. If my original proposal could carry [could be carried] out at all, I will let you know all particulars before-hand. As regards to whereabout the lichen is [was] collected, and the rock on which it grows [grew] were covered with thick tropical plants. The valley is wall [walled] in by high cliffs on both sides within which it rains very frequent. All kinds of vegetables grow wildly. There were many much larger lichens round about but very irregular in shape and difficult to take them off without broken [breaking] into pieces. The one I send you is only a medium-size [sized] ⟨one⟩ among its class, but I prefered [prefer] its better shape and easy[easiness] to take it off from the rock on which it grows. This is about all of it that I can tell you. When ⟨will⟩ you come to Tokyo? Is it possible for you ⟨to⟩ come within the coming two months? I shall looking with pleasure to meet you in the Capital.

Yours very sincerely,
Y. S. Sun

Please return my compliments to Prof. Douglas when you write to him.

To. Mrs. Aoe McGregor
Dec. 9, 1903

Honolulu

Dear Aoe:

Before I took my tour to Hawaii I had sent you a book on China and the Chinese. I think you have received it alright. What ⟨do⟩ you think of this most populous and oldest empire of the world? Every keen observer thinks it is the coming nation, and will be the greatest power of the future, if only its people could be made to realize its own strength and resources and could use it properly.

You told me you are [were] proud that you have [had] the Chinese blood in your vein, then you must take part too to awake the Chinese people from their long sleep into the day of modern progress.

There is a much greater field in China for you, as an educator for the young, than in this Island. Do you have any idea to be a teacher in English for Chinese children in China? I think your service will be more appreciated there and your success will be without bound.

When ⟨will⟩ you come down to Honolulu? I should like to see you very much. Have you anything to tell me? I shall be very pleased to hear from you.

Yours truly,

Y. S. Sun

P. S. I am staying at Young Hotel just now, in room 24, third floor. Come to see me here when you arrive in the city.

To C. E. MacWilliams
July 22, 1904

26, West 9th Street
New York

Dear Sir:

I am a friend of Mr. Wong Sam Ack, Los Angeles, whom you know well. I have been travelling with him from California en [on] route to New York, but he has some business to stay behind at various towns in Arizona and Texas, and I come to New York straight first. I was adivced [advised] by Mr. Wong Sam Ack to call upon to see you as soon as I arrived here and tell you of our object of travelling all over the United States. I just arrived⟨in⟩ this city a few days ago, and looking [looked] forward with great pleasure to see [seeing] you. What is the convenient time for you to meet me at your place? I will come along as soon as I get a reply from you.

With many compliments.

Yours very truly,
Sun Yat Sen

To C. E. MacWilliams

Aug. 31, 1904

St. Louis

Dear Sir:

I am [was] delayed awfully long in my returning journey to New York, and was busy all the time and could not have the article, which you directed me to write, finished until this morning. I enclosed ⟨it⟩ herewith for you to print, but before you do that I want you to correct it carefully and put it in more proper English. I special call your [call your special] attention to the last 5 pages which is [are] written entirely by myself; the other part is written by Mr. Wong [and myself] together ⟨with me⟩. You may sign my name if you think it must be issued with a signature to [on] it.

I'll start for the East from this city with our friend Mr. Wong Sam Ack tomorrow morning. We have to break our journey at [in] different cities, ⟨and⟩ perhaps we may get to New York about a fortnight of time.

With kindest regards and best wishes to you and Mrs. MacWilliams.

Yours very truly,
Sun Yat Sen

To C. E. MacWilliams

Sept. 6, 1904

Pittsburgh, Pa.,

Dear Sir:

We arrived at this city last night and shall [should] stay here for a few days then proceed to Washington and New York.

Did you receive and correct the paper which I sent you from St. Louis? And do you think it will be any good to send it to some magazine to print it first before we issue ⟨it⟩ as a pamphlet. If you think it good, I wish you to send a copy in typewritten ⟨letters⟩ to the *North American Review* to ask them to take it up for their next issue.

With many thanks.

Yours truly,
Sun Yat Sen

To. C. E. MacWilliams

Sept. 15, 1904

Washington, D. C.

Dear Sir:

We were detained at Pittsburgh by initiation work on Sunday and only arrived here last night. We will stay here for at least a few days. Did you publish the pamphlet already? If you did it, please send me a couple dozens. Address as follow [follows]:

    Sun Yat Sen,
    Tsue Lung,
    318 Genn Aven.,
    Washington D. C.

With many compliments and thanks.

Yours very truly,
Sun Yat Sen

To C. E. MacWilliams

Sept. 26, 1904

Philadelphia, Pa.

Dear Mr. C. E. MacWilliams:

Yours of 24th is in receipt, ⟨and⟩ your suggestion of having some Chinese letters on the cover of the pamphlet is very good. But to put the name of Chee Kung Tong on it, I could not be sure whether some of the members may not object to it, and besides, ⟨since⟩ the Chee Kung Tong is only a local name used in this country only, ⟨and⟩ it would not apply the Revolutionary Society general, I prefer the general name Ku Ming Kuan, the revolutionary army [Revolutionary Army]. So in this case I wrote the Chinese letter as Ku Ming Chow, the revolutionary forerunners for the cover of the pamphlet, which is a name general known in China for the movement of the present day. I think this name is more proper for the pamphlet, and no local lodge could raise any question for the privilege of using it.

We will start from here for New York in some afternoon trains tomorrow and will try to call upon you as soon as we can.

Very truly yours,
Sun Yat Sen

To Sugawara

May 9, 1906

Yamasita Do, No. 121C3
Yokohama, Japan

My dear Sugawara:

I have just returned to Japan ⟨for⟩ a few days [ago] and shall be away again very soon. I wish to see you and Mr. Hihata some day early next week. When and where will be convenient for you to meet me?

With the best regards,

Very truly yours,
Sun Yat Sen

To Sewh

Sept. 26, 1906

Saigon

My dear Mr. Sewh:

Since I met you I am greatly impressed by your devoted patriotism and deeply appreciated of your noble offer of service to the cause of our country. If there were more men like you, our country surely would not fall under the Manchu yoke for such a long time. Now it is time for the Chinese people to drive this fallen conqueror out from our land, otherwise China will go to pieces very soon. Though the work is great, it is not a difficult one, for the Manchu race is in its declining and dying condition. They will not remain in China any longer. If we do not come up to get rid of them, some other powers will soon do that for us. Then we will be the slaves of another ruling race.

If you can arouse the Chinese in Java to their patriotism and make them come together with us to work for the salvation of our own country, you will have done a great work for the cause. What is most important now is the sinew of war. At once[Once] we got that, we could make war to drive out our usurper at any time. And this sinew of war can only be got from ⟨the⟩ rich place such as Java. Your work is a noble one and the fate of our nation depends upon the success or failure of it. Be strong and go ahead without hesitation.

Hope God bless and help you. Great success be stored to you.

Very truly yours,
Y. S. Sun

To Sewh

Mar. 17, 1908

Singapore

My dear Sewh:

I was informed by Mr. Lianchye that you want to see me. I shall be very pleased to meet you anytime this week at Mr. Teo Eng Hock's Garden, at Ballestair Road.

Very truly yours,
Y. S. Sun

To Sim Boon Kwang

Jan. 9, 1909

My dear Sim Boon Kwang:

I beg to introduce to you Messrs. Jim and Tan who are workers in the movement in Chowchow. Besides these two there are some others who came together to Singapore to get advice from me. I told them to wait until all other parts are ready, then they can all start at the same time. As you have the intention of going to lead the Chowchow men in the future, these men would be the best rolling masters for the recruiting work. You may find out all the conditions of that district from them.

Very truly yours,
Sun Yat Sen

To Ahchong

Feb. 11, 1910

San Francisco

My dear Ahchong:

I arrived here on Chinese New Year [Year's] Day and have called to see your mother and family. I am exceedingly pleased on seeing your two lovely boys. I have no doubt your Father and Grandma and the whole family in Hong Kong will be pleased to see them too. I should like you to come out and see me here if you can.

With my love and happy New Year to you.

Your affectionate Uncle
Sun Yat Sen

To General Homer Lea

Feb. 24, 1910

38, Spofford Alley,
San Francisco, Ca.

My dear General:

Your letter of the 21st reached me this morning. I will come to see you and Mr. B. as soon as I settle my affair in this city. When I come I shall let you know some days beforehand.

Many thanks for your noble feeling towards our cause.

Very truly yours,
Sun Yat-sen

To Charles B. Boothe
Mar. 21, 1910

San Francisco

My dear Mr. Boothe:

Thank you very much for your kind letter of the 19th inst. and the clipping etc. enclosed in it.

I only arrived in San Francisco this morning, for I had been stopped on ⟨the⟩ way in Bakersfield, Hanford, and Fresno. I am going to sail by S. S. "Korea" tomorrow noon for Honolulu. My address there will be: Y. S. Sun, c/o *The Liberty News*, P. O. Box 1020, Honolulu, Territory Hawaii, and telegraphic address Losun, Honolulu. I hope to hear good news from you soon.

With best regard to you and Mrs. Boothe and Miss Boothe.

I am,
Very sincerely yours,
Sun Yat Sen

To Dr. & Mrs. James Cantlie

Mar. 22, 1910

My dear Dr. and Mrs. Cantlie:

I am sailing from San Francisco to Honolulu today, and will stay there for two or three months. After then I may return to the Far East, or may come again to the United States, according to ⟨the⟩ circumstance that may turn out by the time. My address in Honolulu is as follows: —Y. S. Sun, P. O. Box 1020, Honolulu, Hawaii. I hope to hear from you now and again.

I am enjoying excellent health since I have been in [came to] America, and have been welcome from Chinese communities in everywhere in the United States.

With kindest regards to you all.

I am,
Very truly yours,
Sun Yat Sen

To General Homer Lea

Mar. 24, 1910

On the Sea

My dear General:

In my former letter I informed you that [of] someone posessing [possessing] some very important documents of a certain military Power. Just before my sailing I received a list of the same, herewith I am enclosed with a translation. The list only given [gives] 12 kinds but there are others besides, all amount to more than thirty big books. All are the latest work [works] of the General Staff of the Power. I think it is the most valuable thing that any rivalry Power could get. Would you try to find out whether the War Department of this country would avail this opportunity of obtaining these secret documents?

With best regards,

I am,

Very truly yours,

Y. S. Sun

List:

(1) Orders for mobilization of the active army and navy of all Japan.

(2) Orders of coast defence.

(3) Active orders of high commands during war.

(4) Regulation and orders of telegraphic corps in battle field.

(5) Regulations and orders of the sanitary corps in battle field.

(6) Regulations and orders for Field Artilleries.

(7) Regulations and orders for General telegraphic corps.

(8) Important schedules.

(9) Details of regulations of active officers.

(10) Orders of the Chief Inspector of military training.

(11) Orders and regulations of the line of communication.

(12) Orders for heavy artilleries and siege guns.

Besides the above there are more than ten of other kinds of very important military matters.

To Charles B. Boothe

Apr. 5, 1910

Honolulu, T. H.

My dear Mr. Boothe:

Your kind letter of March 24, with clippings from the *New York World* and *La Follettes*, and a letter of D. Y. are in receipt. I have (read) the *New York World's* article. It is very interesting and enclosed herewith I return it to you.

In regard to D. Y. I did inform him of our conference but did not tell him anything particularly [particular]. I told him that you intended to go to the East soon, so he may hear all from you. Now in this case, I leave the matter entirely to your decision.

My son is well and still studies in school here. I think some day he may come over the States to see you.

With kindest regards.

Very truly yours,
Sun Yat Sen

To Ahchong

Apr. 5, 1910

Honolulu

My dear Nephew:

I [have] safely arrived here a week ago, and saw all our old friends alright. Your cousin Ah Fo is studying in the St. Louis College and at the same time working in the *Liberty News* as a translator. His Chinese is very good. He is a very big boy now.

I have just begun to find way to raise some money for yor [you] and your folks to go back ⟨to⟩ China, but today I received a telegram from your Father says [saying] that Grandma is very sick and ⟨in⟩ danger, ⟨and⟩ want [wants] me to send some money at once, so I have to comply his urgent request first. I am going to send him 1000 dollars Hong Kong money tomorrow. Thus in regard to your case I must delay for a little time, for I can't do two things at once.

With love to you all.

Your affectionate Uncle
Y. S. Sun

To General Homer Lea

Apr. 10, 1910

My Dear General:

I⟨have⟩ arrived here already more than two weeks and [have] received information from C—concerning the affair of C—. The cause of its failure is owing to the too hot-headed men of the first regiment. The time fixed for the uprising was only known to a few of the leaders on both sides; the others ⟨were⟩ only informed that business will[would] start as soon as it can[could] be arranged and did[were] not give[given] any definite date. When the date arrived, we were short of funds to bring in the armed men to the city, and the authorities at the same time got reumot[rumor] of something , and took precaution by having all the munitions of the new army [to be] sent back to the city, and a mechanism of their rifles also taken away so as to render them useless. At that time our men held a council and decided to change the time into the sixth day after the New Year, for the authorities intended to restore the mechanism and munitions on the fifth day, when N. Y. vacation expired and ordinary official business began. And by the sixth day our men can[could] arrive in the city on foot, then a cooperation on both sides, and our business would be a sure success. But on New Year[New Year's] day some dispute happened [to take place] between some men of the 2nd R and the police. The 1st R, however, thought that the real business is going[was about] to begin or have been[were] misinformed that the authorities had discovered the whole affair, and rose as one man [and] marched into the city to attempt to seize the arsenal and recover the mechanism and ammunition, but were prevented and shot down by the T-R garrison. Killed and wounded were more than two hundred. The fight was a most unequal one. The entire force deprived of the mechanism and munitions could not reply a shot and have[had] to retreat [back] to their camp and search for whatever residue arms and munitions. They found a few dozen rifles and 76660 cartridges in the target ground and used that to give a feeble resistance during the third day. The 2nd and 3rd R. saw their comrades slaughtered by the T—but could not render any assistance for they themselves are[were] also deprived of the fighting mechanism. But not withstanding this some of the individuals cast their lots with their comrades and joined the unequal fight. Seven out of the eleven battalions took part in the fight. There were only four that did not take part and they were surrounded before they could do anything. Now the people of the whole K-t- is aroused in [with] indignation against the officials and demand the restoration of every soldier and punishment of the T for the massacre. It is reported owing to ⟨the⟩ fear of a general uprising of all the new army, the government has yielded to the popular demand of K-t. Immediately after the C affair there were mutinies in S- T- and K-s provinces. Now the government is ordering four divisions to be completed in K-t this year so that we shall have more chances to put our men in.

I have just received ⟨a⟩ word from S. C. that wonderful progress has been made along the frontier of Y and K by our agents. The soldiers and people of that region are very enthusiastic in support of the cause and they thought[think] they are ready now to do anything and urge us to start the general movement at once. I have sent ⟨a⟩ word to them to wait until our affair here are settled.

At present there is trouble in Hunan, but I don't know anything about it. But this indicates that the soldiers in the Y are also ready to do anything, if there is no properly directed.

To Ahchong

Apr. 25, 1910

Honolulu T. H.

My dear Ahchong:

How are your folks getting on in Bakersfield? Since I been [came] here I ⟨have⟩ never hear [heard] from you yet. Why not write to me often?

Herewith enclosed I send you a draft of $500 for the passage of your mother, wife and children and yourself to go back ⟨to⟩ China. This is [all] what I can do for you at the meantime. You must go at once without any delay when you receive this money. For Grandma is very sick and wish [wishes] to see you all before she die [dies], so you must be hurry, and do not disappoint me and Grandma and your Father. I have try [tried] very hard before I could get this money, so you must use it only for the purpose I intended. Take the first steamer from any port of United States or Canada. This money will also enable you to pay off some of your debts, if it is necessary for you to do so before you start, but ⟨for⟩ the rest of it you may make arrangement with your creditors and I will do something for you to pay it off in the near future if you will obey what I told you "to go back at once".

Your father is settled comfortably now in Hong Kong. He has land of his own and I will do something very soon to let him have a big and comfortable house, and so all of you may live comfortably together. And when you will be in

Hong Kong I will try my best to support you to finish your medical study in the University of Hong Kong.

Do obey my wish and not delay!

              I am,
              Your affectionate Uncle
              Y. S. Sun

To Ahchong's Wife

Apr. 25, 1910

My dear Niece:

I am now sending to your husband a sum of five hundred dollars for the passage money of you all to go back ⟨to⟩ China at once. When this letter reach [reaches] you the money will arrive also, then you must urge your husband to start the journey immediately without the least delay, for Grandmother is very sick and I wish you all to get to Hong Kong before she die [dies]. Your Father-in-law have wrote [written] to me to get you all back to Hong Kong at once, so I have try [tried] very very hard to get that amount of money for you.

Do as I wish and be quick!

                              I am,
                              Your affectionate Uncle in law
                              Y. S. Sun

Give my best love to the children.

To General Homer Lea

May 9, 1910

Honolulu

My dear General:

I just received news from China today says [saying] that the remnant of the 1st regiment about 7000 men have safely returned to their home in Kanchow, near Kwang Chow Wan, the French Concession. They at once began propaganding work and have already got more than 10,000 followers. They have collected about a thousand rifles with 200 cartridges each from their own district. The rest of the 1st regiment also returned to their respective districts, next numerous to Kanchow men are those of Haifung and Lufung, the two coast districts of the Waichowfu. They also working [worked] in their own villages and also got more than 10,000 followers. At any time the Kanchow and Waichow men are ready for business.

The two undisbanded regiments of the new army in Canton are going to be sent for garrison duty to the Kanchowfu. They [Their] ammunition is still not restore [restored] to them, but when they go off for their garrison duty this must be restored to them. Then we may make good use of those men and their weapons.

Mr. Hu, the party manager in Hong Kong, has went [gone] to Singapore with Messers Hwang and Chao, late regimental commander of Canton, recently.

Letter to Homer Lea, May 9, 1910

I am sorry to tell you that one of my secretaries, Mr. Wang Ching Wei, with some others had been captured in Peking, and Mr. Wang has been sentenced of imprisonment for life. The only hope for him now is the capture of Peking by our army.

I will go to Hilo tomorrow noon and return here in a week [of time]. When ⟨do⟩ you start for the East?

With best regards to you and Miss Power.

Very truly yours,
Y. S. Sun

To General Homer Lea

May 24, 1910

Honolulu

My dear General Lea:

I am going to leave this Islands for Japan on the 30th this month by *S. S. Mongolia*. I shall stay there for a while to wait for news from you and at the same time to do what I can to prepare the way for the future.

I jsut 〔just〕 received information from China that some of our comrades have already taken measure 〔measures〕 to secure concessions for cultivation from French authority in Kwang Chow Wan before they know anything of our proposition out here. The French government there are inviting anyone to go and develope the land, 〈and〉 each application for concession will give 〔be given〕 three acres of land. But application must be sent three months before any answer is given.

I am also informed that there is a certain firm in Hong Kong who would undertake to supply any kind of arms and will guarantee to deliver any part in the coast of Kwangtung Province. Thus it will save us a good deal of trouble of transporting the arms ourselves. If we arrange to buy from that firm, goods can be delivered to the spot where we need before we pay the price. This is the most sure and convenient way, if we could succeed in raising the loan in America, I should like you to see this Hong Kong firm first before we enter into contract with any others. We may use the Hong Kong firm either as a whole supplier or as merely a transporter. For they have ships and godowns in every port in the Far East as well as license to carry and store arms legally to and in anywhere.

My temporary address in Japan is as follows: Y. S. Sun, c/o Mr. K. H. Ike, No. 10, Nakanocho, Akasaka, Tokyo, Japan. I will write again as soon as I arrive there.

With the best regards to you and Miss Power.

Very truly yours,
Y. S. Sun

To Charles B. Boothe
May 24, 1910

Honolulu, T. H.

My dear Mr. Boothe:

I am going to leave here for Japan on the 30th this month by *S. S. Mongolia*. I shall stay in Japan for a while to wait ⟨for⟩ your answer, and at the same time do what I can to prepare ⟨for⟩ the way of working in the near future. My temporary address is as follow[follows]: Y. S. Sun, care of Mr. K. H. Ike, No. 10, Nakanocho, Akasaka, Tokyo, Japan. I will write you again and give you my permanent address, if I establish any, as soon as I arrive there.

With the best regards to you and all your family.

Very truly yours,
Sun Yat Sen

To Charles B. Boothe

June 22, 1910

Tokyo

My dear Beach:

Your letter of May 12, reached me at Honolulu just on the day of my departure from the Islands. I arrived [have been] in Japan ⟨for⟩ already a fortnight, since that time the Peking Government left no stone unturned to get out of this country. The Japanese Government feels rather trouble [troublesome] for my staying here, the minister of foreign affairs positively objected [objects] my presence in Tokyo, but the minister of war have [has] contrary opinion. On the day of my arrival a cabinet meeting took place and the war department prevailed and I was allowed to stay, but that was before the Peking Government try [tried] to do anything. As now the Peking Government impresses the foreign office here so hard, I think I have to leave here on my own accord in order to relieve the uneasiness of the Government here.

Before my arrival some of our leaders have already came [come] to meet me. I told them your view of stopping all premature movement. They all agreed and promised to send word [words] to their own provinces to stop them immediately. I think all such kind of movement can be stopped up to the winter of this year. So we still have many peaceful months to work.

I am preparing to leave here, but friends in connection with the war department wish me to stay a little longer. So my program is very unsettled now, but will write you at once when things are decided.

In case your work is accomplished before I can communicate to you my whereabouts you can cable to Hong Kong as follow:

Chungkokpo, Hong Kong

Ahmi Settled

The agent in Hong Kong will forward such a cable to me at once wherever I may happen to be.

The document signed by representatives of various provinces is ready [in] here. I will send it to you soon.

With my best regards.

Very truly yours,

Chungsan

To Charles B. Boothe

July 15, 1910

Singapore

My dear Mr. Boothe:

I left Japan at the end of June, and arrived here two days before [ago]. During my stay in Japan and on way called at Shanghai and Hong Kong ⟨, I⟩ have met many leaders. They are very willing to comply ⟨with⟩ your wishing by waiting quietly for a time, if there is hope for a successful move soon.

At present, I have no matter of importance to tell you, except that one of our comrades, formerly a captain of a cruiser in the Chinese Navy, is now promoted into the chief command of the whole Chinese Fleet. If time come [comes], I am sure, he would co-operate with us. How is matter getting on in your part, and what is the result of your New York tour? I am waiting eagerly for definite news from you.

My temporary address in Singapore is as follow [follows]:

> Y. S. Sun
> c/o Kong Ye Chiong
> 77 Cecil Street
> Singapore
> Straits Settlements

Cable address:

Enghock Singapore

With my best regards.

                                          Very truly yours,
                                          Y. S. Sun

P. S.

I may pay a visit to Manila in the coming few months. Can you give me introduction to see some of your friends there? And I should like you would [to] ask your friend, the former general in the Philippines, to give me some introduction to the officials there, if you think advisable.

Kang Yu Wei is staying at Singapore at present. He has been here ⟨for⟩ already two months before my arrival.

To Ahchong

July 21, 1910

Penang

My dear Nephew:

Your letter of June 4th reached me here through Ah Fo in Honolulu. Your letter of May 14th did not reached [reach] up to this time. It must have went [gone] astray somewhere.

I cannot send you another three hundred dollars more at the present time. ⟨I⟩ may be able to do it in a few months to come, but not quite sure.

I am very sorry that you cannot return to your Father soon, who are [is] waiting for you all very patiently.

Give my loves to your mother, wife and children and accept the same yourself, from

Your affectionate Uncle
Y. S. Sun

My address:
    Y. S. Sun
    c/o Kong Ye Chiong

77 Cecil Street

Singapore

Straits Settlements

To General Homer Lea

Aug. 11, 1910

Penang

My dear General:

Your letter of June 18 safely reached me here yesterday. The commissioned officers are now recalled back to the army to train new recruits for two divisions of the Kwangtung army, which must be completed within a year of time. Most of them return except a few very mark [marked] men, who are now with me here. We could recover our position in the Canton army very soon and with a much greater strength than before. The numbers [number] of men in the Haifung and Lufung districts are [is] increasing day by day, so I could not tell you the exact number. But it is pretty certain that all able adultmen could be enlisted into the cause. And further east all the districts in Chowchow fu, and Kai Yung Chow are ready to join. This part of Canton produce [produces] the best fighting men. It numbers about several millions. The Chowchow people had once been employed by the England and French armies during their invasion to Peking in 1860, and proved to be the best fighting material. The Taku forts were captured by storming by these Chowchow men.

The villages within the triangle shape of country between Hongkong, Fumoon, and Waichow, having been strongly armed with all their arms, number at least thirty thousand. But ammunition must be provided for them.

The threatening uprising in the Yangtse valley have been stopped by me during my sojourn in Japan, as I have informed yon when I wrote from there. At first they promised to keep quiet up to winter but now I can make them [to] wait longer until our plan for [of] raising funds [is] succeeded [succeeds]. So you can go on with our original plan.

Some trouble is going on in the province of Yunnan now. I have sent a man from here by way of Burma to stop them last week. I think he could succeed in making them keep quiet for a time. Please send me a copy or two of your late book, *The Valor of Ignorancy* as the copy I had have [has] been took [taken] away by a friend.

I intend to stay here for two or three months within that time you may address your letters to me as follow[follows]:

  Mr. Chung San
  c/o Tek Cheang
  197 Beach Street
  Penang
  Straits Settlements

With my kindest regards to you and Miss Power.

            Very truly yours,
            Y. S. Sun

To Charles B. Boothe

Sept. 4, 1910

Penang

Straits Settlements

Dear Sir:

Your letter of June 25, from New York, only reached me here yesterday. I was glad to hear that the result of your visiting to the East is a most satisfactory one. Your former letters to Hawaii were received during my sojourn in Japan. I had replied them all, and besides I had wrote [written] once or twice to either you or the General before I left Japan, in regarding to the rumour ⟨to⟩ which you referred.

In my former letters I either told you or the General that I was just in time, when in Japan, to stop all premature movements in the Yangtze Valley and South China. The leaders from different parts of China all agreed with me to wait until our project in America succeeded.

The signatures which I promised to obtain has [have been] sent ⟨to⟩ you by registered post from Yokohama. I have no doubt it has reached you long before now.

Everything must have been settled by this time. What is the final result now? Is [Does] it succeed or fail, in any case I should like to know the result as soon as possible, so that I may take independent measure [measures] in the future.

If you think that our project of raising the funds will [be] surely succeeded and final settlement is only a question of time, I should like ⟨if⟩ you would advance me a sum of $50,000 American dollars from your own account for the preparatory work. For this will facilitate me to do a great deal of that part of the work, and perhaps ten times of that money may not done [do] the same amount of work [in] a few months later. If you would advance this sum, when the project [is] succeeded [succeeds] you may have twice of it back as interest for the risk you run.

There will be no disturbance take [taking] place in the Yangtze Valley and South China up to the coming winter; so you may be sure that there is nothing to disturb you in the meantime.

I shall be in Penang in the coming two or three months, and within that time I cannot come to meet you, even our project succeed [succeeds], unless the above sum of $50,000, could be sent here beforehand.

Our position among the army in Canton has been recovered since the last failure, and will be much stronger than before within a very short time. The altitude [attitudes] of all other armies in the Empire are the same and with more eagerness to look for a signal of a general movement.

Recently the army in Sin Chiang (East Turkistan) has broke [broken] out into mutiny. This is a part of the previous arrangement of the summer movement with the Yangtze valley, which I have so effective [effectively] stopped in conforming to your advice when I was in Japan. This outlying part of China is too far away from our means of communication, for we cannot use the government telegraph line and our messengers have not enough time to reach there.

With kindest regards.

Very truly yours,
Chungsan

P. S. The telegraphic code (269) which you gave me at Los Angeles, I found it not very suitable for our use. I think we [we'd] better use the A. B. C. Code latest edition with modification of our own design. I suggest to add [adding] 269 to each figure by sender, and receiver can subtract the same in decipher.

    Address: Chungsan
                     c/o Tek Cheang
                     197 Beach Street
                     Penang
                     Straits Settlements

Cable address: Tekcheang, Penang.

Money order also for Chungsan

To General Homer Lea

Sept. 5, 1910

Penang
Straits Settlements

My dear General:

I just received a letter from Mr. B. dated June 25, New York, which gives very encouraging news; but since that time neither of you send me any word, as I had arranged in a letter to you from Japan; so I supposed Mr. B's project might have [been] failed or ⟨been⟩ delayed. I wrote to Mr. B. in reply asking him to send me $50,000 in advance from his own account, if he think [thinks] that the project of raising fund is sured [sure]. Then when the matter ⟨is⟩ settled he may have his money back in two folds as interest for his risk. For I need the money for preparatory work very much, if I can have this sum now I can do [a] work ten times much as the same money can do in a few months after.

As I have told you in my last letter that encouraging news came from every part in China. Co-operation could be easily obtained in many districts along the Kwangtung coast. We can start a movement with a much easier and quicker way than that as [what] we have arranged in the Long Beach Hotel, and with much less expenses. I feel sure that Canton city can be captured from the outset, that will save us all the trouble for a preparation of means and ways to attack it, after the movement is commenced, from outside, for it can be captured by surprise within at any time. In possession of that city we possess at least a hundred thousand of modern rifles and sufficient quantity of ammunitions, and many hundred pieces of modern artilleries, and rifle and cartilage factories, and besides plenty of ready money and vast resources of material supplies. Most of the leaders are very reluctant to do anything other than capture that city from the very start. I think also that that city is the main object from the beginning and besides it is much easier to capture it at the beginning than afterward. The money used for this purpose will be much less than the other scheme which we worked out in A-merica.

Now if Mr. B's New York project failed I want you to try some other way [ways] to get me half a million dollars (gold), for the Canton scheme only, ⟨and⟩ put the others aside for a while, until we achieve our first object. Can you succeed in raising that amount of money in the shortest possible time? If not, try to get as much as you can, but in any case send fifty thousand at once for preparatory work.

Since I stopped the movement of this summer in the Yangtze Valley and South China in conforming to your advice, all our hopes are concentrated in the American project. I shall be much obliged for [to] you to let [for letting] me know at once if your and Mr. B's schemes both failed, so that I may take independent measure [measures] in the immediate future.

With kindest regards to you and Miss Power.

Very truly yours,
Chungsan

Address:

    Chung San

    c/o Tek Cheang

    197 Beach Street

    Penang

    Straits Settlements

Cable address:

    Tekcheang

    Penang

P. S.

If ⟨there is⟩ any money order, also ⟨send⟩ to the same name. In case of telegraphic communication use A. B. C. Code latest edition (5th) by adding 269 to the figure of every word. Find the result and send that as cipher. When receiving any message deduct 269 from each word and the result will be the decipher message.

P. S.

Before starting the movement from Canton it is a [,I think it is] vital important for us to secure a perfect understanding of the English Government. To do this you and I must go to London and work together. If the project of getting money in America [is] succeeded [succeeds] and the 50,000 ⟨is⟩ duly sent to me ⟨, then⟩ I will at once set the others to work and I myself go to London immediately to meet you there. And also have everything [to be] arranged beforehand in the city.

If all your schemes failed get me as many letters of introduction to Manila as you can and send them to me here at once. Much obliges[obliged].

To General Homer Lea

Sept. 29, 1910

Penang

My dear General:

Your letter of August 7, to Hong Kong, is in receipt, Hereafter do not send any letter to the Hong Kong address, but direct to [directly] here.

In regard to Mr. B's appointment as financial agent, if the project could not succeed the same have to be recalled, as I was asked to return the signature in that case.

I want you to go on ⟨with⟩ the other plan we spoke about and try to secure some money for us as quick [quickly] as possible. Under the present circumstances I think a quarter million of gold dollars will be quite enough for the whole thing, even less than that may enable us to do some wonderful work.

Since I returned to the Far East I always try to stop premature movement in every part of China, on condition that I will supply the money in winter. If this condition could not be fulfilled it will be a great blow to my influence. I hope you would urge Mr. B. to send me the sum I asked in a former letter from his account. By this my influence could be saved from discredit. If he can do a little more the whole thing can be carried out to a successful issue.

I am now waiting for your introduction to go to Manila. Did [Have] you send [sent] it already? I have written you to ask for it quite a long time ago [before]. I didn't think I can spare to come over to the United States again at present for everything [in] here are [is] so unsettled. And I [am] fear I shall be unable to stop the uprising in the coming winter, although I still try in that direction, on account of want of money. If this winter movement can be postponed I will come over from Manila in [at] the end of this year.

                Very sincerely yours,
                Chung San

Address:
 c/o Tek Cheang, 197 Beach Street, Penang, Straits Settlements.

To General Homer Lea

Nov. 7, 1910

Penang

My dear General:

Your letter of September 18, and the book and magazines have 〔were〕 duly received some days ago; and after that Mr. B's letter arrived which informed me that syndicate would meet early in October. But that month has already passed and up to this time there is no definite news from them, so I do not expect much from his side. I want you to go on your own way to get the means for our government as soon as possible. Of course I will not wait if any opportunity turn 〔turns〕 up, but it is very difficult to push matter forward without the necessary means. Since I been 〔came〕 here I have improved the condition of the preparatory work ⟨in⟩ many ways. And now we can make a sure success with far less money than we first proposed. I think even a tenth of our original sum would be enough. Can you get that anyway quick 〔quickly〕? I am going to try to raise some money here, if I can get bately 〔barely〕 enough to begin, even far from making of our success, I will start the business at once.

In regard to the translation of your book I will tell my Japanese friend to begin at once. I think we may make something in that way. As to the Chinese edition there will be no hope of making any profit out of it, for Chinese publishers only offer from 3 to 5 Mexican dollars to a thousand words of the best translation because copyright are 〔is〕 not effective in China. Your book after ⟨being⟩

translated perhaps will make about 100,000 words (characters) which only amount to 500 Mexican or 250 American dollars, but at least take one for [to] three months to finish it. But your book contains valuable knowledge which will be indispensable for the Chinese at the present age. I will try to get someone to bring out a Chinese edition after the Japanese edition [is] come [comes] off.

And in regard to your observation of aeroplane in war I have read it several times with much appreciation. All your reasoning are perfectly sound. I agreed with you entirely in your first part but as to part second [two] "as a means of reconnaissance" you missed out one thing that [is] aeroplane and dirigible ballon [balloon] can ⟨take⟩ very good photographs which will help a commander to form a perfect opinion of the enemy's situation. For instance in the battles of Leang Yang and Mukden the Japanese are less one third [one third less] than the Russian commander thought [that the Japanese are more numerous than him]. The Japanese line extending [extended] over 100 miles, which the Russian captive ballon cannot [balloon could not] see. If the Russian had used dirigible or aeroplane to take photograph they could at once detect [out] the Japanese number during these long battled [battles].

And about the Chinese government [in] concerning the force you had trained in America, I think most likely, if such force is still under your command, they would like to get it over and transport it to China and destroy it, as they had done once in the first Wusung Shanghai railway case, to buy it up in the prentention to control the line, but immediately the transaction [is] finished turned up the rails and shipped them together with the locomotors and cars to Formosa and left there to rot. And for the present Government to maintain such force as your four regiments under they [their] service is the most untenable thing under the present situation of China. And I think the whole thing is propped up by Chang Yim Tang, the present Chinese Minister in Washington, for his own good. Be careful for [with] all Chinese you come in contact with in America, and under no circumstances [to] let any one [anyone] know [of] the relation [relations] between you and I.

I hope to hear good news from you soon.

With kindest regards to you and Miss Power.

Very truly yours,
Y. S. Sun

To Charles B. Boothe

Nov. 8, 1910

Penang

My dear Mr. Beach:

Your letter of September 26 is in receipt, but the cablegram you mentioned did not reach me. By what address did you sent it?

October is now over, how is the result of the syndicate meeting? As up to this time there is no definite news from you, I fear, in spite of your hard work for our cause, the New York project might have [been] failed through. Have you some [any] other way to obtain money for us? We are not in need of so large a sum as we first proposed in your house, for many of the preparatory works have [work has] been done since my returning here. I think from one tenth to one fifth of the original amount would be enough to carry out the whole business to a successful end, say half million dollars in gold will just be about the amount we need at the present moment. A small sum must have been easier and quicker to raise than a big one, wouldn't you think so? If you can get this sum within three months from date, it will be just in time for our purpose. After that we will not wait, but take independent measure [measures] to do what we can by any means. In case we could succeed in gaining a permanent footing before you conclude any loan, then the condition of the same must be entirely modified. But if nothing could be done or the attempt failed in our part, then the condition will [be] continued [continue] as we have arranged in Los Angeles.

Letter to Boothe, Nov. 8, 1910

Situation in China is the same so I have no news to tell you.

In regard to memento I agreed with you entirely.

I hope to hear good news from you soon.

With kindest regards.

Very truly yours,
Chung San

Cable address
  Tekcheang
  Penang

To Mrs. Cantlie

Nov. 20, 1910

Penang

My dear Mrs. Cantlie:

Your kind letter of Sept. 22, had been received some time ago〔before〕. I was glad to hear that all your young gentlemen are 〔were〕 getting on so well.

I am very busy recently, indeed, there are 〈a〉 good many things to be done in China; and I could not say definitely when I could pay another visit to England and shall have the pleasure to meet you again there.

My family is with me here now, but my son is still study 〔studying〕 at Honolulu. He will finish his college course by next summer. He want 〔wants〕 to study agriculture after that. Are there any good school 〔schools〕 for that in England?

With kindest regards to you and the Doctor and all my young friends.

Very truly yours,
Y. S. Sun

To Mrs. Cantlie

Nov. 24, 1910

Penang

My dear Mrs. Cantlie:

I [have] posted a letter to you just a few days ago, then I had not the least idea of coming to England so soon. But now I [am] wanting [want] to go to England and America to do some business. I shall sail in a fortnight of time, and expect to see you soon in London. Please keep my coming secret from the Chinese Legation.

In case any one come [anyone comes] to your house to enquire me in the name of Chungsan before my arrival, that man will be a friend of mine. You may treat him so.

With kindest regards to you and the Doctor.

Very truly yours,
Y. S. Sun

To Charles B. Boothe

Dec. 16, 1910

My dear Mr. Beach:

Your letters of Oct. 21, and Nov. 1, 1910, [had] reached me a few days before my departure from Penang. As you did not send any cablegram after your letters, I think the question is decided that we could not succeed in that line.

We are now taking independent measure[measures] of our own to start the great movement in the coming few months. But we are in great need of help at present. Can you do anything for us by your own means? Another few hundred thousand could make us carry out everything perfectly through. But at any case whether we have the money or not, I am sure of our success in the next move.

I left Penang on the 6 December on way to Europe, and will enter the Red Sea by tomorrow. After I finished my business in Europe I will proceed to America and thence to China, I will communicate with you as soon as I reach American shore. If you would do something for us with your own means I will come direct [directly] to see you at Los Angeles.

With kindest regards.

Very truly yours,
Chung San

To Charles B. Boothe
Mar. 6, 1911

Vancouver, B. C.

My dear Mr. Beach:

I intended to write you long before, [this] but ⟨I was⟩ always so busy and so unsettled about future plan that I could not do so. Now I am go [going] to leave here ⟨for⟩ about a week [of time] and will stop over on way in Kamloaps, Galgary, Winnipeg, Toronto and Montreal, thence to New York. I expect to reach New York in a month of time. My address there will be Y. S. Sun, Care of Sing Fat Co., 1127 Broadway, New York. During the meantime communication can be forwarded through Tai Hon Yat Bo, Vancouver, B. C..

As you cannot get for us the necessary funds in time we must start the movement with our own means. I am now working in raising money from my own countrymen and have succeeded in getting more than half we need already, and hope to get the other part along my way east. As soon as money is enough we will set to work at once.

How is your plan of getting money? Is it [there] still any hope of doing something in [on] a smaller scale than our original plan? If so I hope you would do something for us at once. If you could not do anything before my arrival at New York I have to ask you to send back that paper which ⟨was⟩ signed ⟨by⟩ my comrades, registering post to the address which I gave above, for I have promised [to] my comrades to return their signatures in case of failure of raising the intending funds.

With kindest regards.

Yours very truly,
Y. S. Sun

To General Homer Lea

Aug. 10, 1911

My dear General:

Your letters from Washington and Weisbaden are in receipt. I was exceedingly glad to hear that you had made such a great success with the Government and the Senate, and more so to hear that your eyes are getting better rapidly. This last bit of news is most important for it relieves my anxiety very much.

As soon as I received your Washington letter I had at once sent word [words] to my men in China to work accordingly. But before my letter reaches them I have received several cablegrams and letters from them states [stating] that more than ten divisions of the new army outside of Peking are sure, and all the Chinese divisions in the Capital are very promising. Recently one of our men General Wu Lu Chin, is gave [giving the] command of the sixth devision in Peking. And many officers from the Province of Chili hitherto served in the various divisions in other provinces [are] now returned home to take service in the Peking Army in order to work for the purpose of cooperation with the other divisions when the movement took place. Thus you see they are working hard for the same object before they knew our plan. I expect great result could be obtained in that direction very soon.

There are none who would divide power with me at present. All leaders of different provinces are only too welcome [for] me to take up general command, in fact they [their] only fear is that I would not accept that position. Lately I received many letters urging me to return to the East soon and start the movement quick 〔quickly〕. The only thing left to be done now is the way of getting the necessary fund for the starting.

In regard to the effect of the renewal of the Anglo-Japanese alliance to our affair, I don't think it makes any different 〔difference〕 at all. It shows that Japan is not yet ready to take independent action to shape the affairs of the Far East to suit her own purposes. At present her own people is overburdened with increased taxation and the Japanese Government needs perhaps ten years more of time to consolidate and develop Korea and Manchuria, and needs also the money and peace at this juncture. So there is time for us to regenerate China before the new conqueror is ready. And I hope you would be quick to see your English friends and get the means for us to work on.

I am going to leave San Francisco soon and travel eastward again 〈and〉 expect to reach New York on 〔by the〕 end of October.

With best regards to you both.

Y. S. Sun

To General Homer Lea

Sept. 25, 1911

Idaho

My dear General:

Your letter of August 29th reached me here yesterday. I was very glad to hear that your eyes are getting better.

It is still my intention to establish headquarters in Paris or London if I can find the means, General Hwang had [has] not been ordered to Europe yet as he has much to do in China.

Recently there is great trouble happened in Szechwan caused by the railway dispute between the people and government. Our headquarters in the south has [have] been greatly disturbed because there is rumor that the Army in Szechwan has joined the fracas. If that is true our men proposed [propose] to start the Yunnan Army in follow suit first, then the Canton Army after. But I don't (believe) that is true as we never intend that the Szechwan Army should take the initiation [initiative] in the national movement and it was quite unprepared in that respect. According to official report that the new Army in Szechuan disobeyed the Viceroy's order to fight, but did not join the people, it adopts a neutral position, I think that is what really happened.

In regard to how and when and where to obtain the necessary funds, I really cannot form and decision. I only hoping [hope] to get it as soon as possible.

After I ending [end] my journey at New York, I will try to come over to Europe to see what could be done with France and England.

Please write me again to New York address c/o Sing Fat Co., 1127 Broadway.

With my best regards to you both,

Very truly yours,
Y. S. Sun

To Taro R. Otsuka
Oct. 22, 1911

N. Y.

Mr. Taro R. Otsuka
414 S Michigan Ave.
Chicago

Dear Mr. Otsuka:

I have received Mr. Kayano's cablegram. Many thanks to you.

Very truly yours,
Y. S. Sun

To General Homer Lea

Oct. 31, 1911

Homer Lea Savoy LDN:

Li-yuen-hung pro 〔Li-yuen-hung's proclamation is〕 inexplicable, perhaps ambition carry 〔carried〕 by sudden success, but his lacking of generalship cannot hold his own any longer. Organization everywhere 〈is〉 excellent, all looking for me to lead. If financial 〔financially〕 supported, I could control situation absolutely. No strong government could be formed until we get there, therefore loan is necessary.

Nakayama

To General Homer Lea

Nov. 1, 1911

Homer Lea Savoy LDN:

General Hwang arrived Hankow safely. Things [are] much improved. I may take Mauretania Tomorrow.

Nakayama

To Miyazaki

Nov. 28, 1911

Miyazaki:

Return by Denvanha due Hongkong 22 December, can you and Ike meet me there?

Nakayama

To Mrs. Lea
June 27,1912

21 Yates Road, Shanghai

Dear Mrs. Lea:

I am indeed very glad to learn that you and the General had a pleasant trip home, and what makes me more glad still is to hear that the General's health is getting stronger daily and the doctors opine that he will be able to walk about in another time. By the time this letter reaches you, you will be spending your time in the beach, and I have no doubt that a change of air and sunshine will do much to hasten his recovery.

By tomorrow's "Shinyo Maru", my son and two daughters will be leaving for the States to prosecute further studies. Sun Fo will go to the University of California, to take up what course of studies [it] is not yet decided. I trust during his sojourn in the States, he will have occasion to meet your people.

Things in China are gradually getting into proper shape, the bickerings of the political parties in Peking resulting in the enforced retirement of the Premier are nothing very serious. I trust and hope everything will work on smoothly once again before long.

I Have tried to eschew politics as much as possible, I intend to devote all my energies to develop the natural resources of this country, and particularly to the construction of railways. I hope to succeed.

With every kind wish to you and the General,

Yours truly,
SUN YAT SEN

To General Homer Lea
Oct. 13, 1912

491 Avenue Pard Brunat

Shanghai

My dear Lea:

I am very happy to receive your letter of September 15th and also a letter from Mrs. Lea written two weeks earlier, for both of which I thank you very much. I hope your health will continue to improve and we may meet in Paris in about two months from now.

When Mr. Mitchell's telegram came I was up in Peking. It was transmitted by my friend to Peking from Shanghai. I was under the impression that it was a telegram sent by Mr. Mitchell from Shanghai. Accordingly I wired back to him trying to make an appointment for a long interview. On my return I found that Mr. Mitchell had not been to Shanghai at all. Mrs. Lea's letter made it all plain.

The conditions in your memorandum are carefully noted. Several items need to be talked over between us when we meet.

My visit to the north has been a great success as you must have learned from the press. There is far better understanding between the south and the north as a result of this visit. General Hwang has been up there also where he was enthusiastically received too. He is just now back to Shanghai.

Some of the Shansi bankers have approached me to see whether it would be possible to start an industrial bank. It is hoped that they would raise five million dollars for the purpose. I am now exchanging letters with General Yen of Shansi on the matter.

With warmest regards and best wishes to Mrs. Lea and yourself,

Sincerely yours,
Y. S. Sun

To Mrs. Lea
Nov. 14, 1912

Shang hai

Mrs. Homer lea
Ocean Park
California

My dear Mrs. Lea:

I am extremely grieved to learn from the newspapers that General Lea has passed away. I would have sent you a telegram to convey to you my deep sympathy and condolence, but for the fact that until now I never believed in the newspaper accounts to be true.

In losing General Lea I feel I have lost a great and true friend.

Miss Soong wishes to tender you her heart-felt sympathy in your bereavement. I remain,

Yours sincerely,
SUN YAT SEN
(per E. R. S.)

To James Cantlie
May 2, 1913

Shanghai

Mr. Cantlie
140 Harley Street
London

Submit on my behalf following appeal to British Government, Parliament, Governments of Europe, and give same widest publicity in [to] all press.

To Governments and peoples of foreign powers:

As a result of careful investigation by officials appointed by Government to inquire into recent murder of Nationalist leader Sung Chiao-jen in Shanghai, the fact is clearly established that Peking Government is seriously implicated in the crime. Consequently people are extremely indignant, and situation has become so serious that nation is on verge of most acute and dangerous crisis yet experienced. Government conscious of its guilt and enormity of its offence and realising strength of wave of indignation sweeping over nation as direct result of its criminal deeds and wicked betrayal of trust reposed in it, and perceiving that it is likely to lead to its downfall, suddenly and unconstitutionally concluded loan for pounds 25,000,000 sterling with quintuple group despite vigorous protests of representatives of nation now assembled [assembling] in Peking. This highhanded and unconstitutional action of Government instantly accentuated intense indignation which had been caused by foul murder of Sung Chiao-jen, so that at present time fury of people is worked up to white heat and terrible convulsion ap-

Letter to Cantlie, May 2, 1913

pears almost inevitable [inevitably]. Indeed, so acute has crisis become that widespread smouldering embers may burst forth in devastating conflagration at any moment. From date of birth of Republic I have striven for unity, peace, concord, and prosperity. I recommended Yuan Shihkai for Presidency because there appeared reasons for believing that by doing so unification of nation and dawn of era of peace and prosperity would thereby be hastened. Ever since then I have done all I could to evolve peace, order, and government out of chaos created by revolution. I earnestly desire to preserve peace throughout republic, but my efforts will be rendered ineffective if financiers will supply Peking Government with money that would and probably will be used in waging war against people. If country is plunged into war at this juncture it will inevitably inflict terrible misery and suffering upon people who are just beginning to recover from dislocation of trade and losses of various kinds caused by revolution. For establishment of Republic they have sacrificed much and are now determined to preserve it at all costs. If people are now forced into life-and-death struggle for preservation of Republic not only will it entail terrible suffering to masses but inevitably also adversely affect all foreign interests in China. If Peking Government is kept without funds there is prospect of compromise between it and people being effected [affected], while immediate effect of liberal supply of money will probably be precipitation of terrible and disastrous conflict. In name and for sake of Humanity which civilisation holds sacred I therefore appeal to you to exert your influence with view to preventing bankers from providing Peking Government with funds which at this juncture will assuredly be utilised as sinews of war. I appeal to all who have lasting welfare of mankind at heart to extend to me in this hour of need [needing] their moral assistance in averting unnecessary bloodshed and in shielding my countrymen from hard fate which they have done absolutely nothing to deserve.

Sun Yat Sen

To Postmaster
Nov. 12, 1913

26 Reinanzaka

Akasaka

Tokyo, Japan

To Postmaster

Tokyo

Dear Sir:

Please deliver my letters to bearer.

Yours truly,

Sun Yat-sen

To Mrs. Cantlie

Nov. 14, 1913

Tokyo, Japan

My dear Mrs. Cantlie:

I am in receipt of your letter acknowledging receipt of my letter from Japan. I am writing specially to ask you to be careful in your conversation write 〔writing〕 so called "friends" of mine. As to Mr. Addis who is now knighted by the King is not my friend. He was the one who financed Yuan Shih Kai in his undertaking against the South. I fear many pose themselves as my friends in order to gain your confidence, and learn from you certain facts and opinions.

I am not very well acquainted with Minister Lin, and from what I heard of him, I do not think he will be or is on our side for we are certainly on the losing side now.

It gave me great pleasure to hear how well your children are getting along.

Please remember me to Dr. Cantlie. I hope he is not working too hard so as to injure his health.

With sincere regard 〔regards〕, I am,

Yours most sincerely,

Sun Yat Sen

To Mrs. Lea

Dec. 23, 1913

Tokyo

My Dear Mrs. Lea:

I write in the belief that this letter will find you still in London, and so address you through the kindness of our mutual friend Dr. Cantlie.

I am still in Japan. It is sad indeed to see the dear country reverting to the old ways, but fortunately indications are not wanting that a favourable turn of affairs will in the near future. Despotism has again asserted itself and its weight has become more unbearable than even at the time of the primitive Manchus. The pendulum of reaction has reached its limit and the rebound is bound to take place. Perhaps this is the darkest hour before the dawn. I know you and my other friends greatly sympathize with our cause, and this knowledge helps in no small way to encourage me to proceed with our difficult task. The struggle may be long and tedious, but it is sure to win, because right must ultimately prevail.

I have been told that the late general's *The Day of the Saxon* is on sale at most of the booksellers here. This is as it should be. It certainly deserves a hearty reception. Mr. Ike, who, you will remember, translated the *Valor of Ignorance* into Japanese, has written to me to ask you for permission to render also this latest work into Japanese. I do not quite remember whether the late General had verbally given him the right of translation or not, but I thought it best to re-

Letter to Mrs. Lea, Dec. 23, 1913

fer the matter to you. Mr. H. Ike's address is as follow[follows]:

    Mr. H. Ike,

    25, Daimachi, Akasaka,

    Tokyo

I also take this opportunity to present to you the compliments of the season.

                                        Yours truly,

                                        Y. S. Sun

P. S. —My own address is as under:

    S. Toyama,

    Akasaka

    26, Reinanzaka, Tokyo

To Mrs. Lea

June 17, 1914

26, Reinanzaka

Akasaka

Tokyo, Japan

My Dear Mrs. Lea:

I thank you very much for your letter of May 1st. In reference to the translation of *The Day of the Saxon* I think I shall ask a country man of mine to translate it into Chinese in one of our magazines.

As far [for] the condition in China it is similar to the condition existing when I saw you at Long Beach. In all our troubles, finance is the chief difficulty, but I have a means of solving this trouble by means of Department Stores. Could you assist me in this matter by helping me to find organizers who are versed in conducting matters of this nature? If such could be found would they come and help us, thus doing a way with our chief difficulty? As you will know paper currency will be depreciated in value by the merchants in time of war when there is a scarcity of metallic money. But when the Department Stores are once established in each city than [then] we can maintain the value of paper currency. Often one city has a surplus of a certain commodity, for the lack of which another city suffers famine, etc. These can be easily remedied when the goods could be transferred from one place to another. You see now, of what great importance these organizations are for [to] the welfare of the people in time of war.

Another favour that I would ask of [for] you is whether or not the General's friends are still interested in China, and if so I should like to get into communications with them.

Hoping that you are in the best of healths [health] and enjoying [enjoy] Los Angeles. With kindest regards and best wishes, I am.

                Your sincerely,
                Y. S. Sun

To James Deitrick

Aug. 14, 1914

26, Reinanzaka
Akasaka
Tokyo, Japan

Dear Mr. Deitrick:

Many thanks for your kind and welcome letter of July 10th. Undoubtedly you can be of great service to me and my cause in America at this juncture.

First of all, try your best to stop any loan which Yuan Shih Kai may attempt to raise in America. At present he cannot get any more loan from Europe, and I am told that he intends to give great inducements to American Capitalists to secure money which is his only power; and he is going to send his Minister of Finance, Chow Tse Chi, to the United States for this purpose. So please be prepared beforehand in blocking every possible channel from which he may get the money, by telling the American, that Yuan Shih Kai will surely fall before long, even with the support of money. So it is a great risk for anyone to support his Arch-Murderer, besides the people in China hate the Capitalists who ever did give any support to their enemy, and will surely repudiate any concession which might have been given by Yuan Shih Kai.

Secondly, I want you to look for men who are honest and willing to help me in the constructive work of China after the fighting is finished, i. e. when the

Revolution [is] succeeded [succeeds]. The fighting part of the Revolution is an easy matter but the constructive part is of real difficults [difficulty]. You can help me a great deal in that way. And the most important of these is the financial adjustment. For during the Revolution panic is surely to follow and all trades will be at a stand still for lack of money, and more so in China, for the medium of exchange in the commercial centre of the country is controlled by foreign banks. So foreign bankers, such as the Hong Kong Shanghai Banking Corporation, really hold the balance of power in an internal struggle. If we cannot get rid of that money control we are never [be] independent and Yuan Shih Kai is but a mere tool of those foreign bankers.

My way of getting rid of this curse is that the Revolutionary Government must prepare to control the trade, so we can use any kind of money we please and thus we can do away with foreign bankers and be our own master.

In order to do that the Government must (1) organize department stores to conduct distribution; (2) control both the land and water traffic, i. e. to conduct transportation; and last but not least by manufacturing some of the most important goods which hitherto, depend upon foreign supply, i. e. to conduct production.

Thus China can be independent both politically and economically. For this reason, I want you to look for expert men in different lines for me. The most important of all is to look for expert organizers and managers of department stores. For I want to put up a system of such stores all over the country. This will follow the step of the Revolutionary Army. At such time goods can be gotten very easily by the government in form of taxation, contribution and exchange for other goods, the people will be only too glad to dispose of their over-productions or stagnant goods. So we can run a government without asking the people for money.

This will be a great blessing to all the people. Now you see why I lay such emphasis on the department stores. In a former letter I mentioned this to you, but I am not sure whether you have received it or not.

The department store is a common thing in America but in China we have none and no one knows how to organize it and no one knows how to manage it. If it is organized I think it will not be difficult for you to pick out such experts, but they must be men of honesty, great energy and ability.

It would be splendid if you can make arrangement with some of the most influential department store trust and get them to cooperate with this scheme of our's.

In that case we should like them to advance us a sum of at least ten million dollars as initiative war fund, for the franchise given. Is it possible to make such an arrangement? If you think your success in this particular matter is possible, I will appoint you as my agent with full power to negotiate. You may draw up forms of your appointment and conditions of the arrangement for my approval, by return 〔returning〕 mail.

General Hwang's trip is for pleasure and observation. I did not admit him in the next movement, for his last flight from Nanking during the second Revolution disappointed me bitterly. But as a friend and an old revolutionist, for he did a good deal during and before the first Revolution, I still regard him friendly, so I ordered my followers in America to give him welcome, and I hope you will do the

Letter to Deitrick, Aug. 14, 1914

same if you should happen to meet him.

I am busily [busy] preparing for another movement. This time I shall conduct the whole affair personally. As you know the first Revolution broke out before I could reach China. And when I arrived there everything was developing in such a stage that I deemed it wise to accept things as they were. I was only too glad to have it concluded in a peaceful way. But there I committed my mistake by entrusting a wrong man, the arch murderer Yuan.

In the second Revolution I did not take part, for I thought that many there were quite competent to carry out the work to a successful end, for means were more than sufficient for any undertaking of that kind. But too many cooks spoiled the broth! Now the country is in greater danger than ever, and Yuan's absolutism is much worse than the former Manchu rule. Thus I am compelled to take the lead again. You may be pleased to hear that I possess greater confidence than ever before and I am convinced that I can overthrow Yuan's power much easier than I did with the Manchus, and that may come very soon too.

By the way, please find out a certain Henry Clifford Stuart of Washington for me. He wrote me an open letter about paper currency which in a general way I quite agree with him. But we cannot circulate paper currency without department stores. Please find out what sort of a person he is, and, if advisable, get him to cooperate with you in my department store scheme.

Whenever you hear of my success in occupying a foothold in China, you must come to see me at once in order to map out a constructure plan for the industrial and commercial development.

In regard to the Boy & Girl Scout Movement I fully agree with you in its necessity and importance, and I will surely carry it out after I succeed in my undertaking.

With best regards, and hoping for an early reply, I am,

Yours sincerely,
Sun Yat-sen

To Mrs. Lea

Sept. 13, 1914

26, Reinanzaka
Akasaka
Tokyo, Japan

My dear Mrs. Lea:

Your kind letter of Aug. 3rd is at hand, for which I desire to tender you my warmest thanks and appreciation, especially for the great personal interest you have shown in my scheme of department stores.

My plan of such a store is to relieve the financial straits and to facilitate commerce in revolutionary time, for as you well know that China's finance is controlled entirely by the foreign banks. When war breaks out commerce will be absolutely stagnant, thus the people will naturally suffer a great deal. My plan is to avert such sufferings, and it will not be opposed by any person.

Our friend, Mr. J. Deitrick, has written me recently and I have put the entire matter in his hands, so I shall not trouble you anymore about this matter. I am pleased to tell you that my work is progressing favorably. I am confident that the time is near, when the reactionary government will be crushed forever. As soon as you hear that I have succeed [succeeded] in my undertaking or that I have gained a footing in any part of China, I wish and hope that you will come to the East as soon as possible for I need your assistance in various matters of importance.

Again thanking 〔thank〕 you for your esteemed letter, and with kindest regards and best wishes. I am,

                                        Yours sincere friend,
                                        Sun Yat-sen

To Lee Yuan Swee

Oct. 9, 1914

Mr. Lee Yuan Swee 26 Reinanzaka
c/o Chop Ban Seng Akasaka
28 Belfield Street, Ipoh Tokyo, Japan
Federated Malay States

My dear Mr. Lee:

Your letter of Sept. 19th has been received, for which I desire to express my sincere thanks, especially for the whole heartedness you have put in the scheme of raising funds for the cause. Immediately after I got your letter I cabled you the following: "Inform all we have nonconfidence in × ×. Chungsan" — Now I wish to explain the reason which prompted the above message. Sometime ago this man × × × came to see me. I heard that he was working for the cause with a party of his own. He told me he was going back to Canton soon, so I asked him to join our party and work with us. He answered that he was not working for any party but for himself and that his motive for going to Canton was solely to see his family. Mr. Hu Hanmin (Ex.-Gov. General of Canton) tried to persuade him to join us, but in vain. Later I learned that he was in Canton for other reasons than to see his family. When he was here I told him plainly that if he should deceive me, I would expell him from the cause and oppose him in every way. Now I must carry out my decision.

As I wrote you in my previous letter, I write you again now, that all the money collected are to be sent directly to me. So please stop remitting collections to him immediately, He is very deceptive and is not a man to be entrusted with anything. Immediately after the First Revolution, he abused the position that he obtained by executing men by tens of thousands, including Nan Yang people, without submitting them under any form of trials whatever. He has executed more men than even Yuan Shih Kai. For a man who abuses his power we must not extend any assistance, and must keep him out for the good of the cause. It would, therefore, be a hindrance instead of help to our cause, if any help is rendered ⟨to⟩ him.

If you desire to know more about this man you can get informations from Mr. Luk Man Fai.

But if the Nan Yang people are not willing to send to me the collection, I advise them to keep it for themselves instead of giving it to any other man, for it would do harm than good to the cause.

Hoping that you have carried out my instruction, and please inform all the people in various places of Nan Yang of this letter.

With kindest regards, I am,

Yours very sincerely,
Sun Yat Sen

To James Deitrick
Oct. 12, 1914

Shanghai, China

James Deitrick,
Palace Hotel
San Francisco, Ca.

Dear Sir:

Herewith is power-of-attorney in which you are granted certain powers to contract for the opening up and operation of department stores, and other industrial enterprises in China.

Provided that you can arrange it you will dispose of the entire privileges granted therein for a joint-undertaking with the Government of China to establish a system of department stores, upon an advance of ten million dollars to me and my party. This money is to be used for the promotion of affairs of the party and country and within the boundary of China. If, owing to the disturbed financial conditions, you find it inconvenient to secure said sum, then you will use your own judgment as to disposal [dispose] of districts to various persons and for such sums as may be deemed prudent and fair, For example, say the district around Hankow or Nanking or Shanghai, etc. In case of cash transaction you will have the money deposited in a bank in my name and to my credit and have the bank send me certificates of deposit of said monies [money].

In case you cannot find such a party willing to undertake this department store, you are authorized to close up a deal with said party to undertake work in such industrial lines as Mining, Iron and Steel Works, Transportation, Grain Elevators, Manufactures, and Arsenal for the Navy and Army of China, etc., under the same agreements, and with the same understanding that half of its shares must be owned by the Government.

Under your power of attorney, you are authorized to contract for expert men to operate stores for and in [on] behalf of the Government upon such terms as are in vogue in America, added thereunto such additional expense as may be actually necessary to secure such service for China.

The scope of powers sent ⟨to⟩ you are large, but I believe in your tact, wisdom and good judgment and feel that you will carry out the work for me and my country the same as if I was personally present and we could jointly confer upon the important subject.

Yours very sincerely,
Sun Yat-sen

To James Deitrick

Oct. 19, 1914

26 Reinanzaka

Akasaka

Tokyo, Japan

Dear Mr. Deitrick:

Owing to pressure of time I could not answer your letter of Sept. 1st, which is a source of gratification to me. I am happy over this deep interest you have shown for [in] my plan and am most pleased, indeed, to obtain your valuable assistance in this matter of utmost importance.

In my preceding letter I confided in you my plan to establish a system of Dep't. Stores throughout China, under one management. This system of Dep't. Stores is to be materialized immediately after this third revolution, and it is to be a joint-stock company, i. e. half will be Government shares and the other half to be foreign shares. For a certain period of time this system will be under the foreign management entirely, later the natives ⟨are⟩ gradually trained up to take its place.

Since we lack organizer and manager for such a work, I asked you in my previous letter to assist me in looking up such men for this purpose.

To that syndicate or concern who will undertake this matter, half of its shares will be given. In order to do this, we desire such a capital to advance us 10 million dollars for the revolutionary fund. This loan, of course, will be a separate item from the Dep't. Store and cannot be mixed up. The concern which advances this necessary loan, will be given the right to co-operate the Dep't. Store, or if Dep't. Stores ⟨do⟩ not suit their purpose then privileges such as building railroads, mining, etc., [etc.,] can also be accorded in the same manner.

With regard to the powers of attorney, I wish to make clear that no right will be given to the Dep't. Store to issue paper money, for this will be reserved for the Government only. Nor can it be given the exclusive right of export and import as such rights are bound by treaty in China.

Referring to the material supply of arms and ammunitions, it is not so important to us now, for we can get them easily from our enemy. That is to say, to buy their soldiers over with their arms, thereby lessening and weakening the enemy's fighting power while increasing our own. Money can easily accomplish this result, therefore, it is more important to us than materials.

For, should we have the same material as our enemy, we will be at a great disadvantage—but if we buy their soldiers over with money, our enemy will have nothing to fight against us. Thus our success will be assured.

Now, I am working for an immediate movement, the result of which can be known within two or three months. If you should hear of my success, please come right over to plan for the constructive work. If it fails then you will have to work for us in America, to raise the sum that I stipulated above for another bigger and surer movement. In that case I myself will come over to America.

Concerning Gen. Hwang Hsing—he was merely assisting to raise money for our cause. All the money [that are] raised in America are [is] sent to me. With regard to the attitude of the Japanese government, owing to the Anglo-Japanese alliance, it is not favorable toward us. But the Japanese people are in great sympathy with us, and our cause.

In closing, I wish to thank you & Mrs. Deitrick for your kindnesses to my children, which I am sure were greatly appreciated. Hoping to hear from you soon & with kindest regards to you & Mrs. Deitrick, I remain.

Yours sincerely,
Sun Yat-sen

To James Deitrick
Nov. 20, 1914

26, Reinanzaka

Akasaka

Tokyo, Japan

My dear Mr. Deitrick:

Your letter of October 31, has reached me yesterday. And previous ones of September 19, 23, 23, 26, and October 1 and 4, have all due safely. I have to beg your excuse for not answering sooner and one by one, for my English secretary is not here, and I have been very busy for the last few months. Besides, in my last letter, which enclosed the signed documents, I have told you all the important things and there is [are] not much new matters to tell you again.

In the last letter I have told you that I was engaging [engaged] in an immediate project by our own means, of which we were expecting good result everyday. But unfortunately several mishaps have [been] taken place since. Firstly, one of our important leader, Mr. Fan Hung Sen, has been [was] murdered by Yuan's man in Shanghai; he has great influence among the northern troops which garrison Shanghai and it's vicinity. He had gained over a great part of them to our cause. Secondly, the preparation in Hanchow, the capital of Chekiang province, has been interrupted by some detection of the enemy. Thirdly, the movement started a few days ago in Kwang Tung province, on account of short of fund, could not capture the city of Canton simultaneously. Now fighting is going on all over outside districts of Canton, and result is not yet known. All the provinces in West and North China are ready for co-operation, but lack of fund.

Time is again ripe for a general movement such as that of the first Revolution in 1911. And the next time all will be under my direct control. No mistake or half measure should be recurred, and I am sure of a greater success than the first Revolution.

I am in urgent need of money now. Can you furnish a sum of half million or more cash immediately? If this can be forthcoming I can still seize the opportunity within this year or the beginning of the next to make a successful move. If you can get the money for me, besides, at the time secure ten or more the latest type aeroplanes and ship to Capt. Tom Gunn, Manila, immediately. If aeroplanes cannot be got just send the amount of mortors (at least 100 H. P.) with necessary materials and equipments.

With kindest regards to you and Mrs. Deitrick.

Yours very sincerely,
Sun Yat-sen

P. S.

The box of AKOZ medicine ⟨was⟩ received, I will ask some of my friends to try it. If real good, some one will surely ⟨be⟩ willing to be selling agent in this part of the world, please tell this to your friend the Doctor.

To President Wilson

Nov. 30, 1914

Tokyo

Appeal you for humanity sake prevent Morgan company contracting loan for Yuenshikai. Money cannot restore peace in China. Only maintain Chinese Huerta longer. Make peoples suffering more. Yuenshikai turns republic despotat [despotic]. People determine overthrow him. Struggle already began Kwangtung Kwangsi. Other provinces soon follow. Hopking [hoping] strict neutrality from America.

Sunyatsen

To James Deitrick

Dec. 19, 1914

Dear Mr. Deitrick:

Yours the November 14 & 28 have been received alright.

I have sent you a letter on October 20, and another on November 27. The former one must have reached you before you sent your last, but you did not mentioned [mention] about it. In both letters I asked you to raise fund for me quick [quickly]. For we are in great need of money at this juncture. Can you do anything to get from a few hundred thousand to half a million? If you can get it for me now our success will be quite sure. I wish you can get the money for me before you come out here. Is there any possibility for you to do it within three months of time? Please let me know exactly for I want to form plan according to the circumstance. I may go to America if nothing can be done within that time.

With the best regard.

Very truly yours,
Sun Yat Sen

To James Deitrick
Dec. 25, 1914 *

26, Reinanzaka
Akasaka
Tokyo, Japan

My dear Mr. Deitrick:

In my last letter I referred about a letter of the 20th October. I think I was mistaken; it is the 20th Nov. So it cannot reach you when you wrote me on the 28th November. I have no English secretary with me at present. My former lady secretaries, both sisters, the elder one Miss Eling Soong has just married, and the younger one Miss Rosamonde Soong has gone back to Shanghai lately. So I have to do the English writing myself.

In two or three of my former letters I asked you to get money for me immediately. Can you do it? I want you to give me definite answer at once, so that I may arrange my plan for the next year's action.

A happy new year to you.

Very truly yours,
Y. S. Sun

* Post marked Dec. 25th, 1914; received May 10, 1915.

To Mrs. Lea

Dec. 31, 1914

Dear Mrs. Lea:

Your letter of October 16th have been [was] received sometime [some time] ago, as we are going so slow that I have nothing new to tell you. Besides my English secretary Eling Soong has married recently and went back to Shanghai with her sister Rosamonde Soong, both of them ⟨were⟩ educated in America, and fine English scholars, so I have nobody to take charge of my English correspondence at present. I should like to have you come out there to help me, but everything is so changable and I cannot arrange any fix [fixed] plan. But I hope time will come soon for us to do something.

With kindest regard and happy new year to you.

Very sincerely yours,
Y. S. Sun

To Mrs. Cantlie

Mar. 19, 1915

26 Reinanzaka,

Akasaka

Tokyo, Japan

My dear Mrs. Cantlie:

I wish to tender you my grateful thanks for your letter of the 17th February. I can really understand how busy you are at this time and sympathize with the mothers of England fully.

I am busy putting my whole time and energy to my work but at present it doesn't seem that we could commence our operations as soon as we planned. Owing to the intervention and conservative influences of English Government, the Japanese Gov't fear [fears] to show us friendliness. But we are working independently of them and feel assured of success.

You can be of great help to me in England by enlightening the public that [by] helping Yuan Shih Kai, England is indirectly but surely advancing the interests of Germany. For Yuan Shih Kai is the exact prototype of the Kaiser in his tyrannical attitude and in his greed for power and self interests. Yuan Shih Kai is pro-German through and through and if Germany comes out victorious in this war, then China will surely become Germany's dependency. England will not only not gain anything by befriending Yuan, but will certainly lose the ground she has already gained in China. You must make this point clear to your people—that Yuan Shih Kai is pro-Germany.

England has my deepest sympathies in this war. It is indeed deplorable to realize the countless loss of English youths daily and all this bloodshed and sufferings forced upon her by a greedy and grasping power.

With best wishes to you and Dr. Cantlie, I am,

>Yours sincerely,
>Sun Yat Sen

To President of Republic Portugal

Apr. 3, 1915

President
Republic Portugal
Lisbon

Pray Your Excellency advise Macao authorities judge Wongmingtong political refugee following law.

Sun Yat-sen

To Governor of Macao
Apr. 3, 1915

Governor

Macao

Pray Your Excellency judge Wongmingtong political refugee following low [law] & equity.

Sun Yat-sen

To President of the International Socialist Bureau

Nov. 10, 1915

President
International Socialist Bureau
Peoples Palace
Brussels, Belgium

Dear Sirs:

So kind and sympathetic a letter from a source such as your organization cannot be otherwise than act as an invigorating tonic full of encouragement and hope to me and my followers. I wish you to know it has done me much good, and that I am grateful to the Socialists for the noble and valuable service they rendered to our cause. The knowledge that I have many sympathizers all over the world make [makes] my heart glad. We are truly fellow-workers, colaborers struggling against great opposing forces, and having the same unshakable conviction that truth, righteousness, and humanity, will surely conquer evil and injustice at [in] the end.

It will interest you to know that at the end of the first revolution when I was elected President of the Republic, I wanted to organize China after the Socialist idea; but I found myself single handed, for the people were absolutely ignorant on that subject, and my followers who were Socialists were but a handful besides their idea of Socialism was both crude and vague. I realized that I could not reconstruct China with such workers I had in hand, and with no talents to support

Letter to President of ISB, Nov. 10, 1915

me whatever, so I decided it would be useless to retain power; which meant prolongation of war and useless shedding of blood; therefore I concluded peace with Yuan Shih Kai with the understanding that he will govern the Republic, which I labored to bring about with the true spirit of democracy.

I was contrited to hand over the reins of the government to Yuan, in whom I had implicit faith. After twenty years [years'] labor, I had accomplished the task of changing an absolute monarchy into a Republic, and I was impatient to proceed in preparing the way for Socialism by educating the thinking and progressive element.

To my great grief and disappointment, Yuan Shih Kai whom I trusted to carry out the work which he swore he would, did nothing but usurped all power to his own interest, and furthermore he undid every bit of my work by underhanded means, and as soon as he felt strong enough he openly went back on his oath, and attacked the very principles that we mutually agreed he should uphold. Today he is more despotic than any tyrant, and China is more corrupt than ever before. He employed a gang of cut-throats and assassins to do away with his opponents, and many of China's best men were deliberately assassinated. Proofs showing that Yuan was the real author of the crimes went for nothing simply because he is the President. Therefore he has absolute power to kill openly or murder secretly, and no one has right to censure him. When Parliament demanded explanations from him, what did he do but simply abolished the Parliament itself. Members of Parliament were poisoned, executed, and imprisoned.

It seems strange that such state of affairs could happen in this enlightened 20th century in a country whose inhabitants comprises one-fourth of the entire human race; and yet the outside world either does not know them or is indifferent to them. With Yuan's power and money he bought up men and influential newspapers. The representatives of different nations were so busy looking after the proper protection of the lives and properties of their own people, and scheming as to what further interests they might secure in China. Plus the keenest jealousy they entertain between themselves; that they deemed, perhaps, profitable and wise to shut their eyes to all Yuan's dispotism; for after all he is in power, and it is only through his hands they might get what they desire.

But with all Yuan's seeming power he must go for we are determined that he should be crushed, and his days are but numbered. The Manchus were much more powerful than he yet we succeeded in relegating them. Yuan is afraid and that is the reason why he pleases the worried powers for in return he expects them to back him up when trouble comes, which he knows is bound to come. He realizes that he cannot rely upon the support of his own countrymen.

The capitalists believe that to uphold Yuan is to preserve peace in China, but that belief is false, for there has been no peace in China and never will be as long as he continues practicing tyranny and selfishness. In a conditional way—not so clear as this, great disturbance is the order of the day in China, and when I give order to rise a great upheaval, greater than any known in China will be the result, for my men are all ready to start whenever the signal is given them. Yuan's own men and soldiers are turning against him, and that is an added assurance of our success.

Our 2nd revolution was a failure because there was no unity amongst the revolutionists and there was no leader for I took no active part in the movement. Immediately after I resigned in favor of Yuan, I gave up politics entirely, and lost myself completely in studying out the best methods of gradually moulding the

Letter to President of ISB, Nov. 10, 1915

government according to the Socialist idea thus realizing and completing the sole object and ambition of my life I firmly believe that only when China becomes a Socialist state, that our people can be made happier and their drudgeries alleviated. Socialism will cure her ailment.

Our coming revolution will, without a doubt reap success. It is under my direct control and management, and I take the entire responsibility myself. My followers profited by the lessons derived from past failure are working in perfect unison and harmony under my personal supervision.

To overthrow Yuan is but a foregone conclusion and is not difficult; but the task that comes after his downfall, the reorganization of China, is what I am afraid of, for I have no practical talents to assist me in carrying out my long cherished desire of guiding the state to that goal. I will again be handicapped as I was in 1912. I am not justified in plunging the country into another bloody war unless I am assured that I can have good, trustworthy talents to help, and advise me in carrying out my Socialistic principles and policies.

I desire to impress upon you, my co-laborers, that China is the land where Socialism can be carried out into practice, and it is the field that should be worked and used as a model of government after the Socialist idea. China is immensely rich in natural resources, and her teeming millions are eager, earnest laborers, quiet in nature, and are easily led and satisfied. So long they are given work they are happy. Industry is not yet developed, capitalism not yet domineering, and the masses of the people are obedient and lawabiding; so she can be easily moulded into any shape or form. So long has the country been under the monarchic rule that her people have never been taught the difference between social democracy and autocracy.

I appeal to you, my co-laborers, to help me in making China the first Socialist state in the world, by concentrating your attention, energy on China, and contributing talents in various lines and departments of work to help me. I need the assistance of men such as your organization could furnish in this great undertaking.

If you agree to my proposal, will you advise me at the earliest possible moment, so that we can devise practical means to carry out our plan. I should be pleased if you will present my idea to the leaders of the Socialists of all countries, and if it be met with approval I may be able to come to Europe to discuss details with you.

Please impress upon the leaders the necessity of absolute secrecy, for should the worried powers capitalists and financiers be acquainted with this matter, they will combine together and endeavour to nip us in the bud, which will make our battle much harder to fight.

In conclusion, I beg you to remember that it is within your power to help push this great human force to labor like men, and to secure happiness and blessings to millions of human souls.

Hoping to hear from you soon, I remain,

Your fellow-worker,
Sun Yat-sen

To James Deitrick

Nov. 18, 1915

> 109 Harajiku
> Aoyama
> Tokyo, Japan

My dear Mr. Deitrick:

As I have not heard from you for a long time, I have been quite anxious about you. Since your cablegram from Petrograd I was expecting you to turn up here at any moment, and not until I learned of your plan to go to New York did I abandon hope of seeing you.

I wonder with what result you are meeting with the negotiation of a loan. Is there any chance of success? Please let me know as soon as convenient as I should like to give upon hearing from you. I shall write more fully, concerning my work and its progress. In the meantime I close with best regards to you and Mrs. Deitrick. I am,

> Yours cordially,
> Sun Yat Sen

To Mrs. Lea

Nov. 20, 1915

109 Harajiku

Aoyama

Tokyo, Japan

My dear Mrs. Lea:

I crave your pardon for delaying to acknowledge the receipt of two of your kind letters, that of July 27th and Aug. 24th. There is so much work to accomplish and so many things that demand my personal attention that there seems hardly time for relaxation. In this case silence does not indicate lack of appreciation, for almost daily I have your letters in mind and 〔wish〕 for the time to come when I may answer them and tell you something of the progress in my work, since writing you last.

I feel sure that with your deep and personal interest, you would be gratified to learn that all my plans 〈are〉 being worked out splendidly, according to expectations, and conditions, also, are more than favorable.

So the start may come to at any moment, while all my followers are ready to fight for an overwhelming victory or perish in the attempt to obtain liberty.

With reference to the monarchy movement, it is more than unbearable to the Chinese people. But they have no means whereby to express their sentiments or opinions. With the influential foreign papers bribed to distort the true state of facts as they are, natually are reads [read] almost daily that the Chinese people are all anxious for the restoration of a monarchical form of government. However, the warning notes of the Five Powers should be sufficient proofs to all that such is far from right or true. The Powers sent the warnings because they apprehended disturbances within the country and feared for a general uprising against the change! Since the change of the Japanese Cabinet, the policy of Japan towards China has changed perceptibly—Okuma of course remains firm in friendship for Yuan Shih-kai. But the majority of the members have no faith whatever in Yuan Shih-kai or his abilities. So in the storm of opposition, and much against his inclinations, Okuma had to submit to the will of the majority and send a warning note to China at this eleventh hour! Surely this warning could not have been prompted through friendship for Yuan Shih-kai!

As I am progressing most favorably in my work here, and as this is the centre of all our activities, I have altogether given up my idea of lecture tour in the United States. For I am convinced that more good and advantages would result from my stay here than in any other part of the world right now. So in the meantime please do not exert yourself for me in that direction. If that time should ever come I shall then cable you.

Henceforth please address all letters to me at the above address. Hoping to hear from you frequently and with my most cordial regards, I remain. As always,

Your sincere friend
Sun Yat-sen

To Yokashi
Dec. 29, 1915

Yokashi
Hongkong

Your business consult 〔Consult your business〕 with Chowkok.

Coyama

To Chowkok

Dec. 30, 1915

Chowkok

Hongkong

If Yokashi business ⟨is⟩ practicable, let him try ⟨to⟩ apply ⟨to⟩ Hongkong Shanghai bank for 10,000 dollars.

To Mrs. Lea

Jan. 11, 1916

109 Harajiku

Aoyama

Tokyo, Japan

My dear Mrs. Lea:

Your letter date December 30th is received. I am very much interested to learn that you are working in a mining man's office, and right now I wish to say that I hope you will make connections with the mining men in America not the speculators but the expert engineers and the administrators, those who could step right in a work for the government. Since the government will take the initiative to open up mines and develop them and encourage the people to follow step. Those who possess such abilities are needed and please be on the lookout for me.

Time is approaching now, and I feel sure that all our hopes will soon be realized. You doubtless have read about the different provinces which have already declared independence. One province after the other is following suit, as similar to that of the first Revolution. It goes to prove first that my two years of labor has not been fruitless in China, and that, after all, ⟨however⟩ apathetic us the Chinese seen [seem] to be, they are not without conscience or national feeling.

This movement has been a greater task than the first Revolution but the results will be much greater, also, a deeper knowledge of human nature and propelled by past experiences we are wiser than before in all matters.

Yuan Shih-kai has now ascended the throne, virtually but his days are numbered, as all can see. Perhaps before this letter reaches you. There will be astonishing accomplishments in China by our men.

Hoping to hear from you again soon. Please direct mail to Tokyo.

With best regards.

Yours sincerely,
Sun Yat-sen

To Mrs. Cantlie
Jan. 18, 1916

109 Harajiku

Aoyama

Tokyo, Japan

My dear Mrs. Cantlie:

I acknowledge with warmest thanks for your welcome favour of 28th Nov. At about the same time I sent you a letter in care of the College of Ambulance which I trust has safely reached you. Inspite of the trouble in Europe I am sure you are all posted as to the present situation in China. News travel [travels] so rapidly these days that you hear of happenings before my letter could reach you with its predictions.

Yunnan has taken lead in declaring independance and one province after the other is following in quick succession, similar to the First Revolution when we overthrew the Manchu yoke. Yuan Shihkai with his comical crown and title of "Ta Huang Ti" (Great Emperor) cannot raise a hand to suppress the voice of people. Where are all his vaunted abilities and powers to hold the country together?

As you said he has indeed succeeded in deluding many ministers of other nations, but he cannot delude his own country men, whose name he has taken in vain, by declaring that "such is the will of the people". I, also, am surprised that the English have been deluded by him, inspite of his very transparent pro-German tendencies and partialities.

The English officials in Hong Kong, Shanghai and Singapore zealously co-operate with Yuan in persecuting our patriots and act as if they receive orders from Yuan Shih Kai and not from their own Government, as if, Yuan were their master and superior. Such action on the part of English officials here is surely going to bring bad consequences upon their Government. For very soon our party, the younger and progressive elements in China will get into power. Therefore, I beg you will get those of our friends in the Parliament to bring this subject before the Government as soon as possible, and do so in a forcible and strong way.

In the past our people have always looked upon England as a friend and have reciprocated friendliness wherever and whenever possible. Unless such persecutions are stopped and policy changed, henceforth the Chinese people cannot help but look upon England in another light. England is doing herself injustice and injury by continuing her persecutions of our patriots and stand [standing] as our stumbling blocks.

The Eng. Government should not keep her eyes glued to the present and the temporary but look further into the future, if she desires friendship and not enmity from the younger generations of China. Inspite of obstructions and impediments in our way I feel sure we shall reap our success in a short period, much sooner than one supposes.

I hope you and Dr. Cantlie are in excellent healths [health], inspite of the great and fatiguing work you are rendering for a good and noble cause. Please write me to the above address until further notice.

In the meantime I close with my warmest greetings to you and yours.

Yours faithfully,
Sun Yat Sen

To James Deitrick
May 27, 1916

Shanghai

My dear Mr. Deitrick:

I sent you a cablegram immediately upon receiving your letter which was you worded from Tokyo. I came to Shanghai a month ago as conditions here necessitate my presence.

Money is now the chief requisite for my work. For 3 years I have labored to create chances and now the chances have come and just for the lack of money things are slipping out of control. The country is now in a most critical condition and I am anxious to pull China out of this chaos and restore her once more into order and peace. It is not Yuan Shih Kai alone we wish to pull down, for that can be easily done. We must at the same moment clear all his officials away, in order to rid China of their evil influences.

You have read of many provinces declaring independence. But you have not any idea of the true state of things or the conditions leading up to this step. The officials are only holding in for selfish ambitions. We created the circumstances and when they see that unless they declare independence they would be the loser, they suddenly turned turtle and became outwardly in sympathy with us. But as soon as they see Yuan is making a little headway, by means of foreign loans, they go over to his side thus retaining their own positions. Take the example of

Lung Chi Kwang, Tutuh of Kwantung province, He falsely declared independence of his province when he perceived our strength in that quarter, but at the same time he was in secret correspondence with Yuan Shih Kai.

So you see with such treacherous men China would become worse and worse and sink deeper and deeper into the mire. Therefore, we must work to clear them all way and not let a single one enter into service again in the next Government. At the same time our cause is being put in a precarious condition, and would play into the hands of Yuan unless I take a drastic step immediately and put all forces under my control again.

For this purpose I need most urgently a sum of five million gold, for which I cabled you. With this sum I can accomplish the chief desire and object of my life—to restore my country into peace within a short time. For I have determined upon the shortest cut to the goal, and that is to strike at the most vital point—Peking.

Now I hope that you have [a] clearer ideas as to the situation in China and will do your best to help me in obtaining this fund, without which all will be lost. You can arrange terms it [in] your own discretion for I have great confidence in your ability and honour.

Please wire me as to results. My cable address is now changed: "Waicy", Shanghai will reach me and all letters must be enclosed in another envelope with the outside envelope addressed as follows: Mousieur Y. Waicy, 55 Yang King Ping, French Concession, Shanghai.

Hoping to hear good news from you soon. I know you are doing utmost.

Letter to Deitrick, May 27, 1916

With best wish to you and your family, I remain,

                                            Yours sincerely,
                                            Sun Yat-sen

To James Deitrick

July 5, 1916

63 Route Vallon

Shanghai

My dear Mr. Deitrick:

    Since the death of Yuan Shih Kai the situation has entirely changed, so I asked you to await my letter, in my cablegram. If I had the necessary sum of money I could have established the provisional government long before the death of Yuan occurred, and now there would be no question of a compromise between the North and South. But according to the constitution Li Yuan Hung has come up to fill the vacancy. Peace and order is to be desired above all things and so I effected an understanding between the two sides successfully. As Li Yuan Hung is an easy going man, and has not any aspirations for the crown, I believe he will serve the country according to the will of the people, and not usurp his powers to his own personal advantages.

    I am consulted upon all the national and international affairs and though I am not taking any position, yet my influence is as strongly felt as ever, and I possess the great confidence of the people.

    Now, I shall stay out and watch the settling down of affairs and remain in the background, unless strong reason calls me forth again. Since conditions are such please cancel whatever political loans you have proposed to negotiate for me, and also return the papers containing the powers of attorney.

If things settle down for the better then I shall take up the industrial work again. In the meantime please look up such men that we can make use of in developing industries, etc. In that case I shall come over to the United States again, soon, to see the capitalists and to get men of whom we could utilize here.

Concerning Henry Clifford Stuart, I do not know why he tries in various ways to discredit me. Recently he created a great sensation in the Washington papers, through a Mr. Seafield, by advertizing for a last jade idol, supposed to be my talisman. Mr. Stuart claimed to have been authorized by me to institute a search and pay a reward of $10,000 for its recovery, etc. [, etc. .] It is the most absurd and ridiculous piece of senseless invention I ever read of.

I do not know what prompted him to act so. He has sent many letters to me but as I did not know whom he was, I never answered him as far as I could remember.

Hoping to hear from you soon, and with best wishes, I am,

Yours sincerely,
Sun Yat-sen

To Mrs. Lea

Oct. 19, 1916

63 Route Vallon

Shanghai

My dear Mrs. Lea:

Your kind letter of Sept. 6th has reached me, and I am very glad to hear from you again. Relating to your idea of travelling in China, I wish to say it might be done, for with the knowledge you could obtain great good would surely come out of them. And I should be only too ready and glad to help you in any way [were] if within my power to do so.

But travelling in the interior of China is something impossible, You simply have no idea how unendurable are the physical hardships! One has to carry all the household necessities on the road, which necessitate a retinue of servents, the best of the accomadations offered is the worst imaginable. Even for men, travelling in the interior is unbearable, to say the least. I hate to discourage your desire and wish, for I know how disappointed you might feel over it. Besides the expenses would be several times greater than travelling in Europe or America, for the same distance.

However, if you wish to study in the coastal cities, it would be a different matter altogether. In that case I shall think out a way to help you do so. As for the present conditions in China, one could not be too optimistic about them, knowing the undesirable factors that are still disturbing from within, the life of the Republic.

At present I must shut off many affairs before I could be free, whence I shall take a trip to America, but of course there is no telling what might come between that time and now.

In the meantime I send my kindest regards.

Yours very truly,
Y. S. Sun

To Comrades in Singapore

Oct. 31, 1916

General Hwanghsing died this morning. Please inform friends throughout English Dutch Colonies and Rangoon Bangkok Saigon.

Sun Yat Sen

To Comrades in Australia
Oct. 31, 1916

General Hwanghsing died this morning. Please inform friends throughout Australia ⟨and⟩ New Zealand.

Sun Yat Sen

To James Deitrick

Nov. 24, 1916

63 Route Vallon
Shanghai

My dear Mr. Deitrick:

Some time ago I wrote you in care of the Palace Hotel, asking you to return the power of attorney, but as no answer came from you, I fear you are no longer in that hotel or that the letter failed to reach you. And since the papers are important, I have asked Mr. Robert Norman, a confidential friend of mine, to look you up and hand you this letter. Upon receipt of this, please let him have the power of attorney.

As you have not written for a long time I am ignorant as to your doings and whereabouts. I have now in view one of your projects, and desire to carry that out immediately. That is, the agricultural idea. I am going soon to get the Government's consent for lands in the North and wish you would look up all facts, including what machines are necessary and what methods must be adopted by us, and let me know soon. With cordial regards,

Yours truly,
Sun Yat-sen

To President Wilson

June 8, 1917

Shanghai

Since America was foremost in welcoming us as a democracy and her example was the chief factor that influenced China to terminate her neutrality with the Central Powers, America is morally bound to assist our Republic at this critical juncture. A band of traitors under the pretext of declaring war for the benefit of China's interests, but whose real purpose is the restoration of the monarchy are endeavoring to enlist the sympathies and support of the Entente Allies and to obtain from them loans, nominally by joining them as faithful allies, but actually for attaining their own selfish ends. The people knowing the real motive for their sinister action bitterly opposed China's entering the war with the result that militarism, the very evil that is now being fought out in Europe, is employed to subjugate the people and abolish our parliament. [Although] the militarists have the upper hand we are able to vanquish them for ever and preserve our Republic, provided Your Excellency will only now make known the real situation to those friendly powers and exert your influence to gain their cooperation in preventing China from being dragged into the European war. By doing this friendly act we can easily destroy militarism and anarchism in China. May I not count upon Your Excellency's assistance on behalf of the cause of humanity.

Sun Yat Sen

To President Wilson

June 9, 1917 *

Shanghai

Your Excellency: At the same time I despatched my appeal to you came Your Excellency's advice to our statesmen. In the name of my countrymen I beg to express deepest gratitude for Your Excellency's foresight and timely warning. China can never be united or at peace so long as she is held in the grip of militarism and enemies of democracy. We are ready to sacrifice our lives for the extermination of these evil factors and look expectantly to Your Excellency to keep all powers neutral and give us fair play.

Sun Yat Sen

* The date of sending is unknown, here is the received date.

To Baron Kato

June 18, 1917

63 Route Vallon

Shanghai, China

Baron Kato

Tokyo, Japan

My dear Mr. Kato:

I am sending the bearer of this letter, Mr. Tai Tien Chur to Japan, who will inform you of his mission.

I write these few lines specially to you to say that what I am going to undertake [to do] in China, depends a great deal upon you, whether I shall meet with success or failure. And I am absolutely sure that with your assistance I can surely succeed.

We are now prepared to clear away these useless and disturbing elements, who have caused so much miseries, and who have retarded the progress of China. And we are confidently looking to you for aid. Will you not for the sake of Humanity extend to me all the helps [help] that you can give?

With best regards,

Yours sincerely,

Sun Yat-sen

To Mrs. Cantlie

Oct. 17, 1918

29 Rue Moliere
Shanghai, China

My dear Mrs. Cantlie:

I am delighted to hear from you and most pleased that each one of your dear lads has been well. In this time of great sufferings all over the world, one cannot help to think [thinking] that you are especially fortunate and protected by God. I congratulate you most heartily upon the honor that has been conferred on you. I am so glad to learn that the valuable work you and Dr. Cantlie are rendering to the country is recognized and appreciated.

In spite of the manifold responsibilities and duties that surely must befall you, I trust that you have time to keep up with the work that we are doing here. Over a year ago I left Shanghai with the greater part of the Navy to Canton. There I organized the Military Government in opposition to the illegal Government in the North, which is comprised of followers and henchmen of Yuan Shih Kai.

By military force they sought to destroy the Republic and compelled Li Yuan Hung to dissolve the Parliament. Thus the Country has been in turmoil ever since. We are trying to overthrow the same autocratic and military spirit within our Country as that for which so many lives have been sacrificed in the European War.

As soon as the Legal Parliament was convened at Canton I resigned as Chief of the Military Government since my object had been obtained. The mandarin clique at North has set up a bogus Parliament and elected a bogus President in the meantime however there will be no peace until Law is restored and the Constitutionalist cause succeeds.

At present I am devoting my time in [to] writing another book by which I hope to instil new knowledge into the Chinese mind and to revolutionize old theories which we, without questioning their worth or truth, have clung to for centuries, to the stagnation of our mental progress and achievement.

Last year I finished a book on the Parliamentary Law, the book which is in great need here, and I am glad that in many of the schools it is being used as a text book. I hope that I shall have plenty of time to write henceforth, in order to educate the people's minds and teach them their responsibilities as citizens, and their privileges and duties.

From your last letter I discovered that you were not informed of my second marriage which took place in Tokyo three years ago. My wife was educated in an American College and the daughter of one of my earliest co-workers and friends. I am living a new life and enjoying what I missed before: a real home life and a companion and helper.

My former wife did not like to travel about and consequently she never accompanied me abroad in my refugee days. She wanted to settle down with her old Mother and always persuaded me to marry another wife according to the old custom. But the girl I loved is a modern girl and would not tolerate such a position and I myself could not give her up. Thus there was no other way than agree to a divorce with my former wife.

As to the children, my son is with me now and my daughter is still in America attending her first year in college.

I am quite anxious for my wife to know you and enjoy your friendship as I do, and I hope to be able to bring her to England in the near future. I am sending you one of our pictures in the same mail.

Hoping this to find you and Dr. Cantlie in the best of healths 〔health〕 and with warmest regards, I remain,

                                          Very faithfully yours,
                                          Sun Yat-sen

To President Wilson
Nov. 18, 1918

President Wilson

The White House

Washington D. C.

Your Excellency:

I congratulate you on the complete victory you have gained over militarism in this world war. You have done the greatest service to civilization and democracy since the world began.

When you advised China to join you in the war last year I strongly objected because I knew that the militarists in my country would surely utilize the occasion to strangly [strongly] [?] democracy in China. My prediction has unfortunately turned out true.

In the summer of last year while the question of joining the war was before our national assembly the Boxer Chief Chang Hsun undertook a coup d'etat under the secret order of the then Premier Tuan Chi-jui, to force the abolition of parliament and to effect the restoration of the Manchu emperor. Thus they intended to crush democracy at one stroke. But this act was not welcomed by all the powers and was bitterly resented by the people of China. Tuan Chi-jui saw that the movement was foredoomed to failure so he changed front at once by joining the christian general, Feng Yuhsiang, who was already marching with his brigade on

Peking to fight the monarchist. Tuan Chi-jui established himself the chief of this anti-monarchist movement and thus pretended to be the savior of the republic.

Immediately after hearing of the restoration of the monarchy and the overthrow of the republic I left Shanghai, on the 5th July, 1917, with a part of the Chinese navy for Canton, with a view to fight the monarchists. But on arrival at my destination all the work I had intended to do had been done already, apparently by Tuan Chi-jui. I conguatulated [congratulated] him for his patriotic action and advised him to restored [restore] the parliament at once. To my disappointment he ignored my advice and to my surprise I further discovered that he was at the bottom of Chang Hsun's boxer movement to destroy foreign institutions and to uphold the Manchus.

I then took steps upon my own responsibility to reconvene the parliament at Canton, At first I was strongly opposed by the southern militarists also, but realizing that public opinion was with me, they let me have my way. The people of Canton welcomed my proposal and the Kuangtung provincial assembly at once sent out invitations to the members of parliament in all the provinces to come to Canton, and they responded enthusiastically. The southern militarists finding that the constitutional movement being so strongly supported by the people dared not openly come to terms with the north, but they conspired to overthrow democracy in the south as well. Thus, after a year [year's] laboring under unutterable difficulties, I finally succeeded in getting the parliament into quorum, which consisted of the majority of both the houses. During that interval the north sent expedition after expedition to crush the south. Thus the southern militarists were compelled to fight for their constitutional cause with my followers purely in self-defense, although they were not working under my direction. This is the real cause of the war forced by the northern militarists upon the south. But it is not a

Letter to President Wilson, Nov. 18, 1918

war between the north and south, as commonly supposed to be, for half the number of members of the parliament in Canton now are from the north.

It is in fact a war between militarism and democracy pure and simple. The northern militarists knowing well that our cause is just and that we cannot be subjugated by them, created a bogus parliament in order to counteract the one elected by the people to gain public opinion in their territory and thus to throw dust into the eyes of the foreign powers.

Since the change of the cabinet in Japan the supply of money and arms to the northerns has been stopped. Being left helpless, the northern militarists now make overtures to the south for a compromise on conditions that both the bogus and true parliament be dissolved and the official posts of the republic redistributed. The southern militarists welcome this idea, as it enables them to divide the nations [nation's] property among themselves and to crush the people's rights.

It is officially given out from Peking that the United States want China to cease internal war, and if the south does not agree to the terms, the militarists will bring American pressure upon the south. Thus when the world was at war we were accused as anti-war; now, then peace is dawning, we shall likely soon be accused as antipeace by the militarists. We have fought against overwhelming odds and against Japanese money and arms and yet survive; but if the United States moral and physical forces are to be misused as the Japanese by the Peking militarists against an oppressed people, the hope of democracy in China is gone.

Therefore I am compelled to appeal to you personally for the sake of justice, democracy and peace in China, and make known to you our peace terms. We insist all along upon one condition only, that is, our parliament must have full liberty to perform its proper functions. If this simple reasonable and moderate condition is denied we will fight on despite whatever pressure the Peking militarists may bring upon us. For this parliament was won by the blood of the martyrs of our revolution and is the foundation of the republic. We could not suffer to see it ⟨to be⟩ so ruthlessly destroyed by the militarists. Moreover, this was the parliament duty authorized to formulate and adopt a permanent constitution for the republic. Until this special duty is fulfilled and the new constitution promulgated, it cannot be dissolved. When Yuan Shi-kai was preparing his way to the imperial throne he abruptly abolished this parliament. Then the people rose and defeated him. This is now the second time that we are fighting for the same parliament. And this very parliament was first recognized by the United States through your own good self.

May I not look upon you now to save democracy in China as you have done in Europe, by saying just a word for the oppressed people of China to the Peking militarists that the parliament which you have recognized must be respected.

Sun Yat Sen

To Paul S. Reinsch

Jan. 10, 1919

His Excellency Paul S. Reinsch, Peking.

Your Excellency:

I wish to thank you for your note of the eleventh of December which was delivered to me yesterday. As I am greatly interested in the subject of Architecture, I shall be indeed greatly obliged if you will hand that volume of Architectural Plans to Dr. Chiang Monlin when he calls for it.

                                      Thanking you again, I am,
                                      Sincerely yours,
                                      Sun Yat-sen

29 Rue Moliere,
Shanghai,
Jan. 10, 1919.

To Lady James Cantlie

Mar. 20, 1919

29 Rue Moliere
Shanghai, China

Lady James Cantlie
23 Harley St.
London

Dear Lady Cantlie:

I am very sorry to learn of the accident that had happened to your husband but feel greatly relieved to hear that he is not daunted in the least. You both are so full of courage and spirit that it is a great inspiration to me to see how bravely you face everything.

As you are so much interested in the affairs of China and since you have taken a large part in making China of what she is already, I feel sure that you will be interested in all my plans. I am sending you here a copy of my project to develop China internationlly *. I have sent a copy of this to each member of the Cabinet of the British Government also. I hope that you will let me know how the people of England will receive this scheme of mine.

If this plan is favorably received in England, I will make a trip there in the near future. At present I cannot very well leave China as the internal peace is not yet settled.

Hoping to hear from you soon and with my most affectionate regards to you and yours,

> I am,
> Very sincerely yours,
> Sun Yat-sen

* Enclosure is omitted here for the full text is compiled in pp. 130-135 of this book.

To C. E. MacWilliams

Aug. 26, 1919

29 Rue Moliere

Shanghai, China

Mr. Chas E. MacWilliams
New York City
U. S. A.

My dear Mr. Williams:

I am very pleased to hear from you and wish to thank you for sending me the clipping from the *Herald*. There are wonderful opportunities in China for persons with capital and the Chinese people are especially eager for Americans to come and help 〈them〉 develop the Country. So I hope that it will be possible for you to make a trip here in the near future and see for yourself what a lot [there] is to be accomplished here in the opening up of this country.

With regard to Mr. Wong Sam Ack, I am sorry to say that I have entirely lost touch of him and have no idea where he is now.

With best wishes,

Sincerely yours,

Sun Yat-sen

To N. E. B. Ezra

Apr. 24, 1920

29, Rue Moliere
Shanghai

Dear Mr. Ezra:

I have read your letter and the copy of *Israel's Messenger* with much interest, and wish to assure you of my sympathy for this movement, which is one of the greatest movements of the present time. All lovers of Democracy cannot help but support wholeheartedly and welcome with enthusiasm the movement to restore your wonderful and historic nation, which has contributed so much to the civilization of the world and which rightfully deserve [deserves] an honourable place in the family of nations.

I am,
Yours very truly,
Sun Yat-sen

To Dr. & Mrs. James Cantlie

Aug. 10, 1920

Dear Dr. & Mrs. Cantlie:

I am sending you several copies of my recent address which I hope you will have it widely published in England, as it will explain to the great mass [masses] outside [of] China the real situation in China.

I hope that you both are in good healths [health].

With warmest regards.

Yours faithfully,
Sun Yat-sen

To James Cantlie

Apr. 2, 1921

Kwan Yin Shan
Canton

My dear Dr. Cantlie:

I am sending you by the same mail my recent book *The International Development of China* which has just come out of print. As you see I have taken the liberty of dedicating this work to you and Mrs. Cantlie as a slight expression of my gratitude and affection for you both.

I desire very much to have Lord Curzon write a preface to this book and will appreciate very much if you would kindly present my letter and a copy of my book to him personally. I desire to ask you another favor in connection with this book that is to get my book published in England. I am going to have it published in America too. The publisher in London by the name of Jenkins seems to be a very enterprising man. He has written me several times to let him publish any literary work of mine, but I never answered him as I had nothing written in English. Will you please therefore see this publisher for me and arrange with him about the publication of this book? I will give the English copyright to any publisher who will take up the book, but in case none will do so, please write me and I will send you a draft for the purpose of publishing it. In which [that] case please let me know what sum will be sufficient. There are several errors in this book and in the map but I am sending you a corrected copy of each for the purpose of reprinting. I shall be most grateful to you for attending to this matter for me.

I hope that you and Mrs. Cantlie are in excellent health. At present, I am so busy with my work that there seems to be no chance to get away. I should like so much to see your son and I do hope I shall see him when he comes to the East.

It is always a great encouragement for me to hear from you. I enjoyed your latest letter so very much.

With my warmest regards to you and Mrs. Cantlie.

Yours sincerely,
Sun Yat-sen

P. S. Please ask the publisher to arrange a table of contents and index to the back. This book should be printed in a larger type than the original, and with only 30 lines to a page, in order to make a thicker book.

Y. S.

To Mrs. Lea

Aug. 5, 1921

Canton, China

My dear Mrs. Lea:

I am very glad to get your letter of the 14th of May. By this time you must have read of our great success, in ousting militarism from Kwangsi province. This means that one more province has come under me. We are making great progress here. We intend to march to the north and drive out all the super tuchunds [tuchuns] and the Japanese clique. Of course as usual the British government here is putting many obstacles in my way and try to minimize all our important gains.

Jms. Chockman is here and is at the head of the Aviation Corps. He has a little son recently and is very proud of him. He comes to see me often and seems to be very enthusiastic about his work. I shall let him know that you are in Buenos Aires. And I will give you a full account of our work here.

We are eager to hear you come out and help us in the industrial work for women, and as soon as time is ready I will let you know. In the meantime I close with my warmest regards.

Sincerely yours,

Sun Yat-sen

To James Cantlie

Aug. 12, 1921

Canton

My dear Sir James Cantlie:

Many thanks for your letter of June 26 and for your great kindness in seeing about the publication of my book in England. I understand fully the difficulties mentioned in your letter; and if you do not succeed in placing the book for the present, I shall wait for a more favourable opportunity.

I have read Marquis Curzon's letter with great interest and quite understand his difficulty. Of course, in requesting him to write an introduction to my book, it never crossed my mind to try to use or exploit him in the interests of my party. I am convinced that the lines of development defined in my book are the right ones to be followed if China and her incalculable resources are to be made available, at the earliest date and without protracted delay, for the use of her people and for the people of the rest of the world. I want this view to be shared by those who are shaping or who are in a position to influence the large policies of the world in order to get the necessary momentum which shall set my thoughts moving in the mind of men in the direction of work and achievement. That is the only reason why I thought of getting Lord Curzon to introduce the book to the English public.

With you, I think the Miners' Strike and its result will have a steadying [steady] effect on political development in England. Of course, the fundamental common sense of your people is a mighty asset.

With renewed thanks and best wishes,

Very sincerely yours,
Sun Yat-sen

To Lady James Cantlie

Aug. 12, 1921

Canton

My dear Lady Cantlie:

I have to thank you for your kind letters, dated June 26 and July 4, with enclosures. I am glad to know that you have moved into new quarters where you will be able to arrange to entertain occasionally the members of the Chinese community in London. That would be very nice of you; and I am sure it will be greatly appreciated.

I am interested, also, to learn that Sir James has been called in as medical adviser to the new Chinese Minister. Belonging as he does to what we at Canton consider the wrong party in China, Mr. Koo is likely to benefit in other than a medical sense from contact with one who is so devoted to right living like Sir James.

I shall do what I can in the matter of the Child Slavery question in Hong Kong. If China had been permitted to get on in the manner contemplated ten years ago, the Hong Kong reactionaries would not now have been able to defend the evil practice there by referring to its prevalence in China in spite of its prohibition by law. Let us hope that some day, not far distant, the practice will be effectively and generally put down.

I think Mr. and Mrs. Haslewood deserve the greated [greatest] credit for what they have already done in the matter. They clearly belong to the order of workers of whom Wilberforce and Clarkson are the great English representatives.

With my grateful thanks for your goodly prayers and warm wishes for the success of the CAUSE,

Very sincerely yours,
Sun Yat-sen

To Tchitcheren

Aug. 28, 1921

Canton

My dear Tchitcheren,

I have your letter, dated from Moscow, 31 October, 1920. It reached me on 14 June, 1921. I have delayed replying because I desired to see the bearer who received it from you, he having forwarded it to me from Harbin. As the latter is unable to travel to Canton to see me for the present, I have decided to reply to your fraternal greetings and suggestion as to the re-establishment of trade relations between Russia and China.

Before proceeding, I must inform you that this is the first and only letter that I have received from you or any one else in Soviet Russia. During the past two years, there have been several reports in the Capitalist press referring to alleged overtures from Moscow to me. No such overtures have been communicated to me by letter or otherwise. In case any of your colleagues has or have addressed letters to me, be pleased to say that I have received none.

I must tell you briefly what the Chinese situation is. I go back to 1911-12, when my political work found its decisive expression in the Revolution which started in October, 1911, and spread rapidly throughout the country. The Revolution led to the overthrow of the Manchu dynasty and the establishment of the Chinese Republic. I was elected President. After a short term of office, I resigned in favour of Yuan Shih-kai, because friends in whom I trusted implicitly and who then had a more intimate knowledge of Chinese internal affairs than I, had advised me that Yuan Shih-kai was in a position to unify the country and to assure the stability of the Republic, having as he had the confidence of the Foreign Powers. My friends now admit that my resignation was a great political mistake, as it had precisely the same consequence as would have taken place in Russia if Koltchak or Yudenitch or Wrangel had succeeded in replacing Lenin at Moscow. Yuan immediately or soon after began to work for an Imperial restoration with himself as the new emperor. As you know, we defeated him.

Since his death, however, the Great Powers have been assisting, politically and financially, a number of pseudo-Cromwells and Napoleons. The present one is an ex-leader of banditti called Chang Tso-lin. Officially, he is the tuchun or military governor of Manchuria, but in fact, he is the master that the Peking "government" obeys. And in his turn, he obeys Tokio in all essential matters relating to Japan. It is, therefore, correct to lay it down that Peking is practically the tool of Tokio in all questions of high policy touching vital Japanese interests. Moscow must bear this fact well in mind in all its official dealings with Peking. And not until there is a clean sweep in the capital—which will be done when I get there—can Soviet Russia hope to re-establish satisfactory relations with China.

Since the date of your letter, I have been elected President of a National Government, which has been established at Canton. This Government is de jure because (a) it derives its authority from the Provisional Constitution, passed by the first constituent assembly that met at Nanking in 1912, and[is] the sole existing Organic Law of the Chinese Republic, and (b) it has been formed in pursuance of the government-making power vested by the Constitution in the legal

Chinese Parliament which is now in session at Canton. My Government is also de facto in that its authority is recognised [recognized] by the great bloc of provinces in the South-West of China and by other provinces as its jurisdiction extends.

For the present, I am geographically debarred from entering into effective commercial relations with you. If you glance at a map of China, you will observe that the territory now under the jurisdiction of my Government lies south of the line of the Yangtze River, and that between this area and the Manchurian and Mongolian "gateways"—through which alone commercial relations can take place—Chang Tso-lin and his confederates stand in the way. There is and can be no "gateway" via Chinese Turkestan until the construction, some day, of the great trunk line included in my projected system of railway communication for China.

Moscow must wait until I clear up the reactionaries and counter-revolutionists that appear in every country on the morrow of a creative revolution. Your own experiences during the past three to four years will enable you to understand the work before me. I have been at it for the last nine to ten years. I hope to finish it at an early date unless some form of active foreign intervention supervenes. This is not very likely so far as the Great Western Powers are concerned. They are apparently sick of Peking.

In the meantime I wish to keep in personal touch with you and my other friends at Moscow. I am greatly interested in your work, particularly the organisation of your soviet councils, your army and education. I want to know all that you and others can tell me about these things, particularly education. Like Moscow, I want to plant the foundations of the Chinese Republic deep in the minds of the children—the workers of to-morrow.

Letter to Tchitcheren, Aug. 28, 1921

With all good wishes to you and my friend Lenin and the rest who have so greatly achieved in the cause of man's freedom.

Yours very sincerely

Sun Yat-sen

P. S. This letter is being sent to you via London through the Russian Soviet Commercial Mission there. If it reaches you safely and without undue delay, please advise me so that I may in future communicate with you through the same medium. I am arranging for communications from Moscow to be sent me in the same way if they are sent to your Mission in London.

To Mrs. Lea

Feb. 11, 1922

Kweilin, Kwangsi

My dear Mrs. Lea:

 I am very glad indeed to get your letter of the 17th of November as I have not had news from you for quite a long while. It has taken your letter almost three months to reach me! What a long time indeed to get news from the outside world! Indeed the lack of means for communication and facilities for travelling are a great drawback to progress.

 I left Canton on the 15th of October for this city, and although it was only a journey of 500 miles it took me 22 days by houseboat to reach Kweilin! Fortunately the scenery all the way was lovely and more than compensated the tedious trip. Kweilin was formerly an imperial city you know, being the residing of the last of the Chinese rulers. It is rich in historic and romantic interests therefore. Kweilin itself possesses wonderful natural sights, and it has been truly describes [described] that the beauties of Kweilin surpass that of the world. Most of the mountains are made up of limestones, forming range after range of curious scapes. With the help of a little imagination one sees forms and shapes of human beings and animals.

 I suppose you have read by this time of the very sad news of the death of Lady Cantlie. It reached me just after Christmas and has greatly saddened us. She was a woman of great strength of character and lovable in every way. I shall miss her comforting and encouraging letters. Poor Dr. Cantlie! I do not know how he can get along without her now, besides their children are all widely scattered over the world.

I shall not be stationed here long and expects [expect] to start the expedition against the northern militarists very soon. But if you address my letters to Canton, they will be forwarded to me. I hope that soon condition will make it possible and worth your while to come and help China and her people.

Hoping that you are in excellent health and spirits and with kindest regards and best wishes.

> Yours very sincerely,
> Sun Yat-sen

To Paul S. Reinsch

Aug. 26, 1922

29 Rue Moliere
Shanghai

My dear Dr. Reinsch:

I have to thank you for your kind and thoughtful letter of the 21st inst.

I reciprocate your hope that we may meet at Peking at an early date. This is quite possible if success attends certain efforts which are about to be made to secure the "financing" of the Government. You will understand what I mean from the enclosed notes which have been worked into two interviews and cabled to the *Philadelphia Ledger* and *Chicago Tribune* services. The *Associated Press* has also carried a summarised statement of my views; and I have promised the A. P. a "follow-up" interview in which I hope to discuss the same subject in its relation to the decisions reached at the Washington Conference in regard to China.

I should be glad to know what you think of the views expressed.

With the assurance of my high esteem, believe me to be,

Yours sincerely,
Sun Yat-sen

To Maring

Feb. 11, 1923

Dear Comrade,

Yours of 11th inst has reached me, for which please accept my thanks. As regard to my delegate at Mukden, I am sorry to say that he has already left the north.

With best wishes,
Your Sincerely,
Y. S. Sun

To Duff. and Joffe

May 23, 1923

For polpred Peking and Joffe

Will start immediately reorganization party, establish daily papers Canton Shanghai Harbin weekly Peking Shanghai presscorrespondence〔press correspondence〕shanghai and monthly Canton. Develop propaganda among northern soldiers soonest possible. Wanted first instalment〔installment〕 of granted support please wire Moscow immediately.

As to organisation military force northwestern boarder delegates going Moscow soon discuss details.

Regarding railway agreement have given again strong advice to delegates Mukden for acceptance by Chang.

(through Wilde)

Sun Yatsen

To Lim Nee Soon

Sept. 18, 1923

Canton

Mr. Lim Nee Soon
"Marsiling Tilla"
9 Caion Hill Circle
Singapore

My dear Mr. Lim:

Please accept my hearty thanks for your kind invitation to your son's wedding. Since distance prevents my attendance, I wish to offer my warmest congratulations and best wishes.

Yours sincerely,
Sun Yat Sen

To Mr. Borodin

Oct. 28,1923

My dear Mr. Borodin:

Will you please be so kind as to dispatch the enclosed telegram to Mr. Joffe for us, as we are quite anxious over his illness!

With many thanks,

Yours sincerely
R. N. Sun
Mrs. Y. S. Sun

To Rabindranath Tagore

Apr. 7, 1924

Dear Mr. Tagore:

I should greatly wish to have the privilege of personally welcoming you on your arrival in China. It is an ancient way of ours to show honour to the Scholar. But in you I shall greet not only a writer who has added lustre to Indian letters but a rare worker in those fields of endeavour wherein lie the seeds of man's future welfare and spiritual triumphs.

May I then have pleasure of inviting you to Canton?

Yours sincerely,
Sun Yat-sen

To Mr. Borodin

May 14, 1924

Dear Mr. Borodin,

Dr. Sun asks me to write and urge you to return to Canton soon, for there are many questions upon which he wants to consult with you. He says, it is hopeless for you and Mr. Karahan to prolong your stay in Peking, for nothing good will result from it.

Dr. Sun has been sick for several days according to [due to] strenuous work. Although he is feeling much better now, still the doctor orders him to refrain from attending to his usual duties and seeing callers. With such an active nature as he possesses, it has not been without difficulties to keep him dorm.

I had the great pleasure of meeting Mrs. Borodin at Shanghai and hope that she will accompany you down soon.

Looking forward to the pleasure of seeing you both soon and with kindest regards from us.

I am,
Yours sincerely
Rosamonde Sun

To Henry Ford

June 12, 1924

Dear Mr. Ford:

Mr. Hg Jim Kai, the bearer of this letter, informs me that you are likely to visit China in the not distant future. Should you do so, it would give me not a little pleasure to welcome you in South China, where—it is commonly said—much of the intelligence, energy and wealth of this country can be found.

I know and I have read of your remarkable work in America. And I think that you can do similar work in China on a much vaster and more significant scale. In a sense it may be said that your work in America has been more individual and personal, whereas here in China you would have an opportunity to express and embody your mind and ideals in the enduring form of a new industrial system.

I am of the view that China may be the cause of the next World War if she remains economically undeveloped and thus become an object of exploitation and international strife on the part of the Great Powers. For this reason I began, as soon as the Armistice was signed in Europe, to think out a plan for the international development of China with a view to its consideration by the Powers at the Peace Conference in 1919. This plan has since been worked out in my book, "THE INTERNATIONAL DEVELOPMENT OF CHINA", which was published in Shanghai in 1921 and in New York in 1922 by Messrs. Putman's Sons.

I now realise that it is more or less hopeless to expect much from the present Governments of the Powers. There is much more to hope, in my opinion from a dynamic worker like yourself; and this is why I invite you to visit us in South China in order to study, at first hand, what is undoubtedly one of the greatest problems of the Twentieth Century.

                                                          Yours very truly,

                                                          Sun Yat-sen

To Mr. Borodin

Sept. 9, 1924

Canton

My dear Mr. Borodin:

Will you please let Dr. Sun know whether you think Guelbean's "Life of Lenin" is a good account, for he wishes to have it published in [to] Chinese soon.

Very sincerely yours
R. S. Sun

To Monsieur Motta

Sept. 24, 1924

Shaokwan

Monsieur Motta
President
Fifth Assembly
League of Nations
Geneva

Dear Sir:

In view of Mr. Ramsey MacDonald's disquisitions on the independence of Georgia and international peace and justice at recent sessions of the Assembly of the League of Nations, it may be possible interest to the League to know that on Sept. 1st I protested to Mr. MacDonald against the delivery to my government of an ultimatum which threatened hostile British naval action in the event of my government taking the necessary measures to suppress a rebellion at Canton instigated by imperialistic and reactionary interests. To this protest, Mr. MacDonald has not replied.

I understand that his silence [to] mean[means] that British policy in China will continue to express itself in acts of Imperialist intervention in support of counter-revolutionary activities against the national movement which aims at the establishment of a strong and independent China.

Telegram to Motta, Sept. 24, 1924

It is no wonder that after assisting rebels and reactionaries in Canton, Mr. MacDonald goes to Geneva to champion the cause of the counter-revolution in the Republic of Georgia in the guise of an "honest broker" scenting Caucasian naphtha.

SUN YAT SEN

To Mr. Borodin

Sept. 26, 1924

Shiu Kwan

My dear Mr. Borodin,

Dr. Sun asks me to inform you that he can not return to the city at the 28th inst, as first decided upon, according to the following reasons (1) the popular demonstration for the Northern expedition will take place here at [on] the 1st of October, when Dr. Sun must be present and address the masses. (2) As this is a critical time with Chang Tsolin and Lu Yunghsiang, Dr. Sun's departure from the concentration campaigns at this time, [discourage their hopes and] discourages them. Furthermore, Dr. Sun believes it will be better for us to start working among the people here first. It will be certainly easier, for the people are friendly towards us, the good results we get from here will be later reflect [reflected] in Canton. As the people in Canton, are hostile towards us, due to recent events and agitations, it would perhaps be easier for us to wait until their antipathy subsides. As it is, they might suspect us of weakness and fear of them.

With our best wishes,

Yours sincerely
R. S. Sun

To Mr. Borodin

Sept. 26, 1924

Shiu Kwan

Dear Mr. Borodin,

Dr. Sun desires me to inform you that he can not return to Canton yet, as the circumstances here are developing rapidly. More troops are coming to join the expedition. We sent you a letter in care of Soong Tse Veng this morning, explaining the reasons for the necessary postponement which we hope has already reached you.

Our best wishes,

Your sincerely
R. S. Sun

To Mr. Borodin

Oct. 12, 1924

My dear friend,

If general Hsu agrees with my new plan, I will change my former plan of transporting arms to ShinKwan. Mr Liao will tell you what my new plan is. I think it is the best way to deal with the present crisis.

Very truly yours

Sun Yat-sen

To Mr. Borodin

Oct. 12, 1924

Shiu Kwan

My dear Mr. Borodin:

There are two matters about which Dr. Sun asks me to write you: (1) that the only way to save Canton is for him to remain deaf and blind to all the acts there. For the merchant volunteers have the upper hand and hold the key to the situation. If by provoking the issue to a crisis, some hitherto friendly elements will turn against us. Men like Fan Sheksang, Liao Hengcho, Yang Shiming and Li Fuk Ling will at once side with them against this combination, ⟨and⟩ it is evident⟨that⟩ me[we] have not the least chance for success.

In[For] the time being, our prestige will suffer. We have to bear that, although bitter. But if the strike should be continued after the time limit, chastise measures must and will be taken against them.

(2) Reporting[Regarding] the Customs question, Dr. Sun has decided to push the matter to the extreme and if that does not provoke a crisis, then we can be sure of holding Canton secure in our hands.

Sincerely,

Rosamonde Sun

To Mr. Borodin

Oct. 13, 1924

Shiu Kwan

My dear Borodin:

Dr. Sun asks me to write you that certain reports which Mr. Liao Chungkai gave him yesterday caused him to think that [been] keeping himself blind and deaf to all the acts going on in Canton cannot save Canton, but only fear and a reign of terror can.

In this connection. Dr. Sun has decided to act at once. Last night he sent back General Wu Techen's troops to Canton. These men will receive orders from the Committee, but they need more training in street fights, so Dr. Sun hopes you will put your experts to give them some training in this respect.

The recent match of arms and ammunitions will not be removed to Shikwan, according to former decision, not will be employed in rearming General Hsu Chung Chi's troops, and the condition ⟨is⟩ Hsu fights at once, and carries on whatever measures the Committee decides upon. The object of this fight is to crush the traitor's army and the rebellions of merchant volunteers.

Yours sincerely
R. S. Sun

To the Central Executive Committee of the Union of Soviet Socialist Republics
Mar. 11,1925

Peking, China

My Dear Comrades,

As I lie here, with a malady that is beyond men's skill, my thoughts turn to you and to the future of my Party and my country.

You are the head of a Union of free republics, which is the real heritage that the immortal Lenin has left to the world of the oppressed peoples. Through this heritage, the victims of imperialism are destined to secure their freedom and deliverance from an international system whose foundations lie in ancient slaveries and wars and injustices.

I am leaving behind me a Party which I had hoped would be associated with you in the historic work of completely liberating China and other exploited countries from this imperialist system. Fate decrees that I must leave the task unfinished and pass it on to those who, by remaining true to the principles and teachings of the Party, will constitute my real followers.

I have therefore enjoined the Kuomintang to carry on the work of the national revolutionary movement in order that China may be freed from the semi-colonial status, which imperialism has imposed on her. To this end I have charged the

Party to keep in constant touch with you; and I look with confidence to the continuance of the support that your government has heretofore extended to my Party.

In bidding farewell to you, dear comrades, I wish to express the fervent hope that the day may soon dawn, when the U. S. S. R. will greet, as a friend and ally, a strong and independent China and that the two allies may together advance to victory in the great struggle for the liberation of the oppressed peoples of the world.

With fraternal greetings.

Sun Yat-sen

Signed on march 11th, 1925, in the presence of:

Tse Ving Song 宋子文
Wang Ching Wei 汪精卫
何香凝
Sun Fo 孙科
Tai En Sai 戴恩赛
Joau Lo 邹鲁
Hsiang Hsi Kung 孔庸之

OTHERS

The Commercial Union of China Bond

Jan. 22, 1895

The Commercial Union of China

                                                         No. 1 one shares

                                                         Honolulu, H. I.

                                                         Jan. 22, 1895

This Certifies that Lee Toma is the owner of one paid up shares of the Capital back [bank] of THE COMMERCIAL UNION OF CHINA.

Transferable on the backs of the Company by endorsement hereon and suttenes of this certificate.

Lau Chong   Y. S. Sun

    Treasurer   President

R. Grieve, Pr. 209 Manohany St., Honolulu

Autobiography

Apr. 14, 1904

My name is Sun Yat Sen, I was born in Honolulu and went to come [and came] back from Hong Kong to Honolulu in the early part of 1896 or the last part of 1895, I stayed at Honolulu for 4 or 5 months and then came on to San Francisco, arriving here shortly before July. I came in on student and traveler's Sect. 6 certificate which I procured in Shanghai. I came in as a subject of China. I went from San Francisco to London via New York and from there to Japan via [of] Canada. From Japan I came back to Honolulu arriving there about Feb. 1901. They examined some witnesses and admitted me as a native born citizen. I had no papers, I always go to Honolulu without papers. Since I came in here as a Chinese subject in 1896, I have done nothing to again become a citizen of the U. S. excepting [except] that I swore allegiance to the U. S. before I received my passport from the Gov. of Hawaii in March this year, at that time repudiating my citizenship of [my] other nation.

Sun Yat Sen

Sworn to before me this 14 day of April 1904

Ward E. Thompson

The Chinese Revolutionary Government Bonds
Jan. 1, 1906

The Chinese revolutionary government promises to pay the bearer one hundred dollars after one year of the establishment in China or demand at the Treasury of the said Government in Canton or its agents abroad.

1st January 1906

The President

Sun Wen

Certificate for Koki H. Ike

Dec. 12, 1907

No. 6IB, Gambetta Street

Hanoi, Annam

To Whom It May Concern

Greeting:—

I hereby certify that the undermentioned Japanese friend, Mr. Koki H. Ike, is fully authorized by me in regard to the matters of raising funds for our revolutionary cause in China, and of obtaining commissarist [commissariat] or military stores for the same cause.

I also certify that he has joined me for years, devoting his time, energy, and ability to our cause, and that he was on the spot with myself, when I led my men in the actual bombardment of the forts of Chin-Nan-Kwan, Kwang-Si, China, on the Fourth of December 1907.

(Signed) Sun Yat Sen

Certificate for Charles B. Boothe

Mar. 14, 1910

Los Angeles, Califormia[California]

By the authority and consent of the council of the Federal Association of China, I hereby appoint Charles B. Boothe of Los Angeles, California, sole foreign financial agent for said association, and hereby delegate to the said Boothe, full authority to act for and in the name of said association, in the matter of negotiating for loans and receiving monies, also, disbursing same in such manner as may be authorized and agreed upon by the president of said association, and to enter into engagements of any nature, as shall be directed from time to time by the president of the association.

Each and every agreement entered into by said Charles B. Boothe, as said financial agent on behalf of and in the name of said association, shall have the same binding force upon the said [the] federal association, as though signed by the president and council of the said association.

The Federal Association of China
by Sun Wen (Sun Yat Sen)
President

The Chinese Republic

July 1912

(At our request, the Rev. Dr. Gilbert Reid, the distinguished independent missionary, visited Dr. Sun in [on] behalf of The INDEPENDENT. The remainder of this introductory note is from Dr. Reid. He says:

"The character of Dr. Sun Yat-sen, first President of the Provisional Republic of China, and his word in bringing about a revolution against the Manchu Dynasty are fairly well known by the general public in Europe and America, as well as in China. His views concerning the Chinese Republic, and his attitude towards questions of the day in bringing about the development of China, and winning for her a place of equality among the nations of the world, are only alightly known, and anything that can be done to secure an expression of opinion from Dr. Sun on these matters will, I am sure, be welcomed by intelligent observers of conditions in the Far East, and especially by those who believe that a republic is the best form of government for all countries".

"For a long time I have had great admiration for Dr. Sun, and this in spite of the fact that personally I am opposed to all bloody revolutions, and am in favor of agitation thru the application on truth, argument and reason. My admiration for this great revolutionist has been due to the fact that he has been straightforward, persistent, courageous and consistent, taking no position under the Manchu government whilst seeking its overthrow. His purposes have been known for years to the government authorities, and in the face of danger he has held on his course without wavering or fear. The sudden revolution reached a successful conclusion largely thru the plans which have been well laid by this young man from the Canton province. His conciliatory spirit and his magnanimity in securing the abdication of the throne and the end of the Manchu Dynasty have placed him high above his fellows in the esteem of his countrymen and of foreign residents in China."

"During a visit of Dr. Sun to Shanghai, I took the opportunity of asking him to express his views for The INDEPENDENT concerning the Republic, and concerning the present political situation. He received me courteously, but disclaimed any right to speak authoritatively on these matters." The following is a record of the interview. —Editor of *The Independent*)

At present I am more interested in the social regeneration of my country than I am in the questions of party, and politics. Having finished the task of bringing about a political revolution, I am now devoting my thought and energies to the reconstruction of the country in its social, industrial and commercial conditions. I have seen enough of the discord between capital and labor in Western countries, and the misery that besets the multitudes of the poor, that I am desirous of forestalling such conditions in China. With industrial development there will come in an increase of manufacturing, and with this change of conditions there is a danger of widely separating the working classes and those who possess the capital. I wish to see the masses of the people improved in their conditions rather than to help a few to add power to themselves until they become financial autocrats. China thus far has had a large middle class, and we have been free from many of the social defects of prosperous nations in Europe and America. There is need today of developing our own great resources, of bringing in new ideas to the predominant farming classes of the country, and of establishing new industries which will help to deep in circulation our growing capital, and so be ready to give prompt relief to the unfortunate in times of flood and other calamities. These are the questions which now engage my attention, and I am hopeful that something may be accomplished for the good of our people.

I am asked if I have any objection to stating my opinion as to whether a republican form of government is really suited to the Chinese people?

I has been a part of my plan, not merely to bring about the overthrow of the Manchus, but to bring about the establishment of a republican form of government. Democratic ideas have always prevailed in China, and there is no reason why they should be handicapped by a monarchical form of government. The Chinese are not only peace-loving and orderly, but they are imbued with the idea choosing their own representatives in managing their affairs. All that [is] needed is to carry out this idea and to meet this wise by having representatives at the national and in the provinces who represent the people, and, being chosen by the people, will work for the best interest of the people. The difficulties which we are now meeting in constructing a republican form of government which is best adapted to the wide area of our country and to our vast population are unavoidable, but I am sure no other form of government will again be established in China. The Republic of China is here to stay.

In reply to the question whether a party government is an essential part of the Republic, I would say that in China as in all other countries, whether the government is republican or monarchical, parties always exist, and the direction of the government changes from one party to another. China, too, has already begun to have her parties. In fact, there are too many parties and societies, and it would be better if they could combine into two or three strong parties. The definite policy of each party will be determined as the years go by.

In view of the danger in having parties during the present Provisional Government, and the fear that persons will be more zealous for their partiers than for the Republic, and so weaken the efforts at establishing a republican form of government, my own wish is that all parties should concentrate their efforts on thoroly organizing the new government and securing recognition from other governments. After the Provisional Government has ceased, and the first president of the republic has been chosen, it will then be safe to organize into parties. I am in favor of having the executive officers responsible to the national assembly, as in nearly all the European countries. Under this system place must be given to parties, and party rivalry is unavoidable. Just now I recognize that we should all ignore our differences and help to unite all parts of the country. Since I retired in favor of Yuan Shih-kai as President of the Republic, I have done all in my power to support him and to recommend unanimity of action. I know the danger that would come to the country from discord, and so far as I have any influence I will use it for the unification of the country, the welfare of the people and development of our resources.

(Ex-President Sun Yat-sen gave expression to these views with some reserve, as he did not care to appear ill print at the present time. His views are therefore all the more of value.

These views are significant, as being uttered at a time when party rivalries in Peking had caused the rejection of the Cabinet list proposed by the Premier, Lu Cheng Hsiang. The radical element seemed bent on the ruin of the very republic which they had fought to establish. One hope in the midst of the political confusion is found in the moderating influence of ex-President Sun. His self-effacement deserves the praise of men. Being the leading spirit in the revolution, his wishes are respected by all the revolutionists, who now form the party called "Tung Meng", or Union League. Their obstruction to the government action of Yuan Shih-kai and his Premier, will be prevented from working disaster, because Sun Yat-sen is at hand to decide the determining move. As an illustration, during our brief conversation, he suggested General Li Yuan Hung, Vice-President of the Provisional Republic and Military Governor at Hankow, as the best man for Premier and to form a Cabinet. And yet General Li is the head of another party from that of Dr. Sun and his friends. Personally I would recommend Dr. Sun himself as Premier, at least if General Li is unavailable.

For the next few months all attention will be concentrated on bringing to an end the Provisional Government, and on electing the first real Parliament, and the first President. In this time of opportunity for personal ambition, Dr. Sun maintains his modest character, and by moderate but none the less effective methods, helps forward his country to the attainment of republican ideas, contented to remain a private citizen. —Gilbert Reid)

Shanghai, China

Eulogy on the Death of Homer Lea

Nov. 6, 1912

Unfortunately Mr. Lea was physically deformed but he possed a wonderful brain. Although not a military man, he was a great military philosopher, well poise in high military problems. He helped me in a general way on military stratagem with reference to the revolutionary propaganda. He commanded a profound farsight and insight in military affairs and was the author of a couple of books on high millitary tactics and stratagem. Several of the prominent military men paid tribute to his professional production, General Roberts is one of his greatest admirers. He was a thoroughly sincfere [sincere] man and devoted his whole energy to the Chinese Revolution. Honest in his dealings, sympathetic in his opinions, frank and resolute, he had made a large number of friends among the Chinese. He helped me in Nanking until his death.

Interrogatories in the Court of First Instance for the Judicial District of Manila

May 6, 1915

1) What is your present abode?

   26 Reinansaka, Akasaka, Tokyo.

2) What is your present occupation?

   None.

3) Where did you reside formerly?

   491 Ave. Paul Brunat. French concession, Shanghai, China.

4) What was your former occupation?

   President of the Republic of China, and later was the Director-General of the Chinese National Railway Corporation.

5) Why did you change your residence?

   Because I opposed Yuan Shih Kai in his murder of Sung Chiao Jen, the minister of Agriculture and Forestry, and for his contracting the Quintuple Loan without the approval of the Parliament.

   After the Provinces of Kiangsi, Kiangsu, Hunan, Anhwei, Fukien and Kwantung had risen in protest by arms against Yuan Shih Kai, the consuls of Shanghai Concessions were asked by Yuan Shih Kai to demand my extradition, therefore I had to leave China.

6) Why did you leave your former occupation?

   For the sake of peace and to avoid bloodshed I resigned the presidency in favour of Yuan Shih Kai, on condition that he would be loyal to his oath

Interrogatories in the Court of First Instance for the Judicial District of Manila, May 6, 1915

of allegiance to uphold the Republic of China, according to our Constitution. After my resignation, I recommended Yuan Shih Kai to the National Assembly as my successor for the Presidency. I then left politics to take up the Directorship of the Railway Corporation. But during the Southern Armed Protestation, Yuan Shih Kai cancelled the Charter of the Corporation, thus I left my post.

7) State what you know of the manner in which Yuan Shih Kai brought about his election to the Presidency of the Republic of China?

Yuan Shih Kai obtained his presidency by two means: first, by bribery, and second by force. During the time of presidential election, twice he failed to obtain sufficient votes, then he used force of arms by surrounding the Parliament with armed police, and threatened to massacre them if he was not elected. By these two means he at last procured a bare majority of votes in his favour.

8) State if you know how the following persons came to their death: The Commissioner of Police of the city of Canton, Chang Chin Wu, Fang Yi, and Sung Chiao Jen. If you do not know personally state if you know ⟨that⟩ the general understanding in China and elsewhere is as to the manner in which each of the persons named came to his death.

Among the four persons named I know personally two of them: Chen King Wah, the Commissioner of Police of Canton and Sung Chiao Jen; the other two: General Chang and Fang Yi, I had met only once while in Wuchang. In regard to the death of these two generals, they were asked by Yuan Shih Kai to go to Peking to be given positions. When they arrived at Peking, they were invited to dinner at Hotel des Wagons-Lits. On their return home after dinner, as they passed out of the Legations Quarters, they were arrested and immediately executed on the same night. Concerning the death of Chen King Wah, Canton Police Commissioner, on the 15th day of the eighth Moon, he received an invitation from the Governor-General of Canton to dine in celebration of the Moon Festival. When the dinner was finished, the Governor-General showed him a telegram from Yuan Shih Kai which ordered Chen to be shot, for the latter was suspected of conspiracy against the Government. Thus without getting the least satisfaction of being shown the proof, and without a trial of any sort Chen was shot immediately.

Sung Chiao Jen was the leader of the National Party. By telegram Yuan Shih Kai invited him to go up to Peking. As he was starting for Peking at the Railway station in Shanghai, he was shot and mortally wounded. A few days after he died in the Railway Hospital. About the same time the assassin Wu Shih Ying and the instigator Ying Kwei Shin were both arrested by the Police of the French Concession. All papers in Ying's house were seized at the time. Among the papers were found cipher telegrams sent from Peking by the Premier Chao Ping Chun, ordering Ying to kill Sung Chiao Jen and promising him a great reward. At the telegraph office in Shanghai were found telegrams from Ying to Chao, just before and after the crime. The whole affair had a preliminary trial at the Mixed Court in Shanghai, and the murderers were convicted and were handed to the Chinese authority for trial. During the trial in Shanghai, Counsels Douglas (English) and Jernigan acted as counsellors to Sung's Party.

After the assasin [assassin] was handed over to the Chinese authority, the Governor of Kiangsu, Chen Tuh Chun, and the Chief Civil Administrator Ying Teh Hung reported the whole affair in detail to the President, saying that his minister Chao Ping Chun was the prime instigator of Sung's murder and demanded his minister and secretary to come to Shanghai for trial. Yuan Shih Kai highly resented the demand and he discharged these officers from their positions.

Interrogatories in the Court of First Instance for the Judicial District of Manila, May 6, 1915

9) State what you know in relation to the manner in which Yuan Shih Kai exercised his authority as President of the Republic of China in relation to the executive of Laws?

Yuan Shih Kai made himself absolute ruler of China regarded nothing but his own will. Although he swore to support the Provisional Constitution, he himself annuled the Constitution and abolished Parliament, besides arresting members and killing those who protested against his manner of dealings.

10) State what you know about the flight of Chinamen from China and the causes therefore?

Under Yuan's government there is no security of laws; he can arrest men without process of law. Therefore people who hold different opinion from Yuan must get away from the country to save their lives.

11) State what you know about the unseating of members of the Chinese Parliament?

The Parliament advocated republican ideas and wanted to adopt democratic principles in the Constitution. Thinking it too much a restriction upon his power, Yuan Shih Kai abolished the Parliament, pure and simple, in a coup d'etat on the 10th of last November.

12) State what you know of the trials of Chinamen, the tortures of prisoners and the indignities upon those who are sentenced to death both before and after execution under the administration of the law by Yuan Shih Kai as President of the Republic?

During my administration as the first Provisional President of the Republic, I abolished all forms of tortures on trial, but after Yuan succeeded me, he restored all former methods of trial and forms of tortures and in addition to these he invented new ways, such as making prisoners kneel on red-hot bricks and on burning chains, or to hand [hang] up the accused by the four limbs, by tying the toes and the thumbs up, besides many other cruel forms of punishments which were not known during the former monarchical regime.

13) State what you know about the Constitutional Committee and what action Yuan Shih Kai took in relation to it.

The Constitutional Committee was abolished in the same manner as the Parliament, for Yuan accused them as rebels since they desired to uphold the democratic principles upon which the republic was founded.

Joint Statement with A. A. Joffe *

Jan. 26, 1923

Dr. Sun Yat-sen and Mr. A. A. Joffe, Russian Envoy Extraordinary and Plenipotentiary to China, have authorized the publication of the following statement:

During his stay in Shanghai, Mr. Joffe has had several conversations with Dr. Sun Yat-sen, which have revealed the identity of their views on matters relating to Chinese-Russian relations, more especially on the following points:

(1) Dr. Sun Yat-sen holds that the Communistic order or even the Soviet system cannot actually be introduced into China, because there do not exist here the conditions for the successful establishment of either Communism or Sovietism. This view is entirely shared by Mr. Joffe, who is further of ⟨the⟩ opinion that China's paramount and most pressing problem is to achieve national unification and attain full national independence, and regarding this great task, he has assured Dr. Sun Yat-sen that China has the warmest sympathy of the Russian people and can count on the support of Russia.

(2) In order to clarify the situation, Dr. Sun Yat-sen has requested Mr. Joffe for a reaffirmation of the principles defined in the Russian Note to the Chinese Government, dated September 27, 1920. Mr. Joffe has accordingly reaffirmed these principles and categorically declared to Dr. Sun Yat-sen that the Russian Government is ready and willing to enter into negotiations with China on the basis of the renunciation by Russia of all the treaties and exactions which the

Tsardom imposed on China, including the treaty or treaties and agreements relating to the Chinese Eastern Railway (the management of which being the subject of a specific reference in Article VII of the said Note).

(3) Recognizing that the Chinese Eastern Railway question in its entirety can be satisfactorily settled only at a competent Russo-Chinese Conference, Dr. Sun Yat-sen is of the opinion that the realities of the situation point to the desirability of a *modus vivendi* in the matter of the present management of the Railway. And he agrees with Mr. Joffe that the existing Railway management should be temporarily reorganized by agreement between the Chinese and the Russian Governments without prejudice; however, to the true rights and special interests of either party. At the same time Dr. Sun Yat-sen considers that General Chang Tso-lin should be consulted on the point.

(4) Mr. Joffe has categorically declared to Dr. Sun Yat-sen (who has fully satisfied himself as to this point) that it is not and has never been the intention or purpose of the present Russian Government to pursue an Imperialistic policy in Outer Mongolia or to cause it to secede from China. Dr. Sun Yat-sen, therefore, does not view an immediate evacuation of Russian troops from Outer Mongolia as either imperative or in the real interest of China, the more so on account of the inability of the present Government at Peking to prevent such an evacuation being followed by a recrudescence of intrigues and hostile activities by White Guardists against Russia and the creation of a graver situation than that which now exists.

Mr. Joffe has parted from Dr. Sun Yat-sen on the most cordial and friendly terms. On leaving Japan, to which he is now proceeding, he will again visit the South of China before finally returning to Peking.

Shanghai, January 26, 1923

* The statement apparently first appeared in the *China Press* of January 27, 1923. US-DS 761. 93/305, dispatch, Shanghai, Cunningham, Jan. 27 to Peking, Schurman, containing a clipping. *The New York Times* for January 27 carried a digest in an *Associated Press* article from Shanghai dated January 26, the date the declaration was issued.

Resume of Dr. Sun's Remarks at Canton Christian College

Dec. 22, 1923, Confidential

Dr. Sun was invited to speak at Canton Christian College by the president of the Canton Christian College Students' Union without previous consultation with the executives of the College. All that could be done then was to entertain him and make the best of a rather unfortunate situation. He arrived at about 1 p. m., Friday, the 22-d December, and went to lunch with Dr. Baxter (British), who is the executive head here now, in the absence of Mr. Henry. As far as I know, the conversation at lunch was not political.

At a mass meeting of the entire college and middle school, after lunch, Dr. Sun talked for nearly two hours, but kept completely clear of political subjects. His main theme at this time was Chinese students' usefulness to China, and he only touched on America in saying he thought it not objectionable that students should go to America if they couldn't get what they wanted in education here. He objected strongly to these who, having studies in America, continue to travel back and forth between here and there without ever settling down to do constructive work in China—all very reasonable.

After the large meeting, however, a small group of foreigners and Chinese were invited to meet Dr. Sun at a tea at the house of Mr. Chang Wing Kwang, our Chinese vice-president. I was not present at this time myself, but took special pains to learn from those who talked with Sun there what was said. It may not be all that was said, but is accurate as far as it goes.

Resume of Dr. Sun's Remarks at Canton Christian College, Dec. 22, 1923, Confidential

He said that in ten years there would be a great world war, when the nations now oppressed by the imperialists and militarists of the world (subsequent utterances indicate he meant England, America, France, and perhaps Italy) would rise in united power to wipe their oppressors off the map. He said :"Ten years from now you'll see how it feels to have a Chinese fleet in San Francisco harbour." China, he said, was combining with Russia, and would later join with Germany, India and Japan in the final struggle with the nations "on top" now.

Either at this tea or at another time while he was on the campus he spoke of how Britain saw the menace of rising China, and he said that all [all that] Britain feared in China —her advance in commerce, wealth, education, civilisation, her whole forward and progressive movement, etc,—was incorporated and personified in himself; and so England had been out to crush Sun from the start. The extremity of his utterance would seem to indicate almost an unbalanced state of mind, as many of the foreigners felt at the time; at least an extremely dangerous, neurotic state.

To one of the Chinese he remarked: "It's a pity this isn't completely a Chinese institution."

As he was leaving, he said to Dr. Baxter and the foreigners with him: "Well, good-bye, enemies- we may be some day."

From all he said one might gather that his programme now is one of utter bitterness to foreigners, and militarism for China to exterminate all trace of foreign superiority here.

It is difficult to tell the temper of the student body. One feels that at heart they are with Sun, right or wrong, in anything that concerns China as against foreigners, though to us personally, they are still perfectly amiable and ready to talk about the affair objectively.

РУССКИЕ ДОКУМЕНТЫ

Письмо Русселю

8 Ноября, 1906 г.

Токио

Д-ру Русселю.

Дорогой Сэр!

Я с большим удовольствием прочитал Вашу нитересную статью «Китайская загадка». Она произвела на меня очень сильное впечатление. Ваша идея возвышенна и Ваше сердце великодушно. Я редко встречал представителя Запада, который когда-либо так отстаивал идею возрождения Китая и практического обеспечения условий человеческого существования миллионам его страдающего населения, как это делаете Вы. Однако уверены ли Вы, что среди американских капиталистов и экспертов, к которым Вы, кажется, столь настойчиво обращаетесь с этим призывом, окажется много таких, которых можно было бы убедить принять участие в этом благородном деле?

Я опасаюсь, что проблемы Китая слишком далеки от того, чтобы привлечь внимание американцев и европейцев, но я надеюсь, что в результате Вашего благородного призыва бескорыстные люди во всем мире постепенно начнут понимать, что возрождение четвертой части человечества будет благодеянием для всех.

С величайшим уважением и лучшими пожеланиями искренне преданный Вам

Сунь Ят-сен

Письмо Русселю

26 Ноября, 1906 г.

Токио

Д-ру Русселю.

Дорогой Сэр!

Я получил Ваше письмо от 16 с. м. несколько дней назад, но был настолько занят, что не мог ответить раньше.

Возможно, я неправильно понял Вас в связи с Вашим обращением к американским капиталистам, но если имеется в виду не чисто альтруистический подход, я не вижу в этом ничего хорошего. Они не настолько глупы, чтобы совершить коммерческое самоубийство, помогая Китаю обрести собственную индустриальную мощь и стать независимым. Я твердо убежден, что если мы проявим хотя бы малейшую склонность стать на этот путь, то весь капиталистический мир Европы и Америки потрясет крик об индустриальной желтой опасности. Таким образом, совершенно очевидно и понятно, что их интересы состоят прежде всего в том, чтобы навсегда превратить Китай в жертву промышленной отсталости.

Но с того момента, как я и мои товарищи начали движение, мы равным образом развертывали его и в социальной сфере.

Причем, при разрешении социальных проблем мы имеем большие

преимущества по сравнению с нашими западными братьями; ибо в отношении развития современной цивилизации мы все еще находимся в девственном состоянии, у нас еще не появились собственные плутократы и, поэтому, на нашем пути нет таких серьезных препятствий, как в странах с высоко развитой современной цивилизацией.

Китай — страна сравнительно однородная в своей бедности, подавляющая масса его населения всегда живет бедно... Поэтому все, что дает какую-либо надежду улучшить общие условия, встретит общее одобрение. Вплоть до самых последних лет современный прогресс все еще не затронул Китай, до сих пор мы еще не наслаждались его благами и не страдали от его проклятий. И когда мы утверждаем современный прогресс в нашей социальной жизни, мы имеем возможность выбрать то, что соответствует нашим устремлениям. Мы не рассчитываем на помощь извне, как бы ни была она желательна, если она не диктуется чисто альтруистическими мотивами.

Если Вы хотите, чтобы возрождение Китая в конечном итоге ускорило социальную революцию в Америке и Европе, тогда, чем меньше капиталисты будут знать о такой тенденции, тем лучше, не говоря уже о том, что не следует обращаться к ним за помощью в осуществлении того дела, которое в конечном итоге нанесет ущерб их собственным интересам.

Вы правы относительно наказаний за нововведения и открытия, но они ослабели с тех пор, как Китай был открыт для связей с внешним миром. Относительно же заявления миссионеров, я не могу сказать — правильно ли оно или нет, ибо я совсем не располагаю фактами.

Совершенно верно, что до последнего времени революционное движение в Китае носило чисто политический, а не экономический характер. Но оно создает почву для нашего будущего экономического развития.

Я не издавал газету, которую Вы называете «Шихуэйчжуай», и мне неизвестно о распространении такой газеты среди моих соотечественников здесь. Газета, которую ежемесячно издают мои товарищи, здесь называется «Миньбао»—«Народ». Она печатается только по-китайски.

Я буду очень рад возможности время от времени получать от Вас известия.

С лучшими пожеланиями, искренне преданный Вам

Сунь Ят-сен

Социальное значение китайской революции[*]

31 Марта, 1912 г.

Республика утверждена в Китае. И хотя я отказался от должности временного президента Китайской Республики, но это вовсе не означает, чтобы я перестал работать в пользу Республики. Я отказался от первой должности потому, что дела гораздо важные требуют моего внимания.

Китай подчинился владычеству манджуров в течение 270 лет. Попытки восстановления его независимости были многочисленны в течение этого периода. Одной из таких попыток была революция тайпингов 50 лет тому назад, но это была исключительна расовая революция: китайцы против мандчжуров. Если-бы эта революция одержала верх, то страна осталась бы под самодержавным правительством, и такой результат нельзя было-бы назвать успехом.

Несколько лет тому назад мы с небольшим числом друзей собрались в Японии и образовали Китайское Революционное Общество.

Мы приняли тогда три великих принципа: 1) Верховенство китайской расы. 2) Управление народом через посредство народа. 3) Верховенство народа в охране богатства.

---

[*] Из газ. «Le Peuple», 11 июля, 1912 г.

Два первые принципа осуществлены отречением манджурской династии. Нам надо теперь осуществить экономическую революцию. Этот вопрос составляет в настоящее время предмет всеобщей дискуссии, но большинство китайского народа не понимает значение этих слов. Они предполагают, что целью обновления Китая является создать из него могущественную нацию, равную великим нациям Запада.

Не такова цель наших стремлений. В настоящее время нет наций, более богатых, чем Великобритания и Америка, более просвещенных, чем Франция. Англия-конституционная монархия, Франция и Соединенные Штаты—Республики, но пропасть между богатыми и бедными в таких государствах слишком велика, и революционные идеи волнуют их граждан. Если не произойдет социальной революции, то большинство останется лишенным радости и счастья жизни. Теперь это счастье составляет удел лишь нескольких капиталистов.

Масса работников продолжает тяжело бедствовать и не может быть настроена мирно. Революция расовая и революция политического правления легки, но революция общества—дело более трудное.

Лишь народ великих дел способен осуществить социальную революцию.

Мне возразят: "До сих пор ваша революция была успешна. Надо удовлетвориться этим и уметь ждать. К чему браться совершить то, чего не пытались до настоящего времени осуществить Англия и Америка, при всем их богатстве и при всей их науке?"

Но это было бы дурной политикой, ибо в Англии и в Америке цивилизация стоит высоко и промышленность развита. Здесь совершить социальную революцию дело трудное.

Мы в Китае еще не дошли до этого, социальная революция для нас сравнительно легка, мы имеем возможность предупредить наступление капиталистического режима. В капиталистических странах установленные интересы охраняются крепко, и подорвать их трудно. В Китае же нет ни капиталистов, ни установленных интересов, а потому революция сравнительно легка.

Меня часто спрашивают, потребует-ли такая революция употребления военной силы. Я отвечаю: да - для Англии и Америки, нет—для Китая. Стачка английских углекопов доказывает правильность моего утверждения, а ведь эта стачка далеко еще не революция, а просто выраженное народом желание вступить во владение источниками общественного богатства, и осуществить эту цель, видимо, можно только силой.

Возможно, что социальную революцию трудно осуществить, но близко время, когда она будет совершившимся фактом, и мы не хотим загадывать, сколько отчаянных средств, сколько опасности для государства принесет с собой это осуществление.

Если, с самого начала существования нашей Китайской Республики, мы не подумаем о том, как защитить себя от установления капитализма в очень близком будущем, то новый деспотизм, во сто раз более страшный, чем деспотизм маньчжурской династии, ожидает нас и понадобятся реки крови, чтобы избавиться от него. Какая мрачная перспектива!

Одно обстоятельство требует в особенности нашего внимания. Как только новое правительство установится, необходимо будет изменить все правления основания (tous les titres) недвижимой собственности. Эта мера есть необходимая принадлежность революции. Этого требует прогресс. Прежде поземельные собственники платили налог с площади земель, распределенных на три класса: хорошие, плохие и худые. В будущем необходимо будет соразмерить налог с стоимостью земли, ибо качество земли гораздо изменчиво, чем это выражает разница указанных трех классов.

Я не знаю, как велика разница между стоимостью в Нанкине и на Бунде, главной улице Шангая, но при употреблении старой системы мы не сможем установить справедливой оценки. Правильнее было бы облагать налогом стоимость недвижимых имуществ так, чтобы бедные земли платили мало, а высокоценные земли платили много. Земли, которые стоят дорого, принадлежат богатым людям, и в обложении их высоким налогом, не было бы ничего несправедливого. Земли, имеющие самую низкую стоимость, составляют собственность бедных слоев населения, живущих в захолустье, и их следовало бы облагать лишь самым легким налогом. В настоящее время земли на Бунде и крестьянская ферма платят одинаковый налог. Это несправедливо. Чтобы устранить эту несправедливость, стоит соразмерить налог с стоимостью земли. Стоимость земли под постройками в Шангае возросла в 10,000 раз за сто лет.

Китай стоит накануне гигантского промышленного развития; торговля разовьется в громадных размерах, и через 50 лет у нас будет много Шангаев. Будем же настолько мудры, чтобы предвидеть грядущее, и примем теперь же решение, что приращение стоимости (La plus value) недвижимых имуществ останется собственностью народа, который это приращение стоимости создал, а не частных капиталистов, которые случайно сделались земельными собственниками.

Письмо Ленину

6 Декабря, 1922 г.

Шанхай

Дорогой Ленин.

Я пользуюсь случаем, чтобы вкратце написать Вам по важному поводу. Я узнал, что советские вооруженные силы концентрируются на манчжурской границе и готовятся занять Северную Манчжурию.

Я опасаюсь, что эта оккупация будет иметь тяжелые последствия для дальнейших русско-китайских отношений. Для китайского народа в свое время оккупация Северной Манчжурии была очевидным доказательством и свидетельством царизма. Если Вы оккурпируете эту область, то я уверен, мой народ истолкует этот шаг как продолжение империалистической политики старой России.

Я лично не верю, чтобы это поведение Москвы диктовалось империалистическими мотивами.

В самом деле, я убежден, что Вам необходимо занять Северную Манчжурию вследствие недоверия к Чжанг Цзолину.

Но позвольте мне еще раз подчеркнуть, что действуя через меня и со мною, Вы можете заставить Чанг-Цзо-Лин, в пределах разумности, сделать все необходимое для безопасности Советской России.

Письмо Ленину, 6 Декабря, 1922 г.

Следуя этой политике, Вы не только избежите опасной реакции против Вас в Китае, но и поможете мне создать положение, которое облегчит и ускорит совместную работу России и Китая.

Ваше прежнее заявление относительно Китая внушило великие надежды моему народу и склонило их[его] к тому, чтобы смотреть на Россию, как на друга Китая, который обеспечит Китаю возможность национального освобождения от империалистических держав.

Я прошу Вас не предпринимать ничего неразумного, чем была бы, несомненно, оккупация Северной Манчжурии. Я предполагаю послать полномочного представителя в Москву в недалеком будущем, для совместного совещания с Вами и другими товарищами о совместном действии в законных интересах России и Китая.

В то же время я должен вновь повторить, что переговоры с тепершним правительством в Китае не только потеря времени, но, пожалуй, и опасны. Пекин теперь слуга и орудие империалистких держав и поэтому иметь дело с Пекином, значит, в действительности иметь дело с державами. Это опасно, так как всегда возможно, что Пекин и эти державы своими маневрами поставят вас в неблагоприятное положение перед лицом китайского народа.

Вновь приношу уверение в глубоком уважении

С братским приветом Сун-Ят-Сен
Верно: Буракова.

Телеграмма Мотте

24 Сентября, 1924 г.

В виду возбужденного Макдональдом на последних заседаниях Лиги Наций вопроса о независимости Грузии и установлении международного мира и справедливости, Лиге, быть может, будет интересно знать, что 1-го сентября я отправил Макдональду протест против вручения им моему правительству ультиматума, угрожающего враждебными действиями британского флота в случае, если мое правительство примет необходимые меры для подавления восстания в Кантоне, возникшего по наущению империалистов и реакционеров. Макдональд на этот протест не ответил. Как я понимаю, его молчание означает, что политика Англии в Китае будет попрежнему проявляться в действиях империалистической интервенции и в поддержке контрреволюционных выступлений против национального движения, имеющего целью создание сильного и независимого Китая. Нет ничего удивительного в том, что Макдональд, поддержав мятежников и реакционеров в Кантоне, затем отправился в Женеву, чтобы выступить чемпионом контрреволюции в Грузинской республике в качестве «честного маклера», почуявшего запах кавказской нефти. Подписана Сун-Ят-Сеном.